SINAI

SINAI

**EGYPT'S LINCHPIN
GAZA'S LIFELINE
ISRAEL'S NIGHTMARE**

Mohannad Sabry

The American University in Cairo Press
Cairo   New York

First published in 2015 by
The American University in Cairo Press
113 Sharia Kasr el Aini, Cairo, Egypt
420 Fifth Avenue, New York, NY 10018
www.aucpress.com

Exclusive distribution outside Egypt and North America by I.B.Tauris & Co Ltd., 6 Salem Road,
London, W4 2BU

Dar el Kutub No. 25797/14
ISBN 978 977 416 728 7

Dar el Kutub Cataloging-in-Publication Data

Sabry, Mohannad
        Sinai: Egypt's Linchpin, Gaza's Lifeline, Israel's Nightmare / Mohannad Sabry.—Cairo: The
    American University in Cairo Press, 2015.
        p. cm.
        ISBN 978 977 416 728 7
        1. Sinai (Egypt) Description and travel
        I Title
        916.239

1 2 3 4 5   19 18 17 16 15

Designed by Adam el-Sehemy
Printed in Egypt

CONTENTS

PREFACE

Many of the military officers, Bedouin figures, and politicians who I met and interviewed while researching this book, were convinced that the cultural, social, economic, and political isolation of the Sinai Peninsula was a natural outcome of it being a military zone—highlighted by extreme measures such as requiring a military permit to travel in or out of the peninsula between the nationalization of the Suez Canal in 1956, which sparked Egypt's war with Israel, Britain and France, and the full Israeli withdrawal of 1982. It was viewed by most as a rugged battlefield, and treated by consecutive Egyptian rulers as simply a route through which mobilizing armies could pass and the stage of wars with Israel, since its founding in 1948. But after the signing of the Camp David Peace Accords between Egypt and Israel in 1978, and following the full Israeli withdrawal from the Sinai Peninsula in 1982, Sinai remained isolated, its Bedouin population marginalized and its development and economy excluded from the rest of the country.

The military permits of the pre-Camp David era are no longer required, but have been replaced by dozens of security checkpoints that stifle the movement of people more than the difficulty of acquiring permits. The war with Israel came to an end, but throughout the thirty years of Hosni Mubarak's rule over Egypt (from 1981 to 2011), not a single university campus was opened in Sinai (with the exception of a private university owned by a business tycoon with close ties to the military). As for development and investment, aside from beachside hotels and resorts, where Bedouin are mostly not allowed to work, the overwhelming majority of the peninsula's 61,000 square kilometers has remained as lifeless and barren as ever.

To further secure the continuation of its utterly failed policies in Sinai, Mubarak's regime imposed a complete media and information blackout on everything related to the eastern province. For the first twenty years of Mubarak's rule, reporting in Sinai, publishing about its grievances, or even applauding the repeatedly promised (but never executed) development plans, either in state-owned or independent media outlets, had to go through the filters of state security or await a permit from the Ministry of Defense. In the last decade, between 2000 and Mubarak's downfall in 2011, restrictions on the media in Sinai were theoretically lifted within a broader nationwide plan to project an image of democracy. Reporters were allowed to travel freely to al-Arish, Sheikh Zuwayyed, and Rafah, whereas before they had only been permitted access to the southern beaches to cover Mubarak receiving world leaders at the lavish mansions and resorts of Sharm al-Sheikh. However, even after media restrictions were supposedly eased, the consequences of publishing an article deemed annoying to the regime remained: criminal, state security, or military trial accompanied by workplace intimidation and the possibility of losing one's job from a given media institution. Moreover, as I have personally witnessed a number of times at security offices in Sinai, reports were regularly written by security officers and sent directly to newspapers to be published under the names of specific journalists. Not so surprisingly, during the last decade of this Mubarak-style freedom, the most memorable writings about Sinai were those about the Taba, Sharm al-Sheikh, and Dahab bombings in 2004, 2005, and 2006—mainly because of the large number of foreign nationals who fell victim to the terrorist attacks there, and their close proximity to Mubarak's residence in his last ten years in power.

Over his thirty years in power, Mubarak succeeded in equating the Sinai Peninsula, in the minds of Egyptians and the majority of the world for that matter, to the southern beach resorts reserved mainly for foreign tourists; the cliché of the 1973 'victory' against Israel; and a lifeless desert inhabited by Bedouin outlaws and traffickers.

On January 25, 2011, when Egyptian protesters marched through the streets of the capital Cairo and held sit-ins across the country, including around Sinai's security compounds and government offices, the relentless reporters and activists of the peninsula were finally liberated. They broke the barriers of fear, stood in the face of a murderous police apparatus and for the first time, possibly in their lives, documented what happened in Sinai, for the world to watch, even if this was largely ignored as media organizations remained focused on the capital Cairo and Tahrir Square. Mubarak's blackout, financed by billions of dollars allocated to the construction of prisons and torture chambers run by State Security, rather than schools and hospitals, was finally brought down, along with the men who supervised it.

Despite the unprecedented freedoms gained in the aftermath of the uprising, everyone seemed to believe that it was temporary. When discussing this book with trusted contacts in Sinai in the years following the revolution, I encountered genuine encouragement, but also serious warnings. One prominent Sinai activist advised me that "there will be an inevitable price that you will pay for taking such a step." When considering who the book would anger, I was told that it would be easier to look for those who the book would not infuriate.

I decided to pursue the book project; Mubarak's downfall had empowered activists and community figures and led to a precious flow of information. Many would still only talk on condition of anonymity, but were discussing subjects they had never dreamed of whispering even to their closest acquaintances under the oppression of Mubarak's regime—testimonies of torture and police brutality surfaced after years of silence induced by fear. But within the atmosphere of greater freedom, which prevailed until 2013, some of the peninsula's most sensitive subjects remained a taboo. Arms trafficking, which mainly supplied the Muslim Brotherhood's offshoot Hamas in Gaza, was one of the most difficult subjects to discuss or report on, followed by the Brotherhood's murky influence in Sinai and the rise of Islamist militants, whose attacks had started even before Mubarak's downfall.

My investigative reporting in Sinai earned me my first threat in late 2012, around my work on armed Islamists. The atmosphere was severely polarized, and several Bedouin leaders had been assassinated for their public condemnation of the militant groups and their opposition to the Muslim Brotherhood regime. In January 2013, North Sinai-based reporter Muhamed Sabry (despite his name, not a relative of mine) was detained by the military for filming in Rafah; he was put before a military tribunal, sentenced to a suspended jail term, and then released. After the incident, I began learning of threats sent to colleagues one after the other because of their determined reporting across the peninsula.

Right after Morsi's ouster on July 3, 2013, and in the context of the avalanche of terrorist attacks across the peninsula and mainland Egypt that followed, the crackdown on journalists operating in Sinai increased significantly, reaching a peak with the arrest of my colleague Ahmed Abu Draa. Detained on September 5 in al-Arish, a few hours after I left him to travel to South Sinai, he was imprisoned in Ismailiya's notorious al-Azouli military prison for one month before standing before a military trial that sentenced him to a suspended jail term.

As another wave of political and security repression (that continues across Egypt at the time of writing) was unleashed, journalists reporting in Sinai were witnessing what they had predicted in 2011: the freedoms gained after the uprising would be hastily crushed. By the beginning of 2014, reporting in North Sinai became as deadly as living in the villages regularly bombarded by the military and Islamist militants. Egypt's security forces began intensifying their crackdown by arresting foreign journalists and Egyptian reporters visiting from other cities, and transporting them back to Cairo in police vehicles, as was the case with Sabry Khaled, a former photographer for the independent *al-Shorouk* newspaper and Nadine Marroushi, a British freelance journalist.

This book, in addition to attempting to defy the state's insistence on a return to an information blackout, aims to fill in the missing facts that State Security Investigations, along with many other state institutions, work tirelessly to suppress. Since 2011, I have met, interviewed, and traveled and lived with more than 150 people from the northern, central, and southern parts of the Sinai Peninsula. I have also conducted interviews in the Gaza Strip, met with Palestinian sources, including Hamas and Fatah officials, in al-Arish and Cairo, and traveled to Jerusalem and Tel Aviv to conduct interviews with government officials, media figures, and various intellectuals and experts on Israeli foreign policy and Egyptian–Israeli relations. Other interviews were conducted over the phone and internet with sources in all of the above mentioned locations.

In Sinai's conservative tribal community—whose history of oppression and ever-deteriorating relations with the state is coupled with a severe lack of trust in any form of media—it became clear that the most effective method for research was long, unstructured interviews and informal talks. A few of the people interviewed for this book did not begin speaking openly to me until months after our first meeting. I later learned that they had made extensive enquiries about me in different tribal and political circles, both in Sinai and Cairo.

Several of the people I interviewed in Sinai insisted on being identified only by their aliases, and some threatened that there would be "unpleasant repercussions" if I were to reveal their real identities. After the ouster of former president Mohamed Morsi, and the beginning of a vicious military campaign across North Sinai, the vast majority of people spoke only on condition of anonymity, if they spoke at all. Such a position was understandable; in many instances it was not the journalist who was pursued over their field reporting in Sinai's towns and villages, but whomever they interviewed was subjected to severe intimidation that could include detention for days or weeks, for having dared to speak to the media.

Since the Egyptian uprising in 2011, I have traveled and reported in a dozen countries, and have reported extensively in Egypt's most marginalized governorates. Throughout this, I have not experienced a region as blacked-out in terms of the flow of information as the Sinai Peninsula, which also happens to be the core of one of Egypt and the Middle East's most crucial assets: the Camp David Peace Accords. Sadly, the Sinai will never reach the stability we all hope for unless it's liberated from the decades-old stagnancy it has been forced into by consecutive Egyptian regimes.

Many of those criticized in this book will attempt to tarnish its reputation, and there will be others who will disagree with my analysis and opinions. However, I ask the reader to focus on the facts and the accounts of those who continue to endure the unlivable and unjust conditions in Sinai. After all, it is the persistence of the people that will take the peninsula from its turmoil to whatever form of prosperity it might have in the future.

Note on Names and Sources

Many of the people interviewed for this book have had their names changed to protect their identities. They are cited by just a first name or by an alias. The names of some security officials have also been changed, to just a single initial, to hide their identities and to protect the author.

The majority of the reporting for this book was done in Arabic, and all translations into English (unless stated otherwise) are the author's own.

Mohannad Sabry, Cairo, June 2015

ACKNOWLEDGMENTS

Throughout the period of three and half years that it took me to research, report and write this book, I was overwhelmed by the amount of support and assistance I received from family, friends, colleagues, and others whose only connection to me and my work was their belief that the Sinai Peninsula deserves to be a better understood. Without this generous support, whether a short private conversation over a sensitive subject or days of editing and fact-checking, this book would have never been produced.

My never-ending appreciation goes to a few people from Sinai, who were always there whether I required an answer to one simple question or had endless demands while traveling through Sinai's tribal communities. They offered their help whole heartedly despite knowing that by doing so they were putting themselves in harm's way. Now, at a time when people are being detained, or worse, for expressing their opinion over what goes on in Sinai, I will not be able to mention any of their names, but they will always be the unknown soldiers behind the scenes of this book.

Ahmed Abu Draa, a dear friend and respected colleague, was the first person to encourage me to go on with this project. His meticulous knowledge of the Sinai Peninsula's complicated politics and security, and his infinite number of connections within any given town or tribe, were among the top reasons I was able to spend weeks on end every time I landed in the peninsula. Ashraf Khalil, author of *Liberation Square: Inside the Egyptian Revolution and the Rebirth of a Nation*, who walked me step by step into the publishing world, had enough patience for my first-time-author questions, and helped put my expectations within reasonable limits. Charles M. Sennott, the founder and executive director of The

GroundTruth Project, was an endless source of precious advice that on many occasions led to me changing parts of this book. Dan Perry, Middle East Editor of the Associated Press, a dear friend and an expert on Israeli politics and security affairs, was the top, if not the only, reason I was capable of reporting from Jerusalem and Tel Aviv and enabled me to further understand Israel's position on Sinai's unfolding events.

I am also thankful to my friends and colleagues Andrew Bossone, Aaron Ross, Dusan Vranic, Zack Gold, Eman El-Tourky, and many others who helped me in many ways, from providing contacts to revising my initial drafts and sitting for hours to discuss politics and history. I also thank Nadine El-Hadi, my editor whose tireless work and tolerance for my continuous delays will never be forgotten.

Finally, I thank my partner Elena Chardakliyska, who spared no effort whenever I needed her support. She always had enough patience for my travels, mood swings, and moments of depression and despair. I dedicate this book to her.

ABBREVIATIONS

ABM	Ansar Bayt al-Maqdis
CSF	Central Security Forces
EGAS	Egyptian Natural Gas Holding Company
EGID	Egyptian General Intelligence Directorate
EMG	East Mediterranean Gas Company
EMIRD	Egyptian Military Intelligence and Reconnaissance Directorate
FJP	Freedom and Justice Party
IAEA	International Atomic Energy Agency
IDF	Israeli Defense Forces
ISA	Israeli Security Agency
ISIL	Islamic State in Iraq and the Levant
NDP	National Democratic Party
MBTU	Million British Thermal Units
MFO	Multinational Forces and Observers
MSC	Mujahedeen Shura Council in the Environs of Jerusalem
PRCs	Popular Resistance Committees
SCAF	The Supreme Council of the Armed Forces
SSI	State Security Investigations
WINEP	The Washington Institute for Near East Policy

CHRONOLOGY

June 5, 1967. The Six Day War begins: Israel invades and then occupies the Sinai Peninsula, the Gaza Strip, the West Bank, and the Golan Heights.

1968. Egypt's Military Intelligence and Reconnaissance Directorate (EMIRD) starts the covert Sinai Fighters Association.

1968–73. Egypt leads a war of attrition against Israeli troops across the Sinai Peninsula.

October 6, 1973. The 1973 War begins; Egypt launches an offensive against Israel (at that time occupying Sinai), taking back control of the Suez Canal and a strip extending 12 kilometers into Sinai.

October 28, 1973. Sponsored by US and the UN, Egypt and Israel agree to a military disengagement and UN observers are deployed in Sinai.

November 9, 1977. President Sadat lands in Jerusalem on a three-day trip; he remains the only Egyptian head of state to visit Israel.

September 17, 1978. Egyptian President Sadat, Israeli Prime Minister Begin, and US President Carter sign the Camp David Accords at the White House.

March 26, 1979. Sadat, Begin, and Carter sign the Egyptian–Israeli Peace Treaty.

1979. Israel begins its gradual withdrawal from the Sinai Peninsula.

October 6, 1981. Sadat is assassinated by armed members of al-Jamaa al-Islamiya as he attends a military parade in celebration of the anniversary of the 1973 'victory' against Israel.

October 8, 1981. Al-Jamaa al-Islamiya attack the Asyut Security Directorate in Upper Egypt, killing 118 security personnel in less than an hour.

October 14, 1981. Hosni Mubarak becomes Egypt's fourth president.

April 25, 1982. Israel completes the withdrawal of its troops from Sinai, with the exception of the border area of Taba (returned in 1989).

December 8, 1987. The first Palestinian Intifada begins.

1988. Hamas is founded by Sheikh Ahmed Yassin, Abdel-Aziz al-Rantissi, and Mahmoud al-Zahar.

March 19, 1989. Taba is returned to Egypt, after a lengthy legal battle with Israel.

June 8, 1992. Egyptian thinker and renowned author Farag Fouda is assassinated in the first of dozens of terrorist attacks led by al-Jamaa al-Islamiya, the Egyptian Islamic Jihad, and other smaller groups.

July 5, 1994. Yasser Arafat becomes the first president of the Palestinian National Authority, established to rule the West Bank and Gaza Strip after the Oslo Accords in 1993.

June 27, 1995. Mubarak survives an assassination attempt executed by Islamic Jihad in the Ethiopian capital Addis Ababa.

1997. Leading members of al-Jamaa al-Islamiya declare an initiative of ideological recantations that renounce violence.

November 17, 1997. Islamist militants carry out a terrorist attack in Luxor, killing fifty-eight foreign tourists and four Egyptians.

November 18, 1997. Mubarak appoints Habib El-Adly, head of the State Security Investigations (SSI), as minister of the interior to succeed Hassan El-Alfy.

1999–2000. Arafat begins loosening the security grip imposed on Islamist groups across the Gaza Strip and West Bank.

July 2000. US President Clinton invites Arafat to attend a Camp David Summit with Israeli Prime Minister Barak. The talks ultimately fail and the second Palestinian Intifada begins year.

March 7, 2001. Ariel Sharon becomes prime minister of Israel, succeeding Barak.

October 7, 2004. Car bombs target the Hilton hotel in the South Sinai Taba resort and two beach camps in Nuewiba, killing thirty-one and leaving more than 170 injured.

October 2004–2008. Egypt's security authorities carry out a campaign of mass arbitrary arrests under the emergency law.

November 11, 2004. Arafat dies.

January 15, 2005. Mahmoud Abbas, of the Fatah movement, wins the Palestinian presidential elections to succeed Arafat as head of the Palestinian National Authority.

July 23, 2005. Bomb attacks target the South Sinai resort of Sharm al-Sheikh, killing eighty-eight people.

August 15–September 12, 2005. Israel carries out Sharon's military unilateral disengagement plan from Gaza and imposes a blockade on the Strip.

January 25, 2006. Hamas wins the Palestinian Legislative Elections, and the movement's top officer, Ismail Haniyeh, is named prime minister of the Palestinian National Authority.

April 25, 2006. A bomb attack targets South Sinai's Dahab resort, killing twenty-three people.

June 25, 2006. A joint attack by Hamas, the PRCs, and the al-Qaeda affiliated Jaish al-Islam ends in the kidnapping of Israeli Corporal Gilad Shalit.

June 10–15, 2007. Fighting erupts between Hamas and Fatah in Gaza, after President Abbas sacks the elected Hamas government. It ends with Hamas in control of the Strip; Israel and Egypt shut down Gaza's border terminals completely.

June 2007–January 2008. Gaza's humanitarian crisis peaks, due to the blockade imposed by Israel and the closure of border terminals.

January 23, 2008. Hamas blows up the border fence with Egypt, and half of Gaza's 1.5 million people cross into North Sinai.

December 27, 2008. Israel launches Cast Lead: an all out offensive against Gaza that leaves it totally devastated.

August 14, 2009. Hamas unleashes a lethal crackdown on Salafi jihadists in southern Gaza after their most prominent spiritual leader, Abdel-Latif Mousa, declared an Islamic Emirate from his Ibn Taymeya Mosque. The crackdown, which killed al-Maqdisi, led dozens of Gazan jihadists and *takfiris* to flee their homes into the Sinai Peninsula where they found refuge.

2009–2010. Hamas establishes an official umbrella for the smuggling tunnels, the Tunnel Affairs Commission, while Egypt gradually lifts pressure on smuggling operations across the Sinai.

January 25, 2011. The revolution erupts across Egypt.

January 27, 2011. In Cairo, twenty-seven top members of the Muslim Brotherhood are detained.

January 28, 2011. Known as the Friday of Anger, police and protester violence reaches a peak, the country's security apparatus collapses, the military is deployed across the nation, and an all night curfew is declared. The maximum-security prison of Wadi al-Natrun falls under an armed attack that fails to breach its walls.

January 29, 2011. Several prison compounds fall under armed attack and some 23,000 prisoners escape, including Muslim Brotherhood members, Hamas's Ayman Noufal, and Hezbollah's Sami Shehab.

January 30, 2011. The Egyptian military is deployed in Sinai's demilitarized zones for the first time since June 5, 1967.

February 5, 2011. Armed militants bomb the natural gas pipeline supplying Israel and Jordan with gas.

February 11, 2011. Mubarak steps down and hands over power to SCAF.

March 2011. The first sharia courts are publicly opened in Sinai. Meanwhile, SCAF begins releasing Islamist prisoners, including those convicted for terrorist attacks and the Sadat assassination.

March 19, 2011. A constitutional referendum, to replace Egypt's 1971 constitution and hold elections before drafting a new constitution, is approved by 77 percent of the vote.

July 29, 2011. Dozens of armed militants attack security facilities in al-Arish, carrying al-Qaeda banners.

August 18, 2011. A cross-border attack is carried out by Sinai militants on Israeli soil, targeting the military and civilians on the highway to Eilat.

October 18, 2011. With Egyptian mediation, Israeli corporal Gilad Shalit is released by Hamas after five years in captivity; his release is part of a prisoner exchange in which 1,027 Palestinians are released by Israel.

November 28, 2011–January 11, 2012. The Muslim Brotherhood's Freedom and Justice Party and the Salafi al-Nour Party win 74.5 per cent of Egypt's first post-revolution parliament.

January 2012–May 2012. Attacks continue across North Sinai, targeting the gas pipeline, police checkpoints and stations, MFO camps, as well as those opposed to the Muslim Brotherhood.

June 18, 2012. Another cross-border attack takes place on Israeli soil, killing one person; responsibility is claimed by the Mujahedeen Shura Council in the Environs of Jerusalem.

June 28, 2012. The Muslim Brotherhood's Mohamed Morsi becomes president of Egypt.

July 2012. A video statement detailing the attacks on the gas pipeline declares the establishment of Ansar Bayt al-Maqdis.

August 5, 2012. An attack on a Rafah border post kills sixteen Egyptian military soldiers and leaves others injured; the attackers attempt to carry out further attacks on Israeli territory but are eliminated by the IAF.

August 12, 2012. President Morsi replaces his military chiefs: he sacks Defense Minister Hussein Tantawi, Chief of Staff Sami Annan, and EGID chief Murad Mowafi; he appoints Gen. Abdel-Fattah al-Sisi as defense minister.

September 2012. The military launches Operation Eagle II, to crackdown on the rising militancy in Sinai.

September 16, 2012. The militants engage in an armed battle with military and police forces in the town of Muqataa, south of Sheikh Zuwayyed; the state's forces withdraw after coming under heavy fire.

September–October 2012. Morsi orders a presidential delegation, comprising hardcore Salafis and formerly convicted Islamists, to lead a dialogue with Sinai's militants; the delegation ends the military campaign and agrees to a short-lived ceasefire with militants.

23 November, 2012. Morsi issues a presidential declaration granting him unchecked powers and protests break out.

December 5, 2012. Clashes erupt between Morsi supporters and opposition protesters against the presidential declaration in Cairo; the clashes leave eleven dead.

March 2013. The prison break case is activated once again to further investigate the attacks on prisons in January 2011; the court orders investigations into Morsi and members of his cabinet, among others.

April 2013. Rockets are fired from Central Sinai into Southern Israel.

May 2013. Seven Egyptian security personnel are kidnapped by Sinai militants who demand the release of Islamist prisoners; the soldiers are released days later after negotiations between the presidency and military command and the kidnappers.

June 30, 2013. Massive protests, organized by the Tamarrod movement, erupt across Egypt demanding the resignation of Morsi and calling for early presidential elections.

July 3, 2013. Defense Minister al-Sisi ousts President Morsi in a popular military coup; he appoints Judge Adly Mansour, head of the constitutional court, as interim president.

July 5, 2013. Armed confrontations break out between Morsi supporters and military personnel in al-Arish. Simultaneously, several terrorist attacks target military and police positions across North Sinai. Interim-President Mansour declares a state of emergency and an all-night curfew in North Sinai.

August 9, 2013. An Israeli drone targets and kills four militants preparing a rocket launcher in the village of al-Ajra in North Sinai.

August 14, 2013. Egyptian military and police forces begin an all out attack on pro-Morsi protesters camped mainly in Cairo's Rabaa al-Adawiya Square, plus other locations across the country. An estimated two thousand civilians are killed and a country-wide curfew is declared.

August 19, 2013. Known as Rafah's Second Massacre, a terrorist attack kills twenty-five military soldiers in North Sinai.

August 28, 2013. A car bomb targets Sheikh Zuwayyed police station in North Sinai.

September 5, 2013. Minister of the Interior Mohamed Ibrahim survives an assassination attempt in Cairo.

September 11, 2013. Terrorists attack Rafah's military intelligence compound killing six military personnel.

October 7, 2013. South Sinai Security Directorate is hit by a car bomb.

October 10, 2013. Al-Rissa checkpoint, east of al-Arish, is hit by a car bomb.

October 19, 2013. Military intelligence command in Ismailiya is hit by a car bomb.

November 20, 2013. A car-bomb attack on a military bus in North Sinai leaves eleven dead and thirty-five injured.

December 24, 2013. A bomb attack hits the Daqahliya Security Directorate in the Nile Delta city of Mansoura.

January 24, 2014. Bomb attacks hit Cairo's Security Directorate.

January 25, 2014. A military helicopter is shot down by militants in North Sinai.

June 3, 2014. Abdel-Fatah al-Sisi is voted president of Egypt.

Map of Sinai

1

SINAI'S REVOLUTION: FOUR DAYS OF ARMED FURY

Mohamed Atef, a 22-year-old Bedouin from the town of Sheikh Zuwayyed, was the first to be killed by Egypt's police in North Sinai. He received a deadly bullet in the chest as he hurled rocks that probably never reached the armored vehicles of the riot police forces blocking North Sinai's main coastal highway on January 27, 2011. Behind him stood Khalil Jabr,[1] a prominent Sinai activist and a descendant of the revered Sawarka tribe—a seventy-thousand-member tribe that outnumbers any other across this rugged peninsula. For years, Jabr had been one of many relentless activists tagged by Egypt's security authorities as members of North Sinai's 'Active Political Cell.'

Jabr happened to be filming with his cell phone as Atef was shot. He helped carry the bloody corpse before sharing the crude video that spread across Egypt to create an unforgettable icon of the Sinai Peninsula and Egypt's January 2011 revolution. Atef isn't only remembered as among the ranks of the hundreds of the revolution's victims, but also for galvanizing Sinai's armed rebellion that defeated Hosni Mubarak's armed phalanx in less than four days.

The story of this cold-blooded murder traveled across the Sinai in just a few hours, even before the video was uploaded to social media websites and spread across the country. Atef's death was a watershed moment that put an end to two days of peaceful chanting, hurling rocks, and trying to avoid the burning tear gas that had been generously fired since the revolution kicked off on January 25, 2011.

Less than two hours later, dozens of men had gathered a couple of miles away from where Atef was killed to discuss what would come next. The fiery chants echoed from an empty plot of land adjacent to the massive gate of Sheikh Zuwayyed, North Sinai's resilient town of Bedouins, Islamists, and Egyptian–Palestinians. The murder of a young fellow Bedouin had put everyone on edge; as decades of fury boiled over, people were unwilling to bear the embarrassment of letting such a crime go unpunished.

Meanwhile, a Bedouin teenager named Abdallah[2] showed up wearing the traditional *thoub* (robe), masked with his *agda* (traditional headscarf), and wielding a locked and loaded AK-47. He definitely wasn't the oldest or the most prominent amongst the Bedouins, nor was he the only armed man around, but everyone else was still just discussing how to retaliate for Atef's death. He had no political or ideological affiliations, but happened to be more decisive than those around him. Without blinking, he pointed his machine gun at the loathed security compound standing a few hundred yards away and adamantly fired his 7.62-mm bullets at it.

The bullet fired by Mubarak's black-clad riot police at Atef was a declaration of war on ordinary, long-oppressed citizens who dared to protest. It was a clear announcement that deadly force would be used and that the Sinai Peninsula, Egypt's easternmost frontier that runs up and hard against the border with the Gaza Strip and Israel, would be disciplined by firepower. And the bullets coming from a teenager's rifle were the counter declaration that every armed protester heeded. It was a loud call for the 'peaceful' chanters to step aside or immediately gear up for the armed rebellion. From this point on, Sheikh Zuwayyed's main square became a battlefield.

On one side of the coastal highway that slices through the town stood the grim police compound (the one fired at by Abdallah), cordoned off by several armored personnel carriers from which tear gas and live ammunition were fired. The fortified compound and its guards were reminders of years of arbitrary detention, humiliation, and torture. On the other side of the highway stood the homes of a community that had witnessed wars and mobilizing armies from the days of Egypt's Ottoman ruler, Mohamed Ali Pasha, until the town was demilitarized by the Camp David Peace Accords that brought an end to years of Egyptian–Israeli wars.

"It wasn't a protest anymore, by nightfall it had turned into a full-fledged battle; the sounds of AK-47s and the 50 calibers were recognizable.

I felt the rocket-propelled grenades rocking the area and clearly heard the armored vehicles racing around," said Mostafa Singer, who was stranded in a shop a few buildings down from the security compound around which the battle raged. The gunfire and explosions were interrupted by minutes of silence every now and then that were "either for distraction, changing positions, or reloading the guns. The atmosphere was eerie and the power had gone out; the blacked-out scene was interrupted by flashes of bullets whizzing around." He waited for one of those breaks and ran to his house two blocks away.[3]

Mostafa Singer, a prominent North Sinai leftist activist in his forties, was born and continues to live across from the security compound in Sheikh Zuwayyed. An investigative writer and expert on Egyptian–Israeli–Gazan relations, Singer was tagged for almost a decade as a leading member of the North Sinai Active Political Cell. He is an Egyptian descended from the Palestinian Sanajreh clan that partially relocated to Sinai in 1948, where he continues to enjoy a far-reaching reputation among every Bedouin tribe. His relentless activism and fiery writings led him several times to prolonged intimidation-over-coffee sessions at the offices of different security authorities.

A personal friend of Khalil Jabr who filmed the death of Mohamed Atef, he was the first to know of the death. "Jabr was shaken when he told me on the phone; Atef's corpse was in front of him as he talked," said Singer, who by then was convinced that nothing would stop the armed escalation.

Two Days Earlier: January 25

Singer had left his house on the morning of January 25 heading to al-Arish, the largest and most populated city in North Sinai and site of the first planned protest to be held in front of the governor's office. He was disappointed to find that only a dozen of his fellow activists had showed up, and with each one carrying countless red flags in their security files, he knew that the failure of protests would mean the worst imaginable punishment for them from the security apparatus. He decided to go back.

Heading to Sheikh Zuwayyed, Singer encountered a small protest in front of the town's security compound. There were several families of prisoners holding pieces of cardboard they had collected from the trash and written their demands on. "They were women and children, and the men they were protesting for were either in prison or fugitives after receiving one, or several, life sentences on trumped up charges. It was heartbreaking; the tidiest of the children looked like they hadn't changed their clothes in a few years."

"Free my father," "I need my father," "We have become orphans," read some of the poorly made banners.

The 'Government Sheikhs,' a bunch of Bedouin elders hired by the government over the decades, had gotten there before Singer. Enjoying the Mubarak regime's largesse, they obeyed everything the regime ordered even if it meant being despised by their tribal community. Their only mission since talks of protests on January 25 started was to convince the public not to follow the doomed opposition and to remain submissive to the ruling National Democratic Party (NDP), which they had tirelessly promoted for years.

"I arrived to hear them telling the families of prisoners to leave and that their demands had been heard and would be handled. My reply was addressed to the protesters, I told them to hold their ground until their demands were fulfilled: do not leave until your relatives are released," recounted Singer.

He was warned by the Mubarak loyalists that he was putting himself at risk by agitating against the regime. He went next to another protest held at al-Mehdiya, the town south of Rafah inhabited mainly by the powerful and government-loathing al-Menaei clan of the Sawarka tribe. On the way, he called the then governor of North Sinai, General Murad Mowafi,[4] who he had personally met several times in press conferences and interviews, to discuss the protests with him. Singer's call to Mowafi took place a few days before Mowafi was appointed Egypt's spy chief when Hosni Mubarak named the long-time head of the Egyptian General Intelligence Directorate (EGID), General Omar Suleiman, as his vice president.

"I asked Mowafi if he was following the protests in Sheikh Zuwayyed and Rafah, and he said he had heard that I was inciting violence and agitating the situation." The reaction of the governor wasn't surprising: it presents a microcosm of how the Egyptian regime dealt with the protests from the very start.

The regime, which relied mainly on the brutal security apparatus to guarantee its prolonged stay in power, had comfortably listened to and trusted the security chiefs who would have described the boiling-over situation as just another bunch of undisciplined kids who would soon be thrown in jail and taught a lesson. Mubarak's men, and his minister of the interior, Habib El-Adly, thought that January 25 was similar to hundreds of other protests they had crushed over many years, but they were mistaken.[5]

In al-Mehdiya, the man behind that second protest attended by Singer was Ibrahim Abu Ashraf al-Menaei, one of the most powerful, revered, and feared Bedouin kingpins in the Sinai Peninsula, and also a victim of the emergency law. He was detained for three and a half years without trial on suspicion of smuggling activities. The co-founder and head of the independent Sinai Tribes Union, Abu Ashraf's reputation went far beyond Sinai: his name and tribal authority echoed through the Gaza Strip, the West Bank, Jordan, the Negev Desert, and Saudi Arabia. He was respected in every Bedouin community connected to Sinai by blood, culture, or politics.

"Some of my life was wasted in detention without trial; I have first-hand experience with Mubarak's thugs and fully understand what it means to be ripped away from your family. I also understand what it means for your family to be without you," Abu Ashraf told me at his guest house in the center of al-Mehdiya, a hospitable tribal meeting point from which dissent was encouraged. "I was never going to give up on the families of detainees, it was time for us to stand in the face of Hosni Mubarak's tyranny."[6]

When Singer and some fellow activists arrived at the protest led by Abu Ashraf, a little conferring concluded that "no one will ever listen if this little number remained in the village, remote from from government departments and main roads." Agreement was unanimous on moving the protest to join those in front of the Sheikh Zuwayyed security compound. And, as the protests were uniting, well-respected and heavily armed Bedouins from South Sinai's Tarabin and Gararsha tribes were on their way to the northern towns in solidarity with their distant cousins and strongly tied brothers in oppression.

"Generous quantities of tear gas were fired at us continually. From the time of our arrival in Sheikh Zuwayyed in the afternoon of January 25, they were met by rock barrages from protesters. Those were the peaceful hours before Mohamed Atef was killed less than two days later."

The Friday of Anger: January 28

As the battle in Sheikh Zuwayyed slowed down to sporadic gunfire in the hours after midnight on January 27 following Mohamed Atef's killing and the spread of the video taken by Khalil Jabr, calls for the Friday of Anger were spreading virally across Egypt. Several deaths and dozens of injuries were reported in the capital Cairo, the coastal city of Alexandria, and the canal cities of Suez and Port Said.

Exceptional mobilization was taking place in every Central Security barrack across the country, while the capital's security directorate called in reinforcements from almost every other city surrounding it. Cairo was preparing for the deadliest crackdown in the thirty years of Hosni Mubarak's rule. The authorities had planned a nationwide blockage of cell-phone and internet networks and, around midnight, police forces detained thirty-seven top members of the Muslim Brotherhood movement, including the organization's Supreme Guide Mohamed Badie, its then unknown deputy Mohamed Morsi (who later became Egypt's president), and a score of its top officials, while hundreds of thousands of people shared lists of gathering points for the following day's protests over social media websites. Eerie silence prevailed in North Sinai as community figures and opposition activists in the region's capital al-Arish, the resilient Sheikh Zuwayyed, and the border town of Rafah continued fueling the calls within communities for massive protests planned to take off from major mosques the next day. However, assessing how ready the public were was quite impossible. The call demanded that ordinary citizens confront a murderous oppressor who had already shown no mercy when dealing with young rock hurlers. What neither the authorities nor the activists knew was that the communities were already fired-up, armed, and determined to crush the regime.

"Looking at the television feed from Cairo, the deaths in Suez, and the video of Mohamed Atef's death, I felt it coming, it was a revolution," said Singer.

The dawn of January 28, the Friday of Anger, broke on the lingering stench of tear gas fumes and burning tires. Despite the deaths, injuries, and terrifying events of Thursday, people in Sheikh Zuwayyed and Rafah adhered to the sacredness of Friday, the Muslim holiday on which the weekly communal prayer is held after a long fiery sermon that often turns political. Not that the sacredness of Fridays has ever stopped a battle in the long history of Islam; this same peaceful sacredness has acted as an inspiration and sermons can be saturated with enough anger to boost the morale of those preparing for a righteous battle. And for thousands in North Sinai, plus the many who traveled from across the peninsula in support of their tribes and fellow Bedouins, no battle was deemed more righteous than that against Hosni Mubarak.

Akin to deadly confrontations in several major cities across the country, Atef's death in Sheikh Zuwayyed on the third day of the revolution had struck up a tacit unity between thousands of people, despite their contrasting allegiances and varying methods of opposition. Mubarak's ironfisted regime that had been in power for thirty years had created endless animosities from everyone: leftists, Islamists, smugglers, militants, criminals, and apolitical ordinaries. Each had their own reasons for loathing Mubarak's regime and this was not the first time that those reasons became common factors that brought people from all sects and far-flung villages to protest tents erected at the Israeli border or around the fortified camps of the Multinational Forces and Observers (MFO), who are deployed in the Sinai Peninsula to monitor the application of the Camp David Peace Accords signed by Egypt and Israel in 1979.

It was the sudden, spontaneous, and uncalculated armed eruption on January 27 that offered the push to whoever was having second thoughts about attacking the regime at one of its most fortified garrisons. Abdallah, the AK-47-wielding teenager, and dozens of armed Bedouins who converged on Sheikh Zuwayyed's main square were the Sinai version of the roaring chants that echoed across Cairo's boulevards and bridges as people crossed over the River Nile and poured into Tahrir Square. Jabr's crude video documenting Mohamed Atef's death was equivalent to the hours of television feeds showing armored vehicles ramming into peaceful protesters everywhere across the nation.

Going out of his house on the morning of the Friday of Anger, Singer received a call advising him of some of the police's plans for the day: "It was my brother; he told me that people known for their affiliation with the state security were warning that I would be eliminated if I was seen on the street. He was concerned, and I know I was not the only one that received the threat, but it was too late. I told him that it's all empty threats, the situation is out of their control."

Meanwhile in Sheikh Zuwayyed, the sporadic gunfire had once again erupted around the main square where the security compound stood. The façade of the building had already been scarred with bullet holes from Thursday's battle. The only security forces left were those holed up in the armored vehicles trying desperately to fend off the armed rebels and maintain the cordon around the compound.

Al-Arish

The atmosphere was different in al-Arish, as different as its societal formation when compared to other towns in North Sinai. Mohamed Ali Pasha, the nineteenth-century Ottoman ruler of Albanian descent, had reconstructed the Mediterranean capital of North Sinai and renovated its ages-old port, and his son and top military commander, Ibrahim Pasha, had used it as a regular stop for his army when heading to wars in the east or attempting to crush the Bedouin rebels who wouldn't submit to the Ottoman Empire. The fair-haired and green-eyed descendants of intermarriages between Arabs, Egyptians, and Turks make up a sizable portion of al-Arish, along with thousands of Egyptians who emigrated from the Nile Valley to Sinai. The Bedouins normally refer to them as the Arrayshiya.

Furthermore, being the capital of the region and the last city Egypt's military was allowed to deploy in without violating the demilitarization conditions of the Camp David Peace Accords, it hosted the office of North Sinai's military chief, the security directorate, the intelligence directorate, the state security directorate, two major central security barracks, the governorate headquarters, and three major police stations.

"Al-Arish required a completely different approach than Sheikh Zuwayyed and Rafah," said Hassan al-Nakhlawi, a well-known activist and co-founder of the Sinai Prisoners Defense Front, who was also tagged a member of the Active Political Cell, along with Jabr and Singer. "The armed culture is not as rampant in al-Arish, the security grip is tighter, and there was a greater chance of a successful security clamp down that would detain the opposition figures and diffuse any chance of mobilizing the public."[7]

Al-Rifaei Mosque, one of al-Arish's biggest and most central mosques, was chosen as the kick-off point for the city's first major march. The security department had surrounded the mosque with fifteen central security personnel trucks, a worrying sign that some five hundred riot policemen had been mobilized to build a formation big enough to crush any protest in a matter of minutes. The civil defense department had sent two fire trucks and several of the city's top officials were at the scene.

"Several of us toured the city that morning and kept an eye on the riot police forces surrounding the mosque," added Nakhlawi, "we found out that only three of the fifteen personnel carriers were full, the rest were empty, it was just for show. That is when we realized that the regime was receiving harder blows than it could handle."

The atmosphere remained quiet even after the Friday prayers, and Colonel Khaled Okasha, the head of North Sinai's Civil Defense Department responsible for fire brigades, emergency services, and explosives specialist teams, had fire trucks among the security formation cordoning off the mosque. He remained at his office where his emergency landline gave him guaranteed access to his troops and other security offices around North Sinai and all the way to Cairo, despite the communications blackout.

"My troops took the fire trucks back to the brigade not far from the mosque, nothing had happened and we watched the revolution on television, there were feeds from Cairo and other major cities but nothing from North Sinai; nothing was expected to happen in al-Arish," Colonel Okasha said.[8]

Okasha's description was pretty accurate, nothing was expected to happen in al-Arish, given the significance of what was already happening thirty kilometers to the east in Sheikh Zuwayyed and the bloody confrontations that had erupted all over the country. A couple of hours after the Friday prayer, protesters started marching around the city, it was their first major protest and it cut right to the chase: it didn't demand reforms or changing of government officials, it went from a deceptive silence to the roaring chants of "the people demand the downfall of the regime."

Egypt Erupts

In the capital Cairo, the police had lost control in several main districts, especially around the commercial center and Tahrir Square. The bridges crossing the River Nile had witnessed some of the fiercest attacks on protesters, in what seemed to be the regime's last stand to keep them from occupying the epicenter of the revolution. But the police's live ammunition and endless supply of tear gas had proven to be weaker than the resilience of the growing waves of protesters and popular fury that escalated in response to the regime's brutality. It was only a matter of time before the protesters flooded the square.

The cities of Suez and Alexandria, both known for their toughness, witnessed the earliest waves of violence and were the first to fall

completely into the hands of the revolutionaries. Dozens of police stations and regional offices of the ruling NDP were set ablaze, but no
incident was more significant than the protesters' takeover of Suez's
most ruthless and fortified police compound—al-Arbaein. Before sunset
on January 28, residents of Suez had seized the compound's weapons
and started firing tear gas at the riot police.

Coinciding with the retreat of police forces, the first attack was waged
on the massive Wadi al-Natrun Prison Compound situated almost one
hundred kilometers north of Cairo on the highway to the Mediterranean port-city of Alexandria. According to government officials, the
attackers were allegedly armed with automatic machine guns and traveled on pick-up trucks. The attack didn't last long and wasn't effective
enough to breach the prison's security, but it was apparently a test-run
for a bigger attack to follow.

Shortly after sunset, major cable television channels started airing
images of the flames rising from the icon of Hosni Mubarak's power
that stood right off Tahrir Square: the headquarters of the NDP.
While thousands cheered the destruction of the dictatorship's temple
that hosted the offices of the ambitious Gamal Mubarak, whose dream
of inheriting his father's presidential seat was in the process of being
shattered, human shields formed by protesters continued to protect
the famous Egyptian Museum housing the world's biggest collection
of pharaonic antiquities.

The formations of riot police around Cairo had gradually started to
retreat and by this point had vanished altogether—having escaped back
to their barracks or slipped out of their uniforms. And Egypt's military
forces, with its khaki tanks and armored personnel carriers, rolled down
the streets of the capital for the first time in decades.

Right after midnight, Egypt's state-owned national television aired
Hosni Mubarak's first speech addressing the public since the beginning of nationwide protests. As it aired on every channel, silence
reigned in every corner of Egypt as millions watched the speech at
major protest sites.

The 82-year-old Mubarak spoke of reform, understanding the revolution's demands, never being unaware of those demands, and claiming
to have worked to fulfill them every day of his life. He fired his cabinet
and promised immediate reform. It was clear how incapable he was of
perceiving the extent and the momentum of the protests.

Rafah

Less than half an hour after Mubarak's disappointing and infuriating speech, the border town of Rafah, which had watched silently for the first four days of the revolution, was up in flames, rocked by the deafening sounds of high-caliber guns and explosives.

Colonel Okasha was one of only a handful of people able to make and receive calls on January 28 on his secure landline that, in his words, "does not die." He was the first to get a call from his Rafah fire brigade: "They informed me that an attack was about to hit their compound, which hosted the building of State Security Investigations (SSI) as well. I told them to evacuate to the al-Ahrash Central Security Barracks a few blocks away."

The fire fighters survived the attack waged by ordinary Bedouins and radical Islamists, but they weren't the target anyway. Inside the compound was the torture factory officially named the SSI, which was the real target. Situated on the main street of Rafah, it came under heavy gunfire for several minutes before receiving rocket-propelled grenades.

This building also shared a wall with a small mosque built by the government and ironically used by the state security officers before, after, or during torture sessions of detainees. A staff sergeant of the state security forces escaped to take refuge inside the adjacent mosque, thinking that the attackers would be fended off by the sacredness of the house of worship, but this was far from reality. The protesters-turned-attackers followed him into the mosque, cornered him, and one of their bullets ripped through his head to leave a blood-stained hole in the wall behind him.

It is understandable why the attackers did not adhere to the unchallenged reverence a mosque should hold in the Muslim world. For decades under Hosni Mubarak's SSI, infamous for its Religious Activity Department, thousands of people were detained, thrown in dungeons, and tortured for just attending prayers regularly or coincidentally at a mosque tagged as a regular location for radical Islamists or led by a fierce opposition cleric. Mubarak's regime had violated this reverence for decades, and the attackers paid it back in kind.

A few minutes later, after the sergeant's death, a load of explosives was strapped to the fortified gate of the compound and detonated. The explosion ripped through the gate, destroying the walls around it and a part of the building. Hisham Habashi, an 18-year-old resident of Rafah, had been running to his aunt's house adjacent to the state security building, but was hit in the head by a projectile flying from the explosion. He died minutes later.

Once again, neither the staff sergeant nor Habashi were the target; the staff sergeant was a lower-rank officer who might not have been known to his killers, but who just happened to be in the wrong place at the time of armed rebellion. So, too, was the unfortunate teenager who became the collateral damage of the night. The target was Colonel E.,[9] Rafah's infamous state security chief and former South Sinai state security investigator. That name, carrying almost a decade of brutality, torture, and a host of trumped up charges that at times put people on death row, had been carved into the public memory of Sinai. Colonel E. was a name that struck fear in the hearts of ordinary people and concern in the minds of the most feared and armed-to-the-teeth tribal kingpins.

However, Colonel E. was significantly more connected than his staff sergeant. With the attack looming, his informants and smuggling connections, who had delivered monthly bribes to his office over the years, had agreed to smuggle him out of Sinai for an alleged sum of LE1.5 million, or US$220,000, in cash, according to several Bedouin sources from Rafah and Sheikh Zuwayyed. Members of the Rafah-based Barahma and Zaarba clans, both known for their control over dozens of underground smuggling tunnels into Gaza, facilitated his escape in the trunk of a pick-up truck driven by a Bedouin from the village of al-Muqataa, situated south of Rafah. In a few hours, Colonel E. was dropped off in Ismailiya, across the Suez Canal and outside the Sinai Peninsula.[10]

"I swear on the life of my children, if I catch him I will cut his head off with my own hands," said a Bedouin man, who did not want to be named, when asked about Colonel E.[11] He did not say if he was tortured inside that building, but the fury in his eyes was more telling than his words. Inside the charred rooms of the SSI building remained walls emblazoned with countless curses and threats addressed to Colonel E., but nothing was more vivid than the lock-up cells. The lines written with pieces of burned wood picked from the torched building were saturated with hate and fury: "May Allah's curse descend on you, E."[12]

The SSI building was the first to be attacked. The Rafah police station, the immigration department, and a school building that was said to have been used as a hideout by the fleeing police personnel were attacked in a similar manner. Every man in uniform had escaped to the heavily guarded al-Ahrash Central Security Barracks, just like Colonel

Okasha's Civil Defense men, while every other building representing the regime was left behind to be burned by the revolution.

To the Bedouins of Sinai, the torched buildings of different police departments represented nothing but the arms of a regime that excluded and oppressed them. The Bedouins of Sinai have been banned from enrolling in the police and military academies, and even when serving the compulsory military service they were assigned to non-military positions in cafeterias and civil service departments. A history of discrimination saturated the hearts and minds of the Bedouin community with hatred toward the state authorities. Very few police and military officers of Bedouin descent were known to the community, a fact that meant the attackers need not worry their bullets and explosives were being fired at relatives or fellow Bedouins.[13]

The Downfall

On January 29, the remaining police force guarding the police compound of Sheikh Zuwayyed had been battered by days of gun battles; the building was scarred with the bullet holes of the looming first defeat it had tasted since it was built in the early 1980s. As Rafah's government buildings went up in flames the day before, Sheikh Zuwayyed's police compound was receiving high-caliber bullets interrupted by rocket-propelled grenades from the north, east, and west. An unknown number of armed protesters took cover on street corners facing the compound, as bullets coming from the compound's guards hit the façades of buildings across the main strip.

"It was impossible to sleep that night, it was a fully fledged, all-night battle," according to Mustafa Singer. "One of the rocket-propelled grenades was fired in the wrong direction to land a few hundred yards from my house; the sound was terrifying."

Furthermore, it had been impossible to send reinforcements, especially through the highways of North Sinai that were dotted with civilian ambushes waiting for anyone in a police uniform or vehicle. It was clear that if the police had abandoned the capital Cairo then there was no hope for those stationed in North Sinai. By noon, the police forces had fled and the fortified Sheikh Zuwayyed security compound had fallen into the hands of its victims.

In Cairo, the military had cordoned off the massive compound of the Ministry of the Interior, a few blocks from Tahrir Square—the target of the protesters second in line after the NDP headquarters, which was still in flames. It remained untouched as the military succeeded in fending off the revolutionaries. As a command center for the country's crumbling police force, it was in total paralysis and its notorious minister of the interior, General Habib El-Adly was arrested by the military prosecutor on the morning of January 29. The news of the police's defeat had already reached every corner of the country. Some officers, left without orders from their superiors, told their conscripts to get out of uniform and run for their lives.

"I believe they were given those orders in Sheikh Zuwayyed as well. It was impossible for the whole security troop to escape at the same time, they must have gradually fled during the chaos with the help of their local informants," said Singer. "First thing I heard was twenty dead, thirty, fifteen, but nothing confirmed. The one confirmed fact was that the police compound was abandoned."

Among the first to arrive at the empty police compound, Singer and several others found the gates wide open, the corridors empty, the offices intact, and the weapons disappeared. In less than ten minutes after his arrival, dozens of people converged on the building. Looting, burning, or destroying everything in their way, each person had their own way and reason for retaliating. The first to be set ablaze were several police cars parked in the yard surrounded by the fortified walls of the compound.

'People came with no plan other than destroying what they hated and viewed as a symbol of oppression." There were dozens of computers and hundreds of files. But, avoiding the possibility of being accused of looting, Singer decided to stay out of the building, watching as fire ate up the compound's contents.

Several of the Sheikh Zuwayyed activists and community figures believe that the local police informants were among the first to walk into the building and start the fires. The computer systems weren't secured, the hard drives were supposedly full, and the paper files carried the names of officers, informants, detainees, and anyone under surveillance. If the building had remained intact, every document would have been seized by the revolutionaries and used as evidence of years of violations.

"This is what we tried to do hours later, we went through the rubble and sifted through the half-burnt papers scattered outside of the building; the most significant thing we found was ID cards held by the police over the years to intimidate their owners," said Singer.

The policy of seizing and holding ID cards was one of the most common and most effective measures of oppression across Egypt, especially in Sinai. A police officer would simply take someone's ID card so the victim would fear even leaving his house in case he was stopped without it. He wouldn't be able to apply for any official documents, visit a public hospital, or call an ambulance. It was the easiest way for a policeman to strip someone of their freedom without putting them behind bars.

Hundreds of ID cards were found at the police compound; everyone agreed that one of the town's prominent clerics would be responsible for holding them and handing them back to their owners, if they were alive, or ever showed up to retrieve them.

"The only remaining urgent matter was to count and identify those who died in the clashes. The initial count was five deaths since Mohamed Atef and Hisham Habashi, most of which had nothing to do with the clashes," said Singer. One of those who had died had insisted on driving back to al-Arish on January 28, despite being advised not to, and received a deadly bullet to the chest while driving through Sheikh Zuwayyed's main strip. Another had attempted to reach his kiosk in the middle of the battle; he intended to save as much of his merchandise as he could, fearing the kiosk would be burnt with its contents, and he died trying to save his sole source of income.

A third victim was Bilal Eisa al-Akhrasi, a ten-year-old boy living a few hundred yards away from Rafah's al-Ahrash Central Security Barracks—the only government facility still standing, and in which every policeman who survived the rebellion had taken refuge. He had rushed out of his house along with two schoolmates to the sound of the last skirmish that took place on the morning of January 29. Outside the fortified gate, two armored vehicles had cut off the main road and fired in all directions. The ten-year-old was their only victim.[14]

Blackout on Sinai

No one had anticipated such events would take place in Sinai; not Hosni Mubarak, not his security apparatus, not the mainstream political opposition, and definitely not the media. Since the full Israeli withdrawal in 1982 and the practical beginning of the era of peace with Israel, Mubarak's regime had transformed Sinai in the hearts and minds of Egyptians into a symbol of the 1973 victory credited to him and no one but him, with a southern beach friendly enough to host nudists from across the globe. And the rest was written off as thousands of acres of rugged terrain inhabited by bandits and Bedouin outlaws.

The Sinai Peninsula, with its complicated and murky politics, was blacked out by the Mubarak regime. The media's only source of information about the eastern frontier was security officials and what they thought was publishable. It was rare for someone to break through the blackout, and those who dared landed in prolonged state security interrogations at the end of which they were released, if lucky, or thrown in jail.

"All of Egypt was blacked out by Hosni Mubarak. You would read about the tourism and national holidays, but not about the poverty and illiteracy. Sinai has always received worse treatment than the rest of the country," said Hani Shukrallah, a prominent Egyptian writer, editor, and publisher.[15]

He remembered when his late friend, Mohamed El-Sayed Said, a famous political analyst and senior researcher at the state-owned al-Ahram Center for Political and Strategic Studies, attempted to write an analytical piece discussing the advantages of the Egyptian–Israeli peace accords: "He was praising the peace treaty, taking a major risk by doing so amongst a population that loathes the accords, and yet, he ended up in an interrogation by the State Security Investigations just because he wrote about something considered a taboo by the regime. They were paranoid, and Sinai was a no-go zone." Said wasn't jailed, but despite his prominence amongst Egyptian and foreign scholars, he still received a warning.

On the other hand, Masaad Abu Fajr, Sinai's most well-known Bedouin author and political activist, landed in jail several times for his activism and critical writings about the peninsula's affairs, at a time when no one knew what went on in Sinai unless it was published in international or Israeli media.

When the January 2011 revolution broke out, Egyptians, the people and the media, and the overwhelming majority of foreign media networks continued down the same path Mubarak had set us upon decades ago: Egypt is nothing but the capital Cairo and a few other major cities; everywhere else, including the Sinai that borders Israel and the Gaza Strip, is not worth scouting, covering, or mentioning unless the regime says otherwise.

But even those who ignited the rebellion in Sinai had never anticipated the abrupt escalation and the speed with which events unfolded until they were witnessing and taking part in it; all they could do was try to keep up with the momentum, and they did.

"The revolution was never planned, nothing was planned but a few protests and sit-ins calling for the release of prisoners and dropping the prolonged absentia prison terms that had haunted hundreds of Sinai Bedouins for years," said Mustafa Singer. "It started off as a desperate call for reform."

The Official Story

Egypt's security and government officials—without presenting transparent, independent, and unbiased field investigations, or the reason for not presenting them as the basis for their argument—have a different version of the story of North Sinai's revolution. Their version denies that a revolution happened in the first place, but claims that it was an evil conspiracy carried out by the Gaza-ruling Hamas movement and the Egyptian Muslim Brotherhood to topple the Egyptian regime and plunge the country into total chaos.

"All of those attacks were planned and executed by Hamas and the Muslim Brotherhood," said Colonel Khaled Okasha, the head of North Sinai's Civil Defense Department until 2012. "Hamas wanted to free its members in Egyptian jails, the Muslim Brotherhood leaders who were detained wanted to be freed, and the Lebanese Hezbollah coordinated with Hamas to free its members as well."

On January 28, Okasha received a call informing him that the EGID had spotted significant activity at the border with Gaza, dotted with hundreds of clandestine underground tunnels. "The information spread to different security offices in North Sinai and indicated that dozens of Gazans were crossing the underground tunnels, heavily armed and driving four-wheel pick-up trucks." Tunnels have been customized to fit cars since 2009, and were enhanced after 2011 to fit four-wheelers comfortably so cars wouldn't be damaged.

Colonel Okasha's testimony, which was endorsed by a number of security officials, but not by a single civilian from North Sinai, proposes that the Hamas brigade that infiltrated the border on January 28 had miraculously taken full control of the area, waged the massive attack on the Rafah government departments, and then continued to Sheikh Zuwayyed to destroy its security compound before driving some 500 kilometers to Cairo, with their four-wheel drives and heavy armaments, to successfully attack and break open several jails surrounding the capital, including two maximum security prison compounds.

"The plan was executed in cooperation with criminals from Sinai's Bedouin tribes," said Colonel Okasha. "The kinds of weapons they used [machine guns, RPGs, and unsophisticated explosives] were never available in Sinai, but always in the Gaza Strip."

Despite Colonel Okasha's consistent testimony, the facts and numbers in this story have varied from one security official to another since January 2011. The Hamas brigade was said to be an eighty-member force and at other times eight hundred; they controlled sixty kilometers of Egypt's eastern border and at times six hundred kilometers. The various stories, saturated with ignorance, provided proof that some Egyptian security officials and analysts didn't even know the geography of their country's most volatile frontier. If Hamas did control sixty kilometers of the eastern border, then it controlled the fourteen-kilometer borderline with the Gaza Strip and, miraculously, forty-six kilometers of the border with Israel, and, if they, according to other testimonies, controlled six hundred kilometers, then they controlled land and sea borders stretching all the way to Saudi Arabia.

What has been repeated by Egyptian former and current officials, security officers, politicians, and media personalities about what went on in Sinai during the eighteen days of the January 25 revolution is just a failed, and disgraceful, attempt to distort one of the most important phases of the country's history.

"What they are saying is simply nonsense, they are the sort of air-conditioned studio analysts who make up stories, but never dare, or know, how to apply field investigations," said Hassan al-Nakhlawi. "Whoever says those weapons weren't [already] in Sinai doesn't know what Sinai is, even if they were top security officers."

But Hamas isn't innocent either. This revolution was as much of an opportunity for them as it was for their mother organization, the Muslim Brotherhood. They had their own decades-old, marred-by-corruption feud with the Mubarak regime and have exploited their geographical, political, security, and criminal relations with Egypt, especially in the Sinai Peninsula, for over a decade.

"Some Hamas officials reached out to me and a few of my affiliates on January 25. They asked about the atmosphere and proposed planning something to release their prisoners, especially the top ones. They wanted Ayman Noufal,"[16] Abu Arrab al-Sawarka,[17] a Bedouin kingpin heavily involved in the smuggling of weapons to the Gaza Strip, told me. "We strongly refused taking part in any such plans, the situation was expected to explode at any second and we had our own lives, families, and interests to take care of at such an extraordinary time."

Abu Arrab started a discreet initiative among some of the strongest and most feared members of the Sawarka, Tarabin, and Remeilat tribes— the three most powerful who controlled everything happening in the northeastern quarter of Sinai and the border with the Gaza Strip. The network of kingpins unified against Hamas's call, in line with Abu Arrab's counterinitiative, were mainly concerned about the consequences of a blunt Hamas movement into their tribal territories. The Bedouins had been smuggling weapons and goods into Gaza, and they ran the tunnels with a tight grip, but they had absolutely no tolerance for Hamas activity on their turf that could cost them dearly, whether sooner or later.

"We called everyone we could reach, we started with the lower-rank Hamas officers from the Tunnels Affairs Commission and we escalated all the way until we reached Ahmed al-Jaabari, the Hamas' military chief and commander of its armed wing, the Qassam Brigades," said Abu Arrab. "Our message was sharp and clear, shutdown and secure the tunnels from your side, and do not interfere in our domestic issues no matter how volatile it gets."

Abu Arrab and his fellow Sinai Bedouins weren't the only ones approached by Hamas. "They also reached out to Bedouin clans from the outskirts of Cairo. They were a better option as they had members already sharing prison wards with the Hamas, Hezbollah, and other political and Islamist prisoners. Hamas wanted their military chiefs, and whoever helped them wanted their members, jailed for drug smuggling, out."[18]

All smuggling operations had been suspended by the Sinai Bedouins since January 25, and the Qassam Brigades deployed reinforcements along the border. The only incursion that took place was when Gazan armed troops infiltrated the border on January 28. Along with Colonel Khaled Okasha, several others who witnessed or took part in the armed rebellion confirmed this breach, but gave conflicting theories to as why the troops crossed into Egypt.

The infiltration coincided with the first attack on prison facilities on January 28, on the maximum security Wadi al-Natrun Prison Compound, which was later described as a test of the security of the compound and proves that the attacks weren't executed by Hamas operatives. When it happened, the Muslim Brotherhood officers who had been detained a day earlier hadn't yet arrived at the prison; they were still in custody at the October 6 Security Directorate some one hundred kilometers away, and none of the Hamas or Hezbollah members jailed in Egypt were in that prison.[19]

These attacks on prisons were seen by many as the reason for the Hamas breach, not the other way around. "The Hamas troopers came to secure the transportation of their people that would soon be released from jail," said Abu Arrab. "They kept a very low profile and had no interest in what was happening in North Sinai; they had a precise goal that wasn't to be disrupted by anything even if it was as unprecedented as what happened in Rafah and Sheikh Zuwayyed."

Mustafa Singer of Sheikh Zuwayyed, Ibrahim Abu Ashraf al-Menaei of al-Mehdiya, and Hassan al-Nakhlawi from al-Arish, along with many others from different towns across North Sinai, endorsed Abu Arrab's testimony.

Prison Breaks

By January 30, more than 22,000 inmates had escaped from five major prisons that had fallen under synchronized attacks a day earlier. The attacks were heavily armed and in one case bulldozers were used to destroy parts of the prison walls. All five prisons, Wadi al-Natrun, Abu Zaabal, al-Marg, al-Fayoum, and Qena, hosted notorious criminals sentenced to life or on death row alongside political and Islamist prisoners. The top thirty-seven members of the Muslim Brotherhood movement, who were rounded up on January 27, were transferred to Wadi al-Natrun Prison Compound on January 29 despite the initial attack on January 28 and complaints by the warden. Hours after their arrival, it was under attack for the second time.

Mohamed Morsi, at that time an unknown Muslim Brotherhood senior official, called the famous al-Jazeera news channel around noon on January 30. He was allowed enough airtime to describe how they left the prison facility after the administration and security guards fled and left the compound unguarded. They were, according to Morsi, the last prisoners to leave. "We are standing on the highway to Alexandria, in front of the prison gate. We will be waiting here and if you call us in an hour we will update you on our situation," were Morsi's last words on air.

On the other side of the capital, leading Qassam Brigades officer Ayman Noufal, along with a few of his Gazan colleagues, and Sami Shehab[20] of Hezbollah, also walked out of al-Marg prison. Noufal and Shehab had already gotten in touch with their organizations and were both picked up by fellow members amid the chaos right outside the prison. Within a few days, and before the downfall of Mubarak, Noufal and several other Gazans who escaped Egypt's prisons were met by celebrations as they crossed the smuggling tunnels back into their homeland, the Gaza Strip.

Throughout 2011, the prison breaks were said to have been a plan sketched out by Minister of the Interior Habib El-Adly and the SSI department to plunge the country into a state of chaos and nationwide fear that would automatically smear the mass protests as an anarchist explosion and sway the public from endorsing it. Figures in Mubarak's regime had fiercely denied such allegations and, through their rhetoric about how the revolution was a conspiracy, they insisted on the role played by Hamas and Hezbollah to aid their domestic Egyptian partner, the Muslim Brotherhood who sought to topple Mubarak's regime.

But as the former regime lost control over its own men and the media in general, opposing theories emerged. Mubarak's longtime policymaker, advisor, and former Egyptian Ambassador to Vienna, Mostafa al-Fiqqi, appeared on television at a time when he was attempting to neutralize his relations with whichever political current was going to takeover in the aftermath of the uprising, and declared that "opening the prisons was a plan put in place originally to be activated in case of Mubarak's death."[21]

The plan, according to al-Fiqqi, was meant to terrify the public before Gamal Mubarak took over his father's position and used the security apparatus to bring back stability, which would portray him as the savior who rescued the nation at a time of turmoil. "The plan was hastily activated when the unexpected revolution broke out."

Staggering as it was, al-Fiqqi's on-air testimony was seen as speculative. However, it seemed to be corroborated by another that came from Major Amr al-Dardir, Head Investigations Officer of Minya Prison at the time of the revolution. Major al-Dardir's meticulous testimony was also broadcast live when he was interviewed in March 2011 by one of Egypt's most viewed television news analysis shows presented by Hafez al-Mirazi, back then a prominent presenter from the Dream Satellite Channel.

"The only escape attempt took place at Minya Prison on February 14, 2011 [three days after Mubarak's resignation], when prisoners managed to break open four of their cells and took four security personnel hostage inside their wards," said Major al-Dardir during his interview with al-Mirazi. "Ten minutes after we reported the incident, Minya Security Director General Mohsen Murad arrived to the prison compound."[22]

Major al-Dardir said that all communication with the commanders of the Ministry of the Interior was lost during the revolution, but the officers and security personnel of the prison took matters into their own hands and remained in the prison compound for thirty-eight straight days. When the Security Director General Murad arrived, Major al-Dardir requested a minor reinforcement of one central security troop armed only with tear gas to contain the riots, but was shocked when General Murad turned down his request, and ordered him to stand down and let him handle the situation.

Major al-Dardir recalls the conversation:

> At the time I remembered all that we heard about the Ministry of the Interior's plan to intentionally open the prisons, which is something I never believed before that moment General Murad handed me his phone and asked me to speak to General Adly Fayed [deputy minister for general security], who was on the line.
>
> General Fayed said: "I am your brother and I am concerned about you, just listen to General Murad and let him handle the situation."

The major's reply to both superiors was clear: "What you're planning will never happen in my prison, no prisoner will escape under my command."

Major al-Dardir, who refused to mention the names of his military and police comrades "in order not to harm them and to be solely responsible for my testimony," said that he sidelined General Murad and decided to raid the rioting prison wards. During the forty-five minutes of General Murad's refusal to reinforce the prison guards and his insistence they stand down, the number of open cells had reached 113 out of a total 186. Finally, almost an hour later, a successful raid led by Major al-Dardir released all four captive personnel, leaving three prisoners killed and eleven wounded.

Instead of receiving a medal of honor, Major al-Dardir, who was threatened by General Murad at the scene, was suspended two months later. "I conveyed this testimony in detail to the Minister of the Interior Mansour el-Essawy and his successor General Mohamed Ibrahim, I was also questioned six times over the details of this incident by the Prisons Inspection Authority, but I can tell you that we don't have inspections authorities, we have a number of commanders who are led by Habib El-Adly [former minister of the interior] from his prison cell," said Major al-Dardir.

Ending his on-air interview, Major al-Dardir asked several police generals who were being hosted by the television show to explain "how General Nazih Gadallah, warden of the Fayoum Prison whose 4,500 prisoners escaped during the revolution, was later promoted to be deputy minister for prisons affairs? If he couldn't handle his one prison, how did you promote him to head the prisons nationwide?"

Months later, when Egypt's judiciary officially held a trial to investigate the prison breaks during the January 25 uprising, neither Mostafa al-Fiqqi nor Major Amr al-Dardir were even brought in for questioning, let alone to give their testimonies on the record.

A Righteous Rebellion

"If the Egyptian regime admits that this was a popular uprising then they will accordingly be admitting to all of their oppression and crimes, which were the reasons behind the events," said Hassan al-Nakhlawi, who had gone from being a detainee of the SSI to being one of their most relentless enemies through his organization, the Sinai Prisoners Defense Front. For Nakhlawi, whose opinion is shared by thousands of fellow Bedouins, Hosni Mubarak's unchecked security apparatus was Sinai's biggest fear and was the main reason behind the armed rebellion.

The Sinai prisoners' cases go back to October 7, 2004, when a terrorist attack simultaneously hit the Hilton Taba Hotel and two other beach camps in South Sinai, killing 34 and injuring more than 150 people. The bombings unleashed the fury of Egypt's police apparatus led by General Habib El-Adly, Mubarak's long time minister of the interior who had applied the emergency law to its deadliest extent since occupying his position in 1997. El-Adly, the former head of the SSI, succeeded Hassan El-Alfy who was fired by Mubarak at Luxor Airport after the bloody Luxor massacre, committed by Islamist radicals, that claimed the lives of fifty-eight tourists and four Egyptians.

A massive campaign of arbitrary detentions kicked-off a week after the Taba bombings. Whole towns and villages were rounded up and led to detention centers for prolonged torture and interrogation sessions before being transferred to jails across Egypt. According to Human Rights Watch's 2005 report *Egypt: Mass Arrests and Torture in Sinai*, "security forces rounded up as many as three thousand people, including several hundred persons detained solely to secure the surrender of wanted family members."[23]

Some of those arrested as bargaining chips to secure the surrender of their relatives were women and children, which in the eyes of the Bedouins constitutes an unforgivable and unforgettable violation of tribal traditions, a violation to be revenged only by blood.

The security offices around Sinai and jails across Egypt became black holes for the Sinai detainees. "Family members were afraid to 'cause trouble' by pressing officials for information about detained relatives. They learned only informally, if at all, about the whereabouts of their husbands, sons, fathers and brothers from those who had been with them in detention but were now released," said Human Rights Watch's report.

The Sinai Peninsula had never experienced anything on such a scale before. The Taba bombings, which claimed the lives of twelve Israelis, was a slap in the face of El-Adly, the celebrated minister of the interior whose harsh policies were seen to have saved Egypt from the terrorism of the 1990s. According to Nakhlawi's Sinai Prisoners Defense Front, in just a few months the number of detainees had risen to 5,000.[24] Torture was as rampant as ever. Those detained weren't on or awaiting trial, they were arbitrarily arrested by the lethal, unchecked power of the emergency law that had remained in force since the assassination of President Anwar Sadat in 1981.

"At some point, almost every family in Sinai had detained members, my two brothers were among the detainees during the Taba bombings case," said Nakhlawi, who was also detained himself a few years after the bombing over his boisterous political activism.

Long-time reporter Ahmed Abu Draa, a prominent Sinai journalist and a Bedouin member of the Sawarka tribe, was also detained along with his two brothers. "They raided our house at dawn looking for my brother because his phone number was scribbled on a bearded schoolmate's book. They took all three of us," said Abu Draa.

In 2005, details of torture sessions became running stories whispered in every house across the Sinai Peninsula. Beatings weren't considered torture, sleep and food deprivation weren't either. The most common form of torture was stripping the detainee naked, tying their hands together, hanging them by the hands and electrocuting them in the genitals. It was the beginning of winter when the bombings took place and the crackdown began, and tossing cold water at someone hung naked in a concrete cell with electrical wires plugged to their body was an indescribably horrible but common crime.[25]

El-Adly's SSI apparatus, a keen student of the US counterterrorism and homeland security agencies, also dubbed the torture sessions "enhanced interrogation." One the most prominent officers of the enhanced interrogations of the 2004 campaign was Colonel E., the target of the first Rafah attack that destroyed the SSI office on January 28, 2011. Back then, he was a senior South Sinai SSI officer and a lead investigator in the Taba bombings case.

As infamous as Colonel E. was the late General A., al-Arish's state security inspector, who was moved to Ismailiya and died in 2010, months before the outbreak of the revolution. "Most of North Sinai's torture sessions took place in the state security office in al-Arish. It was a slaughterhouse headed by A.," said Nakhlawi, who had first-hand experience of enhanced interrogations. "As for E., he was promoted after his South Sinai time, which put people on death row over trumped-up charges. He was appointed the Rafah head of state security."

Despite dying in 2010, General A.'s legacy outlived him. His villa on the coast of al-Arish was overtaken by several of his Bedouin victims a few days after the disappearance of police forces, while his apartment in Ismailiya was torched by unknown assailants in January 2011. The list of those whose hands remain stained with the blood spilled during the 'enhanced interrogation' sessions contained more than twenty officers and a massive number of sergeants and staff sergeants. Such lists carrying the names, ranks, and phone numbers of the officers were leaked after an attack on the SSI Directorate in the capital, Cairo, in March 2011. Each person on the list was accused by many Sinai victims of personally torturing them during their incarceration.[26]

The same arbitrary detention and torture campaigns continued after the 2005 bombings in Sharm al-Sheikh, the luxurious beach resort where Hosni Mubarak spent the majority of his last ten years, and the

2006 bombings in the world-famous scuba diving town of Dahab. The top reasons for arbitrary detention, other than suspicion of being related to the bombings, were affiliation with Islamist groups, political activism, and refusing to cooperate with the authorities—in other words, refusing to become an informer. Those who managed to avoid detention by escaping into the vast rugged terrain received sentences in absentia for charges varying from drug trafficking to attacking the police force.

As for the military, it was not involved whatsoever in the detention or torture, but it handed down around six hundred prison sentences in absentia to people living in the border areas over accusations of smuggling, some of which were based on police investigations.[27]

"The lucky ones would be transferred to prison facilities. Some detainees prayed for this moment that meant an unknown detention period, but less torture or none at all," said Nakhlawi. "This was the rule except if you were transferred to al-Gharbaniyat Prison, the one I was transferred to."

Nakhlawi was detained in 2006 for his activism against Israel during its short July war in Lebanon. He received several security warnings conveyed through the elders of his family and one night was dragged out of his house before dawn, in his underwear, almost blind without his glasses.

"They partied on me for a few days before I was transferred to the notorious prison. I was still in my underwear when transferred from al-Arish's torture factory to the prison in western Alexandria, and still without my glasses."

'Al-Gharbaniyat,' to where Nakhlawi was transferred, is the decades-old name used by prisoners and guards to refer to the Burj al-Arab Maximum Security Prison Compound in western Alexandria, a prison that over the years became any prisoner's worst nightmare. Those who landed there came out with expertise in endurance and survival, and when transferred to other jails were among the most feared prisoners. No one knows with certainty why this became its name, but Masaad Abu Fajr, a Sinai author and activist who was jailed there several times, explained it in an article published by a local newspaper:

> It's an ancient name used by Bedouins of the western desert to refer to the land on which the prison was built. I asked some of my Bedouin prison mates about the meaning of al-Gharbaniyat, they said it

referred to the large numbers of crows in the area. They also said that not far from the prison is the site of an ancient prison. The land on which it was built is a saline area where no plant grows, they loathed it and never shepherded their cattle through it, and if someone was forced to cross it they would do it hastily as they feared its evil spirits.[28]

It was the first to be built by former Minister of the Interior General Habib El-Adly, who competed with older officers of Egypt's police force by incorporating his American security education with his locally constructed oppression tactics. The massive prison facility is made up of thirty eighteen-cell wards, five of which were reserved for political prisoners.

The stories and torture testimonies coming from behind its walls were terrifying. There were two classes for those transferred to al-Gharbaniyat from all over Egypt: political prisoners, who received better treatement, or criminal inmates, who lived in the worst conditions. Which category the detainee landed under was a matter of luck or depended on how much the officers wanted to humiliate and torture them. Some Sinai prisoners were transferred as political prisoners while their mates and sometimes brothers, who may have been detained at the same time for similar reasons, could be tagged criminal, and the contrast in treatment and conditions was blinding.

Al-Nakhlawi was one of those to document some of al-Gharbaniyat's horrors, after his 2006 experience there, in a written testimony for a local website:

> I watched with my own eyes what several prisoners described as a normal practice. The harshest form of abuse was when prisoners were lined against the prison wall, ordered to strip naked and defecate. Whoever wasn't capable of defecating immediately was brutally beaten by prison guards using thick hosepipes as whips, then a water hose was inserted in their behind and the tap opened fully.[29]

By January 25, 2011, there were around one hundred Sinai detainees in different prisons on different charges, including the Taba bombing case defendants, three of whom were sentenced to death but never executed, in addition to around three hundred sentenced in absentia and who remained at large, and a few hundred military-court sentences, also in absentia.[30]

"The regime turned each one of those victims [detained or sentenced in absentia] into a ticking bomb, their cases never settled over the years, and the regime refused to incorporate them into society. Some of them were innocent people who were forced into criminal activities by the unjust, fabricated sentences," said al-Nakhlawi. His words were confirmed by the first post-revolution minister of the interior, who replaced El-Adly before the downfall of Mubarak: "I know that Sinai suffered an unfair campaign of trials and sentences in absentia," said General Mahmoud Wagdi.[31]

Taking Over Security

Meanwhile, back in January 2011, with every member of Egypt's security authorities in the towns of Sheikh Zuwayyed and Rafah having either fled the peninsula or bunkered down inside the fortified central security barracks, the northeastern quarter of Sinai, stretching from east of al-Arish to the border with the Gaza Strip, was left to be handled by vigilante patrols formed in cooperation between the tribes.

Inside al-Arish, the situation was quite similar, security personnel were forced to stay inside the Security Directorate, the one remaining government compound out of three police stations, the police hotel, and the central security barracks.

Tribal elders, mosque Imams, and revered clerics were coordinating with dozens of youth in residential areas and villages to take over security responsibilities; the only difference between the vigilantes of Sinai and those of Cairo and other cities was the weapons they carried and their traditional tribal attire. Road blocks were formed, areas of jurisdiction were drawn according to family, clan, and tribal territories, and the wise elders kept a close eye on any developments that could lead to the outbreak of tribal disputes.

From then on, protests and marches were held on a daily basis in North Sinai's capital, al-Arish. The small protests that sparked the revolution had transformed into major, organized sit-ins that surrounded the governorate offices in the heart of the city, while many of Sinai's youth left to join the protesters in Cairo's Tahrir Square.

"From that day, North Sinai wasn't under Egypt's control anymore, the eastern border was pushed in some fifty kilometers, to east of al-Arish," said Colonel Okasha, who witnessed the unfolding events, and the downfall of every security and government authority east of al-Arish from his office, where the secure landline was.

A Shock to Tel Aviv

Israel maintained a 'no comment' policy throughout the first days of the Egyptian revolution. The Israeli media was reporting the unfolding events in Cairo and across the country as much as the international media, but government officials refrained from exposing the country's concerns over its neighbor that had remained stable for three decades.

On January 31, Israeli Prime Minister Benjamin Netanyahu broke the silence with his comments in a joint press conference with German chancellor Angela Merkel. Watching the downfall of Egypt's police, the explosive events in the Sinai, and the rising number of deaths across the country, Netanyahu expressed his deep concerns.[32]

Israeli officials and political experts in Jerusalem and Tel Aviv didn't hide how surprised and sometimes terrified they had been to see the blows dealt to the only regime they considered a peaceful neighbor.[33]

"I was surprised by two things: the weakness of the Mubarak regime controlling the streets in the early stages and the courage that people demonstrated," said Ehud Yaari, a prominent Israeli TV personality and an expert on Egyptian–Israeli relations. "It was a given for anybody, someone like me who spent lots of time in Egypt, that the socio-economic situation was leading at some point down the road to some volcanic eruption, but I didn't expect it in 2011."[34]

Yaari explained that Israel believed Egypt would go into political and social turmoil if Gamal Mubarak, who he referred to as "Jimmy," inherited his aging father's seat as president. "We expected problems if Hosni Mubarak died suddenly and we believed that the military and Omar Suleiman [head of Egypt's General Intelligence Directorate under Mubarak] would never allow Jimmy to take over."

The change consecutive Israeli regimes believed would eventually take place wasn't a popular uprising, and they weren't concerned much about Gamal Mubarak's anticipated rise to power because they were somehow confident that their partners in peace, the Egyptian military and intelligence, would contain the explosive situation and hold together what Mubarak had maintained for thirty years.

Contrary to the shock of the politicians, Tel Aviv University's professor of humanities Mira Tzoreff was watching what she had repeatedly said would happen since her 2010 article titled "Restless young Egyptians: Where did you come from and where will you go?"[35]

Speaking in an interview, Professor Tzoreff explained:

I said in 2008 that Egypt's youth are like dynamite. When you have so many highly educated people, jobless, open to the world, not living nor alive as young people should, they become dynamite for any autocrat.

I wasn't that surprised as everybody was here, or in the United States or in Europe, because for them what mattered was Mubarak, but we looked below, to the society. The Arab Islamic society had their own vision and dreams and if they cannot accomplish them they will blow in many ways, call it a revolution, a coup d'état or whatever. They did blow.

The Israelis think the peace treaty is very breakable, and so Hosni Mubarak saved it despite going through many crises like the Lebanon war, the Iraq war and whatever happened in Gaza over the years. He suffered criticism from many Arab countries and yet he preserved the treaty and accordingly he was precious to them.[36]

To Israel, a revolution taking down Hosni Mubarak was equivalent to the bullets that assassinated Anwar Sadat, and if the Camp David Peace Accords weren't killed with Sadat in 1981, maybe they would be brought down with Mubarak in 2011. In both unanticipated instances, Mubarak's dear friend in Jerusalem, Benjamin Ben Eliezer, Israel's former deputy prime minister and member of the Knesset, broke down in tears fearing that it might be the end for the peace with Egypt, a fear deemed legitimate by dozens of Israeli politicians and military men.[37]

2

BOMBING THE GAS PIPELINE: ATTACKING ISRAEL ON EGYPTIAN SOIL

The only one who spoke was a Bedouin native of the Sinai Peninsula; he was masked, but his accent was instantly recognizable. The other five, also masked and armed with AK-47s, did not speak a word. "This has nothing to do with you, leave right now, or you will be shot," the technicians and guards, who happened to be on duty the night of February 5, 2011, at al-Mazraa control chamber of North Sinai's natural gas pipeline supplying Israel, Jordan, and Sinai, were told.

The Toyota Land Cruiser, carrying the five unidentified men guided by the Sinai native, arrived at the pipeline control chamber at around 7:45 a.m. The bombing was apparently planned to the last detail, not that there were many details to be planned. The guards were unarmed and the massive control chamber, located some fifty kilometers from Egypt's border with Gaza, was surrounded by stretches of desert from three sides and a small village several meters from the fourth.[1]

Egypt was in the midst of an uprising and the military was struggling to fill thousands of positions abandoned by police officers who took off their uniforms and escaped from every place where they could be identified as members of Egypt's loathed police force, which became the main target of boiling revolutionary anger.

"We immediately obeyed the order. None of us was willing to resist when ordered by masked, armed men who seemed ready to kill if this is what finishing the job they traveled for required," said Abu Sakl,[2] using the name of his clan from al-Arish, not his real name. He was one of the two guards who were led out of the control chamber, along with the rest of the technicians.

A few minutes after the workers walked out, the masked men had already strapped the explosives to the pipeline, stretched the initiation wire for about a hundred meters outside of the chamber, and successfully taken their first shot at Israel's interests on Egyptian soil. The successful attack was carried out five days after Benjamin Netanyahu expressed his deep concern over the unfolding events in Egypt.

The four-wheel-drive vehicle sped off along the highway leading to the border riddled with smuggling tunnels that have transported the means of life and war to the Gaza Strip over the years. The attackers left nothing but the remaining piece of the initiation wire, and a sky-high pillar of flames that lasted a few hours. The wire was collected by a Bedouin who kept it as a memento of the first of many attacks to hit the pipeline.

"We thought Israel was attacking Egypt, the explosion rocked our houses," said Mohamed Yahya,[3] whose house stands a couple of hundred yards from the chamber. He described how everyone came running out, some jumped out of their beds to the sound of the explosion, while others who lived closer to the walls of the chamber watched their houses burn down while they took refuge at the far end of the block along with their neighbors.

Salman Abu Zeina, who owns a poultry farm several yards from the chamber, heard the explosion from his house a few miles away. "I looked out of my top floor balcony and saw flames while receiving calls from my workers."[4] He arrived a half hour after the explosion to find dozens of dead chickens at his farm and his workers desperately trying to save the rest.

Abu Zeina, who studied chemistry, said he noticed the initiation wire as soon as he arrived at the site, and believes TNT was the explosive material used by the attackers. "What I saw makes me believe it wasn't locals who did this, Egyptians are not familiar with making and handling explosives and it's not a part of their culture. Those who know about such things don't live here; they are either in jail or outside of the country where they can apply whatever they learned."

"It could have been foreigners or members of the radical groups that escaped Egyptian jails a few days before the attack," said Abu Zeina, adding that he knew the guide was a Sinai Bedouin even before hearing the testimonies of those who identified the accent with which they were threatened. "The guide has to be a local; he is their green light through a million issues that could come in their way while driving with explosives in such a tight-knit tribal community. The local element is the only guarantee for foreigners in Sinai."

Up until this explosion, media organizations—local or international, politicians, activists, and the rest of the population were too occupied by what was going on in Egypt's major cities since the beginning of the revolution on January 25, 2011. When the explosives ripped through the pipeline, Cairo was dealing with political and security events unprecedented in the history of the country. Tahrir Square was the epicenter, and Sinai remained on the periphery, unless an explosion ripped through something close or somehow related to Egypt's eastern neighbor and partner in peace, Israel.

Despite the deadly battles that had broken out in North Sinai and destroyed the vast majority of its government facilities, the gas pipeline bombing was the first major news to come out of the peninsula. *Al-Masry al-Youm*'s Sinai reporter Ahmed Abu Draa, and CNN's Mohamed Fahmy were the first to report on the attack.

On January 28, 2011, or the Friday of Anger, Egypt's military tanks and armored personnel carriers were deployed across the country. The military's unprecedented mobilization took place as police forces disappeared after days of bloody confrontations with protesters that killed hundreds and injured thousands of civilians. The military took to the streets with the priority of securing what government officials routinely described as "high-importance and sensitive facilities."

The gas pipeline to Israel, Jordan, and the industrial facilities of Sinai, however, turned out to be facilities neither of high-importance nor sensitive, at least to the Supreme Council of the Armed Forces (SCAF), who took over when Mubarak left office; the regime seemed to suddenly think that North Sinai did not qualify for any form of heightened or exceptional security measures, or it simply could not control it after days of armed attacks on government facilities.

Another Bombing

On July 5, 2011, exactly five months after the first successful attack on the gas pipeline, another bombing rocked another of its control chambers south of Bir al-Abd, a key town west of al-Arish. It was the third successful attack to target the much loathed business with neighboring Israel.

Ahmed Abu Draa had access to the bomb site, although at the time of informing me of this he offered no more information, adhering to the rule of not discussing security or crime, or talking about the authorities while on the phone just in case someone happened to be silently, and without our consent, taking part in our conversation.[5]

The drive from Cairo to al-Arish takes almost five hours, and passes a large checkpoint located at the al-Salam Bridge that crosses the Suez Canal—the largest and most important bridge in Egypt and the northern entrance to North Sinai. Routine checks are carried out at this checkpoint by police and military personnel, using often outdated and unreliable equipment.[6] The checkpoint at al-Salam Bridge isn't any different from other checkpoints along the 230 kilometers of asphalt stretching across the Mediterranean coast of the peninsula, cutting through every city, town, or village. A false sense of heightened security kicks in when approaching these mini-garrisons of tanks and high-caliber machine guns mounted on armored machinery, manned by sweaty, sun-burnt, and always fed-up conscripts clutching AK-47s.[7]

Abu Draa told the driver to turn left onto a dirt road leading straight into the yellowness of the desert. "This is it," he said pointing at two red brick chambers off the dirt road a few hundred yards ahead. Surprisingly, there was no sign of security forces at the freshly attacked facility, not a single man in uniform around the chamber or anywhere near the asphalt approaching the site. The closest security checkpoint was at least twenty kilometers further down the road, and the one before that was more than fifty kilometers back.

The so-called pipeline security personnel were nothing but six Bedouins sitting at what could barely be called a shack, made out of plastic sacks sliced open and sewed together to form a sheet that the Bedouin guards stretched over wooden logs to shield themselves from the smoldering July sun. The Bedouin guards knew Abu Draa, who had filmed the sky-high flames the previous night and lost his shoes as "the soles melted while I filmed the fire."

The guards wore traditional Bedouin *thoubs*, or long robes, and covered their heads with *agdas*, or headscarves. They invited us into their shack where they sat on the sand. None of them mentioned their real names. They referred to each other by their tribes' names: Dawaghri came from the Dawaghra tribe, Bayadi was from the Bayadiya tribe, and so forth. They said the bombers drove their four-wheel-drive vehicles through the southern desert, left the cars and crawled for almost a kilometer to reach both chambers and plant the explosives.[8] Shortly after, one chamber exploded, but the other didn't. The explosives from the second chamber were seized by the authorities as evidence that never helped them identify the attackers.

The exploded chamber was completely devastated: the gate was charred and had been blown-open, while a massive hole was left in the brick wall. The bombers had attached explosives to the main valve and then fled back into the darkness of the Sinai desert. Minutes later the bomb went off, ripping a ten-centimeter wide hole through the pipe extending below the valve.

Mocking the police and military officers that arrived later to lead the investigation, Dawaghri, the one who seemed to speak on behalf of his fellow guards, continued:

> The officers walked around and had no clue what went on or what they should look for, the only thing they had was the six of us, so they started questioning us as if we bombed the chamber. We walked around after sunrise and saw the tracks of eight people who had crawled in, we followed the tracks to find other tracks of vehicles almost a kilometer to the south.

"Following and identifying tracks is something we learn as kids in our desert but those policemen never learned it in the police academy," Dawaghri added with a smirk.

It wasn't surprising that Dawaghri mocked the *hukouma*, which literally means 'government,' but is the colloquial Arabic word Egyptians use to refer to all types of government employees, especially policemen. His attitude was very similar to most Egyptians when speaking about the government, or the pipeline bombings. The guards were left unarmed in the infinite darkness of the Sinai desert, the chambers had no electricity, and, accordingly, the only vision the Bedouin guards had was when they decided to cook or boil some peppermint tea. "We did not hear or see anything," said Dawaghri. "A few meters away from that fire we set for cooking you cannot even see your own hands."

The guards' monthly salaries ranged between LE600 and LE1,000, the equivalent of US$100 to US$160, at the time of writing. None of them were happy with this salary, but, as Dawaghri said, "We have no other option but to starve to death or join the smugglers."

"This is how we live here, this is how the government treats us," said Bayadi, the Bedouin guard from the Bayadiya tribe. "You outsiders don't know anything about what we suffer. We are forced to swallow this bitterness every day and night."

Being called an "outsider" brought no surprise; in fact, it was clear how Bayadi viewed Cairo. Most Sinai natives refer to area of the Nile Valley and the Delta as just 'the valley'—it has the cities, the schools, the hotels and shopping malls, and above all, the government. The Nile was the country-long river, whose rewards had not reached them. Journalists just drove in in their sedans and took their photos with cameras worth enough money to feed their families for over a year.

The Hatred Behind the Bombing

"The Egyptian government was never transparent about the natural gas agreement with Israel," said Ibrahim Abu Elayyan, initially talking in a diplomatic tone. Abu Elayyan is secretary general of the Arab Tribes Union, an association established in 2004 to preserve tribal heritage and address the issues of tribal communities across Egypt. The non-governmental organization went far beyond Sinai; it covered the tribal communities of the western desert, Upper Egypt, and the Red Sea.[9]

"If this deal was legitimate and fair the people might accept it, but we have to know what the government is doing," he went on, also saying that tribal leaders suggested to the Egyptian government that they hire Bedouins and license their arms to secure the pipeline tactically. If the government agreed, he said, the facility would have garnered more respect from everyone including those who may think of targeting it. The government refused and the state-owned Egypt Gas Company, without any coordination with tribal leaders, hired the unarmed Bedouin guards from the chamber that was attacked. When the bombings started targeting the pipeline, Abu Elayyan and others confirmed, some of the guards bought weapons independently for self defense in case they found themselves in a confrontation with the attackers.

Turning abruptly nationalistic, Abu Elayyan went on:

> Even if they agreed and armed the Bedouin guards, how do you expect those guards to protect something they genuinely hate? We consider exporting gas to Israel in contradiction to our national principles and endorsing the enemy who we fought for decades and continue to fight until today. We are not even making any economic or political profit from such an agreement. Exporting gas to Israel is a dagger in Egypt's heart.

This prominent tribesman was not afraid to declare his animosity toward Israel and his total rejection of the peace treaty that millions of Egyptians look down on. But he was not in love with the Egyptian government either:

> The gas pipeline bombing is a clear example of the Egyptian government's failure on different levels. The pipeline runs very close to or through residential areas. We repeatedly advised the government to move the pipeline into the empty desert but they ignored our calls and went on building it through the towns of North Sinai. They built it in the wrong spot and then left it unprotected, it is now accessible to anyone who is angry at the government or Israel, and there is a long list of reasons to be angry at both of them.

Because of that long list, Abu Elayyan believed it was difficult to say "if the bombings were carried out by zealous patriots or by a foreign element. We have to wait for the investigation results, but we have been waiting since the first bombing." Abu Elayyan used a mocking tone very similar to that of Dawaghri, the Bedouin guard. He never spoke of the bombing as a criminal act; he perceived it as a natural reaction to a long list of social, economic, and political issues that negatively affected the tribal population of Sinai. He believed the government was to be blamed for the repeated attacks on the pipeline.

While Israel was receiving gas through the multi-billion-dollar pipeline, Egypt was suffering from gas shortages that kept it from fulfilling the agreement, and a lack of infrastructure to deliver gas to its people. Egyptians were paying black market prices of more than US$6 per gas tank, and Sinai, as always, presented a vivid example of marginalization and lack of development. Driving through Sinai's villages, either in the north, middle, or south of the peninsula, cooking gas tanks can be seen left on highways with a sum of money tied to the handle. Bedouins would sometimes walk for kilometers to leave the empty tanks on the sides of the road, in the hope that the distribution truck of the state-owned gas company would drive by before nightfall to replace them. If not, dinner would be cooked on a wood fire or served cold, or there would be no dinner at all.

In al-Arish, Sheikh Abdallah Jahama's opinion wasn't far from that of Abu Elayyan. A long-time Sinai parliamentarian and former chairman of the Sinai Mujahedeen Association—an association formed by more than seven hundred members of the Sinai popular resistance fighters during the seven years of Egyptian–Israeli war across the peninsula between 1976 and 1973—Jahama predicted that the attacks on the pipeline would continue, for very clear reasons.

Typical of Sinai's Bedouins, Jahama made it his business to spot and familiarize himself with any stranger that wanders around his town. For them, it's crucial to know if the stranger is a welcomed guest or a nosy trespasser. Meeting him at a crowded tea shop in the center of al-Arish, he immediately remembered having seen me a few weeks earlier with political activist and writer, Musaad Abu Fajr, after a long day of reporting at the Rafah Crossing Terminal.

> I did not look at the terms of that agreement with Israel, I don't know if it's fair and legitimate or not, but what I do know is our proverb: if the house needs it then it's forbidden even for the mosque to have it [*illi yerido al-beit, yerham 'ala al-jami'*]. If we need the gas, we should not give it to anyone, and definitely not to Israel.[10]

The tribal elder confirmed that the pipeline was bombed with the help of locals, but was sure that the planners weren't:

> I am confident that no stranger can come here, reach the control chambers in small towns, and bomb them without being spotted. They were helped by locals who knew their way around the desert and towns. This is a very tight-knit community where a stranger stands out and is noticed and remembered, just like I remembered you from the last time I saw you. Although I didn't know who you were, I knew you were not a local.
>
> Listen, we are humans, just like anyone anywhere across Egypt, we have criminals and poor people whose souls are weakened by money when they are in need. Moreover, there is no police or security since January 2011. Everyone is heavily armed and more weapons are flowing into the peninsula due to the security vacuum. I don't think it's strange that a local is hired to commit a crime or if they commit it out of a personal motive.

The Chorus of Disapproval

There are hundreds if not thousands of Egyptians who did support the gas agreement with Israel, or at least supported whatever Mubarak's regime did. But supporters of exporting natural gas to Israel were as unpopular as the pipeline itself, and most people harshly criticized and cursed Hosni Mubarak's regime over it. Discussing the agreement was a topic fueled with so much anger and nationalism that declaring yourself a supporter was a good enough reason for your closest friends to abandon you.

Even Mubarak's regime knew how much anger this murky agreement would stir up if publicized, and while the international and Israeli media discussed the agreement and its implications for both countries, Egypt's media was ordered to ignore the topic as if it never existed. The government succeeded at blacking out the agreement signed between Egypt and Israel in 2005 for three years until the gas had actually started flowing in 2008 through the hundred-kilometer sub-sea pipeline connecting North Sinai's capital al-Arish with the Israeli port of Ashkelon.

Hamdeen Sabbahi, the well-known Nasserite politician who ran for president and lost in 2012, broke the scandal to Egyptians and declared that the government had been exporting gas to Israel at, as he described it, "subsidized" prices. Back then, Sabbahi was a parliamentarian who fiercely, and constantly, criticized Mubarak's regime.

But nothing expressed how loathed and demonized this agreement was in the eyes of Egyptians as much as the statement officially published by al-Azhar Scholars Front on May 5, 2008.

To all of those working for the factories exporting Egyptian gas to the criminal Jews and Zionists:

After God has unveiled the secret intentions of the traitors and uncovering the worst crime of selling the nation's dignity and honor for a reduced price, they sold it and were content with little.

We tell those employees working for these factories—and we believe that, if they are Egyptians, they are unaware—protect yourselves from the curse and wrath of Allah, as well as history's and the people's curse, before becoming a nail in the coffin of Egypt. Protect your children, offspring, and families from the ill-gotten money which you make from aiding those who strive toward destruction. Beware that necessity or need are no justification for committing crimes. And as Allah's prophet said, "Everybody that is nourished on haraam, the fire is more befitting for it." Never sell your honor and dignity to criminals in return for a few worthless pounds. There is no immunity from criminal prosecution, and no guilty criminal is deemed innocent whoever they are. Allah says, *Protect yourselves and your families from a fire whose fuel is people and stones, over which are [appointed] angels, harsh, and severe; they do not disobey Allah in what He commands them but do what they are commanded* [al-Tahrim: verse 6]. For the safety of Egypt and the entire nation, do not obey anyone but Allah. *And do not obey the order of the transgressors, who cause corruption in the land and do not amend* [al-Shu'ara': 151–152].

Do not wrong yourselves and get involved with criminals who swindled and sold everything paving the way to a dark tomorrow, a black tomorrow, and a new ugly occupation which would not be less destructive than the occupation of Baghdad, the capital of the caliphates al-Mansour and al-Rasheed.

With your true willingness to do right and your cooperation in facing this by withdrawal, take the lead and rebel against treachery. If you have sincere intentions, you will never be defeated since no oppressor has power over people's hearts, and *If Allah knows [any] good in your hearts, He will give you [something] better than what was taken from you, and He will forgive you; and Allah is Forgiving and Merciful* [al-'Anfal: 70]. No excuses are acceptable when giving up its rights and belittling its value.

Intend, boycott, and show Allah and history that you have done what you could before the consequences of this crime surround you, and before it brings about destruction on you and your families. Bequeath your children an honorable legacy that befits you. This would be more rewarding than exerting your efforts in a world covered under the veil of treachery and decorated with debauchery. Allah, the Almighty, says, *Indeed, those whom the angels take [in death] while wronging themselves—[the angels] will say, "In what [condition] were you?" They will say, "We were oppressed in the land." The angels will say, "Was not the earth of Allah spacious [enough] for you to emigrate therein?" For those, their refuge is Hell—and evil it is as a destination* [al-Nisa': 97].

Then, have faith in Allah's victory and support since: *Indeed, Allah is with those who fear Him and those who are doers of good* [al-Nahl: 128].

So do not weaken and call for peace while you are superior; and Allah is with you and will never deprive you of [the reward of] your deeds [Muhammad: 35]. If you become loyal to your nation and faithful to Allah, *And to Allah belongs [all] honor, and to His Messenger, and to the believers, but the hypocrites do not know* [al-Munafiqun: 8].

Issued by the Azhar Scholars Front, on Monday, May 5, 2008. [11]

For centuries, al-Azhar has been known for its moderate interpretation of Islam; it has been and continues to be the seat of Sunni Islam looked up to by hundreds of millions of Muslims across the Islamic world. The statement published in 2008, under the merciless regime of Hosni Mubarak, revealed how popular and influential the anti-gas-export bloc was. The way moderate al-Azhar scholars viewed the gas agreement as treachery made it easy to speculate what the more conservative, or rather, extreme, Muslim Brotherhood, Salafis, and jihadists would think of it.

In 2008, months after Egypt's natural gas began fueling Israel's electricity plants, Cairo's administrative court accepted a legal action filed by Ibrahim Yousri, a lawyer, former Egyptian Ambassador to Algeria, and former head of the International Law and Treaties Department. Yousri, who started a famous online campaign, "No to Selling Gas to the Zionist Entity," demanded "full cancelation of the petroleum minister's decision permitting the sale of natural gas to Israel and also scrapping his decision to raise domestic gasoline prices because the difference in expenditure could be covered by the discounts Israel was receiving."[12]

Israel was buying Egyptian natural gas for prices eight to ten times less than prices paid by other countries to various exporters. The intermediary that ran the operation, Hussein Salem's East Mediterranean Gas Company (EMG), was paying Egypt a fixed price of US$1.5 per Million British Thermal Unit (MBTU), and the agreement dictated that the price would remain the same for a period of fifteen years regardless of the varying international market prices or the amount of gas exported.

"In the same year, natural gas was being exported [by other countries] to Japan for $12.5, not $1.5," said Mika Minio-Paluello, an analyst of the London-based energy think-tank Platform, who was featured in "Egypt's Lost Power," an al-Jazeera documentary investigating the details of the gas agreement. "Germany was receiving gas from Russia for over $8 per unit, this is vastly more, up to eight times more than what the Egyptians were receiving."

Minio-Paluello said that when the terms were amended, Egypt received US$3 per MBTU, a price still significantly below international rates. "Egypt in fact lost more money in 2010 with the higher rates than they did in 2008, because they were exporting more gas."[13]

While it agreed to such a staggeringly flawed agreement, Egypt's energy officials were signing deals to import fuel to satisfy its domestic shortages at US$9–10 per MBTU.

According to Minio-Paluello's analysis based on confidential documents leaked to al-Jazeera Network, Egypt received a total amount of US$92 million from Israel when it could have received up to US$773 million if it had sold the same amount for a similar rate to what Japan was paying during the same period, US$12.6 per MBTU. "My calculation says that Egypt lost, over the three years [from 2008 to 2011], $1.8 billion," said Minio-Paluello.

As for Ibrahim Yousri, he scored his first legal win against the government on November 18, 2008. Egypt's Administrative Court announced its first degree ruling to "cancel the government's decision allowing natural gas exports to Israel at prices the government admitted are lower than global rates and also agreeing to conditions of not increasing the initial prices for a period of fifteen years." The ruling was automatically appealed by the government, which appointed dozens of lawyers, in addition to dozens of other lawyers who voluntarily decided to join the defense panel.[14]

On February 2, 2009, the Supreme Administrative Court trashed the initial ruling and accepted the government's appeal. The court indicated that "the decision to sell the natural gas 'surplus' to the east Mediterranean countries, including Israel, was taken by the cabinet as a governing authority, and the decision was within its political duty. It is considered a matter of sovereignty that the constitutional, administrative and regular judiciary decided to exclude from its monitoring duties."[15]

A year later, on February 27, 2010, the Supreme Administrative Court put an end to the ongoing legal dispute and announced a final ruling. Judge Mohamed Husseini, head of the court's judicial council, ruled that "looking into the appeal filed against the government's decision to export natural gas to Israel is not within the jurisdiction of the court because it's a matter of state sovereignty." The court recommended a cancelation of the length of the agreement and the prices related to that period "because the agreement does not include a specific mechanism for monitoring the amounts of natural gas exported and its price." The court ended its ruling by advising the cabinet to revise the export prices according to the higher interests of Egypt.[16]

Mubarak and his cabinet decided to ignore the lengthy legal dispute as if it had never happened. The gas exports continued and the prices and dates were never amended or regulated with a clear mechanism as the Administrative Court had ordered months earlier. And while the court described the whole matter as "exporting the natural gas surplus," Egypt was in fact suffering severe shortages and incapable of covering its domestic demand, which forced most Egyptians to pay what ranged between two and ten times the subsidized prices they should have paid for a tank of cooking gas. Meanwhile, the Bedouins of Sinai, some of whom could see the pipeline from their windows, continued to carry their empty gas tanks for kilometers, hoping they would be refilled before nightfall.

Israel Never Blessed It Either

Since the agreement was signed in 2005 and the construction of the subsea pipeline began, Egyptians were convinced, or made to believe, that Israel was the winning side of the deal. Egypt's nationalists and political opposition considered Israel's move to import Egyptian gas a new chapter in Israel's historic violations against Egypt and sometimes, as they would put it, a continuation of the Israeli occupation of Egypt through the Camp David Peace Accords.

However, Israeli politicians, media figures, and scholars make it clear that the murky gas deal was as unpopular in Israel as it was in Egypt, if not more so, given Israel's pragmatic approach to the whole matter.

Ehud Yaari, a prominent Israeli television presenter and Middle East analyst, was known for his harsh criticism of the gas agreement and of Benjamin 'Fouad' Ben Eliezer, Hosni Mubarak's dear friend and the Israeli minister of infrastructure who signed the 2005 memorandum of understanding with Egyptian Petroleum Minister Sameh Fahmy. It was this memorandum that allowed Egypt's natural gas to be funneled into Hussein Salem's East Mediterranean Gas Company on its way to Israel.

"I will not talk about Fouad. But I will tell you that there was a very powerful lobby from the private sector to get the politicians to vote for it," said Yaari,[17] and the politicians did vote for the required law to give the green light to what seemed to be a Fouad-sponsored business.

Yaari, like several Israeli officials including then Energy Minister Yosef Paritzky, had rejected the idea from the start. Their objection was that Egypt wasn't capable of covering its own needs of natural gas while exporting what it claimed to be a surplus, in addition to the secrecy surrounding the terms of the deal signed with EMG which made it seem suspicious. According to Yaari, "Egypt never fulfilled its contractual obligations of supplying natural gas; it never supplied more than 70 percent of what it was supposed to, never. Mainly because the Egyptian energy market was absolutely mismanaged, and Egypt never had enough gas to sell anyway."

In addition to Egypt's inability to fulfill the terms of the agreement, Yaari believed it wasa major mistake to commit 40 percent of Israel's energy needs to supplies from Egypt. "Mainly because we never knew what will happen after Mubarak, we expected Egypt to go through turmoil if Jimmy [Gamal Mubarak] was to take his father's position. This deal was the result of the efforts of a certain business lobby in Israel who managed to get the deal through and it did cost Israel a lot at the end of the day."

Yosef Paritzky, energy minister at the time of the agreement, was featured in the al-Jazeera documentary "Egypt's Lost Power," in which he explained "the deal was so covert, behind the scenes and un-transparent that it called for attention. The deal was too good to be true and the prices were ridiculous."[18]

He also pointed to the clear affiliation between former intelligence officers from both countries: Salem, a former Egyptian military and intelligence officer, founded EMG with his Israeli partner and long-time business associate Yossi Melman, also a former, intelligence officer. Interestingly, Melman hired Shabtai Shavit, former head of the Israeli intelligence agency, the Mossad, as a Senior Executive of EMG sometime before the agreement was finalized. The trio formed an intelligence umbrella for the business, and facilitated the overcoming of political and legal difficulties on both the Egyptian and the Israeli sides.

Ehud Yaari believes that in addition to the fact that this specific deal was viewed by many Israeli figures as corrupt and shady, it clearly increased Egyptians' anger against Mubarak and, accordingly, increased Israel's concerns that the stability of Egypt's regime was coming to an end.

Meanwhile, professor of humanities Mira Tzoreff watched the Egyptian uprising from her office in Tel Aviv University. Having studied Egyptian society and youth for years, she believed that the natural gas agreement with Israel was one of several reasons leading to the revolt against Mubarak's regime. "This is the meaning of autocracy, not caring about the people. Mubarak did insult the Egyptian people, he insulted his people for his own interests, and this is why I believed the uprising will come and that it was a matter of time." said Tzoreff. "Mubarak turned into a harsh autocrat if you look at the ordinary people, not the ones from Masr al-Gadida [an upscale eastern Cairo district] who don't have to rely on the government.[19]

As for the Sinai and its population, whose lands hosted the gas pipeline, Tzoreff believes that if Israel was to learn something from this experience, "it should learn to change the way it views and treats the Sinai and its population." And in the broader context, learn that "the Egyptian people should be viewed as more important than the regime. The moment you realize that the population has more power than you can imagine then your policy should be directed to the population and not only to the big personalities. The [Israeli] policy must change."

The Masked Men

"Masked men bombed the North Sinai gas pipeline!" This phrase became a staple of every official statement published in the aftermath of every successful bombing that targeted the pipeline. It got to a point where these official statements were so predictable and superficial that they needed only to be skimmed. Most of the time, making a phone call to an informed journalist like Ahmed Abu Draa or a Sinai tribal elder was significantly more informative than whatever the security reports had to say.

How the authorities arrived at the conclusion that the attackers were either masked or men remains an unanswered question. It is a reasonable assumption as most criminals attempt to hide their identities by wearing face covers, but official statements regarding major crimes and national security matters should not be built on hypothesis. Yet, throughout more than twenty attacks between February 2011 and July 2012 on the pipeline, security personnel saw the attackers only once, when a firefight broke out during an attempt to shower the pipeline control chamber in eastern al-Arish with RPG shells, and, even then, the attackers fled safely.[20]

Despite being confident that no one could cruise the mountains and valleys as fast as they did, the attackers adhered to the rule of using a vehicle that would be impossible to trace. Nothing was better than one that would be found parked in front of hundreds of houses in Sinai: a one-cabin Toyota pick-up truck, the top pick of Bedouins that now occupied the revered position of camels in the tribal communities. To further cripple the authorities, the vehicles had no license plates and, in several cases, there was no registration of either the chassis or the engine numbers that could be the authorities' last chance of identifying the vehicle.[21]

After a few successful attacks, the phrase 'masked men' became a running joke throughout the country. It even inspired Egypt's famous satirist Bassem Youssef, as he dedicated a whole episode of his popular TV show "El Bernameg" to mock the Egyptian authorities' failure to fulfill their security duties and protect the pipeline, or arrest anyone related to the attacks.

Colonel Khaled Okasha, who wasn't fond of the 'masked men' phrase, was, until his retirement in late 2012, the first security official to arrive at a bombing scene with his explosives experts. He explained:

> The former regime and the company responsible for this pipeline never secured it because the Sinai Peninsula was held with an iron grip and the security apparatus was in full control. They were confident that no one would attack it before the revolution so they decided to save the millions of dollars they should have spent to build a security system for the project.
>
> Securing a pipeline stretching for hundreds of kilometers across the desert was impossible under the circumstances the police and military have lived through since January 2011, and the company ended up paying for its failure to build its own security system.[22]

The only confirmation, other than official statements, that the attackers were masked came from the only Bedouin guard who actually saw them. A few weeks after a bombing in August 2011, Abu Eid, the Bedouin guard from the bombed control chamber located on the eastern outskirts of al-Arish, agreed to talk:

> It was around 1:00 a.m. when a few masked men, armed with machine guns stormed my house. They sat me down with a machine gun to my

head and told me to take my kids and leave. I feared for my family and children, I took them and ran out immediately. I called the gas company officer and told them what happened; they didn't tell me what to do or what they would do so I called Abu Draa [the journalist and a distant cousin of his, who arrived in time to film the explosion].[23]

Half an hour later, the explosion went off, burning Abu Eid's adjacent yard with all the goats, chickens, and pigeons he raised and sold to make an extra living. Once again, Abu Eid gave us the grim description of how miserable his work and living conditions were, from his "useless salary of $100 a month," to the long dark nights he had to spend protecting a gas pipeline he sees only in silhouette.

Although Abu Eid's testimony did confirm that the bombers were masked, it was also evidence that they knew what kind of explosives they were using and how powerful they were. More importantly, they forced out the Bedouin guard to avoid any collateral damage, which would be a reason for other tribesmen to seek revenge, even if the main target of the attack was a much-hated facility such as the gas pipeline. The 'masked men' were keen on avoiding any grudges with the Bedouin community. They were well aware that if Abu Eid or any of his children were killed by the explosion then their attack on the gas pipeline would have changed from a 'patriotic' act to the start of a chain of retaliations that could have ripped the masks off their faces. They always made sure the only one chasing them was an incompetent security department that had got nowhere through its ongoing investigation into fifteen successful bombings.

Mubarak's Unwanted Business
The natural gas pipeline stretching between al-Arish and Ashkelon was Mubarak's business, born to his closest clique, including his son and potential heir Gamal. Throughout his thirty-year rule, there had been prime ministers and ministers Egyptians viewed as criminal, but no one was as loathed as this new guard of businessmen, and the gas pipeline agreement was deemed to be the most criminal deal the aging dictator had ever adopted.

Throughout the three years before the January 25 uprising—since the gas exports to Israel started—Egypt's military had no role in the agreement, or the strings attached to it. It was a logical strategy because the old generals, who became the ruling Supreme Council of the Armed

Forces (SCAF), were never fond of Mubarak's new guard, whether Gamal, who was being prepared to take over his father's presidential seat, or Hussein Salem, who defected from the military in the 1970s to become the billionaire whose business was more important to Hosni Mubarak than any of his military chiefs. For the aging president, Salem was a partner while the generals were employees.

Since the first bombing a few days before Mubarak's resignation, the military never actually moved to protect the pipeline, making it clear that it was, in the eyes of Defense Minister Mohamed Hussein Tantawi and his council (SCAF), an unwanted business that belonged to Mubarak's era. The military did carry the responsibility of securing what government officials routinely described as "high-importance or sensitive facilities," but this specific facility was left defenseless in a region where anything that related to Mubarak's oppression became a target of furious attacks that did not entail mere rock throwing, but rocket-propelled grenades, high-caliber machine guns, and explosives.

When the scale of the attacks grew embarrassing, after a few bombings, the military gave the pipeline token protection and stationed an armored vehicle with a few soldiers around every major control chamber. These soldiers weren't any better than the unarmed Bedouin guards when it came to protecting the gas pipeline, and the attacks continued as if they weren't there. The stance of the ruling generals wasn't surprising to many Egyptians, as SCAF took over Egypt through one of the bumpiest periods in the country's modern history and faced tireless dissent and unprecedented political turmoil. With Mubarak under arrest and facing legal charges, and Hussein Salem long gone with his offshore assets well protected by his Spanish citizenship, the repetitive bombings failed to sway the military into securing a corrupt business they weren't benefiting from in the first place.

The ruling generals and their military intelligence, still intact and fully operating under the supervision at that time of General Abdel-Fattah al-Sisi, had the needed resources to start a serious hunt for those behind the attacks, and they had the technology and weaponry required to back such a wide-scale operation. They could have stopped the RPGs aimed at the pipeline if they had geared up to defend it, but would then have been accused of maintaining the corrupt businesses of Mubarak and his cronies. Instead, they decided to stand down and watch Israel look for alternatives to Egypt's cheap natural gas.

"Israel begged Tantawi to send reinforcements to Sinai to protect the gas pipeline and hunt the attackers. He never agreed," said Ehud Yaari. "He never wanted the military to become embroiled in Sinai's messy affairs; he left it for the police and kept the military's presence and actions at minimum."

But the police department that once ran Sinai with an iron grip was gone before Mubarak's resignation. The police force in Sinai was rarely seen for the two years after their defeat on January 28, 2011, and their barracks remained scarred with bullet holes from their last battle. Meanwhile, Israel had continued paying prices significantly lower than international rates—when it actually received gas between the frequent bombings that had crippled the pipeline.

However, on April 19, 2012, Egypt's state-owned gas company, the Egyptian Natural Gas Holding Company (EGAS), informed Hussein Salem's EMG that they had turned off the tap. Mohamed Shoeib, chairman of EGAS at the time, told local newspapers that "canceling the agreement was a business matter that had no political motives." He explained that "EMG had failed to pay what it owed EGAS for several consecutive months, which gave the Egyptian side the right to terminate the agreement."[24]

The trial of those linked to the Egyptian petroleum sector and the natural gas agreement went smoothly. Mubarak was not among the defendants, but on June 28, 2012, four days after Mohamed Morsi was declared president of Egypt, Petroleum Minister Sameh Fahmy, who was photographed signing the agreement with Israeli Minister of Infrastructure Benjamin Ben Eliezer, was sentenced to fifteen years in jail along with businessman Hussein Salem, who was sentenced in absentia. A long list of Egyptian petroleum officials shared the cage with Fahmy. Between them, the defendants were fined US$2 billion and were obliged to return US$499 million to the state.[25]

3

SINAI'S ARMS: EN ROUTE TO GAZA

O n June 5, 1967, Israel launched an unprecedented military offensive against Egypt. Within five days its airforce had bombarded military airports and facilities as far as the capital Cairo and the governorates of Upper Egypt, while its ground forces led a ground incursion that occupied the Sinai Peninsula and seized control of the eastern bank of the Suez Canal. When the war broke out, Egypt's armed forces in the Sinai Peninsula were said to have been composed of 100,000 troops, some 900 tanks, 1,000 personnel carriers and armored vehicles, and another 1,000 pieces of artillery.[1]

When the six-day offensive came to an end, Egypt had lost some 9,500 troops, according to Egyptian statistics,[2] and 15,000, according to Israeli statistics.[3] General Mohamed Fawzi—who was appointed commander of Egypt's military to replace Abdel-Hakim Amer, defense minister at the time of the defeat—wrote in his memoirs that Egypt had lost 85 percent of its airforce capabilities, while the majority of its infantry returned from the Sinai Peninsula without their arms or machinery.[4] Stories of troops walking across the Sinai to cross the Suez Canal back into mainland Egypt spread in every neighborhood across the country. Barefoot, broken, and unarmed, they traveled back on foot from a frontier that was said to be impermeable; they were what remained of an army the masses had believed was unbreakable. The defeat and retreat of the Egyptian military from the Sinai was followed by deadly battles between the armored divisions of both Egypt and Israel, battles that cost Egypt further losses. What became known as the Six Day War, and dubbed the *naksa*, or 'setback,' by Egyptians, was the beginning of six years of war between both countries and both a full and partial Israeli occupation of the Sinai Peninsula that continued until 1982.

Dozens of Sinai Bedouins from every tribe across the peninsula, who fought alongside the troops in covert operations overseen by the Egyptian Military Intelligence and Reconnaissance Directorate (EMIRD), arranged hideouts for the officers and field commanders who were pursued by the Israeli military; they dressed them in Bedouin outfits and treated whoever was injured, while hundreds of weapons were buried in the farms and yards around Bedouin houses. Some of those officers remained in Sinai for months before being able to cross back to the western bank of the Suez Canal.

"Those Bedouins were the seeds from which the Egyptian military operations grew back inside the Sinai Peninsula, behind enemy lines," said General Fouad Hussein,[5] who was transferred to the EMIRD and became Sinai Communication Officer in 1968. "The only knowledge I had of Sinai was how to move my battalions across the mountainous or desert terrain. It was a purely military focus that didn't have any regard to the society and the people, but when I started the operation I realized that there were many fighters waiting on the other side."

The Bedouins became the foundation of what was later named the Sinai Mujahedeen Association, a group of 750 recruits that ran an intricate espionage and logistical support network that served the Egyptian military throughout the war until October 1973. In several books written by General Hussein years after the war, he documented stories of how the weapons from the defeat, and the occupied Bedouin population of Sinai, were reused in operations against Israeli military encampments across the peninsula.[6]

On October 6, 1973, Egypt led its counter offensive during which it regained control of the Suez Canal and a vertical strip along its eastern bank inside Sinai. With the airforce bombarding Israeli targets deep inside the peninsula, the Bedouin tribes were once more able to seize caches of Israeli weapons that were buried in a similar manner to those of 1967. Large amounts of the hidden arms were gradually seized by the Egyptian authorities starting in 1973 and after the full Israeli withdrawal in 1982, but the fact that the military was pursuing an unknown amount of weapons in such a massive area made it impossible to estimate what was left behind after years of war.

"After the Israeli withdrawal in 1982 and Egypt's return to full control of the peninsula, those weapons started moving north toward the Gaza Strip," said Mohamed al-Filistini,[7] an Egyptian of Gazan origins, whose family has resided in North Sinai since 1949. "They weren't only the foundations of Egypt's post-'67 operations [against the occupation] but also became the foundation of the Palestinian resistance factions."

Al-Filistini, whose school teachers in North Sinai were Gazan until 1982 when the Egyptian state took over, says the movement of weapons has not stopped in the modern history of Sinai. Born and raised in the midst of war and occupation, this Egyptian citizen saturated with Palestinian resistance beliefs became an ardent follower of the movement of arms across the Sinai and into the Gaza Strip.

The Egyptian military and state security imposed a tight grip on arms across the peninsula back in the 1980s and 1990s. But the remains of years of war were impossible to track down; one shocking example General Mohamed Fawzy described in his memoirs was the withdrawal of 100,000 infantry troops from Sinai on the third day of the war, who, despite being ordered to return with their personal weapons (normally a machine gun and sometimes a machine gun and pistol) and abandon everything else, returned empty handed.[8] The humiliating withdrawal was caused, according to General Fawzy, by Defense Minister Abdel-Hakim Amer's reckless orders that were given without any coordination with the chiefs of staff or even putting together a plan for securing the country's entire ground force. Another example was the large number of landmines flushed out by heavy rains every year or found every time they were accidentally exploded by farmers or cattle.

Some Bedouins became experts in collecting those mines and turning them into poorly assembled explosives, most of which were smuggled to the Gaza Strip for the resistance movements. . . . Back in the 1980s it was just the Palestinian *muqawama* [resistance]. Hamas, the Islamic Jihad, the Popular Resistance Committees, all of this didn't exist, and it took almost a decade for those movements to start to take hold in the popular imagination of Bedouins and Egyptians from Palestinian origins."

Al-Filistini added that up until the mid-1990s, "a pistol or a rusty rifle was considered a fortune for the Bedouin smugglers and the Gazan fighters alike, and was an unforgivable crime in the eyes of Egyptian authorities . . . if someone had just heard of a smuggled handgun and didn't inform the police they would be detained."

Adnan Abu Amer, dean of al-Ummah University's Faculty of Arts and Humanities in the Gaza Strip and a keen researcher of the rise of the Islamist movements of Palestine, said that

> throughout the 80s and 90s, the resistance movement relied on extremely poor resources and the majority of its weapons came from criminal syndicates across Israel, smugglers from the West Bank or through ambushing Israeli troops and stealing their weapons within the Gaza Strip.
>
> Bedouins of the Naqab Desert smuggled weapons to the Islamist fighters as well, but they were old and debilitated. The first advanced attack in Gaza was the murder of Rabbi Doron Shoshanon, January 1, 1992. It was shocking to both Israelis and Palestinians because he was killed using a rifle, and the fact that the fighters had obtained a rifle was extraordinary at the time.[9]

Abu Amer says it was a Carl Gustav rifle, a Swedish weapon from 1916 that at the time was sold in Europe and the US as an antique. Where it came from and how it landed in the hands of Islamist militias is unknown, but up until that time arms as old as World War I were roaming the desert with Bedouins who moved freely between the Sinai and Israel until 1982 when their movement gradually decreased.

From the mid-1990s criminal gangs started controlling the movement of weapons across the Sinai. It became a much more organized process, and the AK-47s brought by these gangs turned the long-buried weapons and flushed-out landmines of the Egypt–Israel war into antiques without a market. They weren't arms traffickers per se, but rather criminals who made money out of anything: they dealt in opium and marijuana, smuggled seeds and agricultural fertilizers across the Israeli border, and later on began smuggling Russian and eastern European sex workers from the resorts of South Sinai into Eilat.

Meanwhile, the Egyptian authorities were focused on tracking down Islamist militants who led terrorist attacks across Cairo and various cities in Upper Egypt. With the Egyptian crackdown on the Sinai Peninsula and a relentless Israeli military presence in the Gaza Strip, those who once breached the border fence went underground and revived the idea of smuggling tunnels that had failed in 1983; they dug the first operational tunnels in 1997, and this time they succeeded.

"We called them rope-tunnels. They were so tight it required a slim person to be able to crawl inside them while digging. Whatever was being smuggled had to be pulled with a rope that extended through the tunnel," explained al-Filistini.

While Abu Amer believes that the tunnels and weapons from Sinai didn't have a major impact on the Islamist militias at that time—for many reasons, topped by Yasser Arafat's widening clampdown that threw the majority of them in jail between 1996 and 1998—al-Filistini says that the tunnels became the northern passage of Sinai's old and newer weapons. Another sign that both researchers referred to was the spread of various kinds of weapons among Gazan families and the increase in violent disputes across the Strip—such as all-out brawls between warring clans that involved digging trenches and bombing houses. It was a frightening phenomenon that continued for years.

1997: El-Adly's Cartel

On November 17, 1997, the head of Egypt's State Security Investigations (SSI), General Habib El-Adly, was promoted to the position of minister of the interior. The promotion took place a few hours after the Luxor massacre during which fifty-eight foreign tourists, three Egyptian police personnel, and one Egyptian tour guide were killed by Islamist extremists. It left the country in a state of shock as this terror attack exceeded the dozens of others that had shaken Egypt since the failed assassination attempt on Hosni Mubarak in the Ethiopian capital, Addis Ababa, two years earlier.

The *New York Times* reported at the time:

> Most of the victims were shot in the head and chest, suggesting an attack that proceeded with discipline and precision, Egyptian investigators said. Some were slashed and hacked with knives, so viciously in one case that a victim's head was nearly severed.[10]

Immediately after the attack, al-Jamaa al-Islamiya published a statement saying:

> Mubarak should accept Islamic rule in Egypt, free political prisoners, and secure the release from a US prison of Sheikh Omar

Abdel-Rahman [the group's spiritual leader, who was convicted in
1995 of conspiracy to execute terrorist attacks in the United States
and has remained in American prisons since].[11]

On the day of the attack, Mubarak flew to Luxor in person and fired
then Minister of the Interior General Hassan El-Alfy.

His replacement, El-Adly was a shadowy figure who had swiftly
climbed the hierarchy of Mubarak's police state to lead the country's
most notorious security apparatus: the SSI that terrorized Egyptians
using the emergency law in place since President Anwar Sadat's assassination in 1981. El-Adly's arrival at the minister's seat came with an
overhaul of policies that represented the beginning of a new era of
oppression and further impunity for the police department.

Facing a rising challenge from radical Islamist groups that had
thwarted the state's attempts to rein them in since the early 1990s—
especially in the impoverished, territorial, and heavily armed region of
Upper Egypt—El-Adly arrived in his office with the conviction that the
terrorists would be impossible to crush using the conventional police
tactics that had led to the demise of his predecessor. It was a dirty guer-
rilla war and the young general turned Egypt's Ministry of the Interior
into an equally dirty operation.

El-Adly's new policy was to conquer the strongholds of Islamists in
Upper Egypt using criminal networks of born-and-bred bandits there.
This new arm of the police apparatus, which was already infiltrated by
the minister's former home, the SSI, knew the terrain better than the
general himself and was willing to accept any agreement with the state
as long as it steered the regime's guns away from them.

Drug lords and arms traffickers became the most protected people
in every governorate south of the capital, all the way to the Sudanese
border. Bandits who had taken refuge in far-flung mountainous areas
returned to their towns and villages wielding their unlicensed weapons.
They were on a hunting mission and Islamist militants were the prey.
And in return for fighting on behalf of the state, various authorities,
topped by the Ministry of the Interior, would turn a blind eye to the
activities of the newly established cartels.

In 2007, ten years after El-Adly's arrival at the minister's seat, a movie
was produced detailing a portion of Egypt's war against the Islamist militants of the 1990s, named "al-Gezira," or "The Island." The film was

based on the true story of one drug and arms trafficking kingpin from Asyut: Ezzat Hanafi, the offspring of the dirty tactics injected into the police system.

The terrorist activities almost came to an end within three years of El-Adly's reign, as the nationwide, brutal crackdown orchestrated by the police department and its criminal arms proved to be very effective. But despite the authorities triumph in their battle against the Islamist insurgency, those years remain a shameful phase in Egypt's history, a phase of unprecedented violations of human rights that claimed thousands of innocent victims and left behind powerful criminal syndicates that El-Adly exploited to entrench his rule over the Ministry of the Interior and that of Mubarak over Egypt.

"He became the most powerful, untouchable member of consecutive cabinets because of the emergency law and security policies that [eventually] brought an end to Mubarak's regime," said Ali Eddin Helal, Egypt's former youth minister and a senior member of Mubarak's National Democratic Party (NDP), describing his long time colleague El-Adly.[12]

During one of the cabinet meetings attended by Mubarak and former Prime Minister Ahmed Nazif, Helal said that El-Adly's answer to the proposition of lifting the state of emergency was simple and straightforward: he threatened to resign. "'It's either me or lifting the emergency law,' he simply said to Mubarak and the whole cabinet."

Soon after the defeat of Islamist militants, which brought the main assignment of the cartels to an end, El-Adly's security apparatus dictated the terms of a new deal. The same immunity would continue as long as the cartels cooperated with the police department in spying operations that were broadened to include not only Islamists but any form of opposition and the community as whole. Members of the cartels became the top promoters of and voters for Mubarak's NDP in municipal and parliamentary elections, and became more responsible for silencing local disputes and opposition than the authorities themselves.

Hanafi's empire in Asyut's Nekheila village continued to grow until he became the country's biggest producer of opium, gaining a reputation that far surpassed that of Sinai, the historic producer of Egypt's opium. Hectares of poppy flowers and cannabis were cultivated within his stronghold that attracted dozens of wanted criminals from every governorate in Upper Egypt and was guarded by thugs armed to the teeth with weapons he had accumulated and dealt in over the years. His house was surrounded by concrete towers over which high-caliber machine guns were erected to secure as far as the edges of the village.[13]

He strengthened his ties with the police apparatus by supplying them with drugs, weapons, and wanted criminals required for cases that were recorded and paraded as the unending successes of the police's tireless work. Both agreements, the former hunt for terrorists and the newer hunt for dissent, became colloquially referred to as "services."

Over more than a decade of El-Adly's operation, the police seized tons of drugs and thousands of arms, but the majority of the government interceptions of smuggling and trafficking operations were recorded against criminals that either fled the scene or weren't there to begin with. Such operations were the fruits of the "services" provided by the cartels.[14]

In 2004, the police besieged Hanafi's village and battled his cartel members for five days before they surrendered. During the vicious battle, machine guns, RPGs, landmines, and unsophisticated explosives were used, while Hanafi ordered attacks on the Asyut Security Directorate and the Upper Egypt railway tracks, and ordered his followers to block major highways in an attempt to deter the police forces.

During the five-day battle, Hanafi made comments to the media accusing "the authorities of plotting to get rid of him despite helping them during the parliamentary elections and supporting them throughout their war against terrorists in the 1990s," reported the BBC. "Hanafi added that he killed large numbers of terrorists on orders of security authorities, adding that he received weapons from the police to execute such missions."[15]

Finally, after El-Adly signed the permit to use police gunships to bombard Hanafi's empire, the gang surrendered and their leader attempted to commit suicide. He survived, but was sentenced to death and executed along with his brother in 2006.[16]

Before Habib El-Adly was appointed minister of the interior, he served in almost every position in the State Security Investigations, which he joined in 1965, four years after he graduated from the police academy. Hosni Mubarak had appointed six ministers before El-Adly, but he outlived them all in the position and remained untouchable for fourteen consecutive years, until Mubarak fired him in the midst of the January uprising in 2011.

El-Adly's Sinai Branch

Up until the late 1980s, the Sinai Peninsula's security was handled mainly by the Egyptian General Intelligence Directorate (EGID) and the Military Intelligence and Reconnaissance Directorate (EMIRD). Both departments have always viewed it as a military zone because the peninsula has been in a state of full or partial war and under full or partial occupation since the Suez war in 1956 when Britain, France, and Israel led an offensive against Egypt in the aftermath of Gamal Abdel-Nasser's nationalization of the Suez Canal. Up until 1982, traveling into or out of the peninsula, even for residents, required a special permit from the military command in Cairo, North Sinai's al-Arish, and South Sinai's al-Tor.

"We [the military] ran the peninsula since the republic was declared [in 1952], and even historically, when Egypt was a kingdom," said General Mohamed Okasha, father of police colonel Khaled Okasha and a former airforce pilot who served for years in the military intelligence and was among those responsible for securing the Israeli military envoys during the peace talks in the late 1970s. "Between 1967 and 1982, there were no police in the Sinai Peninsula. The first police deployment took place after the Israeli withdrawal in 1982 and before that, during the gradual Israeli withdrawal from parts of western and middle Sinai, the military remained in full control even when it came to police work."

"It took a few years for the police structure to spread across the peninsula and the military to start the full transfer of duties to the minister of the interior," added General Okasha, who agreed with many tribal elders that that the SSI was the most active police department in Sinai since the Israeli withdrawal.[17]

The military's control did not wane even after the police started its operations, but when Habib El-Adly was appointed minister of the interior, he overhauled the decades-old system of policing the Sinai along with the policies of Egypt's security apparatus. El-Adly, who had previously served as deputy minister for Sinai affairs took the police deployment in Sinai to another level, and the SSI, armed with the unchecked privileges of the emergency law, became the most feared and loathed among the Bedouin tribes, with offices in every town across the peninsula.

"We knew him [El-Adly] since he was deputy minister, even before he headed the state security," said Abu Suleiman al-Tarabin, a prominent and feared member of the Tarabin tribe, widely known for his smuggling business. "The country had been suffering from terrorist attacks and he was the one who defeated the terrorists. This is how he was able to share Sinai with the military who believed they were the only rulers here."[18]

Abu Suleiman, who always described himself as "a businessman balancing myself between the authorities and fellow tribesmen," is one of several arms trafficking kingpins in the Sinai Peninsula. The 53-year-old inherited the smuggling business from his father and, over the years, took it from camels to Land Cruisers and from trusted messengers to sophisticated handheld transceivers used to spy on police signals. Despite never spending time in jail, he was sentenced in absentia to eighty years for several charges of drug and arms smuggling crimes, a sentence he described as "unjust."

When El-Adly was appointed in 1997, Abu Suleiman says that few weapons were going to Gaza through Sinai and it was the same year the first tunnel was dug between Egypt and the Strip. "Abu Ammar [the late Palestinian leader Yasser Arafat] was still alive and he coordinated directly with the intelligence, Omar Suleiman [head of EGID between 1993 and 2011], and Mubarak. Back then, whatever weapons crossed the peninsula were given the green light from the intelligence services."

High-ranking Egyptian security officers confirmed what the smuggler had told me. General Fouad Allam, former head of the SSI until 1985, said that the Egyptian authorities turned a blind eye to the smuggling of weapons into the Gaza Strip because of political interests.

> Egypt had been the main and only mediator between the Palestinians and the Israelis and I believe that allowing the flow of weapons and the operation of tunnels was a part of how the Egyptian authorities dealt with the complicated politics of the Gaza Strip. It was a matter of political interests and maintaining stability and relations with neighboring states, and Egypt always maneuvered to calm the Palestinian–Israeli issues without losing either party.[19]

As for Colonel Khaled Okasha, who headed North Sinai's Civil Defense Department until 2012, he described it as "Egypt's historic generosity with Gaza, for which it was sometimes thanked, but many times met with ingratitude and used against our interests."[20]

While El-Adly grew closer to Mubarak, the Taba bombing on October 7, 2004, rocked the ever-calm southern shores of Sinai. The aftermath of the attack marked a turning point in the history of security control over the peninsula and revealed that Omar Suleiman's EGID had taken a few steps back and handed a major part of the operations over to Habib El-Adly's SSI, which led the infamous campaign of arbitrary arrests and torture that left an estimated 5,000 victims.[21]

In February 2005, four months after the security's failure to find the Taba assailants, despite the crackdown across the peninsula, El-Adly decided to employ the Upper Egypt tactics of co-opting local networks. He struck a deal with Bedouin elders from several tribes, specifically the most powerful Tarabin in the south, to lead the hunt for wanted attackers who the Egyptian authorities claimed were Islamist members of the Egyptian–Gazan al-Tawhid wa-l-Jihad movement.

Sheikh Atteya al-Kibriti of the Tarabin tribe told the Associated Press's Sarah El-Deeb that "Bedouin tribes signed a 'pledge document' with Egyptian security forces to help them track down wanted militants and provide security cooperation." He added that the Bedouin elders had raised issues of arbitrary arrests with the government as a part of the cooperation agreement.[22]

But the arrangement wasn't as innocent as al-Kibriti described it. Several of the elements the authorities had relied on were, akin to Upper Egypt's Ezzat Hanafi, arms and drug smugglers once hunted by the regime. Among the assets of El-Adly's not-so-covert operation were Abu Suleiman al-Tarabin of South Sinai and Abu Arrab al-Sawarka of North Sinai, who in return for their services received more allowances to continue their smuggling businesses uninterrupted. Egypt's security apparatus did not hide its murky relations with these criminal networks, and, many of them were living freely as they were delegated to operate within the tribal community on behalf of the authorities. As Colonel Okasha said, "these are security bargains and leverages that are applied in every security outfit in the world." To him and many others, it was for the greater good.

The arrangement, which many tribal figures insist succeeded in tracking down and apprehending many militants, did not last long as El-Adly turned against those he had just recruited. Meanwhile the attacks continued, hitting Sharm al-Sheikh in 2005 and the scuba diving town of Dahab in 2006. Backed by the emergency law, the SSI launched another wave of arbitrary detentions that threw many of the collaborators into prison without trial. Those who managed to escape were tried in absentia by state security tribunals, which guaranteed no rights whatsoever to defendants, and handed out long jail terms.

Abu Arrab was apprehended by an emergency law administrative arrest warrant—a warrant signed by the head of SSI or his regional officer that can be renewed indefinitely without the intervention of any judicial authority except for the State Security Prosecution—from his house outside Rafah and transported to al-Gharbaniyat prison in western Alexandria. Meanwhile Abu Suleiman fled to the valleys of South Sinai and was later sentenced in absentia to twenty-five years.

Ripples from Gaza

Almost one month after the Taba bombing, on November 11, 2004, Palestinian leader Yasser Arafat died in a French hospital. The aging and then passing of Arafat, whose authorities had brutally controlled the Islamist factions of the Gaza Strip, had a major impact on movement of arms across the Sinai Peninsula. In the years leading up to his death, the Islamist factions in Gaza, topped by Hamas and the Palestinian Islamic Jihad, were gradually gaining more freedom.[23]

According to Adnan Abu Amer:

> Arafat had loosened the grip on Hamas in the late 1990s in an attempt to pressure Israel right before the failed talks with Bill Clinton and Ehud Barak in Camp David in 2000. Back then it was the first time we ever witnessed members of the Qassam Brigades and other Islamist factions carrying their weapons and moving freely across the Strip. Soon after [the Camp David talks], the Second Intifada broke out and with it Hamas started using tunnels to plant explosives under Israeli military camps and watchtowers. The military arsenal of Hamas was growing; they were buying from criminal organizations in Israel and even from members of the Palestinian Authority, and they started reaching beyond the borders into Sinai.

In Sinai, Abu Arrab and Abu Suleiman explained that weapons were crossing in small quantities until the early 2000s, and this was gradually on the rise. Arafat's control over Hamas and other Islamist factions was lifting and they had started importing shipments of weapons independently. The Gaza Strip was fraught with feuds between Hamas and Fatah, even within Arafat's ranks. Disputes were reaching unprecedented levels with powerful personalities such as Mohamed Dahlan, commander of Gaza's Preventative Security Department, publicly criticizing the aging leader. The majority of arms smuggling at that time was orchestrated by Fatah members and their loyalist clans, as the movement controlled the border area and were the feared authority.[24]

The surge in demand in Gaza, the vicious Egyptian security policies mixed with corruption after the Taba bombings, and the death of Arafat all had a direct and significant effect on Sinai. The smugglers, who were just a few operating under the control of the SSI and the intelligence, expanded their networks and slipped out of the tight control once imposed over Sinai.

> Each one of them [the smugglers] expected this relationship [with Egypt's security authorities] to come to an end at some point. They watched their elders serve the military throughout the war with Israel and get nothing in return, and they watched Upper Egypt's criminals, who are the extension of the Sinai arms smuggling route, strike deals with El-Adly and end up in prison. What they expected happened too soon when the police turned against them in 2005.

Al-Filistini went on that anyone involved in the smuggling networks had started establishing their own shadowy empires, even when their relationship with the authorities was stable. "They never trusted each other, the police had jails to throw them in and the smugglers had the valleys to hide in, or millions of dollars to buy their freedom from the corrupt authorities."

The rise in arms trafficking continued following the death of Arafat until it reached unprecedented levels after Israel's unilateral military disengagement from the Gaza Strip in August 2005, under Prime Minister Ariel Sharon. Months later, on January 9, 2005, Mahmoud Abbas became president through elections Hamas had boycotted.[25] The newly elected president attempted to curb Hamas's rising popularity and military strength through crackdowns led by Dahlan's Preventative Security but it soon proved to be impotent when Hamas gained an overwhelming majority in the Palestinian Legislative Council elections in January 2006.[26]

Keeping an eye on the changing dynamics right across the border, Omar Suleiman's EGID maintained its connection with every faction in the simmering Gaza Strip, including Hamas, whose strongman Ismail

Haniyeh was named prime minister and leader of the Legislative Council's
majority bloc following the victory at the Legislative Council elections.
The nature of Egyptian monitoring of and connections with the Gaza
Strip in the aftermath of Arafat's death remains disputed, and while Gazans
insist that the EGID supported Fatah's Abbas and Dahlan, others stress
that Fatah was enraged by Egypt's public and new endorsement of Hamas.
"Egypt's State Security Investigations and Intelligence Departments are
historical rivals of Hamas, they have jailed them in Egypt for their interac-
tions with the Egyptian Muslim Brotherhood, their mother organization,
and they continued to endorse Fatah as it jailed them in Gaza," said Abu
Amer, who believes that Egypt had requested both Fatah and Israel to
further stifle Hamas and the Islamic Jihad, Gaza's main Islamist factions.

Al-Filistini claims otherwise:

> Omar Suleiman's intelligence officers were at some point hosted by
> Hamas officials in the Gaza Strip; their acceptance of Hamas's hospi-
> tality was a sign of harmony that enraged the Palestinian Authority. I
> believe they were well aware of Hamas's rapid rise that relied to some
> extent on the Sinai as a source of weapons.

The dispute over Egypt's stance on the rise of Hamas existed even
at the level of governments; secret cables leaked by WikiLeaks revealed
that Omar Suleiman was intent on crippling the Muslim Brotherhood
offshoot. The cables said that Suleiman told Israeli defense official Amos
Gilad that he would "do all in his power to sabotage the Gaza elections in order to prevent a Hamas victory."[27] Suleiman apparently never
fulfilled his pledge, or had no intention of fulfilling it in the first place.

While Abu Amer's opinion is backed by a history of animosity between
Mubarak's regime and Hamas and its mother organization in Egypt, the
opposing argument is also backed by a similarly long history of allowances
given by Mubarak to the Islamist opposition in Egypt. Such allowances
were clearly seen in the multi-billion dollar charities and businesses
owned and run by Muslim Brotherhood figures. However, speculation
over the nature of Egypt's relations with Hamas ended when Mubarak
tacitly allowed them to receive weapons and to continue smuggling operations—worth hundreds of millions of dollars annually and fully controlled
by Hamas. The allowances were bestowed at a time when Mubarak and
Suleiman were more than capable of crushing the whole operation.

The Qassam Rockets

By the time Ismail Haniyeh was named prime minister in 2006, Hamas's military wing, the Ezzidine al-Qassam Brigades, were already firing their Qassam III rockets at Israeli military and civilian targets. The Qassam rockets, unsophisticated as they were, were the fruit of years of underground experiments and signaled an unprecedented development in the group's military capabilities.

The first version of the Gaza-made rocket, Qassam I, was a four-kilometer-range rocket that carried a five hundred gram warhead and was first used in October 2001,[28] right after the outbreak of the Second Intifada. The rocket was quite ineffective, but was developed further. In January 2002, Hamas operative Osama Zohadi Hamed Karika was arrested by Israeli authorities at the Rafah Crossing Terminal carrying documents that detailed the development of the Qassam rockets. He later admitted that he was on a trip to Saudi Arabia to obtain funding for the project.[29]

Abu Suleiman says he is skeptical that Saudi Arabia was the final destination; maybe for transit or financing, he says, but he believes the trip was going further. "He could have been on the way to Yemen, Sudan, or even Iran where the serious operations were taking place. This one was arrested but many more weren't."

Abu Amer endorsed the smuggler's argument; he explains that Iran had been cautiously approaching Hamas for a few years before the unilateral disengagement in 2005. "They were sending money, training operatives in different countries, but weren't fully engaged with Hamas yet."

The fact that underground workshops became capable of producing the rocket made it impossible for Israel to stop what had already started, and extremely difficult for the Egyptian authorities to intercept the raw materials required for making such rockets. The manufacturing process required nothing more than some chemical fertilizers, or explosive material such as TNT if available, while the metal body could easily be made of scrap metal melted and reshaped in simple workshops.

Renowned Israeli military scientist and author Azriel Lorber described the unguided Qassam rockets as "extremely simple and based on 'kitchen table technology' and on commercially available raw materials, mostly chemical fertilizers, both for the propellants and the explosives."[30]

When Israel began tightening its grip on the movement of fertilizers, construction materials, and other products defined as dual-use[31]

—incorporated in the manufacturing of explosives and potentially fueling the rocket-making facilities—the smugglers in Sinai started tying sacks of fertilizer, small amounts of explosives, and post-1973 landmines to the ropes extending through the underground tunnels. And in 2005, when the Israeli border police withdrew from Gaza along with the IDF during the unilateral disengagement, it left the Rafah Crossing Terminal and the fourteen-kilometer border with Egypt manned by the debilitated Palestinian Authority police, most of which were polarized by the broadening turmoil and more concerned about their internal disputes than any other policing responsibilities.[32]

During the years of development of the Gaza-made Qassam rockets, from 2000 to 2005, Iran's influence hadn't been evident on the ground in Sinai at all, in comparison to its influence on military knowledge inside Gaza. The smuggling operations continued to rely on a network of intermediaries, mainly the Gaza tunnel owners, who conveyed the list of demanded merchandise to the providers in Sinai. The providers in turn would independently obtain whatever was requested through their own means. It was basically a courier service that had to remain secret in order not to raise suspicion, and the fact that the majority of the required materials were sold publicly across Egypt made the job relatively easy. (See chapter 4 for more detail on the smuggling operations.)

According to al Filistini:

> The fertilizers and simple chemicals were brought in by farmers and ordinary shop owners across Sinai who didn't realize they were supplying the smuggling networks. The more attention grabbing materials, especially TNT, were smuggled from mainland Egypt with the help of anyone willing to do it, drug and arms dealers or even ordinary criminals.

Back then, notes al-Filistini, Hamas didn't have to run any form of sophisticated operation or rely on trusted smugglers that would require more funding and stronger ties. Either the Gaza intermediaries or a farmer in the Sinai, it was all the same as long as the material was delivered without complications. "Those few years of dealing with all forms of criminals were the foundation of the smuggling network that later handled the Iranian weapons coming from Sudan. The few who proved to be the most efficient were the ones who later handled the missiles and anti-tank weapons starting from 2006," explained al-Filistini.

A study published by the Intelligence and Terrorism Information Center at the Israel Intelligence Heritage and Commemoration Center said that, in 2001, four rockets were fired at Israeli settlements within the Gaza Strip. Since then, the numbers have significantly risen: to 35 rockets in 2002, 155 in 2003, 281 in 2004, 179 in 2005 when the Qassam III was announced with a range of twelve kilometers and a fifteen-kilogram warhead, and finally a staggering 946 rockets fired in 2006.[33]

Hamas Takes Shalit, and Gaza along with Him

On June 25, 2006, several members of Hamas's Qassam Brigades, the Palestinian Islamic Jihad, and the Popular Resistance Committees (formed over the years by defected members of Hamas, Fatah, and Islamic Jihad), and members of a formerly unknown group named Jaish al-Islam, or The Army of Islam, crossed an underground tunnel running from Karm Abu Salem in southern Gaza into Israeli territories and engaged in a short skirmish with an IDF patrol. Two of the Palestinian fighters were killed during the firefight that left two Israeli soldiers injured and one in the hands of the Gazan troops.

With a broken hand and an injured shoulder, IDF corporal Gilad Shalit was dragged back into the Gaza Strip through the same tunnel. It was the first time Palestinian factions had abducted an Israeli soldier since 1994,[34] a remarkable operation that signaled not only high-level, secret coordination between Gazan militants, but also the effectiveness of an intricate network of tunnels and underground bunkers built over the years across the coastal enclave.

In reaction to the operation, an Israeli incursion of Khan Younes was ordered by then Prime Minister Ehud Olmert on June 28, three days after the abduction. At the time, Olmert said in a speech in Jerusalem that "all the military activity that started overnight will continue in the coming days. We won't hesitate to carry out extreme action to bring Gilad back to his family."[35]

The Palestinian Authority rushed to deny any knowledge or shared responsibility for the operation. President Mahmoud Abbas called on the international community to intervene and stop Israel's incursion while his cabinet spokesman Ghazi Hamad called the Israeli operation "unjustified."[36]

"Egypt turned from a mediator underestimating one of the disputing parties, Gaza or rather Hamas, into a mediator that is keen on flirting with the side it once looked down on because of their possession of Shalit," said al-Filistini. He added that Sinai Bedouins were jokingly saying at the time that Shalit had probably been smuggled through the tunnels and would be found in al-Mehdiya, the Sawarka tribal stronghold south of Rafah, or some valley in South Sinai. It was sarcastic, but spoke of Sinai's reality: the tunnels were running and becoming more sophisticated, al-Mehdiya was gaining a reputation for smuggling weapons into Gaza, and the valleys of the South Sinai were unreachable by either Israelis or Egyptians.

A year later, in June 2007, a bloody confrontation broke out between Hamas and Fatah across the Gaza Strip and left hundreds dead and injured. Hamas had historically kept a few steps away from politics since its establishment in 1986, until it won the Legislative Council elections in 2006 and the cabinet along with it. Following this victory it decided to take over the Gaza Strip by firepower: killing, injuring, and humiliating their longtime oppressors headed by Mohamed Dahlan's Preventative Security.

Hamas's goal wasn't only to seize control of the Gaza Strip, but to make an example of its opposition, an example that would be carved into the collective memory of Gaza's 1.5 million people. The Islamist movement and its Fatah rivals were both accused of war crimes in the aftermath of the June 2007 battle. Human Rights Watch's April 2009 report, *Under Cover of War*, said several hundred Gazans were "maimed" and tortured in the aftermath of the Gaza War. Seventy-three men accused of "collaborating" had their arms and legs broken by "unidentified perpetrators" and eighteen Palestinians accused of collaborating with Israel, who had escaped from Gaza's main prison compound, were executed by Hamas security officials in the first days of the conflict.[37]

Along with the Gaza Strip, Hamas seized control of the Rafah Crossing Terminal, the smuggling tunnels, and the arms imports from Sinai. 2007, referred to by Hamas as the "Year of Decisiveness," sent the Gaza Strip into total isolation. The terminals with Israel were already shut down from the start of the siege in 2005, following Israel's unilateral disengagement, and the cabinet of Ehud Olmert—who took over as prime minister after Ariel Sharon's illness sent him into a coma on January 4, 2006—gradually elevated the blockade to the extent of suspending fuel, food, and medical supplies.

Some five hundred Palestinian Authority personnel,[38] mostly from Preventative Security, fled into Egypt before Hamas took control of the crossing terminal. Handing over their weapons and IDs to the Egyptian authorities, they were transported under heavy security to the central security barracks in Rafah and remained there under Egyptian security supervision for several months. Right after their escape from Gaza, Egypt sealed the Rafah Crossing Terminal while the SSI started another wave of arrests and threatened severe punishments for any interaction with the Gaza Strip.

"It was a time of such extreme unrest on both sides of the border that we suspended all of our work," said Abu Suleiman. "No one knew if Israel was going to invade Gaza again or if Egypt was ever going to loosen its tight security in North Sinai."

The same fears applied on the Gaza side of the border. Hamid and Akram al-Shaer, two Palestinian residents of Rafah who had been involved in smuggling since the early 2000s, said that uncertainty prevailed and total chaos hit the markets of Gaza. The only thing that happened smoothly was Hamas's quick control of the weapons of the Palestinian Authority.

"Major parts of the Strip were blacked out after Israeli jets hit the power station and markets were running out of supplies as everyone was rushing to buy whatever they could pay for in anticipation of stifling months and severe shortages of goods," said Hamid who suspended his business and closed his tunnel to avoid angering any of the warring sides. "It was clear that Hamas had taken control, but the assassinations and attacks by both sides silenced the whole strip, and it remained silent until it became clear who was in charge."[39]

2008: The Gazan Invasion of Egypt

On January 23, Hamas elements blew a hole in the border fence with Egypt and, within a few hours, tens of thousands of Gazans crossed into Egypt on foot, riding donkeys or bicycles, and in vehicles. The scene was extraordinary and is remembered by residents of North Sinai as the most crowded days in the history of their province. The United Nations had estimated at the time that around 750,000 Palestinians, half of Gaza's population, crossed into Sinai over the period of five days, mainly to buy consumer goods and supplies,[40] while Egypt's chamber of commerce estimated that the total purchases reached US$250 million within three days of the breach.[41]

Days later, when Hamas reached an agreement with Egyptian authorities on resealing the border and closing the terminal except for Gazan returnees, Egyptian president Hosni Mubarak commented on the incident for the first time. "I told them: 'Let them come in to eat and buy food, then they go back, as long as they are not carrying weapons,'" Mubarak told reporters at a book fair in Cairo.[42]

No actual measures were taken by the Egyptian authorities to stop the flow of Gazans into North Sinai, which was astonishing for a regime that had been harshly criticizing Hamas and other Islamist factions for years since their establishment, and stifling their movement through the Rafah Crossing Terminal, Gaza's only door to the world. Even the media reports on the breach, according to many Sinai residents who crossed freely into and back out of the Gaza Strip, seemed to reflect an Egyptian agreement or prior knowledge of the incident.[43]

For the five days when North Sinai was occupied by hundreds of thousands of Gazans, Egypt's security departments fully lifted its control over the northeastern quarter of the Sinai, which was unprecedented. Movement of both Gazans and Egyptians was totally unchecked within the fifty-kilometer area between the border and the western end of al-Arish. Even foreign journalists working in Egypt, who normally required coordination with the EGID and SSI to operate in Sinai and the border area, were allowed to enter Sinai and cross the blown-through fence into Gaza and back.

One journalist who roamed freely between Sinai and the northern end of the Gaza Strip reporting for local and foreign media outlets said, on condition of anonymity, that "it looked like Egypt wanted us to cover the scene and report on what turned into an open-air market for Gazans."

Al-Mehdiya, a stronghold of al-Menaei clan, the fiercest of all branches of the populous Sawarka tribe, was also bustling a few kilometers from the open border. Like every village in North Sinai, dozens of youth moved to the main cities of Rafah, Sheikh Zuwayyed, and al-Arish to buy and sell whatever they could make money out of, but several prominent members of al-Menaei clan had other businesses to attend to: smuggling loads of weapons into the Gaza Strip.

Abu Arrab was in prison at the time, but three of his cousins were running what many residents of North Sinai remember as the largest arms smuggling network in Sinai. The trio, Halim, Eid, and Salem,[44] of al-Menaei clan, had been sitting on an arsenal of Grad missiles, Russian Kornet anti-tank missile launchers, rocket-propelled grenades, high-caliber machine guns, and large quantities of TNT. All three had been working with Abu Suleiman al-Tarabin of South Sinai since 2004 and had successfully smuggled the first few Grad rockets into Gaza during the stifling blockade that Israel and Egypt had imposed since the Hamas takeover months earlier.

"In 2008, Iran was behind it all," said Abu Suleiman. "We had started hearing from Hamas operatives that fighters were getting training in Iran and other countries, then the heavier weapons started appearing, coming all the way from Sudan to stay here in Sinai."

Abu Suleiman said that some of the weapons were stored in Sinai for several months before the border breach in January 2008. Egypt, he explains, was serious about its blockade and the SSI had informants in almost every village across the peninsula. No one was willing to risk their lives for it, until everything suddenly changed.

Forty-five-year old Eid, who takes pride in the fact that he special-ized in smuggling weapons, and, according to him, never smuggled drugs and never "enslaved African migrants as the criminals do," said that smuggling weapons is just "a job, just like being an engineer, but since we don't have jobs like you in Cairo we make a living out of what-ever is available here." He went on: "2008 was the first time we started smuggling large amounts of weapons. I wasn't involved in the smuggling of rockets, I mainly smuggled machine guns, RPGs, and ammunition."

His fellow tribesmen, Salem, also in his forties and Halim, who was twenty-six in 2008, had lavish multi-million-pound villas in al-Mehdiya, surrounded by olive trees. Along with Eid, they gained a reputation for smuggling the majority of the rockets and explosive materials into the Gaza Strip. They said that the weapons were transported through the tunnels and overground in the vehicles, freely crossing the border dur-ing the few days of the breach.

At the time, Hamas operatives were the ones responsible for plan-ning the transport of weapons into Gaza, while the Sinai smugglers were responsible for transport across Sinai and storing them. Although the three smugglers wouldn't give much detail on the means of transport across the border, others predicted that the rockets were most prob-ably transported in vehicles above ground since the tunnels back then weren't as sophisticated as now. Some of the smugglers didn't know what they were smuggling exactly, as weapons were taken apart to ease the transport and to lower the risks of being spotted.[45]

Hamas had built this 'arms only' smuggling network by sifting through all forms of criminals and testing their capabilities throughout the years of blockade that sent the movement's operations underground. They extended the relationship and made the smugglers rich to guarantee their loyalty, and to make sure they never got caught while involved in any other form of illegal business. Some of them became so powerful the Egyptian authorities started recognizing their status within the tribes across Sinai. As for linking them with the Upper Egyptian and Sudanese smugglers, it wasn't much of a challenge: the African smuggling route ran for decades before Iran started arming Hamas and their joint operation was built on an already existing expertise.[46]

It wasn't only weapons that crossed. According to prominent Israeli journalists Avi Issacharoff and Amos Harel, quoting Israeli sources, Iran had taken advantage of the breach and transported everything required for a significant military buildup into the Strip.

> Members of Hamas's military wing smuggled blueprints and other detailed technical instructions into Gaza that will enable the group to develop rockets capable of striking at longer distances. . . . Some 200 Hamas militants who received training in Iran, the Beqaa Valley in Lebanon, and Syria, returned to the Strip through this breach in the wall.[47]

Abu Arrab, who was released from detention a few months after the breach, confirmed that "several Iranian operatives had entered Gaza during that breach. They were in Sinai for days and were hosted by several people in different locations." At some point, he says, "they had two officers from the Qassam Brigades securing them, they moved between different houses and spoke Arabic like we do." Abu Arrab did not confirm if they had been kept by his cousins who smuggled and stored the weapons, but said, "I believe it because at some point I hosted Hamas operatives in a similar manner."

Several months after the breach, in November 2008, Egypt's security authorities apprehended Sami Shehab, or Mohamed Yousef Mansour, who led a Hezbollah cell operating in Egypt for, according to Hezbollah's leader Hassan Nasrallah, "a logistical job to help the

Palestinians get (military) equipment." The apprehension of the cell, and the acknowledgment by Hezbollah's leadership, put an end to the speculation about Iran's role in smuggling weapons across Egypt and into the Gaza Strip.[48]

In al-Mehdiya, when asked if smugglers coordinated the transport of weapons with Hamas prior to the attacks on the border, Eid and Salem refused to answer the question, with a smirk. As for Halim, the youngest and most daring, he said, "with or without coordination, the weapons were going in. Keeping weapons in storage is a risky responsibility and costs thousands of dollars. If Hamas hadn't moved, those who kept the weapons would have sent it in themselves to get rid of the burden."

Al-Filistini, on the other hand, says that Hamas never actually handled the shipments:

> The movement historically outsourced this business to the smugglers in southern Gaza and provided them with immunity to keep them providing the service. Inside the Gaza Strip they provide logistics and security for the smuggled arms, but never appear in the picture. . . . Israel and Egypt have attacked and destroyed the tunnels for almost a decade, have you ever heard of a Hamas operative killed in any of those attacks? The victims are always ordinary tunnel workers that have nothing to do with either the weapons or Hamas, they have a limited job that entails no information whatsoever except for moving a shipment through a tunnel and handing it to whoever will deliver it to a person or a place inside the Gaza Strip.

The smuggling of arms had been growing since Hamas's takeover of the Strip, but it reached its peak during the border breach and throughout 2008. The surge in Iranian military supplies and training was demonstrated throughout the year, most clearly during the Israeli war on Gaza in December 2008 that was known as Operation Cast Lead and continued into January 2009. Hamas's military capabilities had gone from the fourteen-kilometer-range Qassam III rockets to the 122-mm rockets known as Grads, with ranges between twenty and forty kilometers and with twenty-kilogram explosive war heads. This 2008 to 2009 war was the first opportunity for Hamas to demonstrate its possession of and ability to use guided weapons such as the Russian-made Kornet anti-tank missile, in addition to the newly injected knowledge of locally-built improvised explosive devices or IEDs.[49]

In a report published by the Washington Institute for Near East Policy (WINEP), in 2009, Yarom Cohen and Mathew Levitt quoted Israeli intelligence officers:

> Beyond small arms, Israeli intelligence estimates that some 250 tons of explosives, 80 tons of fertilizer, 4000 rocket-propelled grenades, and 1800 rockets were transported from Egypt to Gaza from September 2005 to December 2008. According to Israeli figures, from June 2007 to December 2008, Hamas increased not only the quantity but also the quality of its arsenal in Gaza, improving the performance of its improvised explosive devices and expanding the distance and payload capabilities of its Qassam rocket warheads.[50]

Egypt's Mix of Corruption and Incompetence

Up until the January 25 uprising broke out, the overwhelming majority of weapons came into Egypt through the southern border with Sudan, ruled since 1989 by an Islamist military officer and graduate of Cairo's Military Academy, Omar Hassan al-Bashir. Since his ascent to power, al-Bashir remained publicly supportive of Islamist movements, starting with his alliance with Hassan al-Turabi, leader of the National Islamic Front, and hosting outlawed members of the Egyptian Muslim Brotherhood movement, providing logistical assistance to members of the Egyptian Islamic Jihad and al-Jamaa al-Islamiya in their long dispute with the Egyptian regime, and allowing Osama bin Laden, al-Qaeda's founder and commander, to freely operate out of Sudan for a time.

"Every one of the factions we fought in Egypt had an extension in Sudan, or at least someone working for them," General Mohamed Okasha said. "The Egyptian authorities fought them both here and in Sudan. It was always a source of weapons and men, and a hideout for the militants in times of crackdowns in Upper Egypt."[51]

General Okasha says that various factors came together to form the arms trafficking route between the Sudanese border and the Gaza Strip. He cites the weakness of the central government in controlling the criminal networks and preventing its own officers from engaging in corruption, and the militant activities that led to years of rising instability and an abundance of weapons outside government control as among those factors. However, above all, he says, was Sudan's willingness to allow Iran to operate on its soil.

> The Iranians are freely operating with the knowledge, if not cooperation, of the Sudanese regime from one side, and with the Sudanese trafficking networks from another. Their weapons would enter Sudan through official ports and move to the traffickers who would receive and ship them into Egypt. Such operations are financed by hundreds of millions of dollars in transportation budgets, and from experience we know that those behind arms trafficking, especially Iran, are willing to go far with expenditure and tactics in order to secure their shipments.

WINEP quoted Israeli security and intelligence reports saying that arms travel through a variety of routes that cross Yemen, Eritrea, Ethiopia, and South Africa, and eventually meet in Sudan. The report did not mention how they were transported for hundreds of kilometers to the Sinai Peninsula, but indicated that

> after the material enters the Sinai, it is transferred into Gaza via tunnels underneath the 'Philadelphia Corridor,' the Gaza–Egypt border that runs through the city of Rafah. Less frequently, arms are moved to Gaza via the Mediterranean Sea: the weapons are deposited in waterproof barrels submerged below the surface and tied to buoys eventually retrieved by fishermen.[52]

General Okasha said that despite corruption on both sides of the Sudanese border, which had a significant effect on the authorities' ability to keep up with the influx of weapons,

> the lack of training and development of the security and military institutions was more destructive than corruption. The criminal networks, despite coming from the poorest and most underprivileged communities of Egypt, have far exceeded the state's abilities under the decaying Mubarak administration.

Colonel Khaled Okasha, who also ended his career as a police officer in Sinai, agreed with this theory of his father, General Okasha:

I was responsible for storages of police and civil defense equipment worth LE4 million. It was useless because none of my corporals, sergeants, and the majority of the officers under my command knew how to use it. They had received no training whatsoever on how to use equipment being constantly introduced into the departments.[53]

General Okasha blamed the debilitating military capabilities on the twenty-year defense minister Mohamed Hussein Tantawi, describing him as "a bureaucrat that came to the liking of the coup-fearing Mubarak because of his submissive, uncreative character." Meanwhile the younger Colonel Okasha blamed the police department's deterioration on the fourteen-year minister of the interior Habib El-Adly, describing him as "someone who believed in using fear and brutality rather than security sciences and professional tactics, a minister that was more keen on buying the latest and sometimes unneeded equipment rather than giving proper training on the the use of tactical and up-to-date equipment."

As for the smugglers, both corruption and weakness played in favor of their business. Abu Suleiman said that every challenge he faced was either familiar and had a ready solution, or a solution was found for it in a matter of days, or weeks at most. He also said, "weapons were mainly brought into Sinai on boats crossing the poorly secured stretches of the Gulf of Suez and smaller fishing boats that work along parts of the Suez Canal itself, but that was in case the smugglers were in the southern and middle parts of the peninsula." This was backed up by testimony from both the Okashas. Abu Suleiman went on:

Sinai is the last phase of the operation and is considered an easy job if the shipment successfully crosses the Gulf of Suez. After that, everything is loaded onto pick-up trucks and driven across the mountains and valleys until it reaches the north. "It either goes straight to the tunnels or remains in the villages of Rafah for a while if there is any disruption. The police, military, and naval police officers are constantly taking bribes. They know that the shipment is coming in; either they accept the bribe or refuse it. Accepting a bribe becomes an easier option when you know that [if you don't] someone else will, and it's much easier when the lower ranks know that the higher ranks are corrupt.

According to Abu Arrab, shipments crossed the ferries and al-Salam Bridge in Ismailiya in small and heavy pick-up trucks, and sometimes in shipping containers. He went on:

> Bribes helped and were also used to keep attention away; sometimes a smuggler would pay an officer on the bridge while the shipment was crossing by ferry, or even on a boat in the Suez. The ferries have always been poorly secured and hundreds of heavy trucks cross from both sides of the Suez Canal every day.

Abu Arrab said that many smugglers started customizing heavy trucks with flat steel boxes above which a different material is loaded, mostly construction materials, fertilizers, or even vegetables—things that no one would be suspicious of to the extent of unloading a shipment weighing several tons, whether at the bridge or the ferry. "If the truck is loaded with sand, cement, or construction steel, the flat box becomes completely unreachable unless the shipment is unloaded. And when the security is as weak as this, you can bring anything in a truck as it is never properly inspected."[54]

The corruption and incompetence was never limited to the police and military institutions, but reached far into a regime built on a decades-old bureaucracy. One of many loopholes exploited by smugglers was the port-to-port or transit shipments, which is a container that arrives at one Egyptian port and heads directly to another where it is to depart the country to its final destination. Such shipments, known locally as 'passing cargo,' are the sole responsibility of a registered shipping company and are handled at ports by custom clearance agents, whose responsibility does not exceed recording the departure of the shipment at the exit port.

In a country like Egypt, with numerous sea and land ports, and hundreds of shipping companies and customs clearance agents operating in every city, an unknown number of businesses and officials were involved in forging the records of shipments or providing smugglers with the official 'customs seal' that allows them to load the smuggled arms into containers crossing Egyptian soil. Once the container is sealed and the required documents are complete, it is not subject to any searches at any of the security terminals or checkpoints across the country except for the departure point. Opening such containers outside of the departure port usually requires an official police report and the presence of a customs agent to oversee the police search of an already cleared shipment.

Shipping and transportation businesses were hardly discouraged from engaging in corruption, not only because of the many system loopholes to be exploited, but also the lack of punishments proportional to such crimes. The transit shipments, which allegedly became the smugglers' favorite way of smuggling weapons and narcotics in and out of the Sinai Peninsula over the past decade, are organized by laws that do more to encourage than deter criminal activity. A transport company's punishment for failing to clear a shipment at the departure port is normally a fine that would not exceed a few thousand pounds plus payment of the customs tariffs for the goods, if they were ever fully registered at the entry port.

In the year 2000, a high-ranking security official told Egypt's state owned *al-Ahram* newspaper that the illegally smuggled goods in domestic markets had reached LE7 billion, which reflected a LE 2.5 billion-worth of loss by the customs authority.[55]

Until today, Egypt's security and military officials have denied the involvement of their ground personnel in arms smuggling operations taking place across the Sinai Peninsula. This hard-to-believe argument was in itself a confession of how incompetent the government institutions have become, but, over the years, the Mubarak regime preferred being tagged as incompetent over admitting to the rampant corruption and working on ways to eliminate it. "In December 2007, then-Israeli Foreign Minister Tzipi Livni publicly denounced Egyptian efforts against smuggling into Gaza as 'terrible,' claiming that she possessed videotape evidence of Egyptian police helping Hamas smuggle militants and weaponry across the border."[56]

Days after Livni's explosive remarks, Israeli newspaper *Arutz Sheva* reported that then-Knesset member Yuval Shteinitz, who later became defense minister, criticized the Foreign Ministry and Livni for suppressing the video. The paper said "the recording was originally sent to the Israeli embassy in Washington and would have convinced the US Congress that Egypt is not capable of defending the border ahead of a crucial Congressional vote on foreign aid, Shteinitz claimed."[57]

2011: The Libyan Route

A few weeks after the Egyptian uprising and the resignation of Hosni Mubarak, Libya became the new source of weapons that replaced the decades-old African route. The downfall of Libyan dictator Muammar

Gaddafi, and the disintegration of his military, caused an unprecedented explosion of arms trafficking and smuggling across Libya into every country surrounding it. Billions of dollars worth of military arsenals had fallen into the hands of rebels or were seized by criminal syndicates that operated almost everywhere across Libya's 1.7 million square kilometers.

Reporting from the Libyan border in February, April, May, and August 2011, it became clear that Egypt's poorly secured western border had turned from an amateur 9-mm pistol market into a fully fledged arms trafficking hub. Salloum, the sleepy Egyptian town of a few thousand residents and the main crossing point into Libya, had become the northern entrance of Libyan small arms. The Jaghboub Oasis, some two hundred kilometers south of Salloum, and the Eastern Owaynat Desert in southeast Egypt, both historically known for drug smuggling operations across North Africa, became the floodgates of heavier weapons including high-caliber anti-aircraft guns, rocket-propelled grenades, and surface-to-air missiles.

During the third week of July 2011, Egypt's security authorities reported seizing a shipment of twenty-five anti-aircraft missiles, along with nine shoulder-held launching systems. That shipment was intercepted just one hundred and twenty-five miles out of the capital Cairo. Two weeks later, two truckloads of machine guns, sniper rifles, and ammunition were seized on the northern coastal highway between Marsa Matrouh and Alexandria.[58]

At the time, Egyptian security officials said that the destination to which the weapons were headed was unknown, while Israeli officials reported that they had detected an inflow of SA-7 anti-aircraft missiles to the Gaza Strip.[59] The news was paraded as a successful blow by Egypt to the arms smuggling cartels, but police and military officials had failed to explain how such weapons reached hundreds of miles inside the country, all the way to the edge of the capital. Such interceptions were in fact solid evidence that Egypt's authorities at the time had no control over the arms smuggling operations anymore.

Abu Suleiman said that the weapons seized were on the way to the desert surrounding Cairo's 6 October suburb, where they would be handed over to the eastern desert tribes that geographically extend over the Nile Valley and the cities of Ismailiya and Suez, the two main entrances to Sinai by road, or across the Suez Canal. He described how the desert around 6 October became the intersection of tribal borders as well as highways.

It is connected to every part of the western desert: the southern roads come from the Bahariya and Farafra Oases, beyond which roads reach the Eastern Owaynat region on the Egyptian, Libyan, and Sudanese borders; this same road connects to another stretching north of the Great Sand Sea to Siwa Oasis, behind which is the Jaghboub Oasis at the Libyan border; and the northern roads come from the North Coast and Alexandria, from which the highway extends to 6 October then inner Cairo.

The roads extend for thousands of kilometers all over the western desert of Egypt and are poorly secured except for areas near towns or military bases. The massive desert, through which the network cuts, provides multiple safe routes for traffickers to avoid any contact with the authorities. A simple look at the geography of Egypt makes this clear: the first shipment was seized almost one hundred kilometers outside of 6 October, on the al-Alamein Road, which runs directly to the heart of tribal territory on the North Coast, while the other one was three hundred kilometers away, on the coastal highway outside of Alexandria, which leads to the same point where the first shipment was intercepted.

"It was Gaza that encouraged all of this," Abu Arrab said in Rafah. "The majority of weapons coming from Libya were already paid for by Palestinians and were just cutting through Egypt to reach the Gaza Strip."

Hamas, the Islamic Jihad, and the Salafi–jihadist factions of the Gaza Strip were the first to arrive in Tobrok to buy Gaddafi's arms. The Libyan uprising opened up unprecedented opportunities for them after relying for decades on the African route, which risks interception by several governments and dozens of tribes and crime syndicates. The newly opened line in 2011 stemmed from one country plunged in chaos, Libya, and cut straight through another suffering a total security vacuum, Egypt. In addition to being a more economical option, saving thousands of miles of off-road smuggling, it was also a safer and more guaranteed operation as it was handled only by tribes that have dealt with the Palestinian factions for decades and in many cases were related by blood and by Sunni Muslim, Israel-hating ideologies.

At the Libyan border, smugglers confirmed what Abu Arrab had said. "Their money is always ready, they are very trusted when it comes to buying weapons and four-wheel drives," said one smuggler in Salloum, speaking of Palestinian buyers. He complained at the time that he had been put out of business by the control over the market of smuggling kingpins, which left no room for smaller operations.

"The gradual downfall of Gaddafi's regime satisfied every Palestinian faction," said Abu Suleiman, who managed to travel to Libya in 2011, despite officially being a fugitive from the Egyptian government. "In 2011, the whole region changed, Libya became the source of arms and the smuggling business went 90 percent west [toward the Libyan border]; we rarely handled southern [from the Sudanese border] shipments after the Egyptian and Libyan uprisings." He described the chaos in Egypt and Libya as "Gaza's window that never opened before and will never open again if closed. Hamas and other factions will do whatever they have to in order to import as many arms as possible."

Gaza's effect on the avalanche of weapons coming from Libya into Egypt kept Sinai at the end of the smuggling funnel. The rising jihadist groups in Sinai became more emboldened by the abundance of weapons, which they enjoyed as much as the smugglers and the Bedouin tribes in general. The intertribal disputes grew more hostile as everyone became heavily armed and were encouraged by the full retreat of the police and the gradual retreat of tribal authority in the aftermath of the January 25 uprising.

"Anyone can assess the change in Gaza by looking on the ground in Sinai. If drug dealers and thieves are carrying RPGs in Sinai then you can roughly imagine what the Qassam Brigades have in their Gaza bunkers," said Abu Suleiman.

Misrata Market

In the center of Rafah, Egypt's border town with the Gaza Strip, the Masoura market has been held every Saturday for decades. Merchants arrive from every part of the Sinai Peninsula and beyond to set up stalls at one of North Sinai's most bustling weekly gatherings, while residents come from far-flung towns and villages to shop for a week's or a month's supplies. But in mid 2011, the market was flooded by Libyan vehicles and weapons and came to be referred to as Misrata market, after the Libyan port city.[60]

Libyans that fled the war into Egypt or were transiting through had realized how much profit they could make on their vehicles, especially four-wheel drives, if sold in North Sinai instead of selling them on the border in Salloum, or in any Egyptian city where the buyer's concerns over customs tariffs and re-registering the vehicle in Egypt would significantly lower the price. It was a better bargain for them to drive it to Rafah, where it would be sold for a much higher price before crossing the tunnels into the Gaza Strip.

The market didn't gain its Misrata reputation only because of vehicles, but rather because of the weapons. By May 2011, half of the Rafah market's merchandize was weapons coming from Libya, sold by Sinai Bedouins who had already bought the weapons at wholesale prices.

Abu Arrab, who at some point had sold a few weapons at the Misrata market, said that:

> Automatic and sniper rifles, high-calibers, anti-aircraft 14.5 mm, RPGs and landmines are all available. The machine guns are sold right at the market while the missiles are delivered in different and far-away locations where the sellers hide them. What is being sold at the market is just a fraction of what is crossing the Sinai; the majority of the shipments don't appear here as they are not owned by the smugglers, they are paid for in Libya, and our job is to just secure the shipments until the tunnels into Gaza.

Several traffickers, including Abu Arrab and Abu Suleiman, said that up until 2012, SA-7 missiles, Grad missiles, Russian anti-tank missiles, heat-seeking missiles, and Iranian Fajr missiles were all crossing the Sinai along with tons of other military equipment such as satellite phones and internet devices, handheld transceivers, and uniforms. They estimated the number of people responsible for the Hamas-financed smuggling lines across the peninsula at ten.

The Iranian Fajr-5 rocket, a seventy-five-kilometer range rocket with a ninety-kilogram warhead, was among the 10 percent of weapons Abu Suleiman had said continued to come from Sudan. In October 2012, Israeli jets destroyed the Yarmouk arms manufacturing facility south of Khartoum, which it claimed was a source of arms smuggled to the Gaza Strip. This plant "was 'designated' by the United States as essentially under the control of Iran at the end of 2006 and thereby became the target of sanctions under the Iran and Syria Nonproliferation Act."[61]

In 2007, a year after the designation of the Sudan facility and as Hamas took control of the Gaza Strip, leaked American diplomatic cables revealed that former head of the EGID General Omar Suleiman had promised Israel to "cleanse" the Sinai from arms smuggling, for which he was applauded by high-ranking Israeli military and intelligence officials. In addition to stating that "the Israeli Security Agency (ISA) had, on several occasions, provided Suleiman with detailed intelligence on the names of smugglers," the cables described the Sinai as a "weapons and explosives warehouse" and stressed that "co-operation against smuggling is better with Egyptian Intelligence Chief Omar Suleiman than it is with Egyptian Military Commander Field Marshall Tantawi."[62]

Ironically, this information was only made public when WikiLeaks provided *The Telegraph* with the leaked cables that the paper published on February 9, 2011, the day that Suleiman was appointed vice president of Egypt and two days before Mubarak was forced out of power. By then, the Israeli view of the peninsula had already changed, when the natural gas pipeline stretching through North Sinai was first bombed on February 5, 2011. The transformation of Sinai from a buffer zone into a hostile territory became Israel's top concern while it attempted to adapt to the changing nature of its friendly neighbor, Egypt.

Yossi Kuperwasser, general director of Israel's Ministry of Strategic Affairs, noted that the downfall of Egypt's Mubarak and Libya's Gaddafi, and the unparalleled amount of weapons crossing the Sinai put Israel in the range of Hamas and the Islamic Jihad's deadly rockets.

"Libya's weapons have leaked into several countries, but nothing is more concerning to us than the weapons crossing Egypt into the Gaza Strip," said Kuperwasser from his office in Jerusalem. "The most critical weapons that entered Gaza [coming from Libya and elsewhere] were the long-range Grad and Iranian Fajr missiles." He stressed that what is even more worrying than the flow of weapons is the transfer of Iranian military knowledge that continues to give Hamas and other Islamist factions the ability to locally produce rockets and other forms of weapons. To him, the 2012 war, known as Operation Pillar of Defense, was a vivid example of the rising military capabilities of Islamist groups in the Gaza Strip.[63]

"There were weapons that were relevant to the war and others weren't, but it showed us what the capabilities of Hamas have become," said Kuperwasser.

During this war, which broke out in November 2012, the first Iranian Fajr-5 rocket was fired at Israel, with a range twice that of the Grad and Qassam III rockets formerly used by Hamas and the Islamic Jihad, putting Tel Aviv for the first time ever within reach of Gazan attacks. Until that rocket was fired, war sirens hadn't echoed in Tel Aviv since Saddam Hussein fired his Scud missiles at Israel during the 1991 Iraq war.

4

THE SMUGGLING TUNNELS: BESIEGED BY ISRAEL, GAZA EXPLODES INTO EGYPT

The first underground tunnel between Gaza and Sinai was said to have been found in 1983, only one year after Israel's full withdrawal from the peninsula after almost fourteen years of full or partial occupation.[1] Despite the ineffectiveness of the smuggling operations back then, it concerned the Israeli military, especially with the outbreak of the First Intifada in 1987, five years after the historic city of Rafah, a landing point for armies, merchants, and travelers throughout the history of the Middle East, had been split by the reestablished international border in a Berlin-Wall-like operation that left families divided on both sides of the border. For the decade after the tunnels were unheard of, until 1997 when the phenomenon reappeared in the Strip, which had been occupied by Israel since 1967.[2]

By the end of 1999, Palestinian leader Yasser Arafat had ordered the lifting of the stifling security grip imposed by the ruling party Fatah on its rival Islamist factions operating across the Gaza Strip. Professor Adnan Abu Amer described the development "as a political maneuver to pressure Israeli Prime Minister Ehud Barak and US President Bill Clinton ahead of the Camp David Summit in June 2000." The failure of the trilateral talks—between Israel, the Palestinian Authority, and the US— and the renewed allowances to Islamist militias plunged the Gaza Strip into a wave of violence during which Hamas revived the use of attack tunnels. Digging them around Israeli military encampments in various parts of the Strip, the Islamist militants used the tunnels to plant and detonate explosives under Israeli military watchtowers.[3]

The start of what became Gaza's tunnel phenomenon remains disputed, but older generations from Rafah, on both sides of the border, remember it as a smugglers' idea that was later enhanced into a military tactic by the Islamist fighters from different factions that were forced underground by the relentless Israeli occupation and the increasing crackdowns from the Palestinian Authority. It was then further developed to cope with the rising pressures of the external blockade that began after Israel's military unilateral disengagement in 2005.

"Theoretically it goes back to the 1980s, but it practically started in 1997. One family decided to dig a tunnel that started inside their house and extended it to the house of a relative on the Egyptian side of the border," said Hamid, a 55-year-old Palestinian–Egyptian living on the Gazan side of Rafah. His family, like many others from Rafah, extended to both sides of the border after years of intermarriages between both peoples. "Back then the border line was so thin in some areas you could talk to your relatives [on the other side] if you were loud enough."[4]

In 2000, Hamid dug his first tunnel in partnership with a relative who owned a house right on the border. "It took a few months of digging and ran from the bedroom. After the digging was finished the room was cleaned up and the opening of the tunnel was covered with a carpet and some furniture."

Hamid estimated the number of tunnels dug in a similar manner (from house to house) to be fifteen, but he admits it is impossible to know the exact number because the digging of tunnels was surrounded by secrecy. "If the Israelis suspected that a tunnel ran from a certain house they would immediately raid it, arrest all the men, and bulldoze the house. Many houses were also bombed by the Israeli airforce over similar suspicions."

Palestinian professors of economics Wafiq al-Agha and Samir Abu Mudalalla, who have published several meticulously researched studies on the smuggling tunnels and their influence on Gaza's economy, said that "up until the year 2000, the tunnels were used to smuggle jewelry and narcotics, the most lucrative materials at the time, while rarely smuggling weapons to the armed resistance factions. . . . The tunnels continued to operate in very small numbers until 2007 due to the constant Israeli targeting of the smuggling operations and their owners." Al-Agha and Abu Mudalalla also estimated the number of tunnels operating in mid-2007 at only twenty.[5]

Hamid, the Gazan tunnel owner, and Abu Arrab, the Sinai arms smuggler, who worked together for more than a decade, said that those twenty or so tunnels were built with the knowledge of Yasser Arafat's ruling Fatah movement and the Mubarak authorities in Egypt. What was once used to smuggle jewelry and narcotics, pre-2000, became the main route of smuggling arms to the Palestinian Authority that coordinated directly with the tunnel owners as it attempted to import weapons and ammunition from any source possible.

"During the first four years [of the transformation of tunnel operations, 2000–2004], the tunnels weren't really a necessity for the people of Gaza because all the Israeli-controlled terminals were operating. Gaza was not only importing goods but also exporting to the West Bank and Israel," said Hamid. But when the Israelis withdrew in August 2005, the importance of tunnels began to rise with the imposition of the Israeli blockade that began immediately after the disengagement and the Egyptian blockade that started with Hamas's takeover in mid-2007.

For five years between the outbreak of the Second Intifada in September 2000 and the Israeli unilateral disengagement in September 2005, the Israel Defense Forces (IDF) made it impossible for the tunnels to grow. The ground incursions and house demolitions became concentrated in the city of Rafah, and especially on the borderline with Egypt. Human Rights Watch's investigation of house demolitions in the Gaza Strip indicated that some 1,700 houses where fully destroyed by Israeli forces between 2000 and 2004. House demolitions reached an unprecedented level in 2004, with 298 houses completely razed in an IDF operation that followed an attack by the Palestinian Islamic Jihad that successfully targeted an Israeli armored personnel carrier. A Human Right's Watch report noted that Israel's oppressive military presence in the Strip, especially Rafah, had caused a significant surge in prices of arms and ammunition, putting the price of a single ordinary 7.62-mm machine-gun bullet at US$7, a figure the IDF paraded as evidence for the success of its operation.[6]

Israel's demolition of houses along the border aimed to create a buffer zone and went on until 2004. Hamid, whose first tunnel was destroyed in an IDF operation in 2003, says that before the demolitions began

> tunnels were 150 to 300 meters long at most. After that, tunnels stretched for longer distances that sometimes reached 1,000 meters. The border attacks and demolition of houses and tunnels killed and displaced many people, but in the end it led to enhancing the structure and security of tunnels, the opposite of what Israel had spent millions of dollars to accomplish.

Sharon's Blockade: A Ladder for Hamas

By mid-September 2005, the unilateral disengagement plan enacted by then Israeli Prime Minister Ariel Sharon had been completed and the blockade imposed on the Gaza Strip had reached unprecedented levels. Sharon's disengagement and external blockade plan, which had faced opposition from within the Israeli cabinet and the country's opposition alike, was viewed by many Israeli politicians and analysts as irrational.

Ehud Yaari, who describes Ariel Sharon as "a brilliant military man but a poor strategist," says that "Sharon took Gaza in 2005 and convinced himself that he will throw it in the lap of Mubarak and transfer de-facto responsibility to Egypt. Hosni Mubarak, as was predicted, said I am not catching, and he didn't."[7] Sharon simply wanted to revive the history of Egypt's rule over Gaza, which continued from 1948 to 1967.[8]

Yaari believes that Sharon's plan started faltering when Egypt moved to match Israel's blockade of the Gaza Strip. However, the real effects of the not-so-strategic plan started to surface months later, when Hamas starting flexing its muscles in confrontations with Fatah's remaining authorities in Gaza, and finally took over the whole strip after the bloody battles of June 2007. Meanwhile, Sharon's illness had left him in a coma, and his successor Ehud Olmert had stuck to the clearly impotent blockade policy, which pushed the Gazan population to the edge of starvation.

Sharon's advisor and prominent speaker Dov Weissglas described the policy of besieging the Gaza Strip back then, saying, "It's like a meeting with a dietitian. We need to make the Palestinians lose weight, but not to starve to death."[9]

"The entire architecture of Israeli policy toward Hamas since 2006 has only made the situation worse. After Hamas won the elections they kind of wanted a unity government, but such openings were shutdown one after the other which led to a policy of total isolation which backfired," said Dr. Benedetta Berti of the Tel Aviv-based Institute for National Security Studies.[10]

Israel's miscalculated plan, according to Berti, was to stifle the Gaza Strip to the point that the population, who brought Hamas to power through elections, and the opposition, who were silenced by Hamas's firepower, would rise in a revolution-like wave and topple the movement. But, as she went on, the opposite happened. Hamas continued and took over the Gaza Strip and the policy became only worse. The isolation weakened the middle class of Gaza by shutting down all the factories and accordingly those who could have been against Hamas were impoverished and left helpless. . . . Simply, the idea of besieging them [Hamas] to teach them a lesson only made them stronger and impoverished the people and made them more dependant.

For the six months after Hamas's takeover in June 2007, the Israeli sea, air, and ground siege paralyzed the Gaza Strip. Finding no fuel, residents of Gaza abandoned their cars and the prices of donkeys and horses, which became the most efficient form of transportation, skyrocketed. A popular story circulated in Gaza of a young man who invented a mixture of frying oil and acetone to use as an alternative to liquid gasoline for vehicles and, despite spreading across Gaza, residents loathed the invention due to its unbearable exhaust fumes.

Economists al-Agha and Abu Mudalalla published a shocking analysis of the blockade's impact that drove inflation through the roof, reaching more than 100 percent on various consumer goods. The industrial sector gradually began to stall due to the lack of raw materials and spare parts; by the end of 2008, some 90 percent of Gaza factories were shutdown and the industrial workforce had plummeted from 35,000 to less than 1,000 workers. Gaza total gross domestic product fell by more than 30 percent between 2005 and 2008.[11]

Hamas's January 2008 breach of the Egyptian border relieved Gaza's immediate consumerist needs. Although Mubarak played no active role in helping Gaza's destroyed economy, this breach revealed that he would tolerate any scenario other than Sharon's original plan of throwing responsibility for the Gaza Strip in Egypt's lap.

General Mohamed Okasha, who was an airforce pilot under Mubarak's command during the 1973 war, said "despite Mubarak's failure on many foreign policy levels and his constant submissive policy toward Israel, his way of handling the Gaza challenge was as cunning as that of Israel's. He never accepted even the mention of reviving Egypt's rule over the Gaza Strip, either fully or partially."[12]

Interpreting Mubarak's tolerance, indicated by his reaction to the 2008 border breach, as a green light for the underground tunnel operations, Hamid and his fellow tunnel owners jumped at the opportunity to revive their businesses once destroyed by the IDF. By this time, their service was in high demand and no longer just a clandestine business.

"We started digging again, this time [after the disengagement] there was no IDF and no houses to hide inside, it was all in the areas cleared by Israel's bulldozers," said Hamid. "Some engineers and architects became specialists in managing the tunnel digging operations and workers became specialized diggers."

Hamid says that compasses were used to direct the digging, while long, thin pipes were pierced through the tunnel ceilings, reaching up above ground to locate where the diggers had arrived, with constant monitoring by both the Gazan owners and the Sinai partners. Most tunnels arrived exactly where they were meant to: inside the Sinai partner's farm or back yard, or hitting their house's concrete base. No tunnel has ever missed and emerged within the thin strip of the buffer zone. Some digging operations took up to four months depending on how much was invested; some operations ran around the clock and took as little as ten weeks and, depending on the tunnel's length and dimensions, the capital invested varied from US$80,000 to US$300,000.

"As we dug, Hamas started approaching everyone involved in this new line of work," said Hamid. "They coordinated with everyone, even the families known for being Fatah loyalists, and at the time there was no option but to accept that Hamas was in control."

Sinai Sees Light at the End of its Tunnels
In late 2006, while Hamas was winning the legislative elections and flexing its political and militant muscles across the Gaza Strip, Hussein was jumping between jobs in North Sinai's al-Arish. The then 22-year-old had graduated with a technical diploma that proved useless in a region where there were no industrial facilities or much of an agricultural sector, and where the dozen or so vacancies at government institutions opening annually required several security and tribal connections to get appointed— connections he did not have. His dream back then was to garner enough capital to build a tiny apartment on the rooftop of his family's house.

From working at restaurants and grocery shops to occasional shifts on cargo trucks running weekly between different markets in North Sinai, Hussein made barely enough money to buy his cigarettes and support his family; once every few months he would be able to buy a new pair of shoes or a sweater. In November 2006, a relative of his convinced him to apply for one of the state-sponsored "fresh graduates projects."

"It was humiliating, the projects were basically an indirect government loan that came in the form of a project that most probably would never succeed or make any profit," said Hussein, who realized that his chances of getting onto, let alone succeeding in, any such project were close to nothing. There was a bread-selling project that was basically a cargo motor tricycle and license to buy subsidized bread and resell it in residential areas far from the state-owned bakeries, but there were no open slots. Farming projects required ownership of agricultural land, which he didn't have. Even if he did, he would end up indebted to the state for almost three years and the state took no responsibility for the failure of the project, which if it did fail, would mean a straight road to jail or selling your possessions.[13]

The only open project was for females: 'the productive goat project' that was carried out in every rural area in Egypt and was simply a few goats given to women who were supposed to raise, breed, and sell them. The debt was significantly less and entailed lower risk. Hussein decided to apply under the name of one of his female relatives and through acquaintances at the Social Solidarity Ministry's al-Arish office. Two months later, the rooftop waiting to be his future home was turned into a barn for the little goats.

"I wasn't the only one this desperate, I know men like me who picked parsley and arugula in little farms in Rafah and Sheikh Zuwayyed, and others who served tea and coffee at highway tea shops," said Hussein, who believes he was lucky and probably envied for getting onto such a project.

Before his first goat was sold, in January 2008, Hussein was running between al-Arish and Sheikh Zuwayyed, buying and selling whatever he could for Gazans who crossed into North Sinai during the five-day border breach. During the first few hours, he had struck a deal with his cousin who owns a shop in Sheikh Zuwayyed that he would take responsibility for resupplying the shop every few hours. The sales were unprecedented and he restocked the shop at least ten times in the first three days.

Hussein remembered:

It was a week of continuous work and everyone made a lot of profit, the driver who I hired, the wholesale shops I was buying from for prices better than retail, and finally me and my cousin in Sheikh

Zuwayyed. The border breach was the first time in our lives to make actual profits in North Sinai, it was Allah's mercy raining on everyone, especially the poor who needed it the most.

Mohamed al-Filistini, who also made profit selling consumer goods during the border breach incident, added:

> It was also a political gift for the Egyptian regime, for the year after the border breach, the majority of North Sinai didn't complain about jobs or lack of opportunities. It was the beginning of the real smuggling operations that gradually increased to tens then hundreds of millions of dollars and reached everyone in Sinai.[14]

The massive black economy—feeding everyone from farmers to retailers, wholesalers, drivers, and storage house owners—exploded in the ever impoverished North Sinai and was a new development that lifted a major burden off Mubarak's shoulders. This marginalized border province that complained of discrimination and a lack of government care and attention became a destination for unemployed people coming from as far as Upper Egypt, while the Gaza Strip that protested Egypt's blockade and its support of Israel's oppressive policies, found a middle solution that relieved its ailing 1.7 million people and resurrected its dead economy.

In the months after the breach, hundreds of tunnel openings started surfacing in Rafah. The young men who once picked parsley and arugula in little farms became tunnel owners. The area where the soil was most suitable for digging tunnels extended for eight of the fourteen-kilometer border with the Gaza Strip,[15] exactly between Tal Zaareb, west of the Rafah Crossing Terminal, and all the way to the Jaradat district, east of the terminal. The underground network grew so crowded within a few months that tunnels ran above each other in layers at eight, ten, eighteen, and thirty meters deep, while some Gazan tunnel owners partnered with up to three Sinai recipients and branched their tunnels to reach three different locations on Egypt's side of the border.[16]

Meanwhile, Hussein and his shop-owner cousin fought to secure their positions within the rocketing black economy. The qualifications and connections required for the new openings were much easier to come by than those of the state-sponsored projects at the Social Solidarity

Ministry. Through family connections, Hussein was hired by one Palestinian tunnel owner to become responsible for the purchases of whatever list of merchandise he required and delivering it to the Sinai partner in Rafah. In mid-2008, he practically moved to Cairo where the vast majority of the purchasing was done.

"It was an opportunity that I trained for over the few days of the breach when managing purchases in partnership with my cousin, and the tunnel owner on this side of the border knew a few of my family members who all vouched for me. I started working sometime in March 2008," said Hussein.

Hussein's job was to receive the money wired via Western Union by the Gazan tunnel owner, sometimes on a daily basis, and the list of required items from the Sinai partner supplied along with the specifications for packaging to make sure they crossed the tunnel with minimal damage. He would then do several hours of shopping in Cairo and oversee the loading of his merchandise at Attaba's market that never sleeps, where cargo trucks depart around the clock to different cities across Egypt and neighboring countries. Realizing how tiring it was to cruise between Cairo and North Sinai two or three times a week, he decided to rent a room in Cairo. For almost a year, he traveled to al-Arish once every two weeks or whenever there was an emergency or a family occasion.

> I bought and shipped every consumer good you can imagine to an address in al-Arish where the tunnel owners rented a storage room; the merchandise would remain there for a few hours before being loaded again and sent to Rafah to cross the tunnel. I sometimes sent more than a dozen three-ton trucks per week and slept an average of five hours per day.

For the first few weeks, every packaged food item was on Hussein's list, along with clothing, household appliances, electronics, cell phones, furniture, spare parts for cars, and, his least favorite, special requests for industrial spare parts and agricultural equipment which required trips to specialist shops. In mid-2008, he stopped handling food supplies as several tunnel owners established wholesale shops in al-Arish where they would receive direct and cheaper deliveries from manufacturers across Egypt. Hussein went on:

Attaba, in the center of Cairo, felt like I was standing in Gaza. I was surrounded by several people I knew from North Sinai who did the same exact job for different tunnel owners. We were receiving phone calls from Gaza almost every hour. North Sinai, that was never on the list of destinations serviced by shipping companies, became the most lucrative, so much so that some companies renewed their whole fleet of trucks during 2008.

Hussein, who sometimes handled close to LE half a million per week (US$70,000), was making profits on every transaction. Exchanging foreign currency wired by the Gazan tunnel owner was his first source of income, followed by the relentless bargaining on prices of wholesale goods. His life continued thus for the first several months as he funneled every pound he gained into repaying the loathed debt of the 'productive goat project,' and building the apartment he always dreamt of.

Despite residing far from his family and relying on an illegal business as the only source of income to live off and enhance the living conditions of his parents and siblings, Hussein believed this was his once-in-a-lifetime opportunity to garner as much capital as he could. He was simply one of tens of thousands of men who sought and made a living working in the smuggling industry. By the time he had finished building his apartment in 2009, the Sinai tunnel owner for whom he worked had already bought a farm in the center of which he built a three-story villa with a brand new Land Cruiser parked outside.

A Hamas Umbrella

Within weeks of Israel and Egypt imposing a full blockade on the Gaza Strip, in the aftermath of the Hamas takeover in June 2007, the Islamist movement was in full control of the border with Sinai, both above and below ground. When Hamas successfully executed the border breach and was welcomed for days to "eat," as Hosni Mubarak put it, it embarked on planning the future of the rapidly growing tunnel economy, and entrenching its control over it.

Islamist preachers across the Gaza Strip described the tunnel operations as an act of resistance and paid tribute to those killed in tunnel accidents as martyrs dying to liberate the besieged population. Fighters of the Qassam Brigades and Hamas's police personnel manned the border as it bustled with hundreds of diggers. Hamid's tunnel at this point was already running; his project that was once surrounded by secrecy and considered a threat to his life became one of hundreds of encouraged and applauded businesses. Mahmoud al-Zahar, the co-founder of Hamas who was elected foreign minister of Ismail Haniyeh's first cabinet formed in June 2006, defended the tunnels, saying "we had to build the tunnels since no electricity, water or food is coming from outside."[17]

The Gazan population, especially the tunnel owners, reacted instantly to Hamas's green light and throughout 2008 they imported almost everything that had been banned by Israel. In a few months, half of Gaza's paralyzed industrial facilities were back in operation; the tunnels themselves were said to have given jobs directly to some 13,000 people. It was the first time for the blockaded strip's GDP to increase after years of sinking since the blockade began in 2005.[18]

"We were able to apply everything that we had dreamt of when working undercover," said Hamid. "I installed an intercom system in my tunnel to ease the communication with workers and bought a couple of winches that pulled the merchandise through the tunnel."

Hamid remembered when the workers came up with the idea of filling barrels with goods and rolling them through the tunnels for easier transportation. This risked breaking the goods, so they decided to pull the barrels through one by one using the winches, but, realizing this was too slow, someone finally came up with the idea of slicing the barrels in half to turn them into a boat-like shapes. While being constantly enhanced, the durable plastic boats were tied to each other using metal wires to form an unsophisticated ten-half-barrel cargo train that was attached to the winch and pulled through the tunnel. At the time, the brilliant invention became known as the *shahata*, and it spread fast among the tunnel operators.

Hamid, who had always been too overweight to crawl into the old tunnels, explained this development:

Back in the 1990s, it was a nightmare if the rope used to pull the sacks broke, it meant a slim person would have to crawl inside the tunnel and clear it. "Despite their efficiency, the [pre-*shahata*] workers were too slow for the demand from Gaza that was hungry and impatient. One worker would be able to carry a fifty-kilogram sack if they were strong and healthy, which was rare. But the *shahata* was really an excellent invention; it made us capable of shipping up to

500 or 1,000 kilograms in one go, depending on the packaging, the strength of the winch, and the width and height of the tunnel.

The *shahata*, which was deemed a revolutionizing development in the tunnels industry, went through one more phase of enhancement. Smugglers focused mainly on heavy construction materials, and who also shipped scrap metal and recyclable materials out of the Gaza Strip, weren't satisfied with the dimensions of the plastic half-barrels forming the *shahata*, so they replaced them with a flat, thick, yet elastic sheet of rubber that served as a slider on top of which the bulky shipments were loaded.

Throughout 2008, the tunnels were said to have generated hundreds of millions of dollars in profits that trickled all the way down through the community. The prices of shipping reached as high as US$1,200 per ton depending on the kind or size of the shipment and how much care it required. Smaller shipments were charged at US$30–50 per fifty-kilogram sacks. The proceeds of the tunnels were divided equally between the Gaza and Sinai owners of the tunnel regardless of how many partners were on each side of the border. Workers at the time, who sometimes worked two shifts per day, were receiving a set rate of US$50 per shift, but handling smaller shipments of weapons or narcotics earned up to US$300–500 per job, which would take them a few hours of work.

Workers on the Egyptian side of the border were paid less due to the number of people arriving in Rafah hoping to find a job in this thriving industry. The high competition brought down the shift rates from US$50, as in Gaza, to LE 200 per shift, which was still significantly higher than the salary of the majority of young Egyptians—be they doctors, engineers, or web developers working anywhere across the country.

The tunnel industry went on uninterrupted and unregulated for months, until mid-2008 when Hamas forces started questioning some tunnel owners over the smuggling of weapons and drugs. Hamid said that he and a few others who had operated tunnels since the start, in the 1990s, had expected Hamas to inevitably make this move.

> They kept a friendly relationship in the beginning, but it wasn't because they really loved the tunnel owners or considered them fighters as they claimed, it was just a way for them to extend their authority. When the people became comfortable [with the idea] that the tunnels were Gaza's only window on the world, Hamas moved in to control it.

In November 2008, Hamas declared that it had established the Tunnels Affairs Commission, a department of the Ministry of Interior responsible for regulating, monitoring and imposing taxes and customs on the tunnels industry. The newly introduced Tunnel License was bought directly from the commission and cost US$2,600; Gaza's Electricity Company charged up to US$800 to supply the tunnel with an electricity cable;[19] and the commission ordered the tunnel owners to compensate the families of victims of work accidents with an estimated US$30,000 for each victim.[20]

The commission announced different taxes to be imposed on every item imported through the tunnels, the highest of which were for tobacco and liquid fuel. The punishments for tax evasion and facilitating the crossing of personnel were as high as a fine of US$5,000 and a temporary shutdown of the tunnel, while harsher punishments were applied for smuggling drugs, weapons, and ammunition. Hamas's security also moved to destroy the older unused tunnels that could be used by criminals and freeze the operations of those who didn't acquire the licenses of establishment and electricity.[21]

The newly imposed system was met with little opposition. With up to 9,000 different types of goods banned by Israel being imported by means of the tunnels, a market worth an estimated US$650 million annually had been created and Rafah's unemployment had decreased from 50 to 20 percent.[22] The tunnel owners were convinced that avoiding a confrontation with the ruling Hamas was the wiser option. Minimal skirmishes took place between Hamas forces and a few families who opposed the new system.

By December 2008 and the beginning of the Gaza war, or Operation Cast Lead, the number of tunnels had risen to seven hundred, an estimated two hundred of which were still under construction.[23] This meant a huge increase from the estimated twenty tunnels in operation before Hamas's takeover and the imposition of the full blockade in June 2007. Israel's plan to stifle the Gaza Strip and bring an end Hamas's rule had totally backfired; Gaza's underground explosion into the Sinai Peninsula didn't only relieve the ailing population, but started bankrolling the Islamist movement that was garnering massive profits through its economic control over the smuggling industry.

Mubarak's Wild Card

The Hamas movement in Gaza wasn't the only party that became directly involved in the tunnel industry. On the other side of the border,

Hosni Mubarak's dictatorial regime saw its own political and security interests in the new phenomenon. Hundreds of millions of dollars generated by the new underground market had revived the Sinai Peninsula and in so doing diverted the attention of the Bedouin tribes and their infuriated youth away from the careless regime.

Throughout the year and a half between Hamas's takeover of Gaza in June 2007 and the beginning of Operation Cast Lead in December 2008, the only form of opposition the rugged peninsula saw was two sit-ins held near the Israeli border to demand the release of various people detained without trial on various charges of arms and drug smuggling or ties to the South Sinai bombings in 2004, 2005, and 2006. Back then, very few political activists were jailed, the most prominent of whom was a descendant of al-Remeilat tribe, Masaad Abu Fajr.

The drastic rise in the number of smuggling tunnels and rocketing profits reaped by residents of Sinai created a multi-pronged opportunity for the Egyptian regime. It relieved it of a major portion of its responsibility toward the impoverished population of North Sinai, who gradually came to rely on their new lucrative business. Within a few months, Rafah, Sheikh Zuwayyed, and al-Arish's estimated 200,000 people had not only stopped complaining about the lack of development and state-sponsored solutions, but built their own villas, dug their own wells, and installed heavy-duty pumps and electricity generators that lit their farms. This took them from dependency on an impotent Ministry of Agriculture to relying instead on a constant flow of know-how and technologies imported through the tunnels from the Gaza Strip, that in turn imported from Israel's internationally reputable agricultural sector.

North Sinai's population was the direct beneficiary of the tunnel industry, having been one of the biggest losers when it came to the state system. In just a few months, one of the poorest and least populous Egyptian governorates, with a population of some 400,000, became the gateway to a purely consumerist, US-dollar-paying market almost four times its size.

"The money flowing from Gaza through North Sinai echoed through every Egyptian government and non-government sector," a Mubarak loyalist and multi-millionaire businessman said on condition of anonymity. "The whole government sensed it starting, and the money cycle included everyone from the central bank all the way down to the poor retailers in North Sinai."[24]

The businessman, who hadn't dealt directly with smugglers or their purchase managers in Cairo, but knows that his products were shipped to Gaza, believes that the tunnel economy was considered illegal while every transaction in it was done legally except for the underground shipping. The money arrived from Gaza through wire transfers handled by official businesses and monitored by Egypt's Central Bank. If the money was smuggled, which rarely happened, it was at some point exchanged at officially registered exchange offices and deposited in legitimate bank accounts, while the hundreds of millions of Egyptian pounds circulating in the local market fueled the national economy as much as any other money coming from a legal source.

When grocery stores in the alleys of Rafah started selling products as good as Cairo's upscale neighborhoods, and when the finest and most expensive four-wheel drives were sold in North Sinai more than any other governorate in Egypt, it wasn't done behind the government's back, it was all public and known to the regime, if not capitalized on.

On the ground in North Sinai, the tunnel owners and everyone they employed didn't disagree with the understanding of the Mubarak loyalist businessman. Egypt's legal system did more to encourage than deter this type of illegal business. The punishment for illegally crossing the border was two years in prison, while the punishments for smuggling legal substances were paying the full taxes or customs in addition to a fine that never exceeded LE 2,000. In any case, the evidence required for the punishments to be applied was far out of the authorities' reach, especially in North Sinai, a region known for its debilitated and highly corrupt security. But nothing encouraged the smugglers more than the fact that Sinai was entirely policed by the SSI and its easily manipulated and highly corrupt emergency law, which was used purely to oppress the community rather than secure it and check for illegal activity.

"When Hosni Mubarak showed no signs of closing the tunnels, everyone took advantage of it," said Emad, a 30-year-old clerical worker at Karm Abu Salem Border Terminal by day and smuggler by night. "The state security officers imposed their own rules. They took massive bribes and employed the tunnel owners and workers as informants; as soon as it became widely known that the officers were running the business, the lower ranks did the same, even the traffic police took bribes from the cargo trucks loaded with goods on their way to Rafah."[25]

Emad described the locations of several tunnels that were under the protection of specific SSI officers; he says those officers were considered partners in the tunnels and their bribes were cut from the profits of the tunnel owners on both sides of the border. Abu Arrab al-Sawarka, Abu Suleiman al-Tarabin, and Mohamed al-Filistini referred to more tunnels and named the same officers, plus others. Such stories were common across the peninsula; tunnel owners who boasted their police connections were capable of solving any problem at any given government department, from a delayed driver's license at the traffic department to releasing a detained relative held at any police station in Sinai and beyond. Not surprisingly, several of the SSI officers accused of giving protection to smuggling operations have also been accused over the past decade of overseeing and sometimes committing the horrifying torture to which hundreds of Sinai's residents have been subjected.

In September 2008, Abu Arrab was released after more than three years of imprisonment. Using his friendships and tribal ties to those who had already been smuggling Iranian weapons into the Gaza Strip, it didn't take him long to become one of the most powerful smugglers in North Sinai. Before the war kicked off in December, this Bedouin, who spent his time in prison without trial, had secured a position for himself smuggling two of the most lucrative items: weapons and construction materials.

"The smuggling business was open to everyone as long as they balanced their relationships with the State Security [SSI] officers," said Abu Arrab. "When I was taken to jail, I took an oath that I would come back to business and would never be arrested again, even if it meant being killed at my house."

When asked about such claims, Colonel Khaled Okasha once again said that no security outfit in the world operates without such

> under the table interactions and understandings. Sinai will always remain like this. Its complicated tribal nature and culture imposed this unique security system built on accurately calculated compromises and relations. The political leadership assesses the end result according to what it's seeking to accomplish. And as not a single bullet was shot in North Sinai over five years [between the Dahab 2006 bombing and the 2011 uprising] then the security operation was successful.[26]

That being said, Colonel Okasha stressed that the security apparatus "never creates the strategy but rather applies it after the political leadership decides what it will be and what goals it will serve, a matter that the population rarely realizes."

In addition to the relative social and economic stability that spread across Sinai due to the growing tunnel economy and the success of the SSI in cracking down on radical Islamists with the help of the newly established network of informants, Hosni Mubarak was capable of silencing Hamas's politically motivated claims that his regime had become Israel's partner in blockading the 1.7 million people of Gaza and relieved himself of condemnation for shutting down the Rafah Crossing Terminal.

More importantly for Mubarak, the tunnels' automatic relief of Gaza's economic and humanitarian crises reflected majorly on Egypt's political opposition powers, especially the Muslim Brotherhood movement, that voiced their support of the Gazan population and used its suffering as claws in their fight against the Egyptian regime.

Operation Cast Lead

In June 2008, Egypt brokered a six-month ceasefire between Hamas and Israel; both sides agreed to renew the ceasefire on condition that Israel lifted its stifling blockade while Hamas would continue to stop Gazan rockets fired toward Israeli territories either by its military wing, the Qassam Brigades, or by other factions including Palestinian Islamic Jihad and the Popular Resistance Committees. On December 27, 2008, a few days before the end of the first phase of the ceasefire, Operation Cast Lead, or the War of Furqan, began.

The Israeli Airforce (IAF) jets did the most damage and viciously bombarded the Gaza Strip. On the first day alone, two hundred Gazans were killed and more than seven hundred were injured, the worst record of casualties since 1948. Before the war came to an end on January 18, 2009, some 1,400 Palestinians were killed and more than 4,000 were injured, the vast majority of whom were civilians.

During the first few days of the war, Israel's airforce also bombarded the border with Sinai in an attempt to destroy the smuggling tunnels. The magnitude of the attacks on both sides of the Rafah Crossing Terminal forced Egypt's border security and terminal workers to flee the terminal as its glass shattered along with that of the houses in North Sinai's villages situated near the border. Egyptian ambulance vehicles stationed inside the crossing terminal were forced to evacuate before being able to rescue any Palestinian victims, while ambulances inside Gaza were unable to mobilize due to the heavy and continuous attacks that at many times targeted hospitals and clinics.

"We watched it live from here, any high hill in Rafah gave us a heart-breaking view of the war. Gaza was bombarded in a way we had never witnessed before," said Abu Arrab, who had just started his smuggling business weeks before the Israeli offensive. "It was very shocking. I expected the people to break into Egypt again, escaping death not shopping."

Throughout the war, some 6,000 buildings were destroyed—the majority of which were civilian homes, as well as several health clinics and hospitals—more than 1,500 factories and workshops, power plants, sewage systems, hectares of farms, dozens of greenhouses, and roads. Even the United Nations facilities were bombarded with internationally prohibited weapons, mainly white phosphorus. An investigative report published by Amnesty International in July 2009, *Operation "Cast Lead": 22 days of death and destruction*, described the brutal attack on the UNRWA headquarters in Gaza city after hundreds of civilians fled their homes to take shelter inside the compound hoping that the UN flags and banners were going to save them from the ongoing slaughter.[27]

In the morning of 15 January 2009 several white phosphorus and high-explosive artillery shells struck the UNRWA headquarters in the centre of Gaza City, causing fires which destroyed dozens of tons of desperately needed humanitarian aid and medicines, as well as the workshops and warehouses. Several vehicles were also damaged. A UN worker and two civilians who had taken refuge in the compound were injured. Some 700 civilian residents in nearby buildings had fled their homes and taken refuge in the UNRWA compound earlier that morning, when Israeli forces had intensified the shelling of the area. A worse disaster was only avoided thanks to the courage of UNRWA staff, who drove the vehicles out of the compound under fire and thus managed to prevent the vehicles full of fuel from catching fire and exploding.

As soon as the war came to an end, when Hamas and Israel agreed to an Egyptian-brokered and internationally endorsed humanitarian truce, the tunnels were resurrected. The several tunnels that had

remained unharmed throughout the heavy bombardment started operating immediately, while the majority, an estimated five hundred tunnels
which had been destroyed or damaged, were renovated and back in
operation within record time. The post-war tunnels weren't encouraged
only by high consumer demand, but now also by a devastated population
and a ruling body that needed to rescue itself from a possible domestic
revolt. Dozens of the tunnels were reconstructed and even though they
were not fully financed by Hamas, the movement did provide assistance,
through equipment and free licenses.

Several international organizations estimated the Gaza losses at
US$2 billion, and, according to UN Habitat, it would have taken Gaza
an estimated eighty years to rebuild what had been destroyed during the
2008 war if only relying on Israel's list of goods allowed to enter Gaza
through the terminals.[28] But with a fully fledged smuggling network on
both sides of the border with Sinai, the reconstruction of Gaza began
immediately despite the devastation and the ongoing blockade.

"After the war, we built the real tunnels," said Hamid. The 'real tunnels' became as long as 1,500 meters and sometimes 2 meters wide. The
owners invested more money and started reinforcing the tunnels with
wooden and metal beams to avoid any sudden collapses of the softer
underground layers. Many of the tunnels replaced the once-celebrated
shahata with rail tracks over which metal carts ran in a very similar manner to professional underground mining works. By mid-2009, the new
tunnels had increased their shipping capacity by more than four times
and the most in-demand items on the list were construction materials.[29]

Everyone's business multiplied in proportion to the growth of
demand and the devastation in Gaza. In Cairo, Hussein was booking
double the amount of cargo trucks to what he would normally have
booked in 2008, and the list of merchandise he handled grew to include
a variety of agricultural products and equipment, water pumps, and
heavier industrial spare parts. Abu Arrab's farm, a few kilometers outside of Rafah, turned into a mechanics' workshop where cars and heavy
trucks were taken apart to be shipped into Gaza and reassembled there.
His relationship with Hamas's top officials grew closer in the aftermath
of the war so that he was allowed to cross the tunnels into the Gaza Strip
without any coordination with the Hamas authorities; he became one of
the main handlers of Hamas shipments that included weapons, military
equipment, and massive sums of cash.

In August 2009, after months of purchasing goods in Cairo's whole-sale markets, Hussein received a call from an SSI officer informing him that he was requested to attend a routine questioning at the al-Arish department. "I was afraid and didn't know what to do. I never heard a single good story about the state security in my life, and the routine questioning he told me about seemed suspicious."

Hussein's immediate reaction was to call the two tunnel owners he worked with on both sides of the border, who said "they both know the name of the officer who I was supposed to meet; it was Brigadier N., and they both told me not to worry and go meet him."

Fearing that the SSI could start a hunt for him if he didn't show up for the 'routine questioning,' and concerned over the safety of his family members in al-Arish, Hussein took the advice of his employers. And, as he walked into the SSI office and introduced himself, he realized that it was a set up and that his employers had turned him in as a 'service' to the officers. In return, the tunnel continued to operate.

"There were no introductions; as soon as the reception officer took my ID they started beating me up, I was then blindfolded and locked up for a few hours before they started torturing me," said Hussein as he lifted his shirt up to reveal the scars covering his back and waist, which he said were caused by whipping and electrocution to his naked body. Hussein was tortured everyday for a week before being transferred to al-Gharbaniyat prison without trial; his emergency law detention warrant, signed by Brigadier N., charged him with smuggling.

> I remained in prison for over ten months during which time my family hired a lawyer and appealed my detention. My release was ordered by the prosecution nine times and every time my detention warrant would be renewed by the SSI claiming that I was 'continu-ing my illegal activity from detention.' My family would return and appeal the detention again and restart the whole cycle. I was finally released in July 2010, I never returned to smuggling and I had noth-ing but a few thousand pounds I had saved before my detention.

From Five Hundred to One Thousand Two Hundred

One of Israel's conditions before the ceasefire was brokered in Janu-ary 2009 was for Egypt to start efficiently countering the cross-border smuggling operations that supplied Hamas with weapons and the materials needed to manufacture rockets domestically. Egyptian agreement to this condition translated into a US-sponsored project to build an underground steel barrier that would somehow hinder Gaza's ability to dig tunnels, and, in February 2009, Egypt agreed to start working on the twenty-five-meter-deep barrier under the supervision of US military experts.

Within weeks, Egyptian and American military convoys were carrying outfield trips to the border with Gaza, while the Ministry of the Interior deployed several hundred more central security personnel to reinforce the border patrols and began building more watchtowers and security posts that looked directly into the Gaza Strip.

However, the first thing new soldiers saw would have been Gazans digging tunnels on the other side of the border as Hamas continued as if nothing was happening a few hundred meters away on Egyptian soil. The Tunnels Affairs Commission announced its new Security Coordination Office that was responsible for granting permits to people crossing the tunnels into Sinai and back. Hamas's police and members of the Qassam Brigades were back to manning the border and taxing thousands of tons of merchandise being shipped through the tunnels on a daily basis.

Whatever America promised Israel, and whatever Mubarak's regime promised the American security officials, didn't apply on the ground either in Sinai or in Gaza. Some smugglers in Gaza and Egypt allege that Egyptian SSI officers had confirmed to them that nothing would change and their business would continue as long as they kept the flow of bribes going.

"Egypt was never going to apply whatever the Israelis and the Americans wanted," said Abu Arrab. "The war was very bad and the people were so miserable there was no option for Egypt but to let the tunnels operate to avoid any problems from Gaza, but Mubarak had to lie to the Americans." He explained that the only way for Egypt to stop the tunnels back then was to open the Rafah Crossing Terminal for cargo and passengers, as this would remove the demand for smuggling. With the terminal not open and the blockade in place, every smuggler knew that nothing would change.

Egyptian security forces started raiding a few tunnels and blocking them with solid waste, rocks, and sand, while every week they would seize some of the cargo trucks heading to Rafah. But as soon as a raid was over, the tunnel owners would re-dig the blocked entrance and put the tunnel back into operation. According to Abu Arrab, "this was a part of the show. They had to arrest people and confiscate shipments to make cases that would be paraded as the government's work." Most of the people the SSI detained "were young people who didn't own tunnels, they were either drivers or poor people trying to make a living. I challenge anyone in Egypt, I challenge Habib El-Adly, to tell me about one tunnel owner that was arrested; there are people who own five major tunnels, live in al-Arish, and were never even visited by the police," says Abu Arrab, who could have been describing Hussein's case—it was very similar.

In Gaza, tunnel diggers went deeper—to more than forty meters underground—and a story was circulated of a 15-year-old who cut a hole through the steel barrier using a blowtorch. "They spent millions of dollars to build a barrier and a boy used a torch smuggled through the tunnels to destroy it and run more tunnels," boasted a member of Gaza's al-Shaer clan, prominent for its control over dozens of tunnels along the border.

By the end of 2010, construction works were fueled by tons of Egyptian cement and steel piled on every street in the Gaza Strip, the wholesale storages were full, and retailers were facing no shortages whatsoever, while Hamas was relieved of dealing with the terrible unemployment rates. Before the Egyptian uprising broke out in January 2011, and despite Israel's frequent bombardment of the border areas and the US-sponsored steel barrier, the number of operating tunnels had reached more than 1,200.

What Egypt and Gaza were never able to control fully was the movement of people across the tunnels, once considered a crime by Hamas and carrying a fine of up to US$1,000 per person if not the total shutdown of the tunnel operation. In 2009, it became legal if whoever wanted to cross carried a permit from the Tunnels Affairs Commission, and the fees for permits gradually dropped to US$100 per person. The demand was constantly rising as the Rafah Crossing Terminal continued to prevent movement out of Gaza, even of students enrolled in Egyptian universities or trying to catch their flights from Egypt's airports for study elsewhere.

But along with travelers and students, jihadists and *takfiris*[30] from various factions operating in the southern part of the Gaza Strip found an escape route as Hamas mounted its crackdown on them for their vigorous opposition to the ruling movement. With little security in the scattered villages of North Sinai, the Hamas detractors, along with their radical ideology, found an alternative home.

As General Fouad Allam, the former head of the SSI, put it:

> We never encountered any radical Islamists in Sinai until the tunnels appeared. It has been a route from both sides since it began; the Taba bombing in 2004 was a clear enough sign that an unprecedented threat was appearing in Sinai. There were always criminals, just like any part of Egypt. But there were never radical Islamists in the history of Sinai, they arrived from the tunnels and once they were in, there was little hope of finding them.[31]

5

SHARIA AND TRIBAL COURTS: THE LAW AND ORDER OF THE SINAI PENINSULA

In mid-2010, Asaad al-Beik of al-Arish, a Salafi cleric and founder of North Sinai's Salafi current known as Ahl al-Sunna wa-l-Jamaa, received a warning from the State Security Investigations department ordering him to shutdown his guesthouse, which he had opened around the clock to receive disputing citizens who sought settlements according to Islamic sharia. There were dozens of other guesthouses across the peninsula to which people turned for justice, but they were all customary courts that ruled according to the ancient customs and traditions of the tribal community.

Al-Beik, who remained on the SSI's watch lists for years as an active Salafi preacher, informed the authorities that he would never shutdown his guesthouse and invited them to "send two soldiers to turn people away." To the bearded cleric, it wouldn't only be a shameful act in the eyes of the tribal community, but rather a "blasphemous act of abandoning the sharia laws of Allah to uphold the legislation of mankind."[1]

Fearing a popular outcry, the authorities never closed al-Beik's court that was known back then as one of only two sharia courts in Sinai. The second was run by another Salafi cleric, Sheikh Nayef Abu Moaath al-Theib, some fifty kilometers away in the town of Yamit, closer to the Gaza border. Back then, neither the SSI nor the two clerics imagined that a few months later a popular uprising would break out, bring down Hosni Mubarak's regime, and take the sharia courts to the forefront of Sinai's law and order efforts.

A few days after the January 25 uprising kicked off, the security and government authorities were left in a state of total paralysis, as in every other part of Egypt, and so ordinary citizens took matters into their own hands and formed the 'popular committees' that took responsibility for securing residential areas and fighting acts of looting and vandalism. Al-Beik and al-Theib were two of several Salafi clerics who coordinated with tribal elders to run the vigilante patrols of the popular committees in the towns and villages of North Sinai. Knowing that there would be no SSI officers to hunt them down, dozens of Bedouin Salafi youth joined the vigilante patrols and reported to the clerics.

In the aftermath of Mubarak's resignation, the downfall of his security apparatus, and the takeover of the interim-ruling Supreme Council of the Armed Forces (SCAF), the Salafi clerics, tribal elders, and vigilantes appeared harmonious, united by the goal of imposing law and order across their conservative and heavily armed communities. But despite the common goal, the contrasting tribal and Salafi backgrounds continued to widen the cracks in the temporary harmony struck by the unanticipated uprising.

By March 2011, after the military took over the security responsibilities of Sinai along with the rest of Egypt, the harmony between tribal and Islamist vigilantes came to an end. Enjoying the unprecedented freedoms brought by the downfall of Mubarak's security apparatus, Salafi clerics preached against the unreligious, tyrannical laws of the state and tribal customary courts, and stressed the necessity and inevitability of applying Allah's sharia law. The scene wasn't different from that in Cairo's Tahrir Square, where different political powers, once united by the goal of toppling Hosni Mubarak, began warring from the day of his resignation.

The Rise of Sharia Courts

In March 2011, Sheikh Asaad al-Beik, who had once received threats over his guesthouse-turned-court, erected a sign on the façade of the same guesthouse that read "The House of Sharia Law in al-Arish." He was one of several Salafi clerics-turned-judges who declared the establishment of their Islamic courts in the service of the community.

Outside their courts, men stood in line, patiently waiting their turn to present their cases to the judges they once visited only at night for fear of being spotted by security informants. What was once a security threat to both the judges and people, became a wide-spread phenomenon. In the two months following the January 2011 uprising, six sharia courts were declared in North Sinai's al-Arish, Sheikh Zuwayyed, and Rafah, and they barely contained the rising demand from every town across Sinai.

Beik explained that:

We have been oppressed for years by the tyrannical and blasphemous regime of Hosni Mubarak that jailed us and stood in our way of apply-ing Allah's justice. While their courts used imported laws, the trash of mankind, to strip people of their rights. We now bear the responsibil-ity of bringing people close to their creator, Allah, and providing them with the tools to practice their religion in the right manner through Islamic sharia so as to manage their lives and resolve their disputes.

Al-Beik's house grew crowded from the rising number of visitors who flocked in daily, and this encouraged him to rent a spacious office apartment on one of al-Arish's major streets where he erected his sign above that of the National Bank of Egypt. At the new location in the heart of the city, al-Beik's visitors regularly outnumbered those of the bank operating one floor below him. Outside of the building, a military armored personnel carrier stood in defense of the bank that fell under armed attacks several times after the January 2011 uprising. Al-Beik's massive desk was covered with thick files of cases being reviewed, while the filing cabinets lining the walls of his room and that of his assistant contained hundreds of cases that were already resolved.

Silently working underground for years and constantly dodging the authorities, the clerics had dreamt of going public for over a decade since Asaad al-Beik and Nayef al-Theib accepted their first cases in the early 2000s. By the time their dream was fulfilled in 2011, they had already created a system for the judicial procedures of the sharia courts. The first step taken by the plaintiffs within the newly established Islamic system was signing a consent document, pledging to accept the judge's ruling based on the Muslim holy book, the Quran, and the teachings, or Hadith and Sunna, of Prophet Muhammad, after which each of the disputing parties would introduce their guarantors, who would also sign another document pledging to accept the ruling and taking responsibil-ity for its fulfillment by the parties they were endorsing.

The judge's assistant was responsible for documenting every part of the judicial procedure, from dating the initiation forms of consent, to accurately writing down the testimonies of witnesses, to gathering and documenting the required information in cases of disputes over possessions or cases of trespassing and violations in which external experts are hired to assess values of assets and the cost of damages. In most cases, the judge's religious associates (who would be other judges or clerics) and those of the disputing parties were allowed to witness the procedures, through which each document was signed by everyone: the judge, his assistant, the plaintiffs, and attending confidantes. Copies of the case files were handed to the parties involved and one was kept in the court archive.

Behind the judges, shelves were stacked with hard-cover books of Islamic jurisprudence, exegesis of the Quran and Sunna, and various well-known encyclopedias of Islamic law from which the judges derive the bases for every step taken throughout the process.

According to al-Beik:

Everyone is allowed to ask us or other sheikhs for the basis of the judgment rendered in their cases. They are also allowed to appeal the verdicts and decisions in cases of the emergence of further evidence that was not presented in the initial trial, and they are allowed to choose the judge in the initial trial and the retrial if their appeal is accepted.

After the disputing parties file their claims to the court, an investigation is opened and carried out by the judge, his assistants, and several pious associates selected by the judge, normally Salafi youth who took part in the popular committees and are well-known within the community. As for the witnesses, al-Beik says:

The minimum requirement for accepting a testimony is that they [the witness] regularly pray, which is easy to confirm in a tight knit community where everyone who goes to a mosque is known. This is the minimum of many requirements dictated by the Quran and Sunna, without it the witness would never be accepted by the court.

The sharia courts are not perfect, perfection is only for Allah, but it is better to acquit a violator than to punish an innocent person, which always happens in the state courts who take the testimony of hired criminals and execute innocent people without thorough investigations or knowing that a 1 percent suspicion should end the whole case.

As for the punishments, they consisted only of financial compensation and fines decided according to the amount of damage caused and the kind of violations committed. Punishments covered everything from verbal insults to premeditated murder. Despite the varying degrees of radicalism among the Islamist judges, they unanimously agreed that physical punishments dictated by the Quran and Sunna for various crimes could not be applied without an Islamic state and ruler.

As al-Beik said:

> Contrary to the state courts who generously execute people by hanging, despite their infamously flawed system and the corruption of the authorities, our Islam doesn't allow us to apply the physical punishments until the Islamic state is established. We will continue to hope that we witness this in our lifetime.

For the population of North Sinai, sharia courts were the salvation of a community torn apart by chaos and decades of unjust rule that came with an unchecked emergency law. But for the Salafi clerics who established the courts and became the judges, it was a matter of adhering to Islam or committing blasphemy. Since their establishment, every one of the prominent sharia judges stressed that resorting to the Islamic system became a duty incumbent on all Muslims, as long as they were able to reach them—in other words, Muslims across Egypt.

"It is a very straightforward matter, if you resort to Allah's laws and uphold them then you are Muslim, a *muwahid* [monotheist believing only in Allah], if you resort to any other laws then you are simply a *mushrik* [polytheist] who chooses a different god than Allah," said al-Beik.

To al-Beik and his fellow Islamist judges, the duty of resorting to sharia courts did not apply before the January 25 uprising because they were almost nonexistent and imposed a major threat to whoever ran them or sought them out. But after publicizing the courts and spreading them across the towns of Egypt's eastern frontier, it became a duty which many of the judges even described as a pillar of Islam. In other words, those who chose alternatives to this system were committing what Allah described as an unforgivable sin, unless they repented before death.

"*Judgment is only Allah's; He has commanded that you shall not serve aught but Him; this is the right religion but most people do not know*,"[2] al-Beik quoted the Holy Quran. "This is what Allah told us, this is the summary of lectures that would go on for hours that we could give as a basis to our sharia courts."

Replacing the Tribal Courts

The rise of sharia courts was nothing strange for Sinai's Bedouin community, or even for its residents who originated from different parts of mainland Egypt. For centuries, the tribal community had customary courts that resolved disputes, punished criminals, and oversaw the implementation of inter-tribal agreements.

With the arrival of the different tribes to the Sinai Peninsula centuries ago, the elders of the community were the tribal judges who were sought out by people for justice. The position was seen as sacred so that most judges did not retire, but stayed in their role until death and usually passed their knowledge to their wisest son who would inherit the position. Various tribes were known for specializations in analyzing and dealing with disputes and resolving them, while every tribe had a revered elder who kept an archive (sometimes of physical documents) of major cases and the details of various inter-tribal incidents, and would be sought for clarification and consultation in complicated matters.[3]

Since the days of Mohamed Ali, Egypt's Ottoman ruler, the tribal justice system was allowed by the state, which sometimes interacted with it and used its laws and regulations to control the community. In his book, *The History of Sinai*, written in 1907, Lebanese historian Naum Shoucair documented several cases where the peninsula's military rulers personally used the Bedouins' courts to resolve their issues or to interfere in and diffuse tribal conflicts.[4]

The majority of documented cases are of military commanders interfering and demanding ceasefires between clans or tribes on the edge of war. This is locally known as *ramy al-wajh*, an act that is always respected by the warring parties and disobeying it would land you in a customary trial for disrespecting the peacemaking of a prominent and powerful figure—a crime normally punished by high fines as a violation of the tribal code of ethics.

Following the coming of Hosni Mubarak to power in 1981 and the full withdrawal of Israeli troops from the occupied Sinai in 1982, the regime hired a few dozen Bedouin elders who became known as 'Government Sheikhs.' Unlike the prominent tribesmen who ran the customary courts for centuries and enjoyed the unanimous respect of every tribe across the peninsula, the sheikhs on government payrolls were appointed by the security authorities and, despite their unmatched authority during the three decades of Mubarak rule, their popularity and respect for them diminished.

"The customary courts were negatively influenced by changing dynamics of the community in general," said Yahya al-Ghoul, a prominent tribal judge who inherited his position from his father Sheikh Mohamed. "The courts became dependant on connections, money, and power rather than justice and sacred traditions."[5]

Unlike the free-of-charge sharia courts, the customary judges were entitled to financial compensation, decided according to the size of the case to be reviewed; witnesses were also compensated. This turned a lot of people away from the tribal courts, either because they simply couldn't satisfy the financial requirements or because they were in dispute with others who were significantly richer. And while al-Ghoul commented cautiously on the tainted reputation of the customary courts, other powerful tribesmen were more outspoken about the widespread corruption that led them to the doorsteps of sharia judges.

"There are tribal judges who either stopped working because they refused the state's control over the customary courts or fought to adhere to the respected traditions and tribal justice in the face corruption," said Ibrahim Abu Ashraf al-Menaei, a Sawarka tribe elder who resorted to one of the sharia courts in 2011. "Some of the customary judges made fortunes using their power in tribal courts, disregarding who was a victim and who was a criminal, but what really destroyed the tribal court system was the state's control over its verdicts."

Abu Ashraf and other tribesmen who spoke about the tribal judges hired by Mubarak's authorities as "mercenaries" testified that the security apparatus, which historically upheld the rulings of the tribal courts, began using them to oppress and intimidate anyone considered in opposition to the regime. "Some people were threatened into either accepting harsh and unjust verdicts from the customary courts or facing detention, just because they were in dispute with a police informant or a smuggler with powerful connections at the security departments," said Abu Ashraf.

In an interview with a local newspaper, Abdel-Hadi Eteik, a tribal judge from Sheikh Zuwayyed, admitted that the customary courts were infiltrated by Mubarak's regime over the ten years before the revolution . . . security officers were ordering customary judges to render verdicts in the favor of their collaborators while others turned their courts into businesses to make money. . . . People lost confidence and stopped resorting to the tribal courts and used violence to resolve their disputes.[6]

When the sharia courts were publicly declared in 2011, they were simply a cleaned-up version of the harshly criticized customary courts. Totally free of charge and financed by donations collected from the community and sometimes the plaintiffs themselves, the sharia courts' visitors were served nothing more than tea and coffee, unlike the lavish dinners that were held at the receptions of customary judges, and whether arriving at the court on foot or in a brand new sedan, everyone sat on the floor of the significantly smaller rooms or waited their turn at the door.

By mid-2012, ten sharia courts were operating daily along the coast of North Sinai, while tribal judges, especially those accused of corruption, continued to accuse the Salafi clerics of violating tribal heritage and of relying on the rising powers of the Muslim Brotherhood movement and the Salafi political parties that had seized 74 percent of the Egyptian parliament in the November 2011 elections.

Despite the ongoing criticism, the public's growing acceptance of the sharia courts significantly increased their popularity and at some point the Salafi judges were approached by security officials who demanded their intervention to help contain rising tensions between heavily armed families and clans. Less than two years after their establishment, the Islamist judges were being sought by Sinai's most powerful tribes, including the Sawarka, Tarabin, Fawakhriya, and Bereikat. The half million Bedouins of Sinai had preserved their judicial heritage for centuries and took pride in it, but the need for swift justice was more urgent to everyone than the debate over tribal judges tainted by years of corruption and Salafi clerics accused of spreading radical ideologies.

We're Not the State . . . Yet

Some thirty kilometers east of al-Arish, Hamdin Abu Faisal, a jihadist ideologue who studied Islamic law and jurisprudence while in prison over charges of active membership of radical Islamist groups, hastily rose to prominence as the head of the Sheikh Zuwayyed sharia court, established at his house a few hundred yards from the military checkpoint stationed at the massive town gate. The court was open from early morning to nightfall every day of the week for almost three years between 2011 and 2013, as disputing parties laid out their claims and presented their witnesses and evidence.

The sheikh, who publicly defended the repetitive bombings of the gas pipeline and described it as an act of jihad in defense of all Muslims, believed that sharia courts and the application of Allah's laws were a basic Islamic ritual, equal to prayer, fasting the holy month of Ramadan, and the pilgrimage to the sacred mosque in Mecca.

As Abu Faisal said,

> Our legitimacy is derived from our religion, we don't require a permit from anyone to pray, and we will not ask for a permit to apply Allah's sharia and manage our lives according to the Quran and Sunna. If sharia courts were something alien and rejected, then why are people demanding we establish courts in every town to meet the rising demand?[7]

By August 2013, the sharia courts had spread out to Ismailiya, western Alexandria, Marsa Matrouh, Sharqiya, and Helwan in southern Cairo. As a sign of their rising popularity, several cases processed at state courts were adjourned due to requests from plaintiffs who withdrew their cases and resorted to a ruling from the sharia courts instead. The justice department and the prosecution never officially accepted the sharia courts' decisions as legal documents, but it included them in the settlement procedures in cases which were dropped.[8]

Abu Faisal took pride in such cases and saw them as a tacit recognition by the state of the effectiveness of the sharia judges and courts. "We are hoping and working with the state so we become official registered entities and eventually the rulings we render will be considered legal documents within the framework of the state courts."

After the Muslim Brotherhood's Mohamed Morsi was elected president in June 2012, the clerics-turned-judges were outspoken about their hopes of an Islamic state that would apply sharia on a state level. Abu Faisal said that he enjoyed the relative freedom post-2011 that allowed him and others to operate publicly, but looked forward to the day when "the anti-Islamic laws of the state courts would be replaced with righteous laws of Allah."

Refuting claims that the sharia courts were establishing an alternative system to that of the state, the clerics stressed that no one was forced to resort to them instead of state courts, "but if you look at how empty the state courts in North Sinai have become, you will realize who the people chose."

Minus the execution of murderers, the amputating of the hands of thieves, and the Taliban's Pakol hats, Sinai's sharia courts looked very similar to the ones established in Kandahar before they spread throughout Afghanistan. David Ignatius of the *Washington Post* observed that at some point, the map of Afghanistan's sharia courts was almost identical to that of the hostile strongholds of the Taliban and al-Qaeda. He wondered if Sinai was pacing down a similar road.[9] Relaying Ignatius' comments to both Abu Faisal and al-Beik, they praised the sharia courts of Afghanistan and hoped to see them spread across the Islamic world. As Abu Faisal put it,

> Our God and their God is one, Allah, our Prophet is one, Muhammad peace be upon him, but the difference between us is clear to everyone. We are not imposing the sharia by force and we never thought of doing this, but we continue to do what is possible under the current circumstances of our communities. That being said, Afghanistan remains the land of jihad where our brothers fought for the sake of Allah.

Al-Beik also took pride in the history of the Taliban's Islamist rule:

> they cleansed Kandahar of the chaos and crime that spread after the fall of the Soviet Union, and the Afghan people were the ones who demanded the spread of sharia courts in other regions because of the success and stability they accomplished.

The tribal customary courts operated in Sinai for hundreds of years, why weren't they accused of being a state within a state? It is because this is a war on Islam and anyone representing it. Allah told us in the holy Quran that we will encounter such opposition: *Quite a number of the People of the Book wish they could turn you back to infidelity after ye have believed, from selfish envy.* Despite this loud opposition, President Morsi is on his way to applying sharia in Egypt.[10]

An Executive Arm

Before the rise of sharia courts, the tribal justice system had its own ways of enforcing its rulings, the most effective of which was publicly naming and shaming people who refused to obey verdicts issued against them after they had pledged to submit to the judge's decision, whether it went it in their favor or not. These shaming campaigns were highly effective in the tribal community and in villages of a few hundred people, normally all connected by blood. In many cases, community pressure went beyond just verbal shaming; it would escalate to a unanimous boycotting of those who did not revere the ages-old traditions.

Other means of enforcing the power of tribal courts was the *tawthiq* system, which translates literally into "tying" or "seizing" and refers to an act of seizing someone's possessions—camels, cars, and other valuable possessions—and depositing them with a prominent and trusted member of the community. *Tawthiq* was usually used by one of the disputing parties in order to force their rival into attending the tribal court, and was only permitted after several peaceful attempts to persuade the party in question to attend a customary trial had failed. It was also used after the court's decision was rejected by those found guilty.

With the dwindling respect for customary courts and the rise of criminal cartels across Sinai, during the late Mubarak years the *tawthiq* system gradually transformed from an ancient tradition used in service of the tribal justice system into a weapon used by disputing Bedouins to terrorize each other and impose their will. In the five years before Mubarak's downfall, and the few months after, North Sinai witnessed at least a dozen major cases of *tawthiq* executed by different warring clans.[11] In each of the cases, members of a clan would physically block the roads and highways cutting through their tribal territories and hijack the vehicles and other possessions of members and associates of their rival clans, and several kidnappings took place along with the seizure of vehicles.

Unlike the old customary system, the sharia courts viewed *tawthiq* as one of the worst possible crimes and usually applied harsher punishments for it than for murder. Al-Beik described it as "an act of thuggery that terrorized innocent people just because they happened to be relatives of someone who was a part of some dispute."

In need of field assistance in investigating crimes and violations, verifying testimonies, mediating between rivals, and applying the decades-old naming and shaming system, the sharia courts adopted a number of Salafi youth that had previously taken part in forming the vigilante patrols. They eventually became known as the Rights Retrieving Committee. Comprised of several bearded and well-known men in every residential area in North Sinai, the committee was formed by and reported directly to the judges.

Kuraiem Abu Rukba, a 28-year-old Salafi from the village of al-Sadat, south of Rafah, was one of the first to join the vigilante patrols in January 2011, and he then became a leading member of the Rights Retrieving Committee. He says that if it wasn't for the rising number of people who found no help or protection from the state authorities, he would have never occupied himself with matters that should be handled by government employees and policemen who are being paid to do so.

"The committee was formed by dozens of men who had been serving the community for years. What was an individual voluntary effort before the revolution became more organized under the umbrella of the sharia courts," said Abu Rukba.[12]

In most cases, according to the broad-shouldered Bedouin, the Salafi youth of the committee were the first to be called by anyone who had been robbed, attacked, or fallen victim to any form of crime, the majority of which were the elderly and widows who were incapable of reaching out to the sharia courts directly. After verifying the claims of whoever was requesting the committee's assistance, Abu Rukba and his fellow committee members would report to the Islamist judges and start a campaign within the family or clan of the alleged violator, calling them to report to the court.

Abu Rukba explained that:

We use the influence of the wise and respectable members of the family of the alleged violator and we stress that reporting to the court is an honorable thing to do. We assist the victim in reclaiming their rights and we assist the violator to repent their sins for the sake of Allah. In most cases, the violators reported to the court as soon as their elders and community figures conveyed our messages.

To any member of the tribal community, refusing the court's call is not only seen as a clear confession of the alleged violations but also shows a lack of respect for the sharia courts and the conservative traditions of the whole community. In extreme cases that normally involved known criminals; those who continued to challenge the call risked being outlawed and expelled by their own tribes, the worst possible punishment for a Bedouin as it means that even their closest relatives wouldn't move to protect them or seek revenge against anyone who attacked them.

"We are already successful if we convince someone to attend to the trial willingly, and our job is done when both parties walk out in peace," added Abu Rukba. "Those are the traditions of our community; no one accepts injustice and no one can bear the shame of refusing to compensate those they did wrong."

The public shaming campaigns of the committee did not only apply to the accused and suspected criminals, but also targeted the police department in dozens of cases of robbery, car theft, physical and armed attacks, and trespassing on land and real estate. In dozens of cases handled by the sharia courts, the victims were requested to report their cases to the police stations first, before the court would declare its verdict. Such a step was taken despite the knowledge that North Sinai's police department had been in a state of total paralysis since January 2011.

"We did it to prove to the authorities that we would have never operated if they had fulfilled their duty, and to protect also ourselves if anyone falsely accused us of anything after the sharia courts had ruled against them," added Abu Rukba, who stressed that this procedure was followed mainly in cases of stolen vehicles that were spotted in the villages and towns of North Sinai. If the police failed to react, which was the outcome in the overwhelming majority of the cases, the court would immediately request whoever was in possession of the vehicle to prove that they weren't involved in the vehicle's theft and return it to its owners.

In late 2011, Sheikh Suleiman Abu Ayoub, the judge of Rafah's main sharia court and a powerful leader of the Rights Retrieving Committee, was accused by local media reports of commanding a battalion of six thousand armed Salafis that were enforcing the verdicts of the Islamist courts across the peninsula.[13] The accusations that went viral and were repeated by pan-Arab media outlets were fiercely denied by Abu Ayoub and his fellow judges, who launched a boycott campaign of local media outlets and appeared on several Islamic television channels to refute the claims.

Each of the clerics had their own way of explaining how laughable the claims were. The controversial Asaad al-Beik said that "using force to apply justice is something to be proud of, but such claims are false because we cannot do something considered a punishable sin by the sharia laws we aspire to uphold, raising weapons in the faces of fellow Muslims."

As for Abu Rukba, whose AK-47 always sat beside him in his Toyota pick-up truck, he said that:

> it's known that every Bedouin is armed, it's a part of their culture and a necessity for life in tribal communities like Sinai. And whoever wasn't armed decided to buy a weapon after the uprising and the significant rise in crime.
>
> As for those who spread such claims, do they know how much money and power is required to arm, feed, and control six thousand men? If we had six thousand armed men, united by sharia, we would have liberated Jerusalem.

The Blurry Line

There is no doubt that the vacuum left by the downfall of an already debilitated and corrupt dictatorship created the opportunity for the sharia courts to expand. Over the three decades since the full return of the Sinai Peninsula to Egypt in 1982, the Bedouin community's confidence in the state authorities had continued to diminish. With an oppressive police department and a bureaucratic judicial system that served Mubarak's interests rather than protecting the people, it was less damaging for civilians to forgo their rights than to attempt pursuing them through state institutions. The desperate community provided fertile ground for anyone capable of imposing any form of justice, even if applied by Salafi clerics who blatantly condemned the ancient traditions of the tribal community, and have been accused of backing terrorism since the establishment of the Egyptian republic in 1952.

A former deputy to the minister of justice and veteran judge, who spoke on condition of anonymity about the spread of Shariah courts, admitted that "the state takes the blame for the fact that one of its most volatile regions was living under alternative systems, and the state knew it." He explained that for the last two decades, the Sinai Peninsula recorded some of the lowest levels of crime in spite of the abundance of weapons, the cultivating and trafficking of drugs, and the unending tribal feuds that always culminate in deaths, injuries, and major acts of vandalism. "It wasn't because Sinai was crimeless, but because no one reported to the police and the state never cared."[14]

But what many people saw as a voluntary service offered by honorable people to a community drowning in anarchy meant much more for the providers, the sharia judges. For them, it was a multi-pronged system that entrenched their control over their communities and gradually turned them into domestic political players that served the rising power of political Islam. And at the time when hundreds of apolitical ordinaries applauded the clerics for their community services, the more politicized elite was criticizing them for their murky stance on the more radical Islamist groups that had led armed attacks since the 2011 uprising, and more importantly, their hypocritical view of the Muslim Brotherhood that had seized the majority of parliament and the presidential seat through elections run by what the clerics viewed as manmade laws that contradicted Islamic sharia.

While they established their courts and preached Islamic sharia to ordinary people, the Islamist judges never showed any actual objection to the rising militant and *takfiri* groups who wielded weapons, imposed their authority over parts of the villages south of Rafah and Sheikh Zuwayyed, and were in constant disputes with Bedouin clans.

Nageh Ibrahim, one of the founders of al-Jamaa al-Islamiya that masterminded the assassination of President Anwar Sadat in October 1981, said that "ideologically, the difference between the Sinai sharia judges and the *takfiri* elements is almost nonexistent."[15]

Jailed between 1981 and 2005 after taking part in terrorist attacks in Upper Egypt's Asyut governorate in the aftermath of Sadat's assassination, Ibrahim became one of the leading members of the programs for ideological recantation and renunciation of violence applied in Egypt's jails since the late 1990s. In prison, he met with several of Sinai's Islamists who were mostly detained after the Taba bombings in 2004. He described them as "the most radical and the most reluctant to participate in any of the programs and lectures held in prison. They walked in saturated with *takfiri* ideologies and the majority of them walked out with the same beliefs, if not worse," said Ibrahim, adding that if they had understood sharia in the first place, they would have never have proclaimed themselves as judges. He went on that:

> this is one of the most sophisticated positions in the history of Islam. Nothing qualifies such people, who I personally encountered in prison, to be sharia judges. Neither their characters nor their Islamic academic qualifications, about which we have no idea, are adequate for them to become recognized, let alone to be declaring themselves, as judges.

6

A NEW HAVEN
FOR ISLAMIST MILITANTS

Mohamed al-Saafin, Eid Abu Jreir, and Khalaf al-Khalafat are three among dozens of Sufi clerics that have spread their moderate and spiritual culture across Sinai's tribal communities for hundreds of years. Sufi shrines were erected in almost every town across the rugged peninsula, the birth and death of the revered clerics were celebrated in mosques named after them, and the impoverished ordinaries flocked to their burial sites praying for forgiveness, cures from illness, and blessings for the young.

The majority of Sinai's written history has described its Bedouin communities as fluctuating between non-religious and Sufi at most; the five daily prayers of Islam weren't considered a sign of piety, neither were the slaughter rituals of Eid al-Adha, which the community adhered to as a tradition more than a religious duty.[1]

When Israel occupied the Sinai in June 1967, the Sufi figures, including Abu Jreir and al-Khalafat, were the first to collaborate with the Egyptian Military Intelligence and establish covert Bedouin units behind enemy lines. Their organization, which was later named "The Sinai Mujahedeen Association," grew to include more than seven hundred members, the most prominent of which was Hassan Khalaf, a hard-core Sufi figure of the Sawarka tribe who led countless operations against Israeli forces until his arrest and trial in an Israeli court. After his release in a prisoner exchange agreement, Khalaf became known as the "Sheikh of Sinai's Mujahedeen."[2]

Some fourteen years later, when Israel withdrew its last troops from the Sinai, Hosni Mubarak, who at that time had only been in power for one year, moved to marginalize the Sufi clerics and the fighters who were once honored and granted top Egyptian medals for their service and sacrifice throughout the war. In the eyes of Mubarak, the Sufi clerics, with their nationalist aspirations and commitment to their community, were a threat to his dictatorship and its plans that entailed no development or reforms for the peninsula, but rather aimed to silence the tribal community and transform it into a buffer zone that would keep the Camp David Peace Accords undisturbed.[3]

"'Do you want me to develop the Sinai for billions so Israel destroys it?' This is what Mubarak said when we asked what will happen to the land that we sacrificed our lives to liberate," said General Mohamed Okasha, the airforce pilot who served under Mubarak's command and was later appointed deputy head of the Sinai Development Authority formed in 1982, right after the Israeli withdrawal. "When I complained to my superior, also an army general, he told me to forget it and stop bothering myself and others."[4]

"Mubarak didn't even maintain the economy built by Israel during its occupation of Sinai," said General Okasha. "Their farms had been exporting crops to the world and they built roads across the peninsula. All of this was gone with the withdrawal and Egypt failed to replace it and incorporate the community that had lived under that Israeli system."

Mubarak's regime continued to marginalize the Sinai Peninsula and exclude it from its nationwide development plans into the 1990s, while the Salafi interpretations of Islam were already clashing with Sinai's prevalent Sufi and nonreligious, tribal cultures. And in mainland Egypt, the radical Islamist movements, headed by al-Jamaa al-Islamiya and the Egyptian Islamic Jihad, were gearing up for another wave of terrorist attacks across Egypt. It had taken the groups a decade of convalescence after the deadly crackdowns they faced in the aftermath of their assassination of President Sadat in 1981 and the bloody attack on Asyut's Security Directorate two days later, which killed 106 police personnel and 12 civilians.

These two leading groups, and a few other smaller yet sometimes more radical ones, were galvanized by the jihadist and *takfiri* ideologies of those who departed to join the Mujahedeen of Afghanistan in their war against the Soviet Union throughout the 1980s. The most prominent of these was Ayman al-Zawahiri, who left Egypt after three years in prison on suspicion of taking part in Sadat's assassination and later created al-Qaeda with Osama bin Laden. The stories of jihad and legendary sacrifices of the Egyptian warriors in Afghanistan, who became celebrated figures in their conservative home villages in Upper Egypt, traveled along with thousands of Egyptians living and working in Saudi Arabia, Yemen, and North Africa, where wealthy Salafis preached the incumbent jihad to their youth who flocked to Afghanistan on the path to Allah.

On June 8, 1992, two members of al-Jamaa al-Islamiya assassinated Egypt's prominent thinker Farag Fouda[5] and two months later, on October 21, the group declared its responsibility for the murder of a British tourist in Asyut. The attacks were the first of dozens of terrorist operations across Egypt that targeted tourist facilities and buses, police personnel, Egyptian Copts and churches, and even ordinary Muslim civilians who were viewed by the radical groups as infidels. A year later, in the summer of 1993, the Islamic Jihad carried out two failed assassination attempts that targeted then Prime Minister Atef Sedki[6] and then Minister of the Interior Hassan El-Alfy,[7] and in 1995, it led an assassination attempt against Hosni Mubarak himself during his only visit to the Ethiopian capital Addis Ababa.[8] The failed attack was planned and executed in cooperation with Sudanese and Ethiopian terrorists.

The Luxor massacre in November 1997, which claimed the lives of fifty-eight tourists, three Egyptian policemen and one Egyptian tour guide,[9] was the attack that unleashed Mubarak's fury. Minister of the Interior Hassan El-Alfy was sacked and Habib El-Adly replaced him to start the most lethal crackdown on Islamist movements in the modern history of Egypt. Regardless of their affiliations, thousands of bearded Islamists were put on exceptional state security and military trials and thrown in jails or landed on death row.[10] Back then, growing a beard was the shortcut to detention, while membership to an Islamist group was a crime punishable by fifteen to twenty-five years in prison. Within a few months, however, El-Adly had turned the page on Egypt's Islamist militants of the 1990s.

Sinai's Vacuum

North Sinai, with its poor towns and far-flung villages, was among the first regions for the radical Islamists to flee to. To them, a region at that time tagged by the authorities as free of radical activity and given little attention, if any, was a perfect hideout far from the security's sight and fertile enough ground for practicing the Islamic duties of *daawa*, or the call to Islam.

General Fouad Allam, a former head of the SSI and a mastermind of Egypt's crackdown on Islamists in the aftermath of Sadat's assassination, said that "Sinai was the least concerning region when it came to Islamist militants and radical movements."[11] Based on facts and figures he had gathered through years of security work and campaigns targeting Islamist militants, this was accurate, but what General Allam, and the whole regime for that matter, never worked to counter and control was the spread of radical ideologies. This mission never required arms or finances and was constantly made easier by new technologies that weren't available for the older generations of jihadist and *takfiri* ideologues thrown behind bars.

Khaled Musaid, a Bedouin descendant of the Sawarka tribe, became one of the top importers of the Salafi–jihadist ideology to the peninsula. A dentist who spent his college years in Sharqiya governorate, a historic stronghold for Islamist radicals and the biggest extension of Sinai's Bedouin tribes in mainland Egypt, he was radicalized as a student and returned to Sinai bringing with him the ultra-*takfiri* teachings of the most radical theorists of jihad, such as Muhammad Abdel-Salam Faraj, the founder of the Egyptian Islamic Jihad, and Sayyed Imam al-Sharif, or Dr. Fadl, the physician who fled Egypt in 1982 and joined forces with Ayman al-Zawahiri to rebuild the Egyptian Islamic Jihad from Afghanistan.

Faraj's jihadi manual, *al-Farida al-ghayba*, or "The Neglected Duty," and Dr. Fadl's masterpiece, *al-'Umda fi i'dad al-'udda*, or "The Essential Guide for Preparation for Jihad," allegedly made up Musaid's doctrine that he brought back to the mosques of al-Arish after graduating in 1999. Preaching in different mosques several times a week, he planted the first seeds of what later became Sinai's al-Tawhid wa-l-Jihad group that planned and executed the bombings of Taba and Sharm al-Sheikh in 2004 and 2005.[12]

Musaid was never on Egypt's security watch lists, but through studying the history of militant Islamists in Egypt, and inspired by al-Qaeda's attacks on western interests in different countries, he began building cells that included recruits from his tribal surroundings, the majority of whom were related to each other, sometimes brothers, and came from the most impoverished communities of Sheikh Zuwayyed and Rafah. Living and operating a few kilometers from the border with the Gaza Strip, Musaid and his fellow radicals were in constant communication with the Palestinian side of Rafah, a stronghold for Gazan Salafi–jihadists, who at the time had significantly more developed military experience than the Bedouins of Sinai, and some of them had already pledged allegiance to al-Qaeda.

While the heads of Egypt's militant Islamist movements remained behind bars or in exile, Mubarak's aging autocracy and his severely corrupt police apparatus failed to recognize the spread of the jihadist allure across the internet's countless forums that ranged from cursing the violence-renouncing ideological recantations adopted by the older generations of al-Jamaa al-Islamiya and the Islamic Jihad in Egypt's prisons, to spreading its jihadist theories accompanied by manuals meticulously explaining how to use arms and make homemade explosives.

On October 7, 2004, three vehicles loaded with highly explosive materials drove into the Hilton Taba hotel and two other beach camps in Nuweiba. The massive bombings claimed the lives of thirty-four people, twelve of whom were Israeli tourists, and hours later, a group named Kataib al-Tawhid al-Islamiya or "The Islamic Monotheism Brigades," an armed wing of Musaid's al-Tawhid wa-l-Jihad, took responsibility for the attack that was executed using TNT-based explosives and was led by Palestinian and Bedouin militants.[13]

"The Taba bombing in 2004 was the first terrorist attack we ever encountered in Sinai," General Allam said of the attack that unleashed what the tribes of Sinai later described as the worst security crackdown the peninsula had ever experienced. Back then and despite detaining up to five thousand people[14] from almost every town and village in Sinai during the weeks following the attack, the sheer incompetence of Egypt's security authorities revealed that Musaid and his armed militants never formerly appeared on the security radars of Egypt or Israel, who spared no effort in the hunt for the assailants behind the attacks.

It wasn't until another major bombing hit the tourist resort of Sharm al-Sheikh on July 23, 2005,[15] and claimed the lives of eighty-eight people, the majority of whom were Egyptians, and injured hundreds that Musaid's name began surfacing through the expansive investigations led by the SSI after another wave of arbitrary detentions. Some of the detainees, who had voluntarily surrendered to the authorities under tribal pressure, admitted to being members of the radical dentist's organization, al-Tawhid wa-l-Jihad, but failed to identify the many of their fellow militants who would usually use aliases and operated in independent cells responsible for different stages of planning and executing the attacks.

Weeks after the bombings, Musaid and his military commander Salam Atteya al-Shnoub were killed in an exchange of fire with police personnel as they attempted to escape a security checkpoint in Sheikh Zuwayyed.[16] The death of Musaid did affect the organization, but it by no means brought an end to its rising activities that were inspired by his unprecedented attacks on the tourist resorts, kilometers away from Mubarak's new favorite residence in Sharm al-Sheikh. By the time the dentist-turned-jihadist was eliminated, the influence of Gaza's Salafi–jihadist current was slowly moving to take his place and that of many Egyptian ideologues silenced by the continuing crackdowns. Eight months later, in April 2006, another bombing hit South Sinai's Dahab resort town, killing twenty-three people, five of whom were foreign tourists.[17]

In addition to the vicious security crackdown, Egyptian authorities launched an awareness campaign organized by al-Azhar, the seat of Sunni Islam, with the aim of spreading moderate Islam in the mosques of North Sinai, while several clerics from among Egypt's mainstream, non-violent, and independent Salafi clerics arrived in an attempt to counter the spreading *takfiri* ideologies. While local clerics were behind bars and hundreds of families struggled after the arrest and torture of their relatives, the majority of North Sinai's tribal community didn't even know about the visiting preachers, let alone attend their sermons. To the broader population, the 'moderate preachers' neither stopped the SSI's overnight raids and torture sessions nor did they provide jobs for the unemployed youth.

"Without education, [and with] endemic unemployment and a brutal security apparatus that targeted thousands of innocent people over the crimes of a few radical elements, the easiest thing to preach was *takfir* and jihad," said a Sinai Bedouin, who was detained several times throughout the 2000s, speaking on condition of anonymity. "The fact that I am not a jihadist, but I am still afraid to speak publicly about my rights and the rights of my people shows you that the radical Islamist current is much more effective than we are." To this Bedouin, like thousands of others, "the regime destroyed the moderate community and indirectly fueled the radical Islamists; its harsh policies became the *takfiri* current's justification of everything they preached."[18]

Gaza's Jihadist Influence

Despite the changing dynamics and the rise of Islamist militants, the presence of Mubarak's regime in the Sinai remained limited to the brutal crackdowns that punished the community collectively. Habib El-Adly's SSI realized that it was facing a new jihadist current, unknown to the founding fathers of the Egyptian jihadist movements and operating in a region where no map of radical ideologies or terrorist activities had ever been sketched.

But their challenges weren't only domestic; Israel's 2005 unilateral military disengagement from Gaza liberated the jihadist movements of Palestinian Rafah at a time when Hamas was gradually taking control of the Strip and capitalizing on, if not cooperating with, radical actors in its battle against the ailing Palestinian Authority. Back then, Hamas was still viewed by Gaza's jihadist and *takfiri* groups as the Muslim alternative to the treachery of President Mahmoud Abbas and his state authorities, who they accused of crushing the Islamist resistance movements for the sake of talks with Israel.

A few months after Hamas's takeover of the Gaza Strip, when smuggling tunnels began spreading under the border with the tacit blessing of Mubarak's regime, the jihadist ideology and militants began to move across the border as free and unwatched as consumer goods. With relatives, in-laws, and brothers-in-ideology spread across the towns of North Sinai, the Salafi preachers of Gaza found a new incubating community that was impoverished, desperate, and shared their animosity toward Israel and the oppressive Egyptian regime. Despite realizing the impossibility of operating in Sinai under the tightened security grip of the Egyptian authorities, the jihadist preachers were confident that such oppression was the main tool for promoting their Islamist rhetoric.

In Gaza, the earliest group to declare its allegiance to Osama bin Laden's global jihad network, al-Qaeda, was Jaish al-Islam, or the "Army of Islam." Founded in 2006 by Mumtaz Daghmash, a defected security officer of Fatah's Preventative Security Department, the group allegedly recruited up to two thousand fighters, the majority of whom were members of the Rafah native Daghmash clan. And despite their harsh criticism of Hamas's failure to apply Islamic sharia, the group joined forces with Hamas and Mumtaz Daghmash was said to have been among those who executed the 2006 cross-border attack on an Israeli patrol during which Corporal Gilad Shalit was kidnapped.

But the most powerful Salafi–jihadist preacher of southern Gaza remained Abdel-Latif Mousa, widely known by his *kunya*, or Islamic alias, Abul Nour al-Maqdisi, a physician who graduated from Alexandria's medical school and was a regular follower of the lectures and sermons held by some of the most prominent Egyptian Salafi preachers. Al-Maqdisi was the spiritual leader and founder of Jund Ansar Allah, a Rafah-based organization founded in November 2008 that pledged allegiance to al-Qaeda. Every Salafi–jihadist group in Gaza revered the 50-year-old cleric whose Friday sermons were attended by thousands of youth.

The two groups and their followers declared their opposition to Hamas as soon as it announced its participation in the municipal elections of 2005. To them, elections were a major contradiction to the Islamic sharia laws they sought to apply and their support for Hamas had been conditioned on the movement's willingness to do the same. Relations between the Salafi–jihadist current and the ruling Hamas continued to deteriorate until al-Maqdisi took his opposition to an unprecedented level, publicly tagging Hamas as pagan apostates and declaring the Islamic Emirate in the environs of Jerusalem during the Friday sermon he led on August 14, 2009, at Rafah's Ibn Taymiya Mosque.

Hamas's reaction was swift; it besieged the mosque and dozens of al-Maqdisi followers inside it, and demanded their surrender before engaging them in a battle that lasted for hours. Members of Hamas's police and the Qassam Brigades besieged the broader vicinity of the mosque and led an all-out offensive during which dozens of al-Maqdisi followers were allegedly killed in execution-style shootings. Before the battle came to an end, al-Maqdisi was allegedly killed when he detonated an explosive belt while Hamas officers attempted to detain him at his house.[19]

The death of al-Maqdisi wasn't the end of Hamas's offensive, but rather the beginning of a crackdown on the broader Salafi–jihadist current of the Gaza Strip. In the weeks following the Ibn Taymiya Mosque incident, Hamas rounded up hundreds of jihadists, engaged in clashes with families and clans in Rafah, and confiscated the weapons and assets of various groups. Various organizations affiliated with al-Qaeda declared their resentment of the crackdown, quoting Ayman al-Zawahiri's decades-old condemnation of Hamas and their Egyptian mother organization, the Muslim Brotherhood.

Right across the border, Sinai's *takfiri*s and jihadists, driven underground by Mubarak's lethal policies, weren't just spectators to the slaughter of their fellow ideologues across the border; their villages and mosques became safe hideouts for whoever was capable of fleeing Hamas's offensive via the tunnels. "They were idolized by the Islamist radicals of Sinai throughout their fight against the Israeli occupation or their opposition to Hamas. Their popularity doubled and tripled after the crackdown in Gaza," said Mohamed al-Filistini.[20] Two of his Islamist cousins in Sheikh Zuwayyed were said to have been among the first people to help the fleeing Gazan jihadists and secure their hideouts in villages far from the sight of Egyptian security authorities.

The escape of Gazan jihadists to Sinai in 2009 was very similar to the situation following Egypt's nationwide crackdown in the late 1990s, when militants had fled to Sinai from Upper Egypt. But throughout the decade in between, al-Qaeda had become the inspiration and had accomplished in the global jihad arena what the Egyptian Islamic Jihad and al-Jamaa al-Islamiya hadn't accomplished in over three decades, while the United States had invaded Iraq and Afghanistan and fiery sermons were cursing the West's military intervention in mosques across Egypt.

"There was nothing to counter the radical rhetoric in Sinai," said al-Filistini, "the *takfiris* were publicly leading the prayers in villages and the recorded sermons and lectures of jihadist theorists, including Gaza's al-Maqdisi, were circulating in the poorest communities."

In a region where illiteracy was reaching 50 percent in tribal communities, al-Filistini believes it was much easier for the Islamist preachers to spread any form of ideology. As he put it, "they weren't preaching to doctors and engineers."

In 2010, a year before Egypt's revolution, several mosques in the villages surrounding Rafah and Sheikh Zuwayyed were publicly referred to by residents of North Sinai as *takfiri* mosques, the most prominent of which was in the village of al-Muqataa, widely known as the "Mosque of al-Tawhid wa-l-Jihad," where Mohamed Hussein Muharib, or Sheikh Abu Munir, led the prayers, and along with his AK-47-wielding sons, established a vigilante, Wahhabi-inspired local "Committee to Promote Virtue and Prevent Vice."

1997–2010: The Reconstruction of Jihadists

In June 1997, when terrorist attacks were echoing in almost every major Egyptian city, leading members of al-Jamaa al-Islamiya embarked on a unilateral initiative of ideological recantations through which the muftis and theorists of the group publically renounced their violent and *takfiri* beliefs that viewed the regime and community as apostates and sinners. The era of recantations, known in Arabic as *al-murajaat al-fikriya*, began with dissolving the armed wing of the movement and calling on its members to put down their arms and embrace a new path of peace and remorse over the more than one thousand five hundred people who had been killed in a few years of bloody attacks.

"We were trying to make peace after sparking the war, but my experience taught me that making the former is much more difficult than igniting the latter," said Nageh Ibrahim, a pediatrician and founding member of al-Jamaa al-Islamiya.

After sixteen years in prison, Ibrahim, who co-led the 1981 Asyut attacks that killed 118 people and was arrested and sentenced to twenty-five years, became the most powerful theorist of ideological recantations. Alongside him were Karam Zuhdi, the former emir of al-Jamaa al-Islamiya, Essam Derbalah, the current emir, and Abbod al-Zomor, a member of the movement's Shura Council and former military intelligence officer who masterminded the assassination of President Sadat.[21]

Behind the bars of Egypt's maximum security prisons, the advocates of these recantations began holding daily lectures that retaught the jailed Islamists, analyzed the history of violence, and offered a counter rhetoric of peaceful change even at times of oppression under the rule of tyrannical regimes. But months later, the scale of rejection of this new path among the members of the movement was clearly shown by the Luxor massacre, whose assailants were killed by police forces after they had murdered fifty-eight tourists and four Egyptians. On the other end of the spectrum, the Egyptian Islamic Jihad, which was the most powerful radical Islamist movement alongside al-Jamaa al-Islamiya, declared its utter rejection of the recantations and led an intellectual offensive that at some point tagged those who adopted change as apostates who denied the incumbent duty of jihad.[22]

Less than two years later, Egypt began to show its positive reaction to the revisions program, administered by the security authorities and imitated by different Arab countries including Yemen, Libya, and Algeria. Between the years 1999 and 2007, the Ministry of the Interior had signed off on the release of some 15,000 Islamist prisoners, most of whom were members of al-Jamaa al-Islamiya. Among them was Karam Zuhdi, the former emir of the movement who issued a public apology upon his release, Assem Abdel-Maged, a co-founder of the movement, and Nageh Ibrahim, who led the recantations and lectured to the majority of Sinai's *takfiris* who were detained in the aftermath of the Taba and Sharm al-Sheikh attacks.[23]

Throughout the years of prison lectures and subsequent releases, Egypt's authorities, and those of Yemen and Algeria for that matter, never revealed the methods adopted to guarantee the effectiveness of the ideological revisions program. Beyond the pledge forms signed by prisoners at the offices of the SSI's Radical Movements Department, there was nothing to prove a prisoner's continued adherence to his pledge renouncing violence. In fact, the rehabilitation-like program became exploited by Islamist prisoners who attended the lectures during the day, and held their counter lectures at night, further radicalizing themselves and other ordinary criminals who shared their prison cells. Outside of the prison walls, the reality awaiting the released Islamists or criminals did more to encourage them to recant on the recantations, no matter how many pledges they had signed.

Since the establishment of the Arab Republic of Egypt in 1952, after King Farouk was toppled in a coup led by the Free Officers, the consecutive regimes of Gamal Abdel-Nasser, Anwar Sadat, and Hosni Mubarak adopted some of the harshest methods of excluding members of various Islamist movements, not only from political life, but also from societal participation. The examples of such oppression are countless and the psychological repercussions hadn't only scarred the bearded Islamists, but also their families, schoolmates, and friends. Besides the sadistic torture and inhuman living conditions the prisoners were subjected to inside Egyptian jails, being sentenced for believing in a radical ideology or for membership of an Islamist movement meant that no workplace, state or privately owned, would hire a person even after they had served their jail time, regardless of how superior their educational qualifications were. Being the relative of a convicted Islamist meant a non-negotiable rejection from military service, police and military academies, and top positions at various government institutions.

Montasser al-Zayyat, a prominent lawyer of Islamist movements who once shared a prison cell with Ayman al-Zawahiri in the 1980s, said:

> The released prisoners suffer from the rejection they encounter
> from their societies that fear the security's continued pursuit of them,

which leaves them in a dire social situation. The security authorities took responsibility for helping the Islamist prisoners return to
moderate ideologies, but it never helped them further or worked
to change how the community perceives them, not to mention the
unfulfilled roles of other institutions such as the Ministries of Man-
power and Social Solidarity.[24]

The Ministry of the Interior's reply to the continuous warnings by
Zayyat and other moderate Islamist figures, who described the released
Islamists as a "ticking bomb," was that "it is not responsible for the living conditions of released prisoners," and, needless to say, Mubarak's
regime turned a blind eye to the issue, which involved hundreds of
innocent civilians whose lives were destroyed by long years of arbitrary
detention, without any investigations or evidence, but allowed by the
emergency law.[25]

In 2007, commemorating the tenth anniversary of the Luxor massacre, Sayyed Imam al-Sharif or Dr. Fadl—his alias among the Mujahedeen
in Afghanistan—the world's most celebrated jihadist theorist, followed
in the footsteps of Nageh Ibrahim and declared his version of the ideological recantations named "The Document of Rationalizing Jihad in
Egypt and the World According to Sharia Regulations." The 111-page
document was said to have been inspired by the success of al-Jamaa al-
Islamiya's initiative that led to the release of thousands of its members
and neutralized its relationship with the security authorities. As for
Ayman al-Zawahiri, Dr. Fadl's lifelong partner in the Egyptian Islamic
Jihad and later al-Qaeda, he condemned the document and claimed
that it was "written under the supervision of the Americans and the
Jews."[26] The release of Dr. Fadl's document, which sent ripples through
the jihadist communities across the world, coincided with the gradual
loosening of Habib El-Adly's grip on the Islamist movements, including the Muslim Brotherhood, which was interpreted as a step taken by
Hosni Mubarak and his son Gamal within a broader plan of preparing
the country for the latter's expected succession of his aging father.[27]

The jihadists and takfiris of Sinai, who had been detained and
imprisoned without trials in the aftermath of the Taba, Sharm al-Sheikh,
and Dahab bombings in 2004, 2005, and 2006, remained in prison for
significantly shorter times than any other Islamists. They attended
the lectures of Nageh Ibrahim and followed the release of Dr. Fadl's

document inside the prison compounds where the majority of them remained until 2009. Upon their release, they returned to their communities that, contrary to Upper Egypt which witnessed an unprecedented economic growth in the 2000s, were deprived of the most basic rights.[28]

Up until the early days of January 2011, the effectiveness of more than a decade of religious violence, imprisonment, ideological revisions, and releases hadn't been tested. But what remained etched into the hearts and minds of Egyptian Islamists was the torture sessions of Mubarak's security apparatus that was said to have been a main reason for hundreds of Islamists pretending to accept the ideological recantations. At the time when Nageh Ibrahim and his fellow, violence-renouncing preachers worked to promote their peaceful rhetoric, Mohamed al-Zawahiri, the brother of al-Qaeda's deputy commander, Ayman al-Zawahiri, was sticking to his relentless refusal of the recantations which he deemed as conflicting with Islamic sharia.

2011: Testing the Recantations

Five days into the 2011 uprising, on January 29, several jails were broken open and more than 23,000 prisoners escaped, among them dozens of Sinai Bedouins who were imprisoned without trial for varying periods on different charges, mainly affiliation with Islamist radical groups. Members of an Egyptian militant group named Jund Allah, or the "Soldiers of Allah" (a group different from Jund Ansar Allah of Gaza), which was composed of around forty members who adopted the violent beliefs of the Islamic Jihad and were arrested in 2002, were also among the escapees from al-Marg and Abu Zaabal prison compounds. Both the Sinai jihadists and the Nile Delta natives of Jund Allah fled directly to the northeastern quarter of the Sinai Peninsula and some of them successfully crossed the tunnels into the Gaza Strip. Luckily at the time, the larger number of imprisoned Islamists, including the top officers of al-Jamaa al-Islamiya and the Islamic Jihad, were in the maximum security prisons of Tora and Burj al-Arab, which fell under less violent attacks that failed to breach the military cordons deployed a day earlier.

Two weeks after Mubarak's resignation on February 11, 2011, the Supreme Council of the Armed Forces (SCAF), which took over as the interim ruling authority and was headed by Mubarak's defense minister Mohamed Hussein Tantawi, began an unexpected campaign of pardons and releases for the top figures of the Islamist movements, including hundreds of their lower ranks and ordinary members. Among the first to be released was Mohamed al-Zawahiri (brother of al-Qaeda's Ayman al-Zawahiri), who was detained in the United Arab Emirates in 1999 and extradited to Egypt. The cousins and brothers-in-law Abbod and Tarek al-Zomor, commanders of al-Jamaa al-Islamiya who led the terrorist attacks in the 1980s during which president Sadat was assassinated, were also released and a few months later Dr. Fadl was released along with dozens of other convicted Islamist militants.

Divided into several groups freed in February, March, July, August, and October 2011, Field Marshal Tantawi approved the release of more than 850 prisoners, the overwhelming majority of whom were Islamists imprisoned by administrative detention warrants under the state of emergency in place since 1981. The overall number included more than fifty people from the Sinai Peninsula. In addition to the released prisoners, the ruling military council lifted the names of some three thousand Islamists living in exile—the majority of whom were members of al-Jamaa al-Islamiya and the Islamic Jihad that had operated throughout the 1980s and 1990s in Afghanistan, Chechnya, Bosnia, and Yemen—from security watch lists placed in the nationwide entry ports by the Mubarak regime.[29]

Nageh Ibrahim believes that many of those pardoned and released had held onto their *takfiri* and militant ideology as they walked out of prison and soon after were united with various underground groups that adhered to al-Qaeda's doctrine. He explains that:

> the recantations program applied mainly to al-Jamaa al-Islamiya, but there were many others who never adopted any revisions and were also released, those included members of the Islamic Jihad and various smaller groups. . . . The inactive *takfiri* current was encouraged by the revolution, the downfall of the regime, and the rise of the Muslim Brotherhood as the most powerful organization at the time.

The prominent Islamist lawyer Montasser al-Zayyat told local media that the release of Islamists is explained by the state of harmony between the ruling military council and the Muslim Brotherhood in the aftermath of the Egyptian uprising. "SCAF was relatively weak when it first assumed power and was facing considerable opposition from revolutionary forces, compared to the harmony that marked its relationship with Islamist movements. The move to release Islamist detainees should, in my opinion, be seen in the context of this harmony," said al-Zayyat.[30]

The beliefs of both Ibrahim and al-Zayyat were proven shortly after the release of the top figures of the groups that terrorized Egypt throughout the 1980s and 1990s. Upon his release from Tora Maximum Security Prison in southern Cairo, Mohamed al-Zawahiri declared his complete rejection of the ideological recantations and those who established the program within Egypt's prisons.

"I was threatened by an SSI officer that I will be sentenced to death if I don't uphold the recantations of Dr. Fadl, 'The Document of Regulating Jihad,' and I didn't accept it because it contained many contradictions with Sharia," said al-Zawahiri in an interview with the London-based independent Islamist NGO, al-Maqreze Centre for Historical Studies. As for democracy, he described it as "a complete contradiction to Islam's view of politics and governance."[31]

As for Abbod al-Zomor, who named his book of revisions *al-Badil al-thalith bayna al-istibdad wa-l-istislam*, or "The Third Alternative between Despotism and Surrender," he told local and international media outlets on his release that the violence authorized and committed by him and his fellow members of al-Jamaa al-Islamiya in the past was triggered by the oppression and violence of the regime of President Anwar Sadat, who they later assassinated.

Al-Zomor told the local *al-Shorouk* newspaper:

Sadat's assassination happened against our plans. Our plan was to carry out a revolution in a civil way without blood, but Sadat arrested everyone in September 1981 so we had to move quickly and kill him. When they [al-Jamaa al-Islamiya's senior commanders] suggested killing Sadat I refused and suggested attacking prisons to free political prisoners with a plan to oust Sadat without bloodshed in 1984, but they refused so I had to listen to the majority and we killed Sadat.[32]

Al-Zomor's post-2011 statements, which conditioned the use of violence to the regime's oppression, cast major doubts on the legitimacy of his recantations, or at least their effectiveness on thousands of Islamist followers whose commitment to renouncing violence was impossible to guarantee.

Analyzing the effectiveness of the ideological recantation of al-Jamaa al-Islamiya, prominent Egyptian scholar and researcher of Islamist movements Hossam Tamam wrote that:

> . . . al-Gamaa al-Islamiya's initiative to cease violence was not inspired by a process of ideological reassessment. The declaration of the initiative came in the wake of a decisive military defeat which brought al-Gamaa to the conclusion that it was futile to continue a campaign of armed confrontation. The initiative was the spark that set into motion a train of ideological recantations, not the culmination of such a process. Al-Gamaa's leadership could not, however, afford an extended process of theoretical revision. At the time of its initial recantations the group was in the midst of a crisis and had to act quickly. In addition to the political and military pressures they faced, more than 15,000 of its rank and file were in prison, some 2,000 had died and 100 faced execution. The revision process was not a luxury, as it was for the Muslim Brotherhood, it was literally a matter of life and death.[33]

Commenting on the release of jailed Islamists, Ahmed Ban, a researcher of radical movements and defected member of the Muslim Brotherhood who operated under the organization's doctrine until his resignation, along with hundreds of the movement's youth who defected in protest of the extremist transformation under its radical Qutbi and Salafi leadership of Mohamed Badie and Khairat al-Shater, said that the "random release of convicted militants was reckless and motivated by political interests rather than security measures."[34]

The Salafi control of the Muslim Brotherhood, which gradually intensified until just a few months before the January 2011 revolution and the unprecedented freedoms it granted to Islamists in Egypt, says Ban, led the Qutbi leadership to sponsor the release of Islamists while it offered itself to the world, especially the United States and Europe, as the moderate and highly organized movement most qualified to rule Egypt in the aftermath of Mubarak's downfall. Domestically (under SCAF), they offered to control the more radical Islamist groups and contain them under their political umbrella. "In return for the release, the Brotherhood received full support from all sorts of Islamists, militant or peaceful, throughout the years after the revolution. They became the Brotherhood's strategic reserve."

The ideological and organizational gap between the Muslim Brotherhood and the Salafi currents, which was widened by Gamal Abdel-Nasser's crackdown on the group in 1965 and the execution of Sayyed Qutb, began shrinking in the mid-2000s until it disappeared when the most powerful Qutbi personalities within the group (such as Badie, al-Shater, and Mahmoud Ezzat) won the internal elections between 2005 and 2010, dominated the Guidance Bureau (the ruling council), took over the Supreme Guide's position, and began limiting the influence of other non-Qutbi members known as reformists. Hossam Tamam described the dramatically changing dynamics of the Brotherhood in his book, "The Salafization of the Brotherhood: The Decay of the Brotherhood Approach and the Rise of Salafism," in which he wrote:

> The result of the internal elections resulted in protests from the reformist current within the group and worried the intellectual and political elites within the group and outside of it, due to what many, including the Muslim Brotherhood themselves, considered a hijacking of the brotherhood organization by the Qutbi current, who strengthened their control over the leadership of the group and occupied its most important organizational positions including the position of the Supreme Guide and two of his three deputies."[35]

What Ban described as the Muslim Brotherhood's sponsorship and gradual control over the Salafi currents across Egypt began early on, before the release of Islamists. It was orchestrated through the "Legitimate Council for Rights and Reform," a Salafi led entity established in the last days of the January 2011 uprising. Financed entirely by the Brotherhood's second-in-command and top strategist, Khairat al-Shater, the convention of clerics began a nationwide outreach campaign that promoted the Brotherhood as the most capable of leading political Islam's attempt to rule Egypt.

Soon after its establishment, defections began hitting al-Shater's council in July 2011, the most prominent of which was Nasr Farid Wasel, a prominent al-Azhar scholar who co-founded the council and was appointed as its honorary head. Wasel said that his resignation came "after the council deviated from the goals it was originally established for." His resignation statement criticized the council saying that instead of focusing on social efforts in favor of the nation and people, the council began criticizing the moderate and primary Islamic institution of al-Azhar, delved into politics and began supporting political powers in the parliamentary and presidential elections, which were scheduled to take place months after his resignation.[36]

Almost immediately after Wasel's resignation, the secretary general of the Council, Mohamed Yosri Salama—one of Egypt's most prominent Salafi figures—declared that the Brotherhood-sponsored convention had prepared the new Islamic Constitution agreed upon by the nation's Islamist currents, headed by the Brotherhood.[37]

"The Council was doubted because of the Brotherhood's financial and political domination over it; it had nothing to do with rights and reform as it claimed, and definitely had nothing to do with *daawa* [call to Islam]. It was clearly a political front. We condemned the heads of the Salafi community for participating in it, especially Yasser Burhami," a Salafi activist from Alexandria commented, referring to Burhami, the leading cleric and founder of Alexandria's politically active Salafi current and founder of al-Nour Party that ran against the Brotherhood in the November 2011 parliamentary elections.[38]

The fruits of the Muslim Brotherhood's campaign, which formed the most powerful bloc on Egypt's political arena at the time, appeared rather too soon. Less than two weeks after the downfall of Hosni Mubarak, SCAF appointed the Constituent Assembly charged with amending the Egyptian constitution. As evidence of the ruling military's acceptance of the Brotherhood's offers, or submission to the rising threat they posed backed by the nationwide Islamist currents, Tarek al-Bishri, a well-known Islamic and legal scholar, was made the head of the assembly while Sobhi Saleh, the Brotherhood's most powerful legislator and legal advisor, was appointed as a member. Not surprisingly, no liberal, leftist, or revolutionary figures were among those appointed by Tantawi, simply because of their opposition to the constitutional amendments and the roadmap proposed by the ruling military generals that, if passed, scheduled the deactivation of the 1971 constitution that remained active until 2011, to be followed by parliamentary elections, presidential elections, and then drafting of the country's new constitution.

The speculation over the apparent political harmony between the ruling military and the Muslim Brotherhood and its Islamist affiliates was confirmed by Tantawi's decision to go on with the referendum despite the opposition of the country's revolutionary figures and blocs that had just overthrown Mubarak weeks earlier. The Revolutionary Youth Council, credited for igniting the January 2011 uprising, Mohamed ElBaradei, the former secretary general of the nuclear watchdog the International Atomic Energy Agency (IAEA), and Amr Mousa, Egypt's former foreign minister and a prominent politician, were among dozens who rejected both the amendments, the referendum, and the roadmap.[39] On March 19, a few days after the release of the first batch of hardcore Islamists including al-Zawahiri and al-Zomor, the constitutional declaration sketched out by the Brotherhood-affiliated assembly was passed by an overwhelming 77 percent, a political triumph for Egypt's Islamist current who dubbed it "The Battle of the Ballot Boxes." The Islamist movements across the country promoted the constitutional declaration for weeks before the national referendum on it, calling it the "defender of Egypt's Islamic identity" and accusing the opposition of treachery and waging war on Islam.[40] Passing the March 2011 constitutional declaration, which scheduled the parliamentary elections prior to drafting the county's new constitution, was clearly in the favor of the Muslim Brotherhood as it gave the parliamentary majority unchallenged powers in forming the constitutional panel. Being the most powerful political organization in a volatile country, in addition to their harmonious relationship with the ruling SCAF, it was easy to predict the control of the Brotherhood over the first post-2011 parliament, and the constitutional amendments that followed.

The unmatched reach of Egypt's political Islamist fronts, led by the Muslim Brotherhood and the Salafi current, was displayed even in the farthest and most impoverished communities. In the ultra-conservative town of Salloum, the border town with Libya, hundreds of hard-core Islamists stood in line to vote on the constitutional referendum on March 19, 2011. The majority of them viewed the voting process as sacrilegious, but had made an exception to show their endorsement of and keenness on preserving the so-called Islamic identity. Voters in this ever marginalized region repeated what the Muslim Brotherhood and Salafi figures had being saying on television channels for days: "voting against the declaration is voting against Islam."[41]

"The line between the Muslim Brotherhood's non-violent approach and the militancy of other groups dissolved after the 2011 uprising, especially now that the Brotherhood was ruled by a Qutbi current [followers of

Sayyed Qutb], which is utterly radical Salafi," said Ban, who stresses that Khairat al-Shater, the Brotherhood's deputy leader and its main financier, became the architect of the movement's future relations with Egypt's radical Islamist groups, including the Islamic Jihad, al-Jamaa al-Islamiya, and the more radical, *takfiri* figures such as Mohamed al-Zawahiri.

"Contrary to the former leaders, Hassan al-Houdeibi and Omar al-Telmisani, who refused to adopt any violent approaches, Badie and al-Shater had no objection to striking up affiliations and working with militant Islamists as long as they served the goals of the Muslim Brotherhood," says Ban. And in return for their unprecedented freedom, allowing them to establish political parties and participate in parliamentary elections in coalition with the Muslim Brotherhood, the Islamist movements and figures were mobilized and used against the democratic and liberal political powers.

"Presenting those who participated in killings and terrorist attacks over the 1980s and 1990s to speak throughout the media and portraying them as political figures on Muslim Brotherhood-sponsored channels reflected a clear partnership and sharing of mutual interests," added Ban.

A live presentation of how empowered the radical Islamist current had become was played out the day after Osama bin Laden's death on May 2, 2011. At a mosque in central Cairo's Abbasiya district, hundreds of bearded Islamists gathered to hold mass prayers for Bin Laden, who they referred to as "our martyred Sheikh." Outside of the mosque, an altered Egyptian flag was erected, bearing the Islamic declaration of faith, "No god but Allah, Muhammad is the prophet of Allah," instead of the iconic eagle. Marching for a few kilometers to join a scheduled protest outside of the US embassy, the protest was met by street vendors selling photos of al-Qaeda's founder around the epicenter of Egypt's uprising, Tahrir Square.

North Sinai: The Base of Operations

Whatever influence or political affiliations the Muslim Brotherhood enjoyed with various Islamist groups that turned to politics—such as al-Jamaa al-Islamiya that established the Construction and Development Party soon after the downfall of Mubarak—did not apply in the Sinai Peninsula which required a different approach. Isolated from mainland Egypt and its mainstream political Islamist currents for decades, the Sinai-based radicals remained influenced by al-Qaeda and its affiliated groups either in the Gaza Strip or in the villages of Rafah and Sheikh Zuwayyed. If the Muslim Brotherhood and their affiliates saw Mubarak's downfall as a political opportunity, the Sinai elements saw it as an opportunity to reconstruct their organizational hierarchy and resurrect the incumbent duty of jihad.

On July 29, 2011, several Bedouins dressed in traditional attire held a protest in front of al-Arish's police station to demand the release of relatives detained and sentenced to death—a sentence that was never carried out—for their alleged participation in the 2005 Taba bombings. The protest was led by a Salafi native of Rafah named Hamada Abu Sheita, and, unlike almost every protest held across Egypt, this one began late in the afternoon. Less than an hour after the protesters began chanting, an estimated twenty pick-up trucks and sedans accompanied by several motorbikes carrying dozens of masked and heavily armed men started roaming the streets of the city; several of the trucks were fitted with poles on which al-Qaeda's black flags, emblazoned with "No God but Allah, Muhammad is the Prophet of Allah," were waving.

Armed with Kalashnikovs, high-caliber machine guns and RPGs, the jihadist entourage drove through several of al-Arish's main streets, randomly firing bullets in the air in what seemed to be a declaration of their arrival, before heading directly to the police station in front of which the late-afternoon protest was held. Showering the security facility with bullets, the militia kicked off a street battle that continued for almost nine hours. In addition to the police station, the armed militants also attacked a local bank facility and killed its security personnel. By dawn of the next day, the jihadist attack came to an end after the police forces, backed by military reinforcements, had detained several of the assailants, including three who were injured and transported to the city's hospital under heavy security. Hours later, an official statement announced that five police personnel and three civilians had been killed and twenty-four others injured.[42]

On August 1, three days after the attack, hundreds of copies of a document headlined "al-Qaeda in the Sinai Peninsula," were distributed at dozens of mosques in al-Arish, Sheikh Zuwayyed, and Rafah, demanding the application of Islamic sharia and condemning the Egyptian military over the Camp David Peace Accords. The document was the first public declaration made by a Sinai-based group and was followed by comments from its alleged commander, named Sheikh Awwad, who declared their responsibility for the attack and stated that a Frenchman, a German, and several Palestinians were among the militants.

"Our goal is to establish an Islamic Emirate in the Sinai Peninsula as a first step toward establishing it across the Arab world," Sheikh Awwad told a local independent newspaper. He claimed that "al-Qaeda has been in Sinai for the past ten years and was responsible for the Taba and Sharm al-Sheikh bombings that were wrongly blamed on al-Tawhid wa-l-Jihad."[43]

In reaction to the document and the comments of Sheikh Awwad, North Sinai's governor, General Abdel-Wahhab Mabrouk, made a statement claiming that "affiliates of al-Qaeda in Sinai are under tight surveillance," while the governorate's security chief, General Saleh al-Masry, said that "ten Palestinian elements, including three injured, were detained and the remaining assailants are being pursued."[44]

The statements of the two highest ranking officials in the governorate turned into a public embarrassment when armed relatives of one of the detained injured Palestinians raided the state-owned hospital after his death and retrieved his corpse, facing no reaction whatsoever from the security authorities stationed in massive barracks hundreds of yards away from the hospital.

Less than two weeks later, on August 18, a deadly attack took place on the Israeli Highway 12 running parallel to the border in the Negev Desert and leading to the southern resort of Eilat. Several armed men had breached the Egypt–Israel border fence and fired machine guns and rocket-propelled grenades at a bus, a border patrol, and a civilian vehicle driving on the highway. The attack left eight Israelis dead, including two security personnel, and around forty injured. An Israeli Apache gunship was mobilized to track down the assailants who were disguised as Central Security Forces, the only troops allowed on the Egyptian border by the demilitarization conditions of the Camp David Peace Accords, but, in what Israeli officials described as "an unintended mistake," the gunship fired at an actual Egyptian border patrol, killing six of its troops. At the time, Israel claimed to have killed ten out of the alleged twelve attackers.[45]

No group declared responsibility for the cross-border offensive that was described by Israeli military officials as an unprecedented development signaling that Sinai, an area about which Israel had repeatedly voiced concerns over deteriorating security, was turning into a more openly hostile neighbor. "It was the first attack where terrorists breached the border and targeted Israelis on Israeli soil, and it called for further reinforcements and developing new security tactics," said Peter Lerner, official spokesman of the IDF.[46]

Israeli Defense Minister Ehud Barak stated at the time that "this is a grave terrorist incident in a number of locations. The incident reflects the weakness of Egypt's hold over Sinai and the spread of terrorist elements."[47] He also expressed regret over the deaths of the Egyptian soldiers and ordered the IDF to conduct a military investigation into the incident.[48]

Several Israeli security officials, including Defense Minister Barak, claimed that the attack was planned by the Gaza-based Popular Resistance Committees (PRCs), which were known historically for maintaining a stable and cooperative relationship with ruling Hamas on one side and the Salafi–jihadist current on the other. In 2006, the PRCs had worked with Hamas and the al-Qaeda affiliated Jaish al-Islam in planning and executing the cross-border attack in which Corporal Gilad Shalit was kidnapped. And despite denying Israel's claim, the group applauded the attack in several statements to the press.[49]

On the ground in Egypt, both attacks had different and extremely revealing consequences. At the time when the Salafi-jihadist clerics of Sinai lauded the repeated bombings of the gas pipeline as an honorable act against the Israeli occupation and in defense of the Egyptian people and their resources, the nine-hour-long battle of al-Arish proved to be different. Whether it was planned and ordered by a specific group or executed by independent elements, it embodied the actual power of militants who were willing to wage war against the Egyptian state, even if the victims were mainly Muslim civilians. As for the state authorities, including the military and the intelligence agencies, both attacks revealed that at the time they had little control over both North and South Sinai.

According to General Mohamed Okasha,

> al-Arish's attack, or temporary occupation, proved that no one has control except the well-armed and trained terrorist elements. It was shocking and disgraceful. It tested the ability of the state, and if the assailants already knew it was that weak then it was a catastrophe, and, if they didn't then, now they do and would be encouraged to continue and intensify their operations.[50]

On the political level, Egypt's ruling SCAF faced scorching criticism over their failure to take firm action against Israel after the killing of the six border security personnel gunned down by the Israeli military gunship. Within a few days, public opinion, stirred up by dozens of Muslim Brotherhood and Salafi figures appearing on various television channels, was totally distracted from the fact that two major terrorist attacks had been executed by militants operating freely on Egyptian soil. Two weeks later, an unprecedented protest took place in front of the Israeli embassy, a few kilometers from Cairo's Tahrir Square. On September 9, 2011, one of the thousands of protesters climbed the façade of the twenty-two-story residential building housing the embassy, ripped down the Israeli flag, and hurled it into the cheering crowds. The flag, which was burnt upon its landing among the furious protesters, was followed by hundreds of embassy documents thrown out of a storage room that was stormed by people who managed to break into the building.

Abdel-Aziz, an activist from Sheikh Zuwayyed, commented that:

> It all played out in favor of the militants—the attack on the Israeli embassy was simply interpreted as a result of the operation and promoted to their followers as one step toward establishing the Islamic Emirate. While the regime was occupied by political turmoil on state level and it was losing control over what was actually brewing on the ground in Sinai. . . . Every successful operation by Islamist militants contributed to building the organizational hierarchy of the militant groups; it appealed to jihadists from mainland Egypt and other countries.[51]

The Brotherhood Connection

On January 25, 2012, the first anniversary of the Egyptian uprising, a Sinai-based group named Ansar al-Jihad, or "the Supporters of Jihad," declared its allegiance to Ayman al-Zawahiri, the Egyptian physician who co-founded the world's global jihad organizational-Qaeda and became its chief after the death of Osama bin Laden. The group's declaration, published on various online jihadist forums, didn't take responsibility for any attacks, but praised the August 2011 cross-border attack in Eilat.

Five days later, on January 30, an armed group of Bedouins blocked the highway leading to Rafah and kidnapped twenty-five Chinese citizens en route to their workplace at a North Sinai-based cement factory.

The kidnappers, who took their hostages to a tent erected in the middle of desert depression several miles south of Sheikh Zuwayyed and surrounded by militiamen armed with RPGs and machine guns, agreed to be filmed by Ahmed Abu Draa, the prominent Sinai reporter and descendant of the Sawarka tribe. The lead abductor, Shadi al-Menaei, bluntly laid out his demands on camera: "We demand the release of our fellow Sinai Bedouins who have been jailed by Mubarak for years, we also demand the Egyptian regime to halt all gas exports to Israel."[52]

Al-Menaei named the same five prisoners sentenced to death, a demand identical to that of the protest held in al-Arish shortly before the attack on the police compound. His appearance on camera came after months of stories tying him to the gas pipeline bombings, some of which referred to the 28-year-old militant as the "emir," an honorary title granted to heads of Islamist groups.

The alleged emir, Shadi al-Menaei, was known as one of Sinai's most notorious criminals in the years leading up to the January 25 uprising. Specialized in the trafficking of African migrants, he was detained in early 2010 and transferred to the infamous Burj al-Arab Maximum Security prison in western Alexandria. Like the majority of Sinai's prisoners, al-Menaei never stood trial but was jailed under the emergency law, with an administrative detention warrant. Mingling with radical ideologues behind the walls of the nightmarish prison compound, the man who walked in a criminal was released months later, before the 2011 uprising, a different person: a bearded hardcore *takfiri*.

"The jihadist community accepted him as a new person, a faithful man who was willing to take the path of jihad, and, according to their ideology, they are obliged to help him," said Abu Arrab al-Sawarka, the arms smuggler who is a relative of Shadi al-Menaei yet a fierce detractor of his radical ideology. "He showed commitment and started fighting the criminals he once worked with, which proved that he wasn't pretending or trying to take advantage of the rising jihadist community that appeared after the revolution."

One day after the kidnapping operation, al-Menaei and his armed militiamen released the Chinese workers after receiving a comforting message from the Egyptian authorities stressing the regime's willingness to enact a retrial for the Taba bombing prisoners. Two weeks later, the SCAF submitted to al-Menaei's demands and referred the Taba bombings defendants to retrial. At the time, North Sinai governor General

Abdel-Wahhab Mabrouk, who failed to mobilize an all-out offensive against the armed militants abducting civilians in broad daylight kilometers away from his office in al-Arish, said that "the incident would neither affect the Chinese workers in Sinai or the Egyptian–Chinese relations."[53]

Five weeks later, the prisoners hadn't been released and al-Menaei was, unsurprisingly, once again leading another troop of around fifty armed men to besiege the al-Gora barracks of the Multinational Forces and Observers (MFO). The incident was the first of its kind since the deployment of the MFO in Sinai in 1979 to monitor the application of the Camp David Peace Accords signed by Egypt and Israel.

With the wire fence and the watchtower of the camp in the background, al-Menaei appeared on camera to repeat his demands of releasing the same prisoners as during the siege, while the militants destroyed the electricity cables fueling the camp and forced it to run on generators. This continued for eight days between March 9 and 16. Throughout al-Menaei's second militant operation, less than two months after the first, the Egyptian police and military forces did nothing but avoid using the vital highways running around the camp and fully controlled by the armed elements.

The Muslim Brotherhood wasn't far from the unfolding events in North Sinai. On the first day of the siege imposed around the MFO camp, the former supreme guide of the movement, Mahdi Akef, was among several Brotherhood figures speaking at a conference hosted by Sinai University, a private institution owned by Hassan Rateb, the prominent ally of Hosni Mubarak who was granted exceptional rights to establish multi-billion-dollar private investments in the military-controlled peninsula.

"The Muslim Brotherhood utterly rejects the Camp David Peace Accords with the Zionist entity, but we cannot do anything regarding it until it's discussed by the parliament and judged by the people of Egypt," Akef said during the conference to an audience led by the Freedom and Justice Party's local figures, three of whom held half of the governorates' six parliament seats at that time, contributing to the 47 percent of the post-revolution parliament the Muslim Brotherhood had won during the elections held in November 2011.[54]

In addition to the parliamentarians, there were several prominent Sinai radical Salafis who worked closely with the Brotherhood's financier, Khairat al-Shater, and formed a line of communication that connected Egypt's most powerful Islamist political player to the jihadist community in North Sinai. At the top of the list was a native of Rafah, Kadri, who was released from prison days after the downfall of Hosni Mubarak. Kadri was imprisoned in 2009 over charges of smuggling weapons, a charge confirmed by several local activists. In detention, he shared a prison cell for months with al-Shater in southern Cairo's Tora Prison.[55]

Describing himself as an "ordinary member of Sinai's Salafi current that consists of thousands of members," Kadri noted that the only difference between his current and others across Egypt was their decision to refrain from engaging in any political process, including the establishment of parties or participation in elections as candidates or voters, "because the political system contradicts our beliefs derived from and governed by Islamic sharia."[56]

Immediately after his release, he became al-Shater's top business partner in North Sinai. Paying a short visit to the Gaza Strip during which he met with Hamas's top figures Mahmoud al-Zahar and Ismail Haniyeh, Kadri was granted the exclusive rights of importing cars to Gaza through dozens of tunnels customized hastily after Egypt's uprising to allow the brand new vehicles to cross unharmed. From sedans and SUVs to pick-up trucks used mainly by the Qassam Brigades, Kadri became the first smuggler in the history of Sinai to send double-decker car carriers through the streets of Rafah, in broad daylight. And during his regular visits to al-Shater's office in eastern Cairo's Nasr City district, the Salafi smuggler handled more than business matters: he was a main courier between the Muslim Botherhood's leadership and Sinai's militants.

"We have no organized Islamist groups in Sinai, all of this is media propaganda to portray Sinai as Egypt's Afghanistan," said Kadri at his office in al-Arish. "When the people of Sinai wanted to send a message, they took the Chinese workers and showed them extreme hospitality, then released them when officials promised to release their imprisoned relatives."

His response to questions about any militant attacks was always to deny the existence of organized groups, describing the various attacks as an angry popular act and blaming it on years of oppression under Mubarak's regime, tagging attacks against Israel and the gas pipeline as a courageous act blessed by the Egyptian people. He claimed that some of the attacks on government facilities were masterminded by the Mubarak loyalists, who were using them to tarnish the reputation of the rising Islamist powers.

Meanwhile, on April 25, al-Menaei and his militia once again blocked the highway running through the town of Sheikh Zuwayyed. This time, he wasn't demanding the release of any Islamist prisoners, but was threatening to bomb a scheduled rally of Egypt's Nasserite presidential candidate Hamdin Sabbahi. Interviewed on camera by the independent news page *Sinai Now*, al-Menaei said that "Sabbahi and his campaign aren't welcome in North Sinai after defending the Syrian dictator Bashar al-Assad,"[57] a baseless accusation promoted at the time by media outlets affiliated with various Islamist currents including the Muslim Brotherhood. Without any security intervention from the town's police compound located less than a kilometer away, the rally was immediately canceled and Sabbahi, a prominent rival of the Muslim Brotherhood's Mohamed Morsi in the presidential elections scheduled a month later, ended his campaign trail in al-Arish.

"He is a socialist and a Nasserite, we don't want him promoting his blasphemous ideology here," said Azzam Sinjer, a member of al-Menaei's militia, referring to Hamdin Sabbahi and explaining why he carried his RPG and joined al-Menaei's attack on the presidential rally. "I am against the presidential elections and was also against parliamentary elections, those people want to apply their own laws instead of upholding the laws of Allah. This is blasphemy."[58]

Asking Sheikh Azzam, as the locals referred to him, what he and his fellow Islamists wanted to accomplish, he said "we are working to establish the Islamic emirate and to liberate Jerusalem." Pointing to his two sons sitting across from him, both younger than ten years, he added that "hopefully they will if we don't."

Unlike the two al-Menaei-led operations demanding the release of Islamist prisoners, the last one on Sabbahi's rally was perceived differently by the surrounding communities witnessing the gradual escalation of the militants over the months following the 2011 uprising. The target of this attack, civilians who would attend the rally, including dozens of North Sinai residents who most probably were descendants of the same Bedouin tribes as the attackers, invalidated the justifications promoted by Kadri and his fellow Islamists after every attack on the gas pipeline to Israel or on the hated police apparatus.

According to Abdel-Aziz, the activist from Sheikh Zuwayyed who supported Sabbahi,

The attack on the pro-Sabbahi event was clearly encouraged by the Muslim Brotherhood. The jihadist community doesn't believe in elections, considers it against Islamic Shariah and, to them, Morsi is as sinful as Sabbahi for participating in elections. We cannot separate such an unexpected act from the apparent links between the Brotherhood and the jihadist community in Sinai. After all, the only party benefiting from such an attack was the Muslim Brotherhood and their presidential candidate.

In the capital Cairo, Ahmed Ban, the defected Muslim Brotherhood member, and Nageh Ibrahim, the former officer and co-founder of al-Jamaa al-Islamiya, believed that the rise of militant activities in Sinai played in favor of the Brotherhood's broader political activities. "Hosni Mubarak used the Brotherhood as a scarecrow for years to further entrench his rule and promote himself to the international community; the Brotherhood used the jihadists in an identical manner," said Ban.

Ibrahim, further to Ban's comments, accused the Muslim Brotherhood of "using the jihadist and *takfiri* current as weapons against their political rivals and the ruling military council." The most telling incident, he says, was the sit-in called for by supporters of the ultra-Salafi preacher Hazem Salah Abu Ismail—protesting his expulsion from the presidential race over his mother's American citizenship—which took place around the Ministry of Defense in Cairo's Abbasiya district on April 30, five days after the assault on Sabbahi's rally in North Sinai. It was joined by Mohamed al-Zawahiri who walked around the sit-in perimeter flanked by masked men waving al-Qaeda-like black flags.

On May 2, military personnel backed by police forces and plainclothed thugs led a lethal crackdown on the protesters that left thirteen people dead and scores injured, a move that triggered nationwide anger and criticism by human rights organizations and liberal and Islamist political currents alike. The crackdown wasn't just an irrational attack on the protesters, says Ibrahim, "it was triggered by the killing of a military sergeant who was shot from the minaret of the nearby al-Nour mosque." He claimed his killers were among many *takfiri* militants who arrived along with Abu Ismail and al-Zawahiri's followers, two of whom were Sinai Bedouins and were killed in the violent dispersal.

What Ibrahim said about those killed was almost identical to what was documented by statistics and reports published by different NGOs recording the casualties of different protests. WikiThawra, the independent initiative specialized in collecting and collating information on the thousands victims of the political and security turmoil since January 2011, reported that Special Forces sergeant Samir al-Kayal was killed by a live bullet, while two out of the overall thirteen civilian victims were unidentified.[59]

Two days after the bloody events, the Muslim Brotherhood's top officer and member of parliament Mohamed al-Beltagi declared the Brotherhood's demands: "We demand Farouk Sultan [the head of Egypt's Constitutional Court and the Electoral Commission] resigns from his post and transfers his duties to the head of the Supreme Judicial Council, Hossam al-Gheriyani [a prominent Brotherhood-affiliated judge]."

The rising militancy in Sinai and the murky relations between the Muslim Brotherhood and the jihadist and *takfiri* currents weren't surprising to Ahmed Ban: "In addition to the historically documented involvement of the Muslim Brotherhood in violence, the movement's founder, Hassan al-Banna, said 'we will resort to force when other options become useless' in his writings that became the movement's constitution."

What the Muslim Brotherhood's Qutbi leadership failed to accurately assess was their future ability to control the jihadist current which they capitalized on in the aftermath of the January 2011 uprising, but that would inevitably turn into a threat if the movement's candidate, Mohamed Morsi, became Egypt's president, which he did. During the weeks leading up to the 2012 presidential elections (held in the weeks after al-Menaei's militant operations in North Sinai), the Brotherhood's tone had begun to soften when promoting their stance on sensitive issues such as the Camp David Peace Accords with Israel and the ruling SCAF led by Mubarak's long-time military chiefs. Contrary to what Sinai's jihadist current wished for, Morsi had gone from describing Israel as the "Zionist entity" and "grandsons of monkeys and pigs"[60] to stressing the Brotherhood's respect for international treaties signed by Egypt, and instead of continuing his former scorching criticism of the ruling military generals he began applauding them for sacrificing their lives in protection of the homeland.

Meanwhile, in a scene very reminiscent of Gaza's Salafi-jihadist current excommunicating Hamas upon its decision to participate in the municipal and parliamentary elections in 2005 and 2006, Sinai's radical clerics began expressing their concerns over what they deemed a hypocritical stance of the Muslim Brotherhood that was now neutralizing its anti-Israel rhetoric and, for the second time, participating in a political process contradictory to the sharia laws of Allah they fought to uphold.

Flagships of Jihad

Throughout the eighteen months after the January 2011 uprising, the militant attacks across North Sinai never hit the Egyptian military or its facilities, but continued to target the police forces and the gas pipeline stretching to Israel and Jordan, in addition to the cross-border attack on Eilat in August 2011. The few military personnel killed or injured throughout that period had come under fire only at checkpoints comprised of personnel from both departments. Such a pattern seemed to have been followed to match the tribal community's historic hatred of both the police apparatus and Israel in an apparent public relations campaign aiming to promote the militants as virtuous Mujahedeen whose crosshairs are only pointed at the enemy. In Sinai's impoverished communities, the militant attacks were mostly complemented or minimally criticized and described as avenging decades of oppression.

Meanwhile, one day after the presidential election runoffs between former military pilot and Mubarak's former civil aviation minister Ahmed Shafiq and the Muslim Brotherhood's Mohamed Morsi, on June 18, another cross-border attack took place on Israel's border highway near central Sinai.[61] Two assailants wearing explosive belts and armed with machine guns opened fire on a public bus, killing a 35-year-old Muslim, an Arab-Israeli, and injuring others. While attempting withdrawal back into Sinai, both militants were killed by an Israeli military unit. The next day, June 19, a video spread rapidly across jihadist forums declaring the formation of Majlis Shura al-Mujahedeen fi Aknaf Bayt al-Maqdis, or "the Mujahedeen Shura Council in the Environs of Jerusalem" (MSC); the group declared its responsibility for the attack and threatened an ongoing war against Israel.

The MSC spokesperson, who appeared in the video sitting in front of an al-Qaeda banner and flanked by six heavily armed men, all of whom were masked, said "we dedicate this blessed invasion to the soul of the lion of Islam, the reviver of jihad, and the raiser of the banner, the Sheikh and Mujahid Osama bin Muhammad bin Laden."[62] The statement, which also applauded the "Syrian Mujahedeen" and the "oppressed lions of jihad in the glorious Gaza," was the third indirect declaration of allegiance to al-Qaeda from a group operating in the Sinai Peninsula. After describing the details of the cross-border attack a day earlier, which the group dubbed the "Battle of Triumph for Jerusalem and the Prisoners [in Israeli jails]," the two assailants were introduced as the Egyptian Khalid Salah Abdel-Hadi Jadullah, or Abu Salah al-Masri, and the Saudi Adi Saleh Abdallah al-Hadhli, or Abu Hudhayfa al-Hadhali, before their wills were read.

The declaration forming the MSC revealed a clear conflict within the group's hierarchy, while giving the cross-border attack a name dedicating it to Palestinian prisoners in Israeli jails, the masked speaker reading from a piece of paper bearing al-Qaeda's flag dedicated it to Osama bin Laden. Mentioning the uprisings of the Arab Spring and pledging to fight for the application of Islamic sharia, it was difficult to assess if the group would follow Bin Laden's global jihad campaign, excommunicating Arab regimes and leading attacks against them, especially in Egypt from which the group's debut attack was launched.

Hours after the attack, Israel's defense minister Ehud Barak said that it signaled a "disturbing deterioration in Egyptian control in Sinai" and added that Israel expects whoever wins the presidential elections to "take responsibility for all of Egypt's international commitments, including the peace treaty with Israel and the security arrangements in Sinai, swiftly putting an end to these attacks."[63]

Days after Barak's scorching statement, on June 24, 2012, the Muslim Brotherhood's Mohamed Morsi was officially declared the first freely elected president in the history of the republic. The rise of the Muslim Brotherhood to the presidency of Egypt, a country where they have been prosecuted, jailed, and even executed since their establishment in 1928, came a few days after Egypt's interim ruler, Field Marshal Tantawi, declared the dissolution of the Brotherhood-occupied parliament on June 14, after the Supreme Constitutional Court deemed the parliamentary laws unconstitutional.[64]

The parliament's dissolution was followed by a constitutional declaration drafted and passed by SCAF on June 17, the second day of Morsi's runoffs against Shafiq in the presidential elections. The declaration described as a soft coup enacted hastily by the military generals in anticipation of the Muslim Brotherhood's win, simply stripped the president of any control over the military institution and its related affairs, and granted the military council exceptional rights to interfere in purely political procedures normally handled solely by the president and parliament. In addition to granting the military council exclusive rights to appoint and replace members and commanders of the military without the intervention of the president, the declaration conditioned the president's decision to go to war on the agreement of the heads of the military institution and the defense minister. Moreover, it gave the military council the right to form and activate an alternative constituent assembly in case the operations of the already active one were hindered by any reason, a clear sign of the military institution's intent to share the powers of whoever became the country's president.[65]

Arriving at the inauguration process separately in heavily secured entourages, Egypt's new president Mohamed Morsi and twenty-year defense minister Tantawi drove through crowds of hundreds of Islamists carrying banners emblazoned with altered photos of the Mubarak-appointed military chief performing the salute to the Muslim Brotherhood's member, who went from Wadi al-Natrun Prison to the presidential palace in eighteen months. While the world's governments, and media for that matter, applauded the transparency of the presidential elections monitored by dozens of reputable local and international organizations, and described it as the beginning of Egypt's path to the post-revolution stability, the constitutional declaration was seen by the Muslim Brotherhood organization and its affiliated Islamist movements as a clear announcement of the military's rejection of Morsi as the supreme commander of the armed forces, a position occupied by four officers-turned-presidents since the 1952 revolution and the establishment of the Arab Republic of Egypt.

Ansar Bayt al-Maqdis

On the night of July 19, during the Muslim holy month of Ramadan, two military conscripts were viciously murdered in the middle of Sheikh Zuwayyed's main market. The masked assailants, who fired their machine guns at the unarmed soldiers and fled on a motorbike, were the first to commit a premeditated attack on military personnel. Choosing to kill the soldiers as they walked a few hundred yards away from their checkpoint was evidence that the militants had been watching the perimeter and preplanned a swift murder that avoided a gun battle with the remaining troops. Triggering a wave of anger across the tribal community, whose prominent figures immediately stated their condemnation, the attack signaled a transformation in the militants' battle against Egypt's authorities, even when ruled by an Islamist president. Less than twenty-four hours later, a bombing successfully targeted the gas pipeline for the fifteenth time despite the state's announcement of suspending all natural gas exports to Israel and an ongoing trial of Mubarak's regime officials who oversaw the project since its establishment. Six days later, Ansar Bayt al-Maqdis (ABM) or "Partisans of Jerusalem," declared itself as the new jihadist group responsible for the repeated attacks on the gas pipeline. A twelve-minute video published on online jihadist forums showed several drive-by shots taken during scouting trips to different control chambers of the pipeline, lectures held for militants in combat gear, and footage of the bombers planting explosive packages directly on the pipeline, some of which was taken using night-vision cameras.

In a video titled "And If You Return, We Will," ABM's speaker, dressed in military fatigues, said:

> We bombed the gas pipeline supplying the Zionist entity, and Allah knows that we only did this to protect the resources of the nation and the rights of the people. Allah knows that we never intended any vandalism or violation; we were extremely careful that no one is injured in any of these operations and Allah helped us accomplish them, in addition, we never intended to cut the gas supplies to our families in al-Arish, or the industrial facilities all around Sinai.[66]

Unlike the declaration by the Mujahedeen Shura Council, the title given by Ansar Bayt al-Maqdis and the introduction read by its speaker was a clear message revealing the group's animosity to the Egyptian regime and its will to continue its operations targeting the ongoing normalization between Egypt and Israel. And while the MSC referred to the Arab Spring in general, ABM's statement referred to Egypt's January 25 revolution and quoted Ayman al-Zawahiri's blessings on their attacks on the gas pipeline.

"Praise be to those heroes who bombed the gas pipeline to Israel for the fifth time, those heroes that genuinely represent the dignity of the Egyptian people; the Muslim, patient, and defenders of Muslims and Islam. May Allah salute those heroes who renew the hope in the souls of their nation," said al-Zawahiri's statement published in January 2012 praising the attacks on the pipeline and quoted by ABM's declaration of its existence as an organized movement with a history of more than fifteen successful operations.[67]

From this point on, Sinai wasn't Gaza's backyard or a hideout for wanted jihadists anymore. The peninsula was declared the newly opened field of jihad for Egyptian, Palestinian, and foreign jihadists alike, a home to whoever couldn't operate freely under the stifling grip of Hamas in the Gaza Strip or in mainland Egypt where the historic Islamist movements had established political arms and participated in elections. Egyptian security officials continued to refrain from commenting on the ongoing attacks in Sinai and deny the existence of a growing, organized militancy. North Sinai's security chief, General Saleh al-Masry brushed off the whole matter:

> We don't have organized groups in Sinai, we have people with jihadist ideologies but who do not carry weapons or get involved in militant operations, and according to the democratic principles upheld by the January 25 revolution, we cannot prosecute people for their ideological beliefs. But if anyone dares carry weapons, we will crush them.[68]

Outside of al-Masry's office in the North Sinai Security Directorate, Ansar Bayt al-Maqdis was becoming Sinai's most prominent group with command centers in both southern Gaza and Sinai's northeastern quarter, and Shadi al-Menaei, who led the siege of the MFO camp and kidnapped the Chinese workers, became known as their most powerful field commander.

"They brought together the remainder of so many groups that were stifled by Egypt and Hamas for years. Jaish al-Islam, Jaljalat, al-Tawhid wa-l-Jihad, all of them, they are all Salafi–jihadists coming from different groups," Abu Arrab al-Sawarka said while driving through the dark roads connecting al-Mehdiya and al-Muqataa, the two towns from which some of ABM's most active members came. More than five of his relatives had pledged allegiance to the group. "They all look up to al-Qaeda, adhere to Bin Laden and al-Zawahiri, and among them are Yemenis, Saudis, Sudanese, and Libyans."[69]

Wielding his machine gun while attending funerals and weddings held in the villages, Shadi al-Menaei's reputation traveled to every corner of the peninsula; he had become one of the most feared personalities in Sinai, praised by Islamists and tribesmen alike. Mohamed al-Zawahiri, the brother of al-Qaeda's chief, described him as "a defender of Islam who accomplished what the state failed to, repeatedly hit the Zionists, and fulfilled the wishes of all Muslims," while Sheikh Zuwayyed's sharia judge, Hamdin Abu Faisal, described him as "a pious young man who ardently defends the sharia of Allah."[70]

Despite the unfolding events in Sinai, the capital Cairo seemed to be fully occupied with the ensuing battle between elected president Mohamed Morsi and the military generals over the rule of Egypt. One month after being sworn in, Morsi signed the release warrants of twenty-seven Islamists who were jailed or sentenced to death by Mubarak-era military and state security courts; the group included nine members of the Muslim Brotherhood living in exile and sentenced in absentia, in addition to two foreign nationals, a Saudi and a Syrian. Morsi's decree was met by extreme opposition and accusations that he was serving fellow Islamists from his presidential office, but despite the public outrage against the Brotherhood officer-turned-president, it remains an undeniable fact that the ruling military generals released hundreds of radical Islamists they had once hunted.[71]

7

THE MILITARY UNDER ATTACK

A Massacre in Rafah

On August 2, the Israeli National Security Council's Counterterrorism Bureau renewed its warning against travelling to the Sinai Peninsula, a statement that was followed by similar travel advice announcements made by American security authorities.[1] "The counterterrorism bureau calls, once again, on all Israelis in the Sinai to leave the area immediately and to return to Israel," read Israel's warning that called on families of tourists to urgently get in touch with relatives in Sinai's southern resorts and urge them to return home.[2]

The sudden warning was said to have been triggered by information obtained by the Israel's intelligence units of an impending terrorist attack. Hours later, the Israeli army's Operational Chief of the Southern Command, Major General Tal Russo, responsible for securing 230 kilometers of land border with Sinai, ordered the evacuation of military personnel from the Karm Abu Salem (Kerem Shalom) Crossing. Evacuating the terminal, operated jointly with Egyptian authorities, and reinforcing combat units in surrounding areas suggested that Israel's intelligence operations might have obtained specific details of the anticipated attack.[3]

Around midday of August 5, an Israeli drone targeted two alleged Palestinian militants riding a motorbike in Gaza's southern town of Rafah. An IDF statement published immediately after the drone strike said it was "a joint operation carried out by the Israeli Shin Bet and military against members of a global jihad organization."[4]

The IDF's statement added that the targets of the operation, 19-year-old Eyad Nadi Okeil and 22-year-old Ahmed Sayyed Ismail, were members of the Gaza-based Popular Resistance Committees (PRCs), known for their solid ties to jihadist organizations operating in southern Gaza, and claimed that Ismail was involved in the cross-border attack carried out in June by the recently established Mujahedeen Shura Council. But as the statement stressed the successful elimination of both men, Gazan sources told Israeli newspaper *Haaretz* that Ismail was only wounded.

Several hours later, around 6:50 p.m., 18- and 13-year-old cousins Ahmed and Mohamed, who live in a makeshift shack standing fifty meters away from Rafah's al-Hurriya Military Post, on the Egyptian side of the border, were performing their evening prayers when they heard a barrage of machine-gun fire outside of their humble home that was more of a tent made of wooden logs, metal pipes, and palm leafs covered with plastic sheets. Running out at the sound of shooting, the teenagers were met by a masked militant who fired his weapon in their direction.

"There was a group of around twenty-five men shooting their weapons at the military post, some of them were masked and others weren't. They were all shouting 'Allahu Akbar' in a strange accent," said Mohamed, adding that he and his cousin ran back inside the tent and started screaming "the military is coming," in an attempt to deter the attackers. Seconds later they saw a military vehicle racing down the asphalt road running directly to Karm Abu Salem Terminal, trailed by a four-wheel-drive Land Cruiser, a pick-up truck, and a sedan.[5]

Almost one hundred meters down the road, Abu Sallam rushed out of his house to the sound of gunfire. "I ran directly toward the military post where the attack was happening, I thought some criminals were trying to steal the weapons from the soldiers, but then I saw the military vehicle moving toward me."[6]

"I found myself face to face with the military vehicle, someone inside it screamed 'Allahu Akbar' at me as I turned and ran away from them," said Abu Sallam, a Salafi who confirmed what the teenagers said about the cars trailing the commandeered armored personnel carrier. "I saw the man driving the military vehicle. He didn't wear a mask and wasn't bearded."

Minutes later, the two teenagers, Abu Sallam, and his brother, along with several other residents of the surrounding houses were at the military post carrying the bleeding bodies of the soldiers in two cars whose owners, including Abu Sallam's brother, volunteered to rush them to the nearby Rafah hospital. "I ran to [Rafah's main] al-Masoura checkpoint to inform them, and on the way back we heard the explosion and saw the fire at Karm Abu Salem," said Abu Sallam.

Ibrahim al-Menaei (who has the same name, but is not the same person, as Sawarka's tribal leader Ibrahim Abu Ashraf al-Menaei) was among the first to walk into the military post where the bodies of soldiers and officers were left bleeding. "The attackers hit them as they sat over the Iftar meal [eaten to break fast during Ramadan] they had prepared. Some of the corpses we carried out had fallen directly onto their plates of food," said al-Menaei. "We couldn't make out who was dead and who was alive, except for one soldier who was in shock and later told me that the attackers had kidnapped one soldier and taken him with them inside the armored vehicle."[7]

At the border crossing, standing two kilometers away from the attack site, the commandeered armored vehicle followed by a pick-up truck rammed into the Egyptian gate of the terminal, then maneuvered around the concrete blocks surrounding the gate leading into Israeli territory. The four-wheel-drive vehicle failed to cross through the sandy ground around the concrete barriers while the armored vehicle successfully passed it and continued driving at a speed of seventy kilometers per hour. Israel's Bedouin Reconnaissance Battalion, armed only with machine guns, failed to stop the rogue vehicle, while the IDF's southern command mobilized three tanks and diverted a jet fighter, which ended the pursuit with an air-to-surface missile that brought the commandeered Egyptian military vehicle to a stop. Seconds earlier, the pick-up truck stuck at Kerem Shalom Terminal had detonated an estimated half a ton of explosives it had been carrying.

During the pursuit, several mortar shells fired from southern Gaza exploded in the Eshkol region where the armored vehicle was headed, which was later described as an attempt by the terrorists' accomplices to provide cover for those who successfully infiltrated the Israeli border. Israeli military sources added that two out of a total of seven attackers survived the shelling of the armored vehicle and crawled into the farms surrounding Road 232, on which the vehicle was driving. Minutes later, the militants were gunned down by infantry troops surrounding the area.[8]

Back in Egypt's Rafah, the attack had left sixteen military personnel killed and seven more critically injured, while President Mohamed Morsi called for an emergency meeting with heads of the military and announced a nationwide state of mourning for the victims.

Reshuffling the Military

Two days after the massacre, a massive funeral was held, surprisingly in the absence of President Morsi, led by Defense Minister Mohamed Hussein Tantawi and Chief of Staff Sami Anan. Immediately after the mass prayer held for the victims of the attack in a major eastern Cairo mosque, Prime Minister Hisham Kandil, who was appointed by Morsi weeks earlier, was attacked by dozens of angry people attending the funeral, which forced his personal security to rush him into his armored entourage and flee the scene.[9]

Yasser Ali, the official presidential spokesman at the time, gave an unconvincing justification of the president's absence, saying that he preferred not to interrupt the emotional service with his attendance which would have imposed tightened security and intimidated the crowds attending the funeral. "The president saw it as a people's funeral and preferred to keep it this way; he delegated Field Marshal Tantawi to represent him."[10]

Firmly denying the official line, a military official, speaking on condition of anonymity at the time, said that "the commander of the republican guards [responsible for the president's security] advised him not to go in order to avoid a very possible attack by angry people, which is exactly what happened to Prime Minister Kandil and other Islamist figures who were almost killed by the furious relatives of the victims."[11]

Less than twenty-four hours after the funeral, President Morsi announced the enforced retirement of head of the republican guards, along with the head of the military police and the head of the central security department for failing to secure his attendance. More shockingly, the head of the Egyptian General Intelligence Directorate (EGID) at the time, Murad Mowafi, was also sacked from his position after declaring to the local press that he had been informed of a possible attack days before it happened.[12]

On August 11, six days after the most lethal attack on the military since the Egyptian–Israeli war came to an end in 1974, President Morsi flew to Sinai's border town of Rafah accompanied by Defense Minister Tantawi, Chief of Staff Sami Anan, and Minister of the Interior Ahmed Gamal Eddin. Sharing an Iftar meal with military troops in Rafah, a few kilometers away from the site of the massacre, Morsi pledged to "never, ever rest until we take revenge and bring justice to those killed."[13]

On his return to Cairo, President Morsi began a sweeping reshuffle of the command of Egypt's military: on August 12, he retired Defense

Minister Tantawi, Chief of Staff Sami Anan, and Navy Chief Admiral Muhab Mamish.[14] In addition to the retirement decrees, Morsi annulled the constitutional decree passed by Tantawi during the presidential elections, which had stripped Morsi of any control over the military, and ordered the formation of a constitutional panel to be tasked with drafting the new Egyptian constitution. [15]

The last of Morsi's decisions that day was appointing head of the military intelligence department, Major General Abdel-Fattah al-Sisi, as defense minister after promoting him to rank of general. The exceptional appointment of al-Sisi, despite sacking the others who shared the ruling military council with him since Mubarak's ouster in 2011, was surrounded by utmost secrecy, while any possible responsibility of his—as chief of military intelligence he was in constant coordination with Israeli authorities regarding the border areas and the rising threats in the Sinai Peninsula—for failing to foil the attack was never discussed.

At the time, the official website of the Freedom and Justice Party, the Muslim Brotherhood's political arm, described the little-known officer as "a minister of defense with a revolutionary flavor," a statement that sparked concerns about the possibility that al-Sisi was the Brotherhood's covert element within the military institution. Ironically, the Muslim Brotherhood's cheering of al-Sisi and the public's speculation over his possible ties to the organization took place only ten months before he overthrew Morsi and led the most lethal crackdown on the Brotherhood in its history.[16]

Morsi's decisions to eliminate the most powerful remaining figures of Hosni Mubarak's regime were met by nationwide applause not only from Islamist currents, but also from secular and revolutionary movements who had harshly condemned SCAF (headed by Tantawi and Anan) for the oppressive policies it adopted throughout the eighteen-month transitional period during which they ruled the country by decree.

Egypt's Suspicious Prior Knowledge

While Egypt's authorities were preparing for the mass funeral, Israeli official sources declared that they had shared the information, which they received days earlier, warning of a terrorist attack in the making, with their counterparts in the Egyptian intelligence directorate, headed by Murad Mowafi, who was the first to be sacked after confirming the Israeli claims in his comments to the press.[17] In a string of interviews with several media outlets, including the Egyptian state-owned *al-Ahram* and the

Turkish Anadolu news agency, Mowafi said "we had detailed information about the attacks planned by a *takfiri* group operating in Sinai and Gaza, such information was conveyed to the responsible authorities."[18]

"But we never believed Muslims would kill their fellow Muslims during the holy month of Ramadan," added Mowafi, who had a reputation for irrational verbosity, while in other comments he attempted to shift the blame by stressing that "general intelligence [the EGID] is not an executive or a combatant authority, such an attack doesn't cast any doubts on the capabilities of the intelligence operations."

Mowafi's shocking statements triggered a wave of claims accusing President Morsi of turning a blind eye to the impending attack, which he later used to justify his swift elimination of the top figures of Egypt's military command, including those who weren't in anyway responsible for the security failure or the embarrassment he faced after failing to attend the funeral, such as Navy Commander Admiral Muhab Mamish.

"The head of the general intelligence answers directly to the president and sometimes calls for a meeting attended by military commanders including the defense minister, the chief of staff, and the head of military intelligence," said General Mohamed Okasha, who endorsed Mowafi's statement that the EGID is neither an executive nor a combatant authority. "He was sacked after his comments but he did his job and is the least to be blamed, whether Morsi informed the military commanders and ordered any action remains unknown."[19]

Analyzing the Rafah attack and its murky details through the broader context of Morsi's deteriorating relations with the military command, a deterioration that began with the dissolution of the Islamist-controlled parliament by a constitutional court ruling weeks before the presidential elections in June 2012 and the constitutional declaration passed during the elections, General Okasha said "I am almost confident that Morsi turned a blind eye to the attack so he could use it to get rid of Tantawi and his military chiefs. Hamas's apparent prior knowledge of the attack, the mortars fired from Gaza as cover for the terrorists, and Mowafi's statements all cast major doubts on Morsi's possible involvement in this."

General Okasha, who formerly worked with Field Marshal Tantawi and viewed him as an uncreative officer and a failed politician, believed that the Muslim Brotherhood movement had been in partnership with the ruling military council since the January 2011 uprising, "picking Brotherhood members to amend the constitution, followed by the

Brotherhood's hostile stance toward the revolutionary movements, and, above all, holding presidential elections before writing a constitution, which means undefined presidential powers, were all signs of their harmonious relation with the military."

Weeks before the presidential elections, when it became clear that controlling Egypt came down to controlling the military, this harmonious relationship came to an end, triggering Tantawi's constitutional declaration that simply stripped the president of any form of control over the military institution, "it was a message to Morsi telling him that he will be an honorary president and the military will remain as the actual ruler of Egypt."

For Tantawi and Anan, General Okasha says,

> this was the safe exit which the revolutionary powers were against as they demanded putting them on trial similar to Mubarak. The recent attack which both commanders share the responsibility for, along with their corrupt history within the military institution and over a year and a half of their interim rule, forced them to accept Morsi's offer to retire and remain silent."

Several months later, General Okasha was more confident about his theory as Morsi and his cabinet failed to reveal any further information regarding the attack or the results of the ongoing investigations, despite the fact that the charred bodies of the terrorists killed by the Israeli military were returned to Egypt.

Due to the fact that EGID Chief Murad Mowafi was the first to be silenced after revealing that he "conveyed the warning to the responsible authorities," which directly shifted the blame to the presidency, General Okasha and many other analysts failed to assess the actual responsibility of Defense Minister Tantawi. But, months later, the question was unintentionally answered by Mostafa Bakri, a mouthpiece of the military and a fierce critic of President Morsi, saying that Mowafi had informed the president and "exerted major efforts to convince the military command of launching a campaign in the Sinai Peninsula to counter the rising threat, but Tantawi insisted that military intervention should be the last option and the matter should be handled by the police department." He added that, at the time, Mowafi faced the fury of both Morsi and Tantawi as each took his comments as a direct accusation against them.[20]

On the extreme end of the anti-Morsi spectrum were those who accused him of turning a blind eye to Israeli warnings of the attack and even that the Brotherhood was directly involved in it with the help of their Gaza branch, Hamas. Meanwhile, pro-Islamist speakers promoted an alternative rhetoric, accusing the military commanders of not only failing to fulfill their duty and publicly embarrassing the president by refusing to secure his attendance at the public funeral, but also claiming that Field Marshal Tantawi and Chief of Staff Anan were planning to overthrow the elected president.

The pro-Morsi rhetoric wasn't only fueled by Islamist media outlets and top Muslim Brotherhood figures, such as Mohamed al-Beltagi who referred to the supposed coup plot in a televised interview, but it was also adopted by others viewed as liberal. The local *al-Siyassi* magazine, a subsidiary of *al-Masry al-Youm* news organization owned by Egypt's prominent business tycoon Naguib Sawiris, published a three-page report headlined "Behind the Scenes of the Night of Elimination," while the cover of the issue carried a photo of Field Marshal Tantawi crossed off with a page-size letter X.

The author of the report, Emad Sayyed Ahmed, claimed that "Abdel-Fattah al-Sisi, chief of military intelligence, was informed by the American Central Intelligence Agency (CIA) of intercepted calls between Field Marshal Tantawi and Chief of Staff Sami Anan in the aftermath the Rafah attack, proving that they had began planning a coup to oust President Morsi amid the protests scheduled for August 24." The report added that Morsi's decisions weren't based on his domestic policies, but were rather "an American-sponsored move to eliminate the last Russian-oriented military commanders [Tantawi and Anan] and replace them by al-Sisi who studied at the British military college and the American Army War College," adding that putting this in the light of the military council's neutral, if not supportive, stance on the Russian-backed Syrian regime was the main reason behind eliminating its heads and imposing the Brotherhood's anti-Assad will.[21]

Operation Eagle II

Hundreds of kilometers away from Cairo's political war that began shortly after the attack, the immediate reaction of Rafah's residents and representatives of the Bedouin tribes was to march in support of the Egyptian military, whose murdered personnel they had just carried to hospitals. During the brief march, several people testified to seeing Hamada Abu Sheita—the leader of the protest in al-Arish on July 29, 2011, that was followed by an armed attack on security facilities—driving an SUV with two other men minutes before the attack. All three were said to have been wearing bullet-proof vests.

"They were monitoring the main road from which you can drive to the military post that was attacked. He passed by a shop right before the evening prayers (minutes before the attack took place). The shop owner said Abu Sheita's companions were Palestinians and confirmed that all of them wore bullet-proof vests," said al-Menaei who confirmed that no one from the police, military, or prosecution ever asked for his testimony or that of other witnesses who described the meticulous details of the attack, but were not willing to be quoted out of fear both of the authorities and the militant groups.

Attempting to speak to those who testified to seeing Abu Sheita, including the shop owner based a few hundred meters away from the massacre site, was in vain. Asking a tribal elder why people were so afraid of speaking to the media or authorities about what they had already testified to during the march, he simply replied: "if the military could not defend itself then they won't defend anyone who testifies."[22]

The tribesman's reference to the military's failure to protect itself was whispered in almost every interview or friendly encounter in Sinai over that period. The Rafah massacre wasn't only shocking because it hit the institution carved in the hearts and minds of the Sinai Bedouins as the savior and protector of their land, but also because the army personnel had failed in their first actual, face-to-face encounter with the militants, who regularly attacked the loathed police apparatus.

According to General Okasha:

Politics aside, the attack was evidence of how depleted the Egyptian military's capabilities had become under the two decades of Tantawi's command. If the whole troop decided to sit down for a meal without securing themselves in the most volatile region in Egypt, then we can guess what sort of training they went through and how they came to behave as if out on a picnic, not serving in the border security department and deployed two kilometers away from the Israeli border.

Meanwhile, on Morsi's return from Sinai, the Ministry of Defense declared the launch of Operation Eagle II on August 12. The number 'II' was added to the name of the operation declared a year earlier after the armed attack on al-Arish's police station that had entailed no military casualties and was soon forgotten by the media and the public. This time, the military pledged to eliminate the militant groups operating in the peninsula, shutting down the tunnels to the Gaza Strip, and bringing back the stability lost since the January 2011 uprising. On the highway stretching from the Suez Canal to the border with Gaza, the military's khaki-colored trailer trucks arrived carrying the American-made M1 Abrams tanks and light tanks, and was followed by dozens of armored personnel carriers transporting hundreds of soldiers to reinforce the already existing troops operating under the command of Egypt's Second Infantry Army and its 101 Battalion located in the center of al-Arish.

Throughout the month after the operation began, the newly appointed official military spokesman, Colonel Ahmed Ali, continued to claim a major victory against the militants in North Sinai's three main towns of al-Arish, Sheikh Zuwayyed, and Rafah, and their surroundings. At the time when raids took place during the day and were led jointly by police and military personnel, Colonel Ali's comments were met by widespread denial from the region's residents who accused the authorities of claiming successful raids that never happened.

At the time, only two successful raids were covered by native reporters who competed to embed with the security entourages so as to be the first to document the military's operations. Ahmed Abu Draa was accompanying a troop of police personnel as they raided a shack built inside a deserted farm in the village of Shibana, south of Rafah. Surrounding the farm and slowly approaching the hut made of wood and palm leaves, the troops were met by a barrage of gunfire to which they reacted by firing their machine guns as they docked down on the sandy ground. Seconds later, an explosion took place inside the shack and destroyed its walls to reveal a burning pick-up truck and the five charred corpses of those who were inside the hut. Meters away from the burning site, one of the militants had crawled out, but after receiving a bullet to the leg he was immediately detained and hauled into one of the armored vehicles. As the fire settled, Abu Draa was able to take photos of the bodies and contents of the militant hideout that turned out to be a bomb-making facility. Glassware used in chemistry labs, including beakers, flasks, and funnels, were found shattered around the corpses as the stench of fertilizers, a main component of homemade explosives, rose from the burning hut.[23]

The second documented successful raid took place in al-Arish when a security force raided a mechanics' workshop and seized two hundred and fifty kilograms of TNT that was stored inside it, in addition to rocket-propelled grenades and machine guns.

Some four weeks after the beginning of Operation Eagle II, the military launched a major raid on the village of al-Muqataa, a well-known stronghold of Islamist militants including al-Tawhid wa-l-Jihad's notorious leader Abu Munir. This time, the power and capabilities of the counter-terrorist operation were put to the test after the embarrassment caused by the death of sixteen soldiers at the border post.

A convoy of armored vehicles and dozens of military and police personnel were mobilized on the morning of September 19, with air cover provided by one gunship, but upon their arrival to the village they were met by machine-gun fire and rocket-propelled grenades, while the gunship was targeted by a 50-caliber machine gun. Failing to counter the heavy attacks coming from different directions and blinded by the helicopter's immediate retreat after being hit, the military convey immediately withdrew to the highway leading back to al-Arish. During the brief exchange of fire, one female and one child were mistakenly shot by stray bullets.

Publicly asserting their control over the village, the armed militants embarked on a counter-attack. Riding several pick-up trucks on which high-caliber machine guns were erected, the masked assailants led a brief attack on Sheikh Zuwayyed's police compound before tracking the security convoy back to al-Arish where they headed directly to the North Sinai Security Directorate. While relentlessly firing their machine guns from the ground, several of the attackers fired RPGs from rooftops of residential blocks standing directly in front of the barricaded security facility, leaving a hole in its façade and a bigger scar on the now-fragile face of Operation Eagle II.[24]

A Return to Oppression

Immediately after the Rafah attack in August 2012 that killed the border guards, the military's announcement of leading Operation Eagle II in Sinai to maintain control was met by unmatched popular support; the majority of the tribal community had been calling for government action to put an end to the rising crime that affected, and sometimes paralyzed, the population's daily lives. Since the January 2011 uprising, the only efforts to counter the lawlessness were led by the sharia courts and independent tribal figures, but they barely affected the ongoing disputes and their intervention was always reactive, taking place after the damage was already done. The community's only condition was to be treated with respect and it vowed never to accept the return of Mubarak's oppressive policies which it had rebelled against.

However, those who had called for the authorities' urgent intervention and return to full activity were the first to announce their extreme disenchantment as they saw the military forces, which they had never opposed, leading the same brutal crackdowns once ordered by Minister of the Interior Habib El-Adly. The only difference was that, this time, the crackdown arrived via tanks and gunships instead of police patrols and light weapons.

Among the first targets of the operation was Kuraiem Abu Rukba, a prominent member of the Rights Retrieving Committee who had hoped the police forces would return so that he could quit his vigilante activities. On September 19, three days after the militant counter-attack on the security department in al-Arish, sixteen armored vehicles accompanied by several military jeeps and dozens of security personnel raided Abu Rukba's village, al-Sadat, located on the outskirts of Rafah, toward the Mediterranean coast. After a cordon was stretched around the village, the impoverished Bedouin residents realized that the whole raid had been mobilized to hunt down the 26-year-old Abu Rukba, who wasn't at his family's house at the time.

"They broke down the house's door and barged in looking for me," said Abu Rukba, sitting some two hundred meters away from Sheikh Zuwayyed main security checkpoint that was most probably still on the lookout for him. "When they realized I wasn't there, they dragged my brother Talab out in his underwear. They even strip-searched the older men and women and humiliated them." During the raid, which lasted almost two hours, the security troops broke into more than a dozen houses and ransacked them.[25]

Confident in his innocence, speaking on the record, and allowing his photo to be taken, Abu Rukba accused the military and police of "relying on false information fed to them by criminals who are hired as informants." Hating him for targeting their drug dealing networks with other sharia-courts vigilantes, Abu Rukba believed that the informants reported him to the police in retaliation. "Now me and my three brothers are on the most wanted list, the younger ones are thirteen and fifteen years old."

"They turned me into a fugitive and now everyone thinks I am the most wanted terrorist," said Abu Rukba. "If we sensed any justice in this military campaign, I would turn myself in immediately. But how do you expect me to cooperate with those who raided my house and humiliated my family in a similar way to Mubarak's police?"

Meanwhile, military spokesman Colonel Ahmed Ali was declaring the outcome of the month-long operation, claiming that the military destroyed thirty-one smuggling tunnels in Rafah, killing thirty-two armed militants, and detaining dozens. In reaction to the statement, a running joke spread across Sinai referring to the spokesman as "al-Sah-haf," after Mohamed Saeed al-Sahhaf, Saddam Hussein's information minister who led a misinformation and propaganda campaign via Iraqi national television before and during the 2003 US invasion.

At the time, only twelve corpses were accounted for in North Sinai: the five found inside the explosives lab targeted in the village of Shibana, and the seven bodies received from Israel at Kerem Shalom terminal more than a week after the Rafah attack and transported to the central hospital in al-Arish.

"This is a very tight-knit tribal community; when a fight breaks out between two people in Rafah, people in Sharm al-Sheikh (some three hundred kilometers away) know about it as it's happening," said Ibrahim Abu Ashraf al-Menaei, of the Sawarka tribe, who is head of the independent Sinai Tribes Association. "Saying that twenty people were killed without anyone witnessing operations and clashes, without hearing from their Bedouin relatives, or witnessing their burial is simply a lie by the regime in an attempt to contain their scandalous failure."[26]

As for the thirty-one destroyed tunnels, almost each one of them was hastily reopened after Operation Eagle II was partially interrupted by the rising complaints of Israeli military officials who saw the build up as a threat to the demilitarization conditions deemed as the core of the Camp David Peace Accords. These complaints, also conveyed by the White House, forced Egypt to pull out the majority of the tanks and armored machinery deployed in the border town of Rafah, days after their arrival, while the raids continued in the villages. And as Egyptian military analysts defended the withdrawal and claimed that it was triggered by the inefficiency of tanks in the ongoing pursuit that requires lighter vehicles, Sinai's Bedouins were anticipating the failure of the operation and mockingly saying that the "Eagle" is gradually turning into a chicken.

"The authorities will never be able to maintain security without trusting and gaining the trust of citizens. They should know that imitating the former regime, attacking homes and detaining innocent civilians, is not the way to gain that trust," said Abu Ashraf at his house in al-Mehdiya, which the military tagged as a stronghold of Islamist militants, but did not approach throughout the operation that lasted a bit more than a month. He and others believed that the village was next to be raided after al-Muqataa, but the security's embarrassing retreat after falling under militant fire hindered the plan.

Who Killed the Soldiers?

The Mujahedeen Shura Council in the Environs of Jerusalem were the first to publish a statement denying any responsibility for the Rafah massacre; their statement was published on various online jihadist forums less than twenty-four hours after the attack. "We don't have any relation, near or far, with the attack that targeted the Egyptian army on the border with occupied Palestine on August 5, 2012," said the statement in which the group criticized media outlets for accusing them "and other jihadist organizations operating against the Jews, despite having no evidence except what was said by the spokesman of the Zionist army Avichai Adraee."

> We condemn the calls for an unjust campaign against the truthful Mujahedeen, who proved that their main goal is to fight the Jewish aggressors, while the whole world witnessed how we avoided the Egyptian military when attacking the Jewish forces in the Battle of Triumph for Jerusalem and The Prisoners on June 18, 2012 [the cross-border attack which left one Israeli killed and several injured]." [27]

The MSC statement was the first of several publications detailing the ideological background and the strategies of its operations, all of which stressed and repeated that the organization was strictly involved in the Palestinian–Israeli conflict and that its weapons would never target any of the Arab regimes no matter how the group viewed them. The string of statements, described by many as an operational manual for the members and whoever was willing to join, contradicted the first declaration that announced their establishment and was read by the masked, arms-wielding speaker on June 19, 2012. But nothing was more telling than statement number 19, published on October 10, 2012, which revealed that the group had undergone an ideological conflict between the broad Salafi–jihadist current that was willing to spread its operations against targets beyond Israel, and the domestic Palestinian struggle that aimed to avoid any confrontations with Egypt and other Arab regimes. This conflict, which clearly began during the early phases of establishing the group, ended in favor of the latter.

> We are a Salafi–jihadist current . . . our method is following the Quran and Sunna through the understanding of the ancestors of the nation, we do not permit the [shedding of] blood of Muslims and do not excommunicate them," said the MSC's statement 19. "We have a solid and unchangeable stance from every system or ideology that contradicts the Islamic sharia, such as democracy, nationalism, and the manmade laws. . . our stance from the formerly mentioned wrongful methods does not require excommunication or battling who adopted them, but we criticize them and peacefully call them to return to the religion of Allah . . . our spears are only pointed to the Jewish enemy."[28]

While the MSC continued to distance itself from Egypt's domestic events, another statement was published by a group named al-Salafiya al-Jihadiya fi Sina, or the "Sinai Salafi–jihadist Group," claiming that the counter-attack against the security forces in the village of al-Muqataa was a popular reaction of youth enraged by the violations committed against innocent civilians. The statement continued denying any attacks on the security directorate in al-Arish and accusing the military spokesman of fabricating events and blaming it on the jihadist current.

"For the second time, we stress that the military and police forces are not our target and that our weapons are pointed only to the Zionist enemy except when we are forced to defend ourselves, our families, and our dignity." The evidence for this claim, the statement said, "is that the youth only forced the security convoy to retreat and if they had wanted to eliminate it, they would have. One of the commanders of the security raid, a Major, and we refrain from mentioning his name, was detained by the youth along with his car and two soldiers. They were capable of killing him, but rather they informed him that the military is pointing its weapons in the wrong direction and that the army personnel are not the target of the mujahedeen, they finally released him along with his vehicle and soldiers."[29]

The only group that never published a statement commenting on the attack was Ansar Bayt al-Maqdis, the most active in North Sinai and the one bearing the most lethal record of operations since 2011. Despite their silence, the group declared where it stood by sending clear messages through further operations. On August 31, Bedouins from Rafah found a severed head placed on an intersection of roads leading to the villages, while others found the headless corpse some thirty kilometers away. Hours after the grim news traveled across the peninsula, Ansar Bayt al-Maqdis published a statement taking responsibility for the gruesome murder and naming the beheaded man, Muneizel Mohamed Salama.

The group's statement declared that it beheaded Salama after exposing his involvement in a Mossad operation that successfully assassinated one of their leading commanders, Ibrahim Oweidha Bereikat, on August 26, after taking part in the second Eilat shooting planned and executed by the group days earlier, an attack that left one Israeli soldier killed and another injured. The group claimed that Salama, along with two other Bedouins, were recruited by the Israeli intelligence agency to track down Bereikat and plant a landmine that successfully killed him on his way out of his border village of Khreiza. The group added that Salama's partner, Soliman Hamdan, was turned in by his tribe after admitting to his crime and was killed by Bereikat's relatives in retaliation, while the third, Salama al-Oweida, managed to flee into Israel.

The brutal beheading happened less than two weeks after militants assassinated Sheikh Khalaf al-Menaei, a prominent member of the Sawarka tribe, along with his son Mohamed, one day after he held a massive tribal summit in Rafah to announce endorsing the military campaign declared by the Ministry of Defense. The brutal killings committed in brazen violation of tribal conduct were a direct threat to the whole community that was silenced by the fact that the radical militants operated with impunity.

Months after the operation, Abu Arrab al-Sawarka said that Ansar Bayt al-Maqdis was responsible for the attack, but refused to give any further details.[30] Reaching out to several other sources to fill in the blanks, Mohamed al-Filistini confirmed Abu Arrab's tip, adding that the "full details of the Rafah attack are only known by the Gazan Popular

Resistance Committees (PRCs); they were the first incubator of ABM during its early phases in 2011 when it began as a Sinai-based, covert cell targeting the gas pipeline and Israeli border patrols."[31]

Majlis Shura al-Mujahedeen came to be controlled by Palestinians who successfully marginalized the *takfiri* current to avoid embroiling the whole movement in attacks against Egyptian authorities or in a local feud with Hamas similar to the 2009 case of Abu al-Nour al-Maqdisi. However, ABM was overrun by Sinai Bedouins who harbored decades of animosity and were more inclined to excommunicate and wage war against the Egyptian authorities they viewed as infidels and servants of Israel.

"Some of the attackers did come from Gaza, and the remaining elements that weren't in the commandeered armored vehicle that drove into Karm Abu Salem fled back into the Strip through the tunnels," said al-Filistini of the Rafah attack. "The killing of the soldiers wasn't part of the plan, though."

Al-Filistini says that the group's plan was to commandeer the weapons of the soldiers and the armored vehicles that they would then drive into Israel to execute the main attack which would be immediately perceived as an Egyptian military attack. "Something went wrong, some of the soldiers tried pulling their weapons on the militants, which triggered the shooting in which the sixteen soldiers were killed."

The remarks by al-Filistini, who has solid connections with many of the Palestinian armed factions in the Gaza Strip, tied in with Ibrahim al-Menaei's claim that the "soldier who was in shock later told me that the attackers kidnapped one soldier with them inside the armored vehicle." This suggested that the militants didn't barge in shooting, but began the killing spree shortly after their arrival.

"Hamas could have led Egypt to the details of this attack, but they didn't, or did and Egypt never declared the details," added al-Filistini, who confirmed that Hamas did capture the wounded 22-year-old Ahmed Sayyed Ismail, the PRCs member who survived the Israeli drone strike in Gaza hours before the attack. "ABM never commented on this attack because they understood that the tribes would have immediately waged war against them. Back then, the community continued to have hope in the military that they viewed as Sinai's savior."

"It was too early for ABM to publicly excommunicate and allow the killing of Egyptian Muslims," added al-Filistini, whose assessment was proven to be right throughout the year of Morsi's rule and after his ouster.

8

MORSI AND AL-SISI: A BATTLE IN SINAI

Immediately after the Rafah attack on border guards in August 2012, almost every prominent figure of Egypt's anti-Brotherhood media rushed to accuse the organization and its Gaza branch, Hamas, of perpetrating the unprecedented massacre. Various official statements made by Hamas's spokesmen and top figures denying any responsibility for the attack were in vain, and on Egyptian television channels former military officers, who occupied a great proportion of airtime as commentators and analysts on security matters, called on the Egyptian military to shutdown the smuggling tunnels and bomb the Gaza Strip if required. These belligerent calls were met by utter disgust not only from Egypt's Islamist factions, but also revolutionary, leftist, and liberal powers who had publicly staged protests across Egypt in support of the Palestinian factions and people since the Second Intifada in 2001.

Hamas's reaction to the rising hostility was blunt. "We fear an explosion in Gaza if the blockade and demolishing of tunnels is continued," said Youssef Farahat, a leading member of the movement,[1] while Ismaiel Haniyeh conditioned the shutdown of the tunnels on the opening of the terminals.[2] The statements demonstrated how emboldened the movement had become by the arrival of its mother organization, the Muslim Brotherhood, at the presidency of Egypt. Further complicating the situation, the Islamist movement refused to cooperate with the Egyptian authorities, especially the military whose relations with the ruling Brotherhood were already deteriorating, in their demands for the extradition of several people based in Gaza and suspected for their possible connection to the attack.[3]

As for Israel, despite sustaining no casualties in the attack, it succeeded in handling it efficiently by killing the militants. Official spokesman for the IDF, Lt. Colonel Peter Lerner, described the incident as an "unprecedented development in the militant activities along the Sinai border, an attack that led the Israeli military to apply newer measures to the border security operations across the country, not only the border with Sinai."[4] But like Egypt's authorities, no government official accused Hamas of being part of the Rafah attack, or any other that took place in the Sinai Peninsula since the downfall of Hosni Mubarak.

Israel's major concern was Hamas's intentional policy of ignoring the jihadist movements of southern Gaza that began operating in the Sinai Peninsula immediately after the downfall of Mubarak's regime in 2011. Since then, Hamas viewed the political and security transformation taking place in Egypt as an opportunity to neutralize its relations with the jihadist opposition by allowing their free movement across the border, a plan with which the movement successfully avoided Israel's deadly retaliation for the continued attacks as they were launched from locations outside of the Gaza strip. However, this simultaneously led to a drastic deterioration in their relations with the Egyptian military and intelligence agencies.

"Involved is a big word; they didn't take the necessary measures to prevent the attack," Yossi Kuperwasser, director general of Israel's Ministry for Strategic Affairs, said from his office in Jerusalem. "Sometimes they have control over the tunnels, and sometimes they don't—maybe its incompetence or more of turning a blind eye."[5]

Further to Kuperwasser's claims, the deputy chairman of Hamas's Political Bureau, Mousa Abu Marzouk, who between 2011 and 2013 resided in a fortified villa swarming with Hamas operatives a few blocks away from President Morsi's residence in eastern Cairo, said that his movement "does not have full control over the border area; the control is fairly good west of the Rafah crossing terminal, but there is no control to the east due to Israel's continuous attacks on any security forces in the areas closer to Karm Abu Salem."[6]

Hamas's demand of Egypt that the smuggling tunnels be left untouched had been fulfilled not only by the military campaign's withdrawal from Rafah after Israel's official complaints to Egypt about the troop build-up in Sinai, but by Morsi's decision in September 2012 to curb the security crackdown in North Sinai and delegate a group of

Islamist figures to kick-start a dialogue with the peninsula's Salafi–jihad-ist groups and to investigate the attack.

A Morsi-Brokered Truce

Morsi's delegation, which he hand-picked to exclude members of his political rivals the Salafi al-Nour Party, was represented by Magdi Salem and Nizar Ghorab, the two prominent lawyers of Egypt's jailed Islamists and former members of Islamic Jihad, who had themselves spent almost two decades in prison over their alleged involvement in militant activities.[7]

Upon their arrival in North Sinai in a lavish entourage of Mercedes sedans bearing government license plates, the lawyers, who were accompanied by thirteen other undisclosed figures, held a meeting with several Sinai-based jihadists in al-Bahr district of Sheikh Zuwayyed. Sharia judge Hamdin Abu Faisal, who attended the meeting, said that "Fifty Sinai-based Islamist figures participated in the convention that wasn't meant to amend the ideological perceptions of the peninsula's Islamist current, which was the first to condemn the attack."[8]

Meanwhile, Magdi Salem told the local press that "the Sinai Salafi–jihadist current confirmed that it had no connection to the attack," and added that the delegation will lead more visits to Sinai in order to "open a new page and bring the Salafi–jihadist current and the political leadership closer." As for Nizar Ghorab, he demanded that the state "refer those responsible for the attack to a fair trial and to limit the military operations by the legal system."[9]

What neither Abu Faisal nor the Islamist lawyers mentioned at the time was a second, secret, meeting held in the village of al-Muqataa, the shared stronghold of al-Tawhid wa-l-Jihad and Ansar Bayt al-Maqdis, which was attended by Shadi al-Menaei and several other hardcore militant figures. And, like the first one, the identities of all those involved were never made public, and neither were the details of the alleged evidence proving the innocence of the Sinai-based militant jihadists. But upon the return of the delegation to Cairo, the sharia court head Abu Faisal made a shocking statement saying that "Sinai's Salafi–jihadist current will suspend all operations against the Zionist entity in order not to embarrass President Morsi, in return they expect the suspension of the military operations that randomly detains both the guilty and innocent."[10]

Casting major doubts on the effectiveness of Morsi's truce-seeking delegation that legitimized Sinai's militant groups by bringing them to official negotiations, Abu Faisal's statement was rejected by Abu Hamza al-Masry, a Sinai Saladist-jihadist cleric, saying that the attacks against Israel will not stop and that "denying responsibility for the Rafah attack doesn't mean that the Salafi–jihadist current will give up its sharia-based principles and certainly doesn't mean signing any agreements that will limit its operations by a state-pleasing framework."[11]

Meeting with Magdi Salem, the speaker of the delegation, several months later in his Cairo office, it became clear that the delegation was in fact leading a baseless, evidence-deficient campaign to defend the armed militants against any suspicions, while using the attack as a weapon against the Muslim Brotherhood's and Hamas's political detractors. "I personally investigated the attack and met with many Islamist figures in Sinai; my conclusion was that Mohamed Dahlan's footprints were all over it. He has many agents in Sinai and there is no doubt he was behind the attack," said Salem, blaming the massacre on Hamas's most loathed rival and former head of Fatah's Preventative Security Department that ruled the Strip before its takeover in 2007. Voluntarily and without revealing any of the alleged evidence he gathered, Salem added: "we are not trying to conceal any truths, but Sinai's Islamist current is innocent of this attack."[12]

Asking why the Egyptian authorities and President Morsi never revealed such information despite their repeated pledges to expose the terrorists, Salem said that "Dahlan's involvement along with an intelligence agency of an Arab country might have complicated the matter and accordingly the presidency decided not to reveal its details."

Referring to the United Arab Emirates as the "Arab country," where Dahlan lives and serves as an advisor to the UAE's crown prince Mohamed Bin Zayed al-Nahyan,[13] Salem continued to defend Hamas, although he admitted that Sinai had become a safe haven for Islamist armed militants. "Hamas has no involvement whatsoever in Sinai's repeated attacks, but Gaza's jihadist currents are more likely to cross the tunnels and run operations from Sinai."

Morsi's policy at the time was undefined: neither the presidency, the government, nor the Muslim Brotherhood had declared if the delegation was tasked with brokering a ceasefire with Sinai's jihadist groups, if it was threatening them, or if it was appeasing them with promises of integration within the larger political and social system. In any case, the presidential initiative didn't only prove to be an utter failure, but also a total defeat for Egypt's military and police who stopped Operation Eagle II and submitted to the Muslim Brotherhood presidency driven by its own interests and whatever terms the jihadists had dictated during the secretive meetings before limiting their militant operations. Furthermore, neither the presidency nor the security authorities were given any guarantees that such an agreement would stand.

It wasn't until June 2014 that former US Secretary of State Hillary Clinton published her book *Hard Choices* and shed some light on Morsi's perception of the growing threat in Sinai. During a meeting in July 2012, weeks before the Rafah attack, Clinton said the Muslim Brotherhood's elected president told her not to worry about Sinai's jihadists because they wouldn't feel the need to continue their militant campaign after the Brotherhood's arrival at power. In her book, Clinton described Morsi's view of the situation as "either shockingly sinister or shockingly naïve."[14] Two months after *Hard Choices* was published, in August 2014, *The Atlantic*'s veteran foreign-affairs reporter Jeffery Goldberg asked Clinton what she wasn't sure of at the time of her meeting with Morsi: was it sinister or naïve?

> I think Morsi was naïve. I'm just talking about Morsi, not necessarily anyone else in the Muslim Brotherhood. I think he genuinely believed that with the legitimacy of an elected Islamist government, the jihadists would see that there was a different route to power and influence and would be part of the political process. He had every hope, in fact, that the credible election of a Muslim Brotherhood government would mean the end of jihadist activities within Egypt, and also exemplify that there's a different way to power. . . . The debate is between the bin Ladens of the world and the Muslim Brotherhood. The bin Ladens believe you can't overthrow the infidels or the impure through politics. It has to be through violent resistance. So when I made the case to Morsi that we were picking up a lot of intelligence about jihadist groups creating safe havens inside Sinai, and that this would be a threat not only to Israel but to Egypt, he just dismissed this out of hand, and then shortly thereafter a large group of Egyptian soldiers were murdered.[15]

Further to Clinton's testimony, several former Egyptian Islamists, especially the adherents of the ideological recantations renouncing violence, agreed that Morsi was naïve or rather too innocent to handle the complicated situation, but others in the Muslim Brotherhood leadership certainly weren't. "Khairat al-Shater [deputy head of the Muslim Brotherhood] saw the militant jihadists as a weapon that would be used against their opponents; they decided to outsource the violent activities to other groups instead of doing it themselves," said Nageh Ibrahim, the al-Jamaa al-Islamiya co-founder and military commander who had preached the ideological recantations since 1997.[16]

To the ruling Muslim Brotherhood organization, headed by extremist Qutbi Islamists the Supreme Guide Mohamed Badie and his deputy and strategist al-Shater, there was no "Bin Ladens vs. Muslim Brotherhood" as Clinton put it, but rather an ambitious goal of imposing authority over Egypt. Through this project that would recognize and deal with whoever served it, even if it was militant *takfiri*s, the Brotherhood's approach to Egypt was very similar to Hamas's in the Gaza Strip, who were in full partnership with the Salafi–jihadist and al-Qaeda aligned groups, although relations with the more radical groups began deteriorating when they ran in and won the 2005 elections. A vivid example of the ongoing cooperation was their joint operation with Jaish al-Islam, one of Hamas's top detractors, in abducting Israeli corporal Gilad Shalit in 2006. What the Muslim Brotherhood failed to understand was that Gaza's scenario, despite it being led by their most powerful offshoot, was simply impossible to apply in Egypt.

According to Ahmed Ban, the defected Muslim Brotherhood member,

> Egypt is not Gaza, the Muslim Brotherhood doesn't own and run the military institution like Hamas runs the Qassam Brigades. But they used the same tactics with militant groups: we will give you the freedom to operate as long as you don't threaten our bigger project and we might crackdown on you if you do.[17]

Ban wasn't the only prominent researcher of Islamist movements to stress the blurriness of the alleged line separating the Muslim Brotherhood and other extremist and militant groups, ideologically or operationally. One year before Egypt's revolution, in 2010, renowned scholar Hossam Tamam wrote:

The Muslim Brotherhood's stance on violence is decided by their stance on politics and how deep is their political involvement. . . . The Muslim Brotherhood dosn't reject the idea of armed jihad, either against the occupation or the non-Muslim state, but they never get personally involved in this jihad and prefer that others carry it out. For this reason, when the jihad movement began against the Soviet occupation of Afghanistan, the Brotherhood decided, after major conflicts, to refrain from delving into military efforts and stopped at logistical and financial support.[18]

What the Muslim Brotherhood failed to accurately assess was how capable they were of striking an agreement with puritanical *takfiris*, who viewed the Brotherhood and Hamas as pragmatic politicians at best, but more often as hypocrites and infidels who failed to apply Islamic sharia and accepted the manmade legislature.

Who Rules Sinai?

After the Islamist delegation's return from North Sinai, several Coptic Christian families who had lived in Rafah for decades started receiving death threats that forced them to flee the border town and remain temporarily in al-Arish. The whole matter was said to have been started by a personal dispute between a Coptic shop owner and his Bedouin neighbor, after which his shop fell under heavy machine-gun fire and leaflets were found all around town urging Copts to leave or risk being killed. At the time, the sharia courts, which regularly claimed to be seeking justice and serving Muslims and Copts alike, did not interfere to protect the threatened families and neither did the authorities. Despite statements of condemnation made by the Coptic Church of al-Arish and the National Human Rights Council, Prime Minister Hisham Kandil brushed off the whole incident and claimed that "some of the families willingly left Rafah" as he ordered the authorities to provide the required security for anyone facing threats.[19]

Days after the Rafah incident, on October 5, 2012, President Morsi paid his third visit to the volatile region in two months, one day prior to the thirty-ninth anniversary of Egypt's 1973 war with Israel. Further proving the failure of the state's control over the border regions of the peninsula, the president limited his visit only to fortified al-Arish and failed to fulfill his promises of visiting the border town of

Rafah due to the deteriorating security situation. Furthermore, in an attempt to absorb the anger of representatives of Sinai's Bedouin tribes who attended his speech held at the governorate headquarters, Morsi declared that "every sentence in absentia formerly issued against Sinai residents will be revised," a pledge he never fulfilled. He added that he hadn't signed off on the death sentences issued for the suspected elements in the July 2011 attack on al-Arish's police station, which were declared by the criminal court hastily after the Rafah attacks in August 2012. The statement, cheered by the audience in al-Arish, echoed differently in Cairo, where the justice ministry considered the statement a clear challenge to the authority of judges, further revealing the rift between the presidency and the state institutions.[20]

Meanwhile, a similar version of the Muslim Brotherhood's approach to the Sinai-based jihadists, which rarely received adequate media coverage or popular interest, was happening in the capital. On October 6, 2012, President Morsi ordered the 1973 victory celebration to be held at eastern Cairo's soccer stadium with an audience of around 70,000 people. Hours before the country's most important annual celebration began, Morsi met with the wife of assassinated President Sadat, Jihan al-Sadat, to inform her that he had granted Egypt's highest medals to the late president and several army commanders who served under his command during the war in 1973.

But as the celebration began in the stadium, located a few hundred meters from where President Sadat was assassinated in 1981, it turned out to be an insult to Egypt's military institution and the tens of thousands of soldiers that sacrificed their lives during the fourteen years of full or partial war with Israel. Morsi entered the stadium on a presidential vehicle, alleged to be the same one Sadat rode during the same celebration decades ago, to a cheering crowd of tens of thousands of his supporters waving the flags of Egypt, the Muslim Brotherhood, and its Freedom and Justice Party. Shamelessly, Tarek al-Zomor, al-Jamaa al-Islamiya's top officer who was sentenced to twenty-five years in jail in 1982 for taking part in the assassination of Sadat, sat among the audience. Needless to say, former Defense Minister Tantawi and former chief of staff Anan, who were sacked weeks before the celebration, weren't among the audience, and neither were hundreds of veteran military personnel who had been the celebration's guests of honor over the past thirty-nine years.

"I wasn't invited but the killers were," said General Okasha, who was leader of a squadron of jet fighters throughout Egypt's active war with Israel between 1967 and 1973.

During his speech, that continued for almost two hours, Morsi claimed to have succeeded in applying unprecedented reforms in various political and economic fields, and, as if inviting convicted militants wasn't enough, he equated the transfer of power from the Supreme Council of the Armed Forces to him through the June 2012 elections to Egypt's military triumph in 1973, leaving Egyptians wondering if he was referring to the military generals as defeated enemies.[21]

The clear animosity between the Muslim Brotherhood-controlled presidency and the military institution, as shown by this celebration, continued to prevail on the ground in Sinai, even under the command of Defense Minister Abdel-Fattah al-Sisi, who had been hand-picked by Morsi.

Four weeks after the stadium fiasco, in November 2012, Prime Minister Kandil announced the passing of new landownership laws for Sinai, to put an end to six decades of depriving the peninsula's population of their rights to register the ownership of their land, farms, and real estate.[22] The new law, which limited the certification process to those who could provide proof of citizenship for themselves and their parents, and excluded those who were dual nationals, was welcomed by the majority of Sinai's mainly Bedouin community.[23] However, in a clear challenge to the decree passed by Morsi's cabinet, Defense Minister al-Sisi passed his own, independent military law in December 2012,[24] banning all transactions, sale, purchase, farming, or construction, in areas of military jurisdiction and the five kilometers lining the border with Israel. The only exception indicated by the military law was the already existing residential area of Rafah and, even there, ownership was only allowed for already existing property, but not for the land on which it was built.[25]

Days after both laws were passed, the residents of Sinai realized that nothing had changed on the ground as the ministries of defense, interior, and General Intelligence, whose approval was required before any transactions would be certified, continued to impose severe conditions the people couldn't meet. The most important of these was providing evidence of parents holding only Egyptian citizenship, a condition impossible to fulfill by the Bedouin community whose older generations had lived until the 2000s without registering births or marriages, or even obtaining national ID cards.

The conflicting messages delivered to the population of Sinai by both the presidency and the military was a major disappointment for some half a million people who hoped that their marginalization and treatment as second-class citizens would end with the arrival of an elected president following a revolution that supposedly aimed to turn the page on decades of oppression.

"Morsi will lose the support of Sinai's Bedouin tribes if he doesn't fulfill the promises he gave us," said Ibrahim Abu Ashraf al-Menaei. Criticizing Morsi as weak and indecisive, he continued that his top priority should be

> declaring that we are fully recognized Egyptian citizens by immediately allowing us to unconditionally own our lands and houses that we died defending for years. If Morsi cannot apply a landownership law and won't drop the hundreds of unjust sentences we received over the years, like the Islamists he pardoned, then he should realize that Sinai's Bedouins will view him as another Mubarak.

The 2012 Gaza War

On November 14, 2012, an Israeli airforce strike killed the Qassam Brigades' military commander Ahmed al-Jaabari, whose last public appearance was in 2011 at the Rafah Crossing Terminal as he walked Gilad Shalit to the Egyptian side after six years of captivity in the Gaza Strip. The assassination of Gaza's strongman, who had survived various Israeli attempts to eliminate him over several years, was the beginning of what Israel dubbed Operation Pillar of Defense. This vicious bombardment began with the killing of al-Jaabari and continued for one week, before a ceasefire was brokered by President Morsi. During this war, Hamas, for the first time in its history, fired its long-range missiles at Tel Aviv. (Reflective of how far the Gaza Strip and Hamas depend on Sinai, al-Jaabari was killed while driving a 2012 Kia Cerato brought from Egypt through the smuggling tunnels.)

As soon as the war started, President Morsi recalled Egypt's ambassador from Tel Aviv and ordered the full opening of the Rafah Crossing Terminal, offering full assistance to victims of the war. Hours later, Morsi made a public speech, broadcast by Egypt's state-owned television on

November 16, in which he harshly condemned the devastating attacks on Gaza, referring to Israel as the "enemy" and "aggressor," while wagging his finger and pledging that "Gaza and its people are not alone," and threatening a "people and leadership's anger that Israel would not be able to face."[26]

Morsi's political intervention was accompanied by facilitating the arrival of dozens of Egyptian doctors and tons of medical supplies in Gaza through the Rafah Terminal less than twenty-four hours after the war started and an official visit by Prime Minister Kandil, who made a public speech in front of Gaza's al-Shifa hospital despite the ongoing Israeli shelling. This was met by fierce condemnation across Egypt as the cabinet had previously failed to take any real action following a road accident involving a school bus that killed fifty-one children in Upper Egypt's Asyut governorate on November 17, the third day of the war in Gaza. The Muslim Brotherhood regime's interest in what happened beyond the eastern border and its rushing to defend their powerful offshoot Hamas, contrasted with the reaction to the deadly crash by various government officials, including Prime Minister Kandil, who blamed it on decades of corruption and incompetence left by the former regime of Hosni Mubarak. Morsi's only mention of the horrific accident was in a one-minute speech during which he ordered the prosecution and punishment of everyone responsible.[27]

The attack on Morsi's regime intensified after Sameh Seif al-Yazal, a former intelligence officer and co-owner of one of the region's most powerful security companies, known for his close ties with Egypt's military institution, made a controversial statement on Egypt's widely viewed CBC satellite channel claiming that the government authorities began erecting shelters for Gazan refugees in the Sinai towns of Rafah and Sheikh Zuwayyed. "If the Palestinians enter Sinai, they will never leave. It will be similar to Jordan and Lebanon."[28]

Al-Yazal's statements were fueled by the Egyptian, and especially the Sinai Bedouin, obsession with an alleged Israeli plan to diffuse its ongoing war with Palestine by expanding the Gaza Strip into a portion of Sinai that extends for almost fifty kilometers between the border town of Rafah and east of al-Arish. This conspiracy theory was rooted in a research paper written in September 2008 by retired Major-General Giora Eiland, who served as head of the Israeli National Security Council from 2004 to 2006, and was widely reported on in Egyptian and Palestinian media outlets and online forums. The paper published by the Washington Institute for Near East Policy (WINEP) and titled "Rethinking the Two-State Solution," proposed a land swap between Egypt and Israel through which Gaza would be expanded into the formerly mentioned area and allowed to build a sea and airport while enjoying sovereignty over the territory, and in return Egypt would be granted a part of the Negev Desert along its borders with Israel.[29]

Eiland's proposal apparently wasn't viewed as absurd by all Israelis as it was preceded by statements made by Ashkenazi Chief Rabbi Yona Metzger, in which he called for establishing a Palestinian state in the Sinai desert. At the time, Israel's top-selling newspaper *Haaretz* reported that "Metzger called for Britain, the European Union, and the United States to assist in the construction of a Palestinian state in the Sinai Desert."[30]

Following al-Yazal's statement, various government officials rushed to deny building any shelters and accused the mainstream media of spreading false news, but the reaction of Sinai's tribal kingpins was more practical. "I will send my sons and their cousins to burn those shelters if they ever found them," said Abu Ashraf al-Menaei, pointing at two of his sons sitting in front him at his house in the village of al-Mehdiya. "The only way to resettle Gazans in Sinai is to kill us first."

Further to al-Menaei's claims, the leftist al-Karama Party's representative in North Sinai, Khaled Arafat, told the daily *al-Watan* newspaper that "what the west [Europe and the US] failed to do is now being accomplished by the Muslim Brotherhood. The ruling authorities proposed this plan to several of Sinai's figures and we told them that 400,000 Bedouins would not allow this conspiracy and will stand in defense of Rafah. This plan is the beginning of real treason." Emad al-Bolok, the North Sinai coordinator of the Popular Current, a coalition of leftist and revolutionary movements established by former presidential candidate Hamdin Sabbahi, told the same paper that "the Muslim Brotherhood intends to give Hamas a portion of Sinai, an act that comes within the ideological framework of the organization that doesn't believe in borders between Muslim countries."[31]

In Jerusalem and Tel Aviv, several Israeli government officials stressed that Giora Eiland's proposal, which continues to fuel the ongoing controversy, doesn't in any way represent the Israeli government, while other sources speaking on condition of anonymity bluntly wondered why Egypt is so opposed to the idea of allowing Gaza to use facilities on Egyptian soil to relieve itself from the imposed blockade, such as an al-Arish air and seaport.[32] Such comments were very reminiscent of Ariel Sharon's ambitious plan of shifting the responsibility for the Gaza Strip to Egypt after the unilateral disengagement in 2005 and the beginning of the blockade.

As if President Morsi wasn't facing enough condemnation over his stance on the war in Gaza, the Muslim Brotherhood's Supreme Guide Mohamed Badie made further explosive comments during a lecture at a famous Cairo mosque, saying "I don't see any problem in hosting Palestinian refugees in Sinai, there are hundreds of refugee camps in Jordan and Lebanon."[33]

In spite of the fact that no refugee shelters were built in Sinai's border areas and the whole matter was never anything more than an exaggerated media claim met by extremely unwise Muslim Brotherhood statements, the situation worsened further as members of the Brotherhood-dominated constitution-drafting assembly proposed an article granting the president the right to amend the country's territorial borders after the agreement of the majority of the lower and upper parliament houses, an easy-to-fulfill condition with Islamist dominated legislative authorities.

Article 153 of the controversial constitution draft read:

> The President of the Republic represents the State in its international relations. The President ratifies treaties after taking the approval of the cabinet. A treaty does not have the force of law except after the approval of the House of Representatives and the Senate. The majority of the members of both the House of Representatives and the Senate shall approve the treaties of peace, alliance, trade, navigation, and all treaties that lead to amendment of the territory of the State or concerning the rights of sovereignty or bearing the State's treasury expenditures that are not provided for in the budget. [34]

It was later amended after triggering nationwide accusations against the Muslim Brotherhood of harboring intentions to compromise not only Egypt's sovereignty in the Sinai Peninsula, but also in the disputed region of Halayeb and Shalatin on the border with Sudan, the southern neighbor ruled by a Muslim Brotherhood affiliate, Omar Hassan al-Bashir.

Such concerns continued to rise throughout Morsi's remaining months in power, especially after his official visit to the Sudanese capital Khartoum in April 2013, when an audio recording circulated on various media outlets showing Sudanese Minister of the Environment Hussein Abdel-Qader Helal saying that "President Morsi showed willingness to return Halayeb and Shalatin to Sudan." The shocking statement allegedly triggered Defense Minister Abdel-Fattah al-Sisi to delegate chief of staff General Sobhi Sedki on an official visit to Sudan. Sedki's visit was followed by repeated military statements to the local media saying that the disputed region is fully Egyptian and there will be no compromise over it.[35]

More than a year after Morsi's ouster, further statements made by Palestinian president Mahmoud Abbas claimed that the Muslim Brotherhood president seemed to have had no objection to the idea of resettling the population of Gaza inside Egypt. "He told me, 'how many are they [Gaza's population], 1.5 million, we will put them in [the Cairo district of] Shubra,'" said Abbas in a televised interview on Egypt's CBC satellite channel.

Although the Muslim Brotherhood and President Mohamed Morsi took no actual steps toward resettling Gaza's population in the Sinai, or surrendering any of the disputed southern territories to Sudan, the Islamist regime's actions, such as the proposed constitutional amendments, and statements by its leading figures rekindled the decades-old fears of Egyptians and gave their detractors further opportunities to intensify their attacks at a time when the regime's popularity was already sinking.

Sinai Goes Against Morsi

The Bedouin tribes of Sinai, despite promising their support to President Morsi in meetings held with their representatives in al-Arish and the capital Cairo, began to express their disillusionment after months of waiting for their demands of reform and integration to be fulfilled. The presidential promises—the most important of which were retrials and pardons for hundreds of Bedouins unjustly sentenced under Mubarak, allowing landownership, and applying peninsula-wide economic reforms—were never fulfilled at a time when the Muslim Brotherhood regime was sparing no effort to support Hamas by hosting the reconstruction summit held after the 2012 war.

During the last week of March 2013, the tribes of Sinai announced a summit to be held at the Valley of Firan, in the mountainous south, to voice their opposition and criticism of the regime. On April 5, the massive summit tent was erected some fifty kilometers into the valley, deep in the territory of the southern al-Gararsha tribe. Before the Friday noon prayer, dozens of Bedouin leaders, representing every tribe in the peninsula, arrived in their four-wheel drives and pick-up trucks, and included those who had met with Morsi three months earlier at the presidential palace in Cairo. Driving for hundreds of kilometers to attend the summit, the prominent tribesmen were sending a clear message to the regime, while political and security officials, even those of the governorate of South Sinai where the summit was being held, were nowhere to be seen.

According to Masaad Abu Fajr, prominent Sinai activist and al-Remeilat tribe descendant who was jailed under Mubarak:

> We will never concede to being anything less than fully recognized citizens that partake in the administration, development, and building the future of Egypt. We have proven ourselves throughout the wars and the revolution and now is the time for change. If reforms aren't implemented immediately, we will fight the government through every peaceful means. We will force the government into fulfilling our rightful demands if they continue to turn a blind eye to our misery after our historically documented struggle.[36]

Abu Fajr's statements came after those of Sheikh Ahmed al-Herish, a powerful leader of al-Gararsha tribe that hosted the summit on his tribe's territory after mediating the safe release of kidnapped tourists three times since the 2011 uprising. Pounding the table in front of him, al-Herish yelled through the microphone, accusing Morsi's government of "failing to apply any reforms and marginalizing the Sinai as much as Mubarak did for three decades."[37]

The speeches of al-Herish and Abu Fajr, who were referred to usually as 'politicians,' drew smirks on the faces of other tribesmen known in Sinai as 'militarists,' who attended the conference out of respect for the tribes, but made it clear that it would have no effect whatsoever on the worsening relations between the community and the state. Despite the significant distance between the two poles of the revered tribal leadership, both seemed to fully agree on giving Morsi and his regime an ultimatum before severing their relations with the state and taking the peninsula's matters into their own hands.

"We have already decided to stop the tribal mediation to resolve problems such as the kidnappings," said Sheikh Salem Eneizan of the heavily armed al-Tarabin tribe a few days before the summit, while riding in his khaki-colored, one-cabin Land Cruiser pick-up truck. The trunk of his vehicle was loaded with blankets, a teapot, two Kalashnikov PK7.62 mm machine guns, and two olive-green metal boxes of ammunition emblazoned with "7.62 mm NATO BALL ON CLIPS," while a black Czech-made 9 mm CZ75B pistol sat beside the gear stick.[38]

"I will not talk about development until every Sinai Bedouin jailed or sentenced under Mubarak is granted a retrial or a pardon. We are no less than Morsi's friends who he released without explaining why them but not us?" Eneizan said, referring to the dozens of Islamists who were released after Mubarak stepped down in February 2011. Eneizan's willingness to engage in an armed battle with security forces was explained at the summit by his close friend Ibrahim Abu Ashraf al-Menaei of the Sawarka tribe.

"The regime is apparently unaware of the worsening situation; if this continues there will be a war between the tribes and the state," said Abu Ashraf, who had personally met with President Morsi as part of the delegation and warned him that "the Bedouin community is running out of patience and if they lose hope in peaceful change they will take up their arms and no one will be able to contain such a situation."

Morsi brushed off Abu Ashraf's warnings and the escalation vowed at the Bedouin summit was never fulfilled when, weeks later, the truce between the Muslim Brotherhood and North Sinai's militant Islamists came to an end with the abduction of seven security personnel on May 16, 2013.

Once again, the tribal leaders found themselves in a situation where there was no option but to fully endorse the state, mainly to prove they had no relation to the militant activities. Hours after the abduction, Defense Minister al-Sisi ordered the mobilization of dozens of troops and military vehicles to surround the villages south of Rafah and Sheikh Zuwayyed, where the kidnapped personnel were believed to be kept, and flew Apache gunships in a show of what was to come. On the jihadist end of the spectrum, members of the militant ABM began planting landmines on the main roads leading into their strongholds of al-Mehdiya and al-Muqataa.

Hours after the abduction of the one military and six police conscripts, who were on their way out of the Rafah Crossing Terminal where they were deployed, a video was published by the kidnappers showing the victims blindfolded, reciting their names and ranks, and begging President Morsi and Defense Minister al-Sisi to release Islamist prisoners in a prisoner swap similar to that of Gilad Shalit in the Gaza Strip, naming only one specifically: Hamada Abu Sheita, who allegedly led the 2011 attacks on al-Arish police station and was detained weeks before the abduction. Once again, and in spite of the audacity of the video that enraged Egyptians and drew harsh criticism, President Morsi ordered the military campaign to stand down and work on releasing the abducted conscripts without harming them or their kidnappers.

"We will secure their release because we don't need any problems with the military," Abu Arrab al-Sawarka said at the time, confirming that ABM never ordered the kidnapping, and adding that "some of their affiliates did it independently, which will encourage them to agree to releasing them unharmed."

In the village of al-Mehdiya, Hussein al-Menaei, a prominent member of the Menaei clan and father to one of Ansar Bayt al-Maqdis' militants, decided to personally sponsor the mediation initiative. Declaring the village a safe zone, al-Menaei hosted two delegates from the military intelligence and two jihadist representatives, including Shadi al-Menaei, the most prominent figure of ABM, for a several-hour-long meeting in the yard of his house, which successfully led to the release of the victims a day later. "I did it for personal reasons, I believed that this incident could destroy the relationship between us and the armed forces," he told the *Washington Post* after describing Morsi as "unfit to sell potatoes."[39]

Celebrating the release of the soldiers in a military airbase in Cairo, Morsi was filmed receiving the released conscripts, demanding a hunt for the kidnappers, and calling on the Bedouin tribes of Sinai to surrender their weapons to the state. The president's appearance did nothing to reverse the shame of negotiating, for the second time, with militants who paraded the whole incident as evidence of their authority over the North Sinai enclave and their ability to twist the state's arm, even when its military gunships were flying above their heads.

In mid-June 2013, millions of Egyptians were signing the petition of a group called Tamarrod, or 'Rebellion,' which demanded Morsi to step down and call for early presidential elections. Meanwhile, calls for a revolt against the Islamist president on his first anniversary in power were spreading across Egypt. Among Sinai's Bedouin, like much of mainland Egypt, it was no surprise that even those who had voted for the Muslim Brotherhood's Morsi and promoted him across their towns had turned against him and publicly declared their utter disgust at his call for them to surrender their arms.

"Are you [Morsi] going to secure Sinai if we hand over our guns? It was the tribal firepower, authority, and self-restraint that released the soldiers and the tourists without any losses. That call reflects the crippled mentality of those who think that surrendering guns would stabilize Sinai," Ahmed al-Herish, whose Gararsha tribe had, on his orders, paralyzed South Sinai's highways and mountainous routes three times to force the release of kidnapped tourists, plus another time when two of his cousins were killed at a police checkpoint. Sitting under an olive tree in the ancient town of St. Catherine's, al-Herish took pride in the fact that Bedouin tribes had carried weapons since their arrival in the peninsula some 2,000 years ago. "It was never for aggression and crime, never against the government; it was always for security and justice. Security for places like this monastery that demanded our protection and we committed to it centuries ago," he said, pointing at St. Catherine's Monastery a few hundred yards from where he sat.[40]

Al-Gararsha, al-Herish's massive Sunni Muslim tribe that controls the Valley of Firan, continued to take responsibility for securing several Orthodox monasteries and churches in their mountainous enclave, while al-Jebaliya, their neighboring tribe that occupies the town of St. Catherine's and its surrounding villages, moved from Upper Egypt's desert some 1,400 years ago to impose a secure perimeter around the St. Catherine's Monastery. Outside of the ancient building, a member of al-Jebaliya chuckled when I asked him about Morsi's call: "we will surrender the weapons when the police stop begging for our help every time something happens around Sinai," he said.

In the restive north, the militarist tribesmen viewed Morsi's call differently; they were in the middle of a simmering situation that would inevitably boil over in the form of an all-out war between the military and the armed jihadists while the community would be the main victim.

At a time when the whole country was polarized by political turmoil and Morsi's insistence on excluding anyone who was not an affiliate of the Muslim Brotherhood while brushing off the nationwide calls for revolt, the Bedouins of North Sinai were offering to assist the military in eliminating the militancy and maintaining control over the peninsula.

"The authorities are already using our arms and respected authority over the community to resolve issues they fail to handle, and we prove ourselves every time we are called for help, but they refuse to officially acknowledge us," said Ahmed Abu Zeina, a respected member of the Sawarka tribe, who believed that forming a Bedouin battalion within the ranks of the military and police forces would be the ultimate solution to Sinai's ongoing problems. "You would see disciplined officers satisfying the community with their knowledge of the local culture and imposing security with their experience of the terrain and the tribal conflict resolution they committed to for decades. All of what we do now in closed rooms would be done officially in government departments."[41]

Abu Zeina's call, which was repeated by dozens of tribal figures since the January 2011 uprising, has been effective in many countries with large tribal communities, such as Saudi Arabia and other Arabian Gulf States, or Morocco and Algeria in North Africa. The more telling example was right on Egypt's eastern borders: Israel's Bedouin Reconnaissance Battalion that operates under the IDF's southern command and was the first to come in contact with the attackers of August 2012. A former military general, who operated for years in Sinai and continued to have solid relations with the military institution under al-Sisi's command, had a rather shocking response to Abu Zeina's idea. "They want a Bedouin battalion so they can serve their cousins who are involved in all sorts of criminal activities," said the officer, on condition of anonymity, despite the fact that his operations in Sinai during the Israeli occupation would have been impossible without the assistance of the covert Bedouin elements under the command of the military intelligence.[42]

The condescending reaction of the former officer was representative of the defense and interior ministries who failed to initiate any form of communication with the tribal leaders or community activists since the beginning of Operation Eagle II in August 2012. They also began smearing them through false allegations and a hateful media campaign because of the Bedouins' continued opposition to what they saw as the

state's incompetent policies. It simply added insult to the Bedouin community's decades-old injury of discrimination and seclusion.

"The Egyptian state despises the Bedouins, they refuse us even when
we stretch out our hand to help the authorities," said Ibrahim Abu Ashraf
al-Menaei. "The police want us to be informants, but we should never
demand recognition, a decent job, owning our lands, or being treated
with respect. We will never accept this."

Morsi's Prison Break, Again

In February 2013, seven months after Morsi became the first elected
president in the history of Egypt and two years after the attacks on
prisons in January 2011, the Ismailiya Misdemeanor Court launched
an investigation into the attacks and the escape of some 23,000 prisoners. This included President Morsi himself, who walked out of the
Wadi al-Natrun Prison along with thirty-six high-ranking members
of the Muslim Brotherhood organization who had been administra-
tively detained on January 24, 2011, one night before the outbreak of
the uprising.[43]

The premise of this legal action was built entirely on the remnants
of the Mubarak regime's attempt to smear the January 25 uprising by
claiming it was a preplanned conspiracy. Such rhetoric began on September 13, 2012, when Egypt's former head of general intelligence
General Omar Suleiman offered his testimony during Hosni Mubarak's
trial over the killing of hundreds of peaceful protesters during the uprising. Back then, Suleiman said "communication between Hamas and the
Bedouins of Sinai were detected and was followed by the movement
of groups through the tunnels on the border with Gaza. There was an
agreement to supply the Bedouins with weapons in return for assistance
in freeing Hamas elements from Egyptian prisons. This was exactly on
January 27 and the Bedouins prepared the atmosphere for the escape
plan by attacking the police station of Sheikh Zuwayyed and firing randomly in the areas surrounding the tunnels."[44]

Aside from the fact that the Egypt's judiciary never attempted to
collect the testimonies of hundreds of Sinai Bedouin who were eyewitnesses, participated in the events, and categorically denied Suleiman's
theory, it also failed to take into consideration the remainder of Suleiman's testimony in which he confirmed that no intelligence detected the
Muslim Brotherhood's plans to participate in the January 25 uprising.

"Through the EGID's monitoring of Facebook, we detected that protesters came from different sectors, the majority were from the Kefaya movement, April 6, We Are All Khaled Said, and various other political powers, but we were accustomed to such protests," said Suleiman, adding that during a cabinet meeting attended by Prime Minister Ahmed Nazif, Minister of the Interior Habib El-Adly conveyed his opinion regarding the anticipated protests, "but luckily all intelligence confirmed that the Muslim Brotherhood won't participate and accordingly they [the cabinet] expected it to be a passing protest, like former ones."

"In case of the Muslim Brotherhood's participation, El-Adly confirmed that he would abort this attempt by detaining several of the movement's leading officers," said Suleiman.[45]

Contrary to what Mubarak's loyalists were promoting, the full testimony of General Omar Suleiman, if it was ever supported by any concrete evidence, proved that the Muslim Brotherhood weren't a part of the attacks on prisons across Egypt, and, if they were, the immediate question to be raised was why Mohamed Morsi, a suspected criminal, became the president of Egypt and appointed many of those who escaped prisons along with him as ministers and governors. The second most important question was why Egypt's security authorities, including the military institution that took over the responsibilities of securing the country hours before the attacks began, failed to protect the prisons and obstruct the infiltrating Hamas fighters who, according to Suleiman, took their time burning North Sinai's security facilities to the ground before driving some five hundred kilometers to the capital and breaking open its maximum-security prison facilities.

The only trusted answers were the testimonies of Sinai's eyewitnesses: "if Hamas elements did infiltrate the border, they came to transport their elements out of Egypt. They had no hand whatsoever in Sinai's uprising."

But all of the above didn't matter to the judicial panel of the Ismailiya Misdemeanor Court investigating Morsi's alleged escape, neither did the testimonies of prison officials and some of Mubarak's closest allies who publicly declared that the prison breaks were nothing but one of the the security apparatus's plans to maintain its iron-fisted control over the country in case of Mubarak's sudden death, a plan that was hastily activated to break the revolutionary momentum of January 2011 (see chapter 1).

In May 2013, Colonel Khaled Okasha voluntarily testified in court to what he repeatedly said months earlier. And despite his earlier comments that he "watched the revolution on television from his office in al-Arish," he walked into the courtroom to claim that the Rafah and Sheikh Zuwayyed attacks were carried out by Hamas's armed militants. A local newspaper quoted Colonel Okasha saying that "the four-wheel trucks used by militants carried Gazan license plates," but never explained how he was capable of knowing, let alone confirming, such information.[46]

Some of the testimonies confirming the state's knowledge of the Muslim Brotherhood's preplanned attacks on prison facilities, which were ruled by the court as viable evidence, were in fact incriminating of Egypt's judicial and security authorities that didn't only turn a blind eye to such information during the eighteen months of relative stability under the rule of the Supreme Council of the Armed Forces, but moved on to oversee the presidential elections that ended in Morsi's election.

On June 23, the court ordered another investigation by the prosecution into the prison breaks, stating that it had no authority to rule in such a case due to its judicial nature as a court of misdemeanors.[47]

Sinai's Run-up to Morsi's Ouster

Days before the planned nationwide protests calling for ousting President Morsi on June 30, 2013, the militant Islamist groups in North Sinai were preparing for an inevitable confrontation. As the Muslim Brotherhood's Freedom and Justice Party called for marches in support of the Islamist president, it was clear to the militants that their Morsi-brokered truce—which was led by the radical Islamists of the presidential delegation and decreased the militant operations in Sinai—had come to an end, an end that ushered a looming return of deadly crackdowns by security authorities.

The volatile situation in Sinai wasn't far from the developments in the capital Cairo, where clear references to the possibility of adopting violence had been spreading across Egypt for weeks. In reaction to the anti-Morsi Tamarrod, or Rebellion, campaign, the Muslim Brotherhood and various affiliated Salafi powers initiated a counter-campaign named Tagarrod, or 'Impartiality,' and delegated al-Jamaa al-Islamiya's leading figure Assem Abdel-Maged, who was jailed for two decades after taking part in the murder of 118 police personnel in the city of

Asyut in 1981, to be its organizer. The pro-Morsi campaign's logo was, not very surprisingly, a Kalashnikov.

Despite claiming to have renounced violence while in prison, the convicted terrorist Abdel-Maged appeared on television in mid-June to publicly threaten Egypt's Coptic Christians. Speaking on an Islamist satellite channel, Abdel-Maged claimed that the anti-Morsi protests were planned by extremist Copts and made his on-air threats, saying "do not sacrifice your children, the Muslim public opinion will not tolerate toppling the President."[48]

A week after Abdel-Maged's statements, the Muslim Brotherhood called for a demonstration at the Rabaa al-Adawiya mosque in eastern Cairo under the slogan "Renouncing Violence," during which Tarek al-Zomor, another top figure of al-Jamaa al-Islamiya who was sentenced to jail in 1982 for his role in the assassination of Sadat, pledged to crush Morsi's opposition.

"They threatened us with [demonstrations on] June 30, and we tell them that they will be crushed on that day, it will be the knockout," said al-Zomor, whose threats and those of Abdel-Maged didn't fall far from Morsi's. In a 47-minute speech made by the then-president on June 2, in reaction to a 72-hour ultimatum issued by Defense Minister al-Sisi, he clearly stated that "if my blood is the price of defending legitimacy, then I am fully willing to sacrifice it."[49]

On June 30, as millions marched through the streets of major cities and surrounded the presidential palaces in Cairo, concerns rose of a possible outbreak of violence across North Sinai in support of or in coordination with certain elements of the Muslim Brotherhood leadership. "Within this extreme right-wing segment of Islamists, the ones who concern us the most are those who adopt similar ideologies to the Muslim Brotherhood's Qutbist current," said Ahmed Ban, the defected Muslim Brotherhood officer.

"Such groups, cells, or fellow movements in Sinai are tightly controlled by the Muslim Brotherhood's top Qutbist and strategist, Khairat al-Shater, and he will not hesitate to use them as he used the movement's youth to attack opposition protesters at the presidential palace in December 2012," Ban added, referring to the deadly clashes that erupted in front of the presidential palace in Cairo after a call from al-Shater.

Ban's concerns were legitimate, but despite al-Shater's clout and charisma, Sinai's militants had already turned against the Muslim Brotherhood and began operating according to their own interests, an escalation proven by the rockets fired on Israel's southern port-city of Eilat in April 2013 and the abduction of security personnel a month later that caused a severe deterioration of relations between Morsi and the military institution. "He is a *kafir* [infidel]. He recanted by not applying the Islamic sharia, which is the main reason why we supported him and brought him to power," a bearded driver and native of Rafah said days before the nationwide protests kicked off. "Morsi didn't fail. He is capable of applying Allah's sharia, but he is not doing it."[50]

The difference between the operations of Sinai's militants under Morsi and what was anticipated if he was deposed was drastic. For the two and a half years since the uprising toppled Hosni Mubarak in January 2011, the Salafi–jihadist current hoped that the transformation and the rise of political Islam would somehow lead to the establishment of an Islamic state, while the promises of the Muslim Brotherhood leadership delayed the outbreak of a wave of militancy far more lethal than that of the 1990s in Upper Egypt, not because they trusted the Brotherhood or President Morsi, but rather because of the immunity they enjoyed throughout his time in power. The looming end of the Muslim Brotherhood's reign meant the beginning of a brutal military campaign in the peninsula and a retaliative return of the police forces that were once defeated and chased out of North Sinai; a campaign that wouldn't be held back by an Islamist president anymore.

In January 2011, the Salafi–jihadist groups of North Sinai began fighting for their ideological beliefs, a fight that entailed dialogue, compromises, and relative flexibility, but after the intervention of the military institution and its clear intention of toppling the Brotherhood's Morsi, the fight transformed into one purely for existence.

9

TERRORISTS UNLEASHED BY MORSI'S OUSTER

On July 3, 2013, Defense Minister Abdel-Fattah al-Sisi led a widely popular coup against Egypt's first elected president, Mohamed Morsi.¹ The military's move against the Muslim Brotherhood regime saved the country from plunging into civil strife, but wasn't just a spontaneous intervention in defense of the people as many of al-Sisi's loyalists insist, it was rather a calculated plan to seize power and, within days, the top figures of the Muslim Brotherhood were either detained or fearfully bunkered behind thousands of followers massed at eastern Cairo's Rabaa al-Adawiya Square. In Sinai, before any other part of Egypt, al-Sisi's move quickly proved that it was the beginning of a new dictatorship that surpassed Hosni Mubarak's worst doings over the period of three decades' rule.

Two days after Morsi's ouster, on Friday July 5, 2013, a military unit fired its weapons at more than a hundred pro-Morsi protesters who attended the Friday sermon in front of the governorate building in al-Arish, leaving more than a dozen unarmed civilians injured by the live ammunition used. In return, supporters of the ousted president picked up arms and attacked the military troops surrounding the governorate headquarters before seizing it and erecting their Morsi-supporting banners on its façade. A dozen miles away and a few hours later, jihadist militants began fulfilling their threats of an all-out assault on security forces, as a synchronized attack targeted six different security checkpoints in the areas surrounding al-Arish and Sheikh Zuwayyed, leaving one soldier killed and six more injured, while four police personnel were gunned down in two separate attacks blocks away from the morning's clash site.²

Before dawn of the next day, interim president Adly Mansour, head of the Supreme Constitutional Court, who was installed by al-Sisi to run the transitional period, declared a state of emergency and an all-night curfew throughout the volatile North Sinai. Police and military forces applied a shoot-to-kill policy against anything moving after curfew, including animals and stray dogs in the farms surrounding the security posts.[3] Sinai's worst nightmare since Mubarak's era was once again activated: a wave of random arrests on checkpoints deployed on the majority of highways connecting the towns and villages across the province, while military Apache gunships roamed the skies on an hourly basis.

The deadly attacks continued to target military and police facilities and personnel throughout the months of July and August 2013. One hundred and sixty separate attacks using firearms, rocket-propelled grenades, landmines, and explosives were documented by news outlets and military spokesman and Ministry of the Interior statements.[4] This period witnessed the highest number of attacks ever documented in the peninsula, with a concentration in the three major towns of al-Arish, Sheikh Zuwayyed, and Rafah, and their surrounding villages and highways. According to the figures of the ministries of defense and interior, seventy-six military and police personnel were killed and 103 were injured. During the same period, twenty-four civilians were killed by random fire from militants, and two (known for their ties with the authorities) were assassinated in targeted hit-and-run attacks.

The popular reaction in Sinai to the dramatic explosion of armed attacks was divided between those who condemned the brutal crackdown and blamed it for the outbreak of violence, and those who sided with the military's move against the Muslim Brotherhood regime and the militants that had enjoyed a year of immunity under the now ousted president, Morsi.

On July 10, 2013, a terrifying incident turned many of the military's supporters against it. The military's official spokesman, Colonel Ahmed Ali, published a statement on his official Facebook page claiming that General Ahmed Wasfi, the head of Egypt's Second Field Army, which controls North Sinai, survived an assassination attempt that targeted him while on a field inspection tour of Sheikh Zuwayyed's security facilities and checkpoints. "Armed assailants fired their weapons at General Wasfi's vehicle, in return, the security personnel fired back." The statement added that two of the assailants fled, while another was arrested and a young girl was found injured in their car and died as soon as she arrived at a local hospital.

"By analyzing the incident, it became clear that terrorist elements are using children as a tool of media war against the armed forces in order to distort facts and export a fabricated picture of the situation in Sinai, which is used by the media to accomplish suspicious goals," said Colonel Ali's statement, which was removed shortly after its publication.[5]

On the ground in Sheikh Zuwayyed, yards away from the attack site, a very different story was confirmed by several eyewitnesses who spoke with local reporters, including prominent activist and writer Mostafa Singer. Denying the military's statement, the witnesses said the vehicle belonged to a local resident who attempted to avoid the security checkpoint, fearing the inevitable intimidation and the random shooting. The checkpoint's military personnel immediately pursued the driver and showered his vehicle with bullets, killing his four-year-old daughter Aya al-Sayyed.

The Egyptian Center for Social and Economic Rights launched an immediate investigation into the incident. Relying on local reporters and volunteers who documented the testimonies of eyewitnesses, the center published a denial of the military's claim and called for an immediate investigation into the killing of Aya al-Sayyed. The center's call was in vain and was neglected by media outlets despite the grim details it revealed.[6] Since this murder and the military's shameless attempt to cover it by fabricating an 'assassination' story, many of the Sinai residents who once supported al-Sisi's move against Morsi began to realize that the unfolding events far exceeded the widely feared police brutality and arbitrary arrests—this time, it was a lethal and blindly indifferent military clampdown.

The ongoing violence in Sinai was echoed by events in the capital Cairo, as each side of the warring political camps attempted to capitalize on the deadly events. Commenting on the attacks, the Muslim Brotherhood's top officer Mohamed al-Beltagi told reporters in the heart of the Rabaa al-Adawiya sit-in that "the violence in Sinai will stop as soon as al-Sisi reverses what he did and as soon as Morsi is back to his position as president."[7] The statement was immediately circulated across media outlets and interpreted as a clear announcement of the Brotherhood's control over the militant groups in the Sinai Peninsula, an interpretation that was far from accurate, but was used to garner further support for al-Sisi's campaign. Meeting with al-Beltagi several times and attending conferences in which he spoke, it was clear that he lacked diplomacy and regularly made comments that shed serious doubt over his organization's stance on violence. Confidently saying that violence would stop if Morsi was reinstated was nothing more than an empty threat. At this point, neither the military nor Morsi were willing, or even capable, of reversing the situation or striking another truce with Sinai's militants.

On al-Sisi's end of the spectrum, various military sources listed Morsi's umbrella control over the Sinai militancy as the main reason behind al-Sisi's move against him. After a string of meetings with military, police, and intelligence officials, Hamza Hindawi, Cairo bureau chief of the Associated Press wrote:

> The reason, the officials said, was because of profound policy differences with Morsi. El-Sissi saw him as dangerously mismanaging a wave of protests early in the year that saw dozens killed by security forces. More significantly, however, the military also worried that Morsi was giving a free hand to Islamic militants in the Sinai Peninsula, ordering el-Sissi to stop crackdowns on jihadis who had killed Egyptian soldiers and were escalating a campaign of violence.[8]

Al-Sisi personally confirmed Hindawi's writings in an interview with the *Washington Post*: "The security procedures that were in place to prevent terrorist elements and weapons from entering the country disappeared with president Morsi. So they found a very free and fertile environment to work in."[9]

What al-Sisi and his intelligence officers said was true; the free hand given to the Sinai militants by Morsi was reported openly during his time in power, while the local and international media organizations and even governments continued to belittle the impact of this rugged province on Egyptian politics and security. However, what al-Sisi and his security officials failed to recognize, let alone stop, was the increasingly clear signals of the military's violations that seemed to be happening with a similar impunity to that of the armed militants during Morsi's time in power and after his ouster.

On August 5, exactly one month after the post-Morsi avalanche of attacks, Colonel Ali published a video detailing the successes of the military campaign in fighting the peninsula's militancy. Colonel Ali's latest figures indicated that 103 suspects had been detained and were under investigation, sixty terrorists had been killed, and sixty-four injured, in addition to 120 smuggling tunnels destroyed along the border with Gaza, four houses used as hideouts demolished, and thirty-eight vehicles used by terrorist groups in attacks on security forces confiscated.[10]

From that day on, it became clear that the Egyptian military would not be abiding by any legal framework while operating in the Sinai Peninsula. The military spokesman, Colonel Ali, became the judge and jury, whose statements transformed hundreds of people into statistics, classified them as terrorists or criminal elements, and decided that destroyed houses and confiscated vehicles were unquestionably used by terrorist groups. Moreover, the fact that the Egyptian military operated with its own separate judiciary and prosecution systems, in which thousands of civilians faced military trials in the aftermath of the 2011 uprising, meant that any decisions made during the military campaign weren't subject to any state or independent monitoring.[11]

The August of Transformation

Days after Colonel Ali boasted of the alleged accomplishments of the military campaign, Israel moved to briefly shutdown Eilat Airport after warnings from Egypt's security authorities of possible militant attacks. Shortly after, on August 9, a troop of five militants were targeted by an air-to-surface missile in the North Sinai village of al-Ajra, near the Israeli border. Four of them were killed while preparing several rockets to be launched at Israeli territories. Minutes after the operation, several of the world's major media organizations quoted unnamed Egyptian military sources confirming that the terrorist cell was eliminated by an Israeli Air Force drone.[12]

After publishing an initial statement saying that the Egyptian military was investigating the explosions in the village of al-Ajra, Colonel Ali began denying the Israeli drone claims and said that the militants were targeted by Egyptian gunships.[13] Despite Egypt's desperate attempts, it failed to quash the already spreading story, but what really exposed the fabrications of the Egyptian military, for the second recorded time in less than a month, was the fact that the bodies of the four militants, who were all native Bedouins of Sinai, were immediately retrieved by the group behind the attack: Ansar Bayt al-Maqdis. As usual, the military spokesman failed to answer many questions, the most glaring of which was how there was enough time for more terrorists to retrieve the bodies when the Egyptian forces had supposedly pinned down and eliminated the terrorists.

Before the end of the day, ABM published a statement on jihadist forums mourning its dead members, three of which were from the Sawarka tribe's strongholds of al-Mehdiya and al-Muqataa, and the fourth from the Tayaha tribe, specifically from the village of Khreiza, the hometown of ABM's commander who was killed in the Israeli covert operation after taking part in the August 2011 attack in Eilat. Unlike ABM's former statements that came with assurances of only targeting Israel and never pointing its weapons at the Egyptian troops, this one carried a different message that revealed a drastic shift in the group's strategies: it condemned Egypt's coordination with Israel which it described as "treachery" and "protecting the interests of Zionists and Americans."[14]

Two days later, dozens of vehicles carrying hundreds of people drove through the villages south of Rafah to accompany the corpses of the militants to their burial site. Waving the black flags of ABM, the jihadist-led funeral was an unprecedented scene that was widely interpreted as a declaration of tribal support for the militant organization.

Speaking to a Sawarka tribal leader, who joined the funeral despite his serious rivalry with the militant organization and the wider jihadist current, he said that the incentives of those who joined the funeral were many, "the top reason was the fact that it was an Israeli attack, the Bedouins of Sinai would support anyone that fights Israel, even if it's a terrorist or a criminal. The hatred of Israel is ingrained in the hearts of Bedouins."[15]

But that wasn't the only reason; there were incidents in 2011 and 2012 when Israel targeted Islamist militants and Egyptian border-security troops and there wasn't even a mention of a funeral, let alone hundreds of people publicly showing support. The tribesman explained why this time it was different: "The regime's allies were being killed one after the other and everyone in the villages south of Rafah and Sheikh Zuwayyed was concerned that there will come a time when they could be in the position of Khalaf al-Menaei or Abdel-Hamid Selmi," he said referring to al-Menaei, who was assassinated in August 2012 after holding a conference in support of the military and Selmi, a former Mubarak-era parliamentarian who was assassinated only two days before the Israeli drone attack. Alongside these two prominent community figures, several informants known for their close ties with the security authorities were assassinated in different locations in North and Middle Sinai since the downfall of Mubarak in 2011. For many residents in the villages, left to face the militants and knowing that the state authorities would not, or could not, protect them, it was an unfortunate yet life-saving decision to come out in support of ABM, even if that support was not genuine.

He added:

> Without any efforts to understand the influence of the deadly conflict on the Bedouin population, the funeral scene was intentionally used to smear the tribal community. It was one of many tactics used by the regime to convince Egyptians and the world that Sinai's tribes, especially those living in the border areas, are terrorists or at least supportive of terrorism. It was their plan to avoid any condemnation for their continued violations and crimes against innocent civilians.

The tribesman's allegations of a planned smear campaign was not a baseless conspiracy theory, and, in fact, days later in the capital Cairo, a media campaign began attacking some of Sinai's most respected figures and accusing them of mobilizing militias and harboring the terrorist groups, especially those who loudly condemned the military's violations. One of several such reports was published by the English-language state-owned *Al-Ahram Weekly* on August 15, saying:

> The shift in strategy began to be put into effect in Sheikh Zuweid which, together with Rafah, is a hotbed of terrorist activity in Sinai. The region has been transformed by new tribal leaders into a patch-work of zones of influence. These new leaders emerged following the 25 January Revolution, their new found wealth culled from the arms trade and the trade of goods via Sinai–Gaza tunnels. They call themselves "independent sheikhs" and display their economic and political clout through the construction of lavish villas and by engaging personal militias.[16]

The report, which was dismissed by experts and analysts even in Washington DC and Tel Aviv who wondered why the Egyptian regime didn't begin strategic cooperation with tribal heads instead of igniting animosities with them,[17] contained a dozen factual errors and apparent fabrications (such as claiming that Israel's Defense Minister Moshe Ya'alon denied the drone attack, which never happened). It clearly aimed at tarnishing the reputation of the independent Sinai Tribes Union, which had been established in an effort to counter the corruption of regime loyalists referred to in Sinai as "Government Sheikhs." Headed by Ibrahim Abu Ashraf al-Menaei, the Sawarka tribesman who regularly cooperated with the regime and publicly declared his will to join hands with the military campaign despite the ongoing assassinations of other tribesmen by armed militants, the union, which continuously called for reform and condemned the wrongdoing of any state institution especially the military and the police, seemed to have become excessively annoying for a regime that was intent on operating with impunity.

Al-Menaei, the main target of the smear campaign, should not have had any difficulty denying allegations that he was working with the militants. His role and that of tribal leaders in freeing the kidnapped tourists and most recently securing a safe release of the abducted soldiers in May 2013, should have quashed such claims. As for the allegation of harboring militants, he admitted that the tribes didn't do much to fight them, because

> what is happening now is different, it is not kidnappers carrying a few guns; we are seeing organized groups with countless men and heavier guns, and no tribe is ready to go to war and sacrifice its members knowing that no one will defend us. It is the state's job and is definitely out of our capabilities. . . . We are currently suffering between militants who bring instability to our towns, and a state that cracks down randomly on everyone, including innocent citizens. If the state with all its power and institutions continues to desperately hunt the militants across the country, how do they expect us, ordinary citizens, to find, fight, and defeat them?

Speaking to a former senior official of the state owned *al-Ahram*, he briefly commented on the report saying that "some reporters in various media outlets are widely known for being a mouthpiece of the security authorities." But the situation wasn't as simple as he put it; this time, the regime's message echoed loudly in the ears of al-Menaei and his fellow tribal leaders, who continually offered to cooperate with the security authorities only if the worsening violations ended. It didn't only

mean the regime's refusal of al-Menaei's tribal propositions of cooperation—and, with the backing of the state, the tribes could have effectively
crushed the militancy within months and with minor collateral damage—but outrageously portrayed him, along with many opposition
figures, as a criminal who would sooner or later be hunted down.

Rabaa al-Adawiya

While al-Sisi's regime continued to widen the disastrous gap separating
it from Sinai's tribal community, it moved on August 14 to clear, using
lethal force, the months-old sit-in of Morsi's supporters in eastern Cairo's Rabaa al-Adawiya Square, Giza's Nahda Square, and various other
protest sites in different cities. In a crime unmatched through the history of Egypt's consecutive military dictatorships since 1952, hundreds
of police and military forces, armed with live ammunition and riding
war machinery including armored personnel carriers and Humvees
mounted with automatic, remote-controlled machine guns, attacked the
protest sites, killing close to two thousand people in less than twelve
hours and injuring thousands more. More then eight hundred of the
deaths took place in Rabaa al-Adawiya Square; forty-three police personnel were also killed by armed protesters.[18]

The August 14 massacre was a transformative moment after which
the militant groups of North Sinai publicly declared open war not only
on the Egyptian military and police forces, but also their supporters and
whoever was suspected of collaborating with the authorities. One day
after the bloody dispersal, while Cairo's hospitals, morgues, and dozens
of volunteering doctors and activists were counting and attempting to
identify the rising number of corpses, more than a dozen armed attacks
targeted security forces in different locations in al-Arish and Sheikh
Zuwayyed, killing fifteen security personnel and two civilians, and injuring many others.[19]

On August 19, Sinai's militants exhibited tactical and intelligence
capabilities that had not been shown in any of their attacks inside Egypt
since their rise in January 2011. Less than fifteen minutes after end of
the nightly curfew at 7:00 a.m., a few armed militants stopped two civilian transport busses carrying twenty-eight central security conscripts on
their way to Rafah's al-Ahrash Barracks. This time the militants weren't
planning an abduction, but immediately ordered the men, still in their
civilian clothes, to kneel and shot them in an al-Qaeda-style execution

on the side of road before fleeing the scene. Three of the conscripts survived with serious injuries and within hours the bloody photos were on the front pages of every newspaper in Egypt.[20]

Various testimonies and investigations revealed that the conscripts, unable to travel to their barracks due to the all-night curfew, had spent the night in al-Arish's central transport station. As soon as the curfew was lifted, they set off on their two buses, which had already been spotted by the militant groups who operated inside the region's supposedly secure capital that hosts the command centers of every security apparatus operating in the governorate. The drivers of the buses, who weren't harmed, told investigators that the militants knew exactly what they were looking for. Divided into three groups, the first forced the buses onto a side road running through an empty stretch between the villages and sealed off the road behind them, another group did the same a few hundred yards ahead to stop any incoming traffic, while the third, which stopped the buses and forced the conscripts out, was responsible for the execution.

The attack, dubbed by the media as Rafah's "Second Massacre" (after the first in August 2012), wrecked the military spokesman's propaganda campaign during which he boasted of the ongoing elimination and arrests of militants. The military command immediately canceled all holidays for officers and soldiers deployed around Sinai and applied strict measures on the movement of personnel, which since that time have only been allowed to move around in armored entourages under air cover from Apache gunships. The heightened security measures continued to further suffocate the region without any regard for the well-being of some 200,000 citizens living in the northeastern quarter of the peninsula, where the overwhelming majority of attacks and security clampdowns took place.

In the region's capital of al-Arish, the curfew continued to paralyze the city from 7:00 p.m., while in Sheikh Zuwayyed, Rafah, and the surrounding villages and highways, the curfew began as early as 4:00 p.m. and a shoot-to-kill policy was in place for anything moving in the vicinity of checkpoints and security facilities. Since the state of emergency was declared in the aftermath of Morsi's ouster, at least a dozen civilians have been killed at different checkpoints, only one incident of which was recognized by an official military statement, which blamed him for failing to stop at the checkpoint.[21]

In the weeks after Rafah's second massacre, the total shutdown of al-Salam bridge crossing over the Suez Canal directly into North Sinai meant the trip from Cairo to al-Arish's western edge took almost eight hours, double the usual time. People would sometimes have to wait in their vehicles at checkpoints for hours and face aggression from the officers. In one instance, a driver complained to an officer about warning shots being fired at him while he approached a checkpoint on the outskirts of Sheikh Zuwayyed, and, in response, "he [the officer] threatened that the next bullet would hit the car, and the one after would kill me."[22]

While the security personnel were busy holding up innocent civilians at checkpoints, militants were preparing their next attacks. At 10:00 a.m. on Tuesday, August 27, the first suicide bomb to hit the Sinai Peninsula since the 2004 and 2005 bombings of Taba and Sharm al-Sheikh went off. Four heavily armed groups mounted the rooftops of different buildings with strategic views of the Sheikh Zuwayyed police compound. Mahmoud, a resident of the town, had walked out of his house to a tea shop that looked onto the still-under-construction building one of the groups had turned into a stage from which they would launch their attack.[23]

"Looking out of the tea shop's gate, I saw three men climbing up a building that was under construction yards from where I sat. One carried an RPG, the second carried a machine gun, and the third carried a large video camera. They wrapped scarves around their faces and wore olive-green camouflage pants," Mahmoud testified, after warning me not to publish his real name or the next militant attack would put an end to his life. "It's not the first time I witnessed shooting, and the best thing to do was to find a safe spot, and hide. So I ran into a mechanic's shop a few steps away from the tea shop. Others had also seen the armed men; we all started screaming at people to take cover."

Seconds later, one shot was fired from the concrete skeleton and was followed by the deafening sounds of heavy machine-gun fire and rocket-propelled grenades. "Recalling the events, and hearing the stories from neighbors and friends who saw the other armed groups, I believe the first single shot was a call for all groups to start the attack, and they all did immediately after that one shot."

The sound of gunfire whizzing over the heads of hundreds of screaming civilians, who were on their way to the town's bustling Tuesday market, turned out to be nothing but a distraction. An explosives-loaded sedan raced through the main boulevard before exploding at the gate of the fortified police compound, ripping through the gate, parts of the compound's walls, and an armored vehicle standing right behind it in the yard of the police facility. Right after the explosion, Mahmoud and others hiding in the mechanic's shop saw the militants walk out and through the ally cutting between residential buildings and leading to the bustling market street. Several other people said they witnessed the armed, broad-shouldered militants fleeing in vehicles that waited for them amid the chaos of the market.

Mahmoud and another witness, Ali, who saw the escaping vehicles, agreed that no one would dare describe the vehicles that carried the attackers away. "They would first be detained for questioning, which is always humiliating, and would be in danger if they were ever released," said Ali. Indeed, military and police reinforcements arrived minutes after the explosion to impose a cordon around the police compound and detain hundreds of people inside it. Stripping them of their phones and wallets, everyone was asked one question: what did you see?

As the chaos subsided, it became clear that the suicide bomber had detonated the vehicle less than two meters from the compound's gate. No casualties were recorded on the security's side, while several civilians were injured and dozens of shops surrounding the attack site were fully or partially destroyed. Since that day, the central area of the town of Sheikh Zuwayyed, instead of undergoing the social and economic rehabilitation it needs, has been fully shutdown. The wider vicinity of the police compound has been cordoned off with barbed wire and concrete blocks, shop owners have never opened their businesses again, and snipers stationed on the rooftop of the scarred building indiscriminately shoot at anyone who falls in range of their crosshairs.

The Blackout

Immediately after the Sheikh Zuwayyed bombing, Ibrahim Abu Ashraf al-Menaei decided that his attempts to strike any form of understanding, let alone cooperation, between the military-led regime and the tribal leaders were futile. Sitting at his guesthouse with his cousin Mohamed Abu Bilal al-Menaei, a Salafi Bedouin who has led an armed campaign against human traffickers since 2011 and successfully saved hundreds of victims, they decided to call for a tribal convention that would bring together figures from all sectors of the community with the aim of pressuring the regime into overhauling its brutal policies that continued to inflict major harm on the community while failing to curb the rising militancy.

The convention was held on September 1, 2013, and was attended by almost fifty representatives of tribes, political activists, Salafi clerics, and even radical Islamists. Before the end of the convention, held at Abu Ashraf's guesthouse, he received a phone call from a security official threatening him over his continued condemnation of the regime and the ongoing military campaign. Two days later, the regime responded to the calls of al-Menaei and his fellow tribesmen, in its own way.[24]

Shortly after sunrise on September 3, military gunships fired missiles at several houses in the villages of al-Muqataa and al-Touma, south of Sheikh Zuwayyed. The attack was followed by the usual Colonel Ali statement, this time saying twenty-three terrorists were killed in the attack, "in addition to destroying several buildings the terrorists used as hideouts and shelling a vehicle carrying three terrorists that attempted to escape."[25]

The false statement of Colonel Ali was immediately exposed by Sinai reporter Ahmed Abu Draa, a native of al-Muqataa village that was shelled by air-to-surface missiles during the early morning offensive, who said:

> I documented the airforce attack on the villages of al-Muqataa and al-Touma this morning. What I witnessed is the destruction of six civilian homes in both villages and the partial destruction of a mosque in al-Muqataa. Four civilians were injured, one of whom was taken to Sheikh Zuwayyed's hospital where military forces detained and transferred him to the military hospital.[26]

Two nights after Abu Draa posted this statement on his Facebook page, he was detained and transferred to al-Arish central military base, officially named the 101 Battalion, where he was photographed with several other detainees and his picture was published hours later by the independent news website *al-Youm al-Sabea* with a caption reading "arrested terrorists."[27] As for *al-Masry al-Youm*, the independent newspaper which Abu Draa worked with for over five years, it published a brief and belated statement after North Sinai Press Union threatened a full strike in protest of Abu Draa's arrest, while the national Press Syndicate abandoned him by announcing that he was not a registered

member and would not be represented by the syndicate's defense lawyers. Within days, Abu Draa was transferred to the military al-Azouli
Prison, a maximum-security facility located in the center of Ismailiya's
al-Galaa Camp, the headquarters of Egypt's Second Field Army where
General Ahmed Wasfi oversaw the ongoing operations. Held in soli-
tary confinement in an underground concrete cell with no windows or
sunlight, he was referred to military trial on charges of spreading false
news about the military.

During Abu Draa's imprisonment, the military continued to target
more villages, killing more civilians and burning down more houses,
while the ferocious attacks by militant groups continued to invalidate
the successes claimed by Colonel Ali and the pro-regime media that
submitted to the blackout imposed on Sinai. On September 5, Ansar
Bayt al-Maqdis executed its first attack in the capital, targeting Minister
of the Interior Mohamed Ibrahim with a car bomb as his entourage left
his residence in eastern Cairo's Madinat Nasr district. General Ibrahim
survived the attempt on his life, but, back in Sinai, landmines, RPGs,
and suicide bombers continued to harvest the lives of security personnel. ABM's coordinated attacks on armored vehicles and four-wheelers
killed six military personnel on September 6 and 7, while a previously
unknown group named Jund al-Islam, or the "Soldiers of Islam," claimed
responsibility for two explosive-laden vehicles that ambushed the Military Intelligence Camp in the border town of Rafah, killing eleven
officers and soldiers, and destroying major parts of the facility.[28]

In a press conference on September 15, the military spokesman
Colonel Ali claimed that "the military operations in Sinai are strictly
targeting armed elements and insuring minimal damage for civilians."
Listing the names of a dozen villages targeted since the beginning of the
operation in July, he said that police and military forces "hadn't entered
the villages of Mehdiya, Madfuna, and Nage Shibana since the year
2002, which made security forces intent on cleansing such areas that
pose a threat to national security."[29]

Standing adjacent to a wall-sized screen playing video footage, photos, and interactive maps, Colonel Ali presented the latest statistics,
saying that the number of detained terrorists and criminal elements
had reached 309, while 601 houses and shacks, in which the majority of
Sinai's most impoverished people lived, were destroyed during the raids.
For the first time since 2011, the military spokesman accused Hamas,

saying that "grenades bearing the Qassam Brigades seal were seized along with fatigues and other military equipment used by the Islamic Resistance Movement, Hamas."

Once again, Colonel Ali's denial of targeting civilians came hours after the burial of civilians killed by the military. This time, it was four children, two women, and one man who were killed by heavy tank shelling that began early on the morning of September 13 during a ground incursion into the village of al-Lefeitat, south of Sheikh Zuwayyed. In an attempt to break the media blackout, al-Jazeera Mubashir Misr, a branch of the Qatari-owned al-Jazeera network, aired video footage taken from the bombarded villages, where two people confirmed the death of their relatives. Interviewing Ibrahim Abu Ashraf al-Menaei over the phone, he described what happened as a "disgrace that will haunt the Egyptian regime for hundreds of years," and confirmed the destruction of around sixty homes in the villages of al-Mehdiya and al-Muqataa.[30]

Some ten days after his comments, Apache gunships turned his home, his son's, and the family's guesthouse, which once hosted revolutionary figures, journalists, politicians, and hundreds of impoverished people, into rubble. But it wasn't only Abu Ashraf; Mohamed Abu Bilal al-Menaei's house, which had been a safe shelter for hundreds of trafficked African migrants he had saved over the years, was also bombed into the ground. Both houses, along with dozens of others and hundreds of makeshift shelters inhabited by the poor, were dismissed by Colonel Ali as hideouts for terrorists.

Abu Ashraf and Abu Bilal never spoke of the destruction of their homes, never even posted its photos on their social media accounts, but continued to risk their lives by hosting journalists and facilitating their communication with the impoverished victims. Like everyone, they fled the villages every time the military ground incursions began hunting down and rounding up anyone who wasn't capable of fleeing. Infuriated by even minimal exposure of its crimes and indiscriminate shelling, North Sinai's security forces became rabid, paranoid of anything that seemed to be monitoring; it started a hunt for journalists attempting to reach the area where the military campaign committed the majority of its crimes. Before the end of September, photographer Sabry Khaled and reporter Azza Maghawri were taken from their hotel rooms in the middle of al-Arish, detained, and released after being assaulted by security personnel, and ordered to immediately leave the Sinai Peninsula.[31]

On October 5, Abu Draa was sentenced to a six-month suspended prison term by a military tribunal. He walked out of al-Azouli Military Prison, which had become the most recent source of Sinai's nightmarish stories of torture and death at the hands of prison guards, to find out that his village of al-Muqataa, along with a dozen other villages south of Sheikh Zuwayyed and Rafah, were now the region's most deadly places.[32]

Egypt's al-Qaeda

During a convention of military commanders on October 1, 2013, Defense Minister Abdel-Fattah al-Sisi admitted that the "measures applied are stifling the lives of civilians" and pledged compensation for any buildings destroyed. His pledge was never fulfilled, and his words were contradicted by the military spokesman and field commanders who continued to insist that, without offering any insight or evidence, anything targeted in Sinai was unquestionably terrorist in nature.

General Ahmed Wasfi, who became locally known in Sinai as the "Shed Burner," in reference to the number of impoverished homes destroyed over months of deadly raids, appeared in a televised interview on October 3, during which he claimed that 95 percent of the smuggling tunnels were destroyed and that if it wasn't for the civilian residents of the region, his forces would have finished this job in half a day but they didn't in order to avoid inflicting any harm on innocent people.[33]

These statements of the two most important Egyptian military commanders at the time (al-Sisi and Wasfi) were met by an immediate reply from Sinai's militants, who countered that the military campaign's most significant accomplishment over three months of operations was nothing more than devastating the lives of civilians. On October 7, one day after the annual celebration of the October 6, 1973 victory, Ansar Bayt al-Maqdis targeted the South Sinai Security Directorate with a car bomb that killed five and injured more than fifty people. The attack, despite being the second outside of North Sinai, was the real turning point, showing that ABM, the most organized terrorist organization in Egypt, had spread its operations to other governorates. On October 10, another suicide attack targeted al-Rissa Checkpoint in eastern al-Arish, killing four civilians and injuring five others,[34] and, on October 19, the third suicide attack outside of North Sinai took place in Ismailiya when a car bomb targeted the Ismailiya Military Intelligence Camp.[35]

ABM's attacks throughout the month of October, which targeted military and police facilities hundreds of miles away from their strongholds in North Sinai, presented striking evidence that the group's capabilities were not only increasing, but that they were empowered by covert cells in different governorates that remained below the radar of Egypt's security outfits. The use of independent cells imitated al-Qaeda's decades-old tactic of centralization of decision and the decentralization of execution, which meant that top commanders would give orders, but would not take part in the planning or execution of the attacks. This rule was applied to the fullest extent by al-Qaeda's Osama bin Laden and Ayman al-Zawahiri, who sometimes did not know the identity of the field commanders or foot soldiers until the operations were completed. Since the September 2001 attacks on the United States, bin Laden and al-Zawahiri were forced to further adhere to their rule due to their geographical isolation.

In addition to the sophisticated al-Qaeda tactics, the published videos circulating in jihadist forums and documenting ABM's attacks on the Minister of the Interior, the South Sinai Security Directorate, and a third one that took place on November 20 in which an explosive-laden vehicle was remotely detonated on the highway to target a military transport bus killing eleven personnel, imitated al-Qaeda's Islamic State in Iraq, ISI, that transformed after the outbreak of the Syrian civil war to become ISIL, the Islamic State in Iraq and the Levant.[36]

On October 26, ABM published a video showing the details of the failed assassination attempt on Minister of the Interior Mohamed Ibrahim. The video revealed that the attack was executed by former Egyptian military man Major Walid Badr, who was dismissed from the army and then traveled to Afghanistan, Iraq, and Syria where he joined al-Qaeda. In the 30-minute video, the former military officer, dressed in his military uniform, called for war against Egypt's security authorities and condemned the Muslim Brotherhood for engaging in the country's post-2011 elections. In addition to running segments of speeches of Bin Laden and al-Zawahiri, the video played parts of former speeches made by Abu Mohamed al-Adnani, the official spokesman of ISIL. Two more videos documenting the attacks on South Sinai's Security Directorate and the military transport bus played segments of speeches made by Abu Omar al-Baghdadi, the former head of ISI, originally an al-Qaeda offshoot in Iraq, who was killed in a joint American–Iraqi operation in 2010.[37]

The direct references to commanders of al-Qaeda's branch in Iraq and Syria (which became a competitor and detractor of its former spiritual leader Ayman al-Zawahiri when it transformed into ISIL) had not previously existed in the propaganda of the ABM at any point since its rise in 2011, and clearly showed that the group was incorporating a new wave of jihadists, many of whom were believed to have recently returned with vast experience of fighting in Syria and Iraq. The new recruits weren't only capable of raising the group's lethal capabilities to much higher levels of sophistication, but were apparently influential enough to steer their rhetoric to show signs of allegiance to different figures that had begun competing with the long-isolated Ayman al-Zawahiri and the deceased Osama bin Laden, in a race to control the global jihad scene.

The transformation of ABM wasn't surprising as the relationship between Egyptian jihadists and al-Qaeda in Iraq had existed for years. Up until 2010, the deputy chief and military commander of ISI was the Egyptian Abu Ayyub al-Masri, a student and member of al-Zawahiri's Egyptian Islamic Jihad since the 1980s, and allegedly an expert in car and roadside bombs who flourished in bin Laden's Afghanistan camps in the 1990s. He later became one of the top officers of Abu Musab Zarqawi, the founder of al-Qaeda in Iraq. A US-led attack killed al-Masri in April 2010 along with his chief, Abu Omar al-Baghdadi, who became regularly shown in video statements by ABM.

Abu Omar was succeeded by Abu Bakr al-Baghdadi as the leader of ISI, whose territory and control surpassed that of his predecessor after the Syrian revolution quickly turned into a nationwide civil war in 2011. In June 2013, al-Baghdadi declared that ISI had expanded into Syria to incorporate the Nusra Front (the Syrian branch of al-Qaeda) and become the Islamic State in Iraq and the Levant, ISIL. His decision was fiercely rejected by the Nusra Front Emir Abu Mohamed al-Julani and al-Qaeda's Ayman al-Zawahiri, but their opposition had little effect on the ground, where many of al-Julani's followers abandoned him and pledged allegiance to al-Baghdadi, who declared himself the Caliph of Muslims, and his group, ISIL, as the new Caliphate. Hundreds, if not thousands, of Egyptian jihadists have arrived in Syria for what they see as a jihad against the regime of Bashar al-Assad, and now also against anyone who is not a member of ISIL.[38]

In late 2012, a hardcore Salafi Bedouin from Rafah confirmed to me that many of his jihadist acquaintances left Egypt as early as mid-2011 en route to Syria, and had not been seen since, as far as he knows. More-over, hundreds of thousands of Syrian refugees have continued to arrive in Egypt and roam freely since 2011, many of them arriving directly from Jordan's Aqaba seaport to South Sinai's Nuweiba seaport.[39] There have been no solid statistics estimating the influence of the Syrian mili-tants and Egyptian returnees on Sinai's and Egypt's insurgency, mainly due to the impossibility of pursuing such subjects under the nationwide crackdown on the media by al-Sisi's regime. However, that said, their influence was vividly seen in ABM's rhetoric and the ever-increasing sophistication of its terrorist attacks.

Besides its growing recruitment capabilities and the covert links ABM proved to have across Egypt, a successful assassination attempt on November 18, which targeted undercover state-security Lt. Colonel Mohamed Mabrouk as he drove out of his house in the capital Cairo, suggested that the group was capable of infiltrating the most protected departments of the country's security apparatus. The investigations into the murder of Mabrouk, details of which were published by local media outlets, claimed that an officer stationed at a Cairo traffic police depart-ment was responsible for supplying ABM operatives with intelligence, including Mabrouk's address and car license number.[40]

The results of the alleged investigation, reported by the state-owned *al-Ahram* and several other news outlets known for being controlled by the regime, were far from convincing. Lt. Colonel Mabrouk was declared, after his death, to be the SSI officer in charge of the Radical Activity File, a position that has been surrounded by utmost secrecy since its establishment decades ago, as whoever occupied it would be a target for assassination by radical Islamist groups. Under such a threat, a former SSI source said on condition of anonymity that "any officer related to this specific department normally operates and lives with a different identity, resides at a house registered under a different name, drives a vehicle reg-istered with information that has no relation whatsoever to their job or real identity, and in most cases even their closest relatives do not know the nature of their real work."[41] This makes it close to impossible for a traffic police officer to be able to reveal the identity of Mabrouk, as the state-owned media claimed, quoting government officials.

The former SSI source, like many analysts who cautiously hinted at the case, believed that ABM's infiltration was significantly deeper than just hiring a traffic police officer. In an attempt to directly link the Muslim

Brotherhood, various government officials announced that Mabrouk was the lead investigator into the cases of the 2011 prison breaks and espionage with Hamas, with which Morsi and dozens of the Brotherhood's leading figures were charged.[42] Despite claims that the suspected traffic police officer showed signs of sympathy toward the Muslim Brotherhood, there was no solid evidence linking the ousted president's mother organization to the assassination of Mabrouk. Soon, the whole case disappeared from the press and government officials ceased to speak of it until ABM hit again on January 28, 2014, executing an identical operation in which Deputy Minister of the Interior General Mohamed Said was killed.

Across the towns and villages of North Sinai, the military's bloody clampdown was offering unprecedented opportunities for ABM. The bombarded homes, unlawfully murdered civilians, and the stifling conditions under which tens of thousands of people lived created the perfect incubator the regime once accused the Bedouin tribes of providing. Capitalizing on the population's growing resentment toward the extreme violations of the military, a statement published by ABM's sophisticated media arm on November 9 called on the residents to join the ranks of the group in their fight against the state authorities.

"Where do you stand in the battle of Islam? We've never known you to be incapable or submissive. . . . By Allah, you have no option but to stand in the line of your sons, the Mujahedeen, as they are the keenest on you, our religion is one and our battle is one," said a soft-toned statement that was published in reaction to unconfirmed news of the regime's plans to evacuate the border town of Rafah to create a buffer zone with the neighboring Gaza Strip. Incorporating different verses of the Quran, the statement clearly addressed the ultraconservative yet unarmed members of the community.[43]

As one Sheikh Zuwayyed resident commented:

> They already proved their strategic capabilities, which rely mainly on an incompetent and criminal regime, but recruiting more people is not the problem, it is thousands of people that have lost their homes, farms, jobs, and relatives who will let militants pass in front of their houses even if a little bit of collaboration with the authorities [by alerting them] would save a hundred soldiers. People feel that it is not their fight, they view both the military and the terrorists as aggressors that destroyed their lives, and looking at what is happening, I cannot blame them.[44]

Capitalizing on Terrorism

Since Hamas's triumph over its rival Fatah in the municipal and legislative elections in 2005 and 2006, the movement had continually accused the iron-fisted regime of Hosni Mubarak of applying a blockade on the Gaza Strip equal to that of Israel. There is no doubt that Mubarak did apply a superficial blockade above ground by the continual closure of the Rafah Crossing Terminal, but the massive network of tunnels that operated around the clock from mid-2007, through Mubarak's downfall and until the ouster of Morsi in July 2013, relieved the Strip to the extent that broad sectors of the population lived as if the blockade, either Israeli or Egyptian, never existed. Furthermore, it generated hundreds of millions of dollars that financed Hamas's relentless control over the coastal enclave.

On July 3, 2013, when al-Sisi moved to eliminate Muslim Brotherhood rule over Egypt, it was clear that Gaza's Hamas movement, the closest of the Middle East offshoots to the command in Egypt, stood first in line after the ouster of Morsi and the Brotherhood's Guidance Bureau, and was desperately trying to avoid the looming domino effect. Surveying several former Muslim Brotherhood officers, they all agreed that Hamas was on the ambitious general's hit list right after the global capital of the Muslim Brotherhood, Cairo.[45]

Surely, and very hastily, the situation worsened for Hamas as it plunged into a severe economic crisis three months after the military clampdown began in Sinai. By October 2013, the most powerful branch of the Muslim Brotherhood was incapable of paying salaries to thousands of its employees, its economy was blown back to the depression of pre-2007, and major parts of the Strip were once again living in darkness due to fuel shortages that brought the Strip's power plants to a stop. The devastating repercussions inflicted on Hamas by the ongoing military operations in Sinai included paralyzing the underground smuggling tunnels as a result of their continuous destruction, and the general stifling of North Sinai by the curfew and the brutal campaign that truly began after Morsi's ouster—a development that eliminated the movement's only remaining source of funding. Furthermore, the Egyptian authorities began accusing the movement and its military wing, the Qassam Brigades, of standing behind the ongoing terrorism activities in Sinai. Accompanying the official accusations, a vicious media campaign was waged against Hamas with hours of television shows occupied by so-called military and security analysts who fueled a hateful campaign demanding military action against the Gaza Strip.[46]

Between the downfall of Mubarak in 2011 and the ouster of Morsi in 2013, Hamas managed to destroy what was left of its relations with the Egyptian military. Facilitating the escape of their men in the aftermath of the prison breaks on January 29, 2011, orchestrating major arms trafficking operations after the outbreak of the Libyan civil war, and their refusal to cooperate with Egyptian authorities in cracking down on the rising jihadists moving freely between the Strip and North Sinai were among the publically stated reasons that transformed Hamas in the eyes of the Egyptian security authorities from a regional wild card they could play in their dealings with Israel into an unwanted player that should be, along with its mother organization, eliminated. But Hamas's activity on Egyptian territory had gone on for years before the 2011 uprising, and in the cases of the smuggling tunnels and the movement of arms, it was to a large extent enabled, if not sponsored, by Mubarak and the military's policies underpinned by decades of corruption.

There is no question that Hamas's post-2011 actions, which were encouraged by its blind confidence that the Muslim Brotherhood would rule Egypt forever, were a blunt violation of the conditions dictated by Egypt's ever-ruling military institution on Hamas's freedom, and they have put the movement in the worst situation it has ever faced. But to accuse it of sponsoring terrorists simply, and tellingly, contradicts the deep-rooted animosity between Hamas and the Salafi–jihadist movements in general. If anything, Hamas attempted to reverse the damage to relations with Egypt it caused and softened its tone in the aftermath of Morsi's ouster, on which it refused to comment, stressing that it will not interfere in Egyptian matters. But its attempts at reconciliation have been in vain.

"Of course it is not in Hamas's favor to lose Egypt, they are suffering a lot but it's more complicated," said Yossi Kuperwasser, general director of the Israeli Ministry of Strategic Affairs, despite his unmatched animosity toward Hamas. "On one hand they have to keep the relationship to be able to operate and on the other hand they are a part of the Muslim Brotherhood, which is confronting the regime in Egypt."[47]

However, despite the claims of aiding Sinai's militants, the real reason behind Egypt's hostility was the fact that Hamas was one of the main cornerstones of the counter-revolution's rhetoric that, since the downfall of Mubarak, has continued to claim that the January 25 uprising was a conspiracy planned and executed by the Muslim Brotherhood and their militarized Gaza branch. Without a shred of evidence or investigation, the counter-revolutionaries have accused Hamas of attacking the police facilities of North Sinai, leading attacks on prison facilities across the country, and killing both protesters and police personnel in Tahrir Square throughout the eighteen-day 2011 uprising. And, now, Hamas was being used to justify why Egypt's military campaign had, over the period of six months, failed to crush the rising terrorism.

Promoting this nonsensical conspiracy theory—that attributed Egypt's uprising against a tyrannical regime to the Muslim Brotherhood and Hamas, while denying the role of civil society, revolutionary movements, and hundreds of thousands of people—was the channel through which the post-Morsi regime led its broader clampdown on anyone who supported the January 2011 uprising that had aimed to bring an end to the military's control over Egypt since the establishment of the republic in 1952. In Cairo, the fruits of the military-backed regime's strategy were being reaped. On November 26, the panel appointed by the transitional government to draft a new constitution to replace the one passed under Morsi in 2012, voted in favor of articles allowing military trials for civilians. Outside the walls of the upper parliament, the revolutionary youth, who had brought an end to Mubarak's reign and marched in protest against writing the military trials into the constitution and giving a legal umbrella to unchecked military powers, were brutalized and detained under an anti-protest law passed weeks earlier.

This broader crackdown on political opposition and mobilization, which had paved the way for al-Sisi's toppling of Morsi, was no different than bombarding the houses of Ibrahim Abu Ashraf al-Menaei, the month-long detention and military trial of Ahmed Abu Draa, or the total media blackout imposed on North Sinai as the military gunships claimed the lives and homes of civilians. It was part of a nationwide plan to eliminate dissent, whether it called for constitutional reform and an active democracy in the capital Cairo, or exposed decades of corruption and dirty politics in the Sinai Peninsula and the crimes committed by the ongoing military campaign.

A few months after Morsi's ouster and the beginning of al-Sisi's war on terror, it became clear that the military was capitalizing on the ongoing terrorist attacks and using them as a weapon to entrench its rule and retaliate against anyone who took part in disrupting the status quo maintained over thirty years by Mubarak's dictatorship.

The Path to al-Sisi's Presidency

For a few years after the Taba bombing in 2004 and the massive wave of arrests that followed it, stories were commonly told across the Sinai Peninsula of sadistic torture at the hands of police personnel behind the walls of western Alexandria's Burj al-Arab Maximum Security Prison, locally known as al-Gharbaniyat. Seven years later, when the January 2011 uprising toppled Hosni Mubarak and put his minister of the interior Habib El-Adly on trial, the population of Sinai believed that the torture legacy had crumbled along with its masters. By the end of 2013, al-Sisi's military-backed regime proved everyone wrong. Egypt's Second Field Army command in Ismailiya, known as al-Galaa camp, and its 101 Battalion in the heart of al-Arish, not only replaced al-Gharbaniyat as the most notorious torture factories, but quickly garnered a terrifying reputation for being the black holes into which prisoners disappear with no guarantee of ever walking out alive.[48]

Since the toppling of Morsi on July 3, arbitrary arrests became systemic. Dozens of people were arrested on a daily basis at checkpoints across North Sinai or during raids by military and police personnel. The 101 Battalion, located in the highly secured center of al-Arish in a setting reminiscent of Baghdad's Green Zone, was the first stop for detainees. After spending various periods of time, ranging from a few hours to several days, the majority of prisoners were transported to al-Galaa camp of the military command in Ismailiya, where they landed in the maximum security al-Azouli Military Prison.

Fearing the possibility of being arrested along with their relatives, families of prisoners ceased to inquire about them and the only source of information about their fate was to wait for someone to be released, which rarely happened. Hearing the frightening stories of torture and sudden disappearance, facing a military trial, regardless of what the sentence might be, became the hope of anyone upon their arrest.

On September 4, 2013, the first case of unlawful death in detention under the rule of interim-president Adly Mansour and the military command of al-Sisi, was documented by researchers at the Egyptian Center for Economic and Social Rights (ECESR). Days after the arrest of 28-year-old Abdallah Abu Rabaa from al-Arish, his family received a call from the authorities requesting they come to receive his corpse from the local morgue. No similar incidents were documented since that day, not because the lethal torture had stopped, but because the corpses of those killed in military custody were not transferred to the morgue; instead, they were just thrown on the side of any of the roads running between North Sinai's villages for people to randomly find and attempt to identify. On November 1, ECSER documented the first such case, when the corpses of two men were found in the village of al-Shallaq. Bearing signs of severe torture, one of the corpses was identified as a member of the Sawarka tribe while the other remained unidentified.[49]

Terrified by the fact that millions of Egyptians gave their blessing to the crimes the military continued to commit in the name of its so-called "war on terror," the population of Sinai's deadly northeastern quarter was isolated, incapable of anything but hoping for the terrorism to come to end. But the painful reality was that there was no shred of evidence of the light people looked for at the end of the tunnel.

"This is not a war on terror; this is blindly bombarding everything regardless of what it is. Civilians, militants, and even camels are a target," Abdel-Rahman, a Bedouin from one of Rafah's destroyed villages said. "The military has no plan, no tactics, and they are proving that they have no idea who or what to fight."

Abdel-Rahman, who moved his family to al-Arish as soon as the military campaign began in September, believed that "militants control the land by spreading their informants who would walk through a checkpoint unnoticed. They know of the military raid before it even leaves the barracks in al-Arish or Sheikh Zuwayyed." [50]

His words accurately described the dynamics of hundreds of attacks that took place over months. Almost every day, armored vehicles, tanks, and dozens of troops would launch attacks on the villages south of North Sinai's main towns of al-Arish, Sheikh Zuwayyed, and Rafah, but before the arrival of the armed convoys to any given location, the militants would be long gone and ordinary civilians would be left in the line of the military's fire. The only exceptions since the beginning of the campaign were a handful of incidents where the military engaged in confrontations with militants, or embarked on tactical raids that proved successful. One of them was when al-Tawhid wa-l-Jihad's leading figure, Abu Munir, was surrounded and killed along with his son, and several other suspected jihadists were swiftly eliminated. However, as soon the

the raids were done, whether they took place during the day or at night, ABM's militants would resurface to target checkpoints and security facilities or plant explosives.[51]

The only way for the state to succeed, added Abdel-Rahman, was to reverse the situation and do what Ansar Bayt al-Maqdis was doing: "takeover the territory, remain in control, and show that your only target is the enemy."

Lifting the stifling measures applied throughout the day and night, securing people's businesses and well being, holding dialogue with tribal kingpins and youth, and deploying troops in every village under the protection of armed Bedouins would have pushed every militant into the desert where they would be easily crushed—even if that meant carpet bombing these vast and uninhabited areas. As Abdel-Rahman said:

> Creating life and stability in cooperation with the locals and making them feel that they are fighting for their lives alongside a state that protects them would have saved hundreds of lives and crushed the terrorists in weeks. This all should have happened months ago, before the killings and destruction, I doubt it will be possible now.

Without knowing it, he gave an identical prescription to that Abu Ashraf al-Menaei had given to the state authorities more than two years earlier, and both were displaced and their houses bombed to the ground for doing so.

His doubts about the military campaign's success have been proven so far, and North Sinai's hopes for terrorism to come to an end were destroyed throughout the months of violence. On December 24, 2013, only two days after publishing a statement calling on police and military personnel to abandon their posts, Ansar Bayt al-Maqdis targeted the Security Directorate of Daqahliya in the Nile Delta. The bomb attack, which killed fifteen and injured some one hundred and fifty people, was the most lethal since the ouster of Morsi.[52] The next day, al-Sisi's regime found its long-sought-after excuse and moved to officially designate the Muslim Brotherhood a terrorist organization.[53]

The Daqahliya attack did not encourage al-Sisi to admit his failure and overhaul his policies, and tagging the Muslim Brotherhood a terrorist organization did not stop the attacks. Hours before the 2014 anniversary of the January 2011 uprising, ABM hit the heart of the regime with an explosive-laden vehicle that targeted the Cairo Security Directorate for the first time in the history of Egypt.[54] The next day, January 25, 2014, another ABM attack downed a military helicopter with a man-portable, anti-aircraft missile on the outskirts of Sheikh Zuwayyed, marking the first successful attack on Egypt's airforce since 1973.[55]

In Cairo, al-Sisi was apparently occupied by a far more important matter than bombed security directorates or the downing of military gunships; he was planning his run for Egypt's presidency. Instead of sacking every military and security commander responsible for the failure in curbing the terrorist attacks that hit the heart of the capital, the Supreme Council of the Armed Forces made an announcement saying "the council cannot but look, with utmost respect and honor, on the desires of the masses of the Egyptian people demanding the nomination of General Abdel-Fattah al-Sisi for the presidency of the republic."[56]

10

THE IMMINENT THREAT

In March 2014, Defense Minister Abdel-Fattah al-Sisi officially announced that he would run in the presidential elections. During the same month he also removed General Ahmed Wasfi, the Shed Burner who oversaw the bloodiest security campaign in the history of Sinai, from the command of the Second Infantry Army and appointed him as head of the Training Authority of the Armed Forces. The sudden transfer of Wasfi, which was widely considered as a euphemized sacking, triggered controversy over the real reasons behind al-Sisi's move to eliminate one of his most trusted field commanders.

Failure to stop the attacks and presiding over systematic crimes against thousands of people in North Sinai was never believed to be a possible reason behind Wasfi's booting out. The broad debate referred to only two possible theories: the first was Wasfi's repeated comments to the media, which were used against the military institution, in which he defended al-Sisi's move against former President Morsi. In a televised interview in October 2013 Wasfi said:

> Did General al-Sisi get any promotions? Did any of us members of the supreme military council get any promotions? Did General al-Sisi become a prime minister, a president, or even form a presidential council and become a member of it? A military coup is when military men seize the leadership of a country.[1]

A few months later, what Wasfi had denied began happening, exactly as he predicted. Interim-President Adly Mansour, inexplicably and against all military norms, announced the promotion of al-Sisi to the rank of Field Marshal, a rank only granted to officers who have served as top military commanders at times of war. Not long after, al-Sisi declared his candidacy in the presidential elections.

The second theory, which circulated mainly in Sinai, proposed that Wasfi was removed from his position because of two media reports published by Reuters and the *New York Times* that managed to bypass the near-impenetrable blackout imposed by the military and get some reporting out on the level of harm inflicted on civilians by the military campaign—a scandal that embarrassed al-Sisi's regime, which apparently didn't care about the campaign's failure as much as it did about reporting on it.[2]

Whatever the reason behind the sacking, it led to no change in the regime's plans for Sinai. When the military operation began in September 2013, there were random raids that targeted the villages of southern Rafah and Sheikh Zuwayyed. But in just a few weeks, General Wasfi coined a number of collective punishment methods which were used over the nine months of brutal operations until his transfer, and continued to be applied to the letter by his successor, General Ahmed al-Shahat.

The top method used by the military was to obliterate the villages south of Rafah and Sheikh Zuwayyed using Apache gunships, tanks, armored vehicles, and overnight shelling by artillery fired from the military barracks. The military command simply tagged the villages under constant fire as strongholds of Ansar Bayt al-Maqdis. This was a flawed accusation that disregarded the fact that when terrorist attacks exploded in the aftermath of Morsi's ouster, the numbers of militants were estimated by various tribal sources to be negligible, in comparison with hundreds of families whose houses were bombarded and were forced to flee. More importantly, the militants rarely operated, convened, or launched attacks from the populated areas, as proven by the fact that the military very rarely engaged in confrontations with armed elements when raiding such areas. The main targeted villages were al-Mehdiya, the stronghold of al-Menaei clan from which a few ABM figures came, followed by al-Muqataa, al-Touma, and al-Lefeitat, all four of which were flattened by heavy shelling, leaving a scene very similar to that of Syrian towns bombarded by the army of Bashar al-Assad.[3]

The next method was, coinciding with the raids on villages, to suspend all cellular and internet communications both in major cities and the villages. The military's justification for such a measure was to ban the informants of militant groups from tracking down the security entourages. The blackout strategy was immediately sabotaged by militants who began relying heavily on closed-network handheld transceivers, even when detonating remotely controlled improvised explosive devices, and used Israeli cellular phone networks that actually provided more coverage in North Sinai than Egyptian carriers. In fact, the suspension of communications that sometimes continued for more than twelve hours a day did more harm than good for the military forces as it eliminated the possibility of ordinary civilians reporting any suspicious movement of militants within their communities.

In addition to destroying the southern villages and suspending communication networks, the houses in the vicinity of any given attack site were the first to be punished for not spotting and informing the authorities before militants took their shot, despite the impossibility of warning the authorities due to the communication blackout and the fact that civilians would have become an immediate target for the militants if they had exposed them. Such punishments were applied to dozens of families whose houses happened to be close to the main roads and highways where militants planted landmines. Since the very first time a landmine exploded under a military vehicle in September 2013, the troops would pay a visit to the closest house, evacuate it, detain its male residents, and destroy it on the spot, mostly with a tank shell fired from close range.

Parallel to these top three measures, the military's bulldozers began razing hundreds of acres of productive farmland on which the majority of the region's population survived. In spite of millions of pounds of capital invested over the years by hundreds of families in this land, the destruction continued and was justified by the possibility of the stretches of farmland providing a hideout for militants. By May 2014, the Agriculture Ministry's North Sinai deputy, Atef Matar, unsurprisingly declared that "350,000 trees were harmed."[4]

Under such conditions, life in towns or villages east of al-Arish became unbearable. The all-night curfew and shoot-to-kill policy followed by military and police checkpoints and facilities made no exceptions, even for ambulances and medical staff. To further worsen the situation, fuel supplies were suspended to all gas stations in the towns of Sheikh Zuwayyed and Rafah, while the closure of the highways forced residents to commute through rugged back roads cutting through the villages, extending travel times to hours for even short distances.

Fertile Ground

One month before al-Sisi's inauguration, an alleged covert operation comprising unidentified armed Bedouins tracked down Ansar Bayt al-Maqdis's most prominent military commander, Shadi al-Menaei, and assassinated him near the village of al-Maghara in central Sinai. The operation was celebrated across Egypt's media outlets that presented it to the public as signaling the imminent end of the terrorist organization.[5] At the time, the regime offered no physical evidence proving its claims and several government sources confidently stressed that the military command never released the photos of al-Menaei's corpse in order to protect the Bedouin assassins, and their clans, from the inevitable retaliation of ABM. According to a source with strong ties to intelligence, the regime decided to allow a wave of speculation that was triggered by the group's statement denying the death of al-Menaei.[6]

The official story wasn't convincing, but ABM did not quite manage to disprove it. They published poor-quality photographs of al-Menaei supposedly reading the news of his assassination on a laptop. The authenticity of the photos was never independently verified, but it raised the question of why ABM, with its sophisticated media apparatus, failed to publish a video of al-Menaei himself denying his death.

Al-Menaei transformed into a legend; people spoke of him leading operations and parading his troops in the villages south of Rafah, but no one ever testified to coming in direct contact with him or even seeing him from afar. In July 2014, almost two weeks after al-Sisi's ascent to the presidency of Egypt, ABM attempted to further deny the death of al-Menaei by publishing a half-hour video detailing the August 2011 cross-border attack that killed several Israeli soldiers near the southern resort of Eilat. The video, which showed al-Menaei describing the operation he allegedly spearheaded three years earlier, did not address the claims of his assassination and was suspected of being filmed before his alleged death.

Osama Ali, referred to as Abu al-Walidin in ABM's July 2014 video, was one of the leading militants who executed the Eilat attack. He also happened to spend a few days at the Rabaa al-Adawiya Mosque, not far from his house in eastern Cairo, in February 2011, days after Mubarak's downfall and the beginning of the Libyan revolution. This mosque, which witnessed the massacre of the Muslim Brotherhood supporters in 2013, was chosen back then as the Cairo center for a humanitarian aid campaign overseen by Muslim Brotherhood officials in support of the besieged towns of eastern Libya. Ali, a bearded, long-haired, pious man in his late twenties, stood out among a few dozen Egyptian and Libyan youth who volunteered to collect, organize, and load tons of donations on trucks heading to the border town of Salloum. Waving the Libyan revolution's flag, he chanted for hours on end in front of the massive mosque compound, until the aid convoy departed en route to Libya.

He had also participated in the January 25 revolution in Cairo. "I spent eighteen days in Tahrir Square without a shower, I finally showered after Mubarak's downfall," Ali said at the time. "Now that I have tasted freedom, I want to see one nation, I want an Islamic State that doesn't differentiate between Libyans, Egyptians, or Tunisians."[7]

Returning from Salloum, Ali was looking for work in Cairo.[8] A few weeks later, during the last week of March, he was once again waving the Libyan flag during a protest held in front of the Arab League Headquarters on the edge of Tahrir Square, demanding foreign military intervention against Gaddafi's regime.

All recent attempts to reach Ali's family or friends after watching the recorded message in which he called for jihad and martyrdom were in vain. There was nothing left of him but a Facebook account that was last updated in July 2011, some two months before his death in the cross-border attack. How Osama Ali had gone, in a matter of five months, from searching for a job in the capital Cairo to becoming an ABM fighter who fired his RPG at an Israeli Air Force gunship that was hunting his fellow militants in the desert of Eilat remains a mystery.

Knowing whether ABM approached Ali at Rabaa al-Adawiya Mosque or in front of the Arab League required information that was buried along with him and his commander, Shadi al-Menaei. Whether the group recruited him or he volunteered to fight for his dream of establishing the Islamic State will remain unknown. But Ali's story was revealing of the extent of Ansar Bayt al-Maqdis's reach inside Egypt at a time of unprecedented hopefulness in the aftermath of the January 2011 uprising.

Al-Sisi's Reign

Since he led the ouster of Morsi, Defense Minister Abdel-Fattah al-Sisi continued to repeat his warnings that terrorism would continue, and to pledge that the war against it would too. What he said was accurate, not because al-Sisi offered any evidence to back his regime's claims that Sinai's militancy was backed by external powers such as Hamas and his political rivals, but because his 'war on terror' was the main source of empowerment for militant organizations.

By the time al-Sisi was named president in June 2014, Ansar Bayt al-Maqdis had changed its attack policies: the number of shoot and run operations that targeted security checkpoints and facilities across North Sinai on a daily basis began decreasing and were replaced by less frequent yet far more lethal attacks. On July 19, 2014, the group's armed militants ambushed a military post in the Farafra Oasis, hundreds of kilometers deep into Egypt's western desert, and killed twenty-one military personnel. The attack took place nineteen days after five military personnel were killed in a confrontation with smugglers at the same post.[9]

Three months later, on October 24, 2014, ABM led another attack in broad daylight on Karm al-Qawadis military post, on the southern outskirts of Sheikh Zuwayyed.[10] The attack took place a few days after the post was reinforced with tanks and armored vehicles. They killed thirty-one soldiers and officers, some of whom were shot as they fled the scene, while one was executed as he begged his killers for mercy. The terrorists raised their flag over one of the tanks as they commandeered the weapons and ammunition of the post.[11]

In reaction to the Karm al-Qawadis attack, the most lethal since the 2011 rise of ABM, an emergency meeting of Egypt's National Defense Council declared a three-month-long, all-night curfew, from 7:00 p.m. to 7:00 a.m., in North Sinai's capital al-Arish, which had been exempted from the curfew in Sheikh Zuwayyed and Rafah since it began in July 2013. The military command blamed the attack on infiltrators from the Gaza Strip and announced the start of the gradual evacuation of the border town of Rafah in order create a buffer zone with the aim of shutting down the remaining underground smuggling tunnels. Over the weeks following the decision to evacuate and erase one of the world's most ancient towns, the military forces destroyed some two thousand houses in the one-kilometer area lining the border with Gaza.

Fearing an outbreak of hostilities in the densely populated Rafah, the Egyptian regime ordered financial compensation of LE700 to LE1,200 per meter of construction destroyed to the forcibly displaced residents. Beyond the compensation, no plans were made for temporary residence to shelter the displaced families, alternate schools to take the children, or a state-run initiative to revise the government records of more than ten thousand citizens.[12] Receiving the orders of an AK-47 wielding officer flanked by his tank and obedient conscripts, a population that survived the region's wars and political turbulence over the centuries was left with no option but to bundle up their lives, stand aside, and watch the military's technicians install sacks of explosives that demolished their history.

The weeping of the elderly and of children, the squandered futures of youth, and the voice of reason warning of catastrophic repercussions didn't matter to al-Sisi. Neither did the fact that thousands were already displaced by the brutality of the ongoing military campaign, as he was surrounded by the cheering elite of the capital Cairo. Soliman Gouda, an infamous writer, said the following in an opinion piece published by the country's leading independent newspaper, *al-Masry al-Youm*:

> If Sinai will continue to be chronic headache, let us destroy it, burn it, turn it into fire, and let us chase them around it, from its first inch to the last, until no living creature is left on its land. Its northern people shall depart, if required, so we exterminate any living creature left behind them, without exceptions.[13]

The likes of Soliman Gouda, whose geographical knowledge of Sinai, let alone sociological, political, or economic, remains highly suspect, were the only ones given unconditional freedom to speak and publicly incite aggression and violations of constitutional, legal, and human rights. When the decision to erase the easternmost border town was taken and executed overnight, contrary to development plans that haven't been implemented since 1982, none of Sinai's most knowledgeable activists, politicians, or community figures spoke their mind. Even journalists and researchers of the peninsula's current affairs refrained from saying anything beyond the clichés publishable by the mainstream media tightly controlled by the al-Sisi regime.

The desperation and threats, the dozens of activists and journalists thrown behind bars, the draconian military tribunals and prisons, and Ansar Bayt al-Maqdis's sharpened knives that began beheading civilians it deemed collaborators with the Egyptian military was enough to silence everyone. "Time will be the judge of that," was the only reasonable comment after al-Sisi's decision to evacuate and raze the historic town of Rafah, a decision that blessed the futile policy of collective punishment and gave it the go-ahead to reach farther across the community.

Nothing was more unfortunate for tens of thousands of people than realizing that the only way for their point to be proved, the only way for Cairo's cheering elite to hear the warnings of North Sinai's youth and the weeping of its displaced elderly, was for another terrorist attack to strike and destroy the illusions spread by a military regime that refused to admit that Rafah's tunnels, a product of the regime's own policies, constituted the smallest of dozens of endemic, decades-old reasons behind the flourishing insurgency.

It wasn't long before time did judge the efficiency of the all-night curfew, the continued shelling of villages, and the creation of a buffer zone. Less than one month after the Karm al-Qawadis massacre, during the second week of November 2014, Ansar Bayt al-Maqdis pledged allegiance to Abu Bakr al-Baghdadi's Islamic State in Iraq and the Levant, ISIL, and declared the establishment of the Sinai Province as the Egyptian branch of al-Baghdadi's caliphate.

The Sinai Province's first major attack took place on January 29, 2015, four days after the fourth anniversary of the January 2011 uprising. Intent on breaking all of their former records, a synchronized operation targeted the military's North Sinai command, the 101 Battalion, in the center of al-Arish with explosive-laden vehicles and suicide bombers, while its armed elements waged attacks on the Security Headquarters, the police club, the military hotel, and eight different checkpoints spread between the towns of Sheikh Zuwayyed and Rafah. According to the military's statements, thirty-two officers and soldiers were killed—among them was Brigadier Sayyed Ahmed Fawzi, commander of North Sinai's leading 12th Armored Infantry Brigade—and 105 others were injured.[14]

A statement about the attack, by the newly-appointed military spokesman, Brigadier Mohamed Samir, said that:

As a result of the successful blows dealt by the armed forces and the police to the terrorist elements in North Sinai, and the failure of the terrorist Muslim Brotherhood organization to spread chaos during the celebrations of the January 25 revolution, an attack was waged by terrorists on facilities of the armed forces and security authorities in al-Arish using explosive-laden vehicles and mortar fire. [15]

The Countdown

In the years after the Taba, Sharm al-Sheikh, and Dahab bombings in 2004, 2005, and 2006, it became normal for Sinai's residents to hear the screams of Bedouins being tortured inside the SSI offices. But even back then, when close to five thousand people were reportedly detained from almost every corner of the peninsula, people spoke of their agony to reporters and human rights lawyers from some of the most respected local and international organizations.

While Hosni Mubarak spent the last few days of his reign in the luxurious mansions of Sharm al-Sheikh, the southern resort built and owned almost entirely by Hussein Salem, the Egyptian-Spanish business tycoon and the mastermind of Egypt's corrupt natural gas deal with Israel, the mothers and children of the far-flung villages were terrified to even seek information on the whereabouts of their detained husbands and fathers. Back then it was the short-lived al-Tawhid wa-l-Jihad and its little-known founder Khaled Musaid that sparked the peninsula's terrorist activity, which Habib El-Adly and his SSI officers decided to eliminate by launching their campaign of brutal oppression that, until 2013, was thought to be the worst in Sinai's history.

The victims of those years were the poorest, the most marginalized, and the Bedouins who for years, fearing detention and worse, refrained from stepping foot on the main roads around their villages, let alone going near a big resort like Sharm al-Sheikh. This experience became the seed that grew into a rebellion. And it was El-Adly and the heads of his security apparatus that secured Mubarak's lavish residence and golf course standing minutes away from the simmering volcano of Sinai's disgruntled tribes. And, according to Omar Suleiman,[16] Mubarak's confidante and former head of the Egyptian General Intelligence Directorate, El-Adly was the one who vowed to crush the protests scheduled for January 25, 2011, a few days before his black-clad central security forces were fleeing in the face of North Sinai's fury.

Four years on, instead of leaked videos showing the torture of civilians inside police stations, two photos of dead Bedouins were published on October 10, 2014, by military spokesman Mohamed Samir, who claimed they were terrorists hunted by the ongoing military campaign.[17] Not so long after, on October 28, and in a strikingly similar manner to years of such leaks under Mubarak's rule, a video, taken by one of the torturers in military uniform, showing the same two men, their blue and grey Bedouin *thoubs* stained with their own blood, being brutalized by military personnel at an unidentified location, spread online. The two Bedouin men were later identified as Yousef Eteik and Ahmed Freig from the village of al-Mehdiya.

There was change, indeed. Those who detained, tortured, killed, and fabricated stories to cover their crimes weren't the state security, their head wasn't Mubarak's El-Adly, or even al-Sisi's minister of the interior, Mohamed Ibrahim, whose tenure recorded the highest number of unlawful killings of protesters in the modern history of Egypt.[18] They were rather the military personnel whose al-Arish's 101 Battalion, Sheikh Zuwayyed's al-Zohour camp, and Rafah's Military Intelligence base had stood untouched in January 2011 when dozens of police facilities were burnt to the ground in North Sinai and hundreds more across Egypt. They were the Egyptian military personnel that were, four years ago, met by the cheering of Bedouins who hadn't seen them in the country's only demilitarized border zone since the beginning of the war with Israel in 1967.

Just a few weeks later, on November 29, 2014, Hosni Mubarak and his sons, Habib El-Adly and his commanders of the pre-2011 police apparatus, and Hussein Salem and his co-defendants in the natural gas agreement trial were all acquitted of all charges of killing protesters and squandering the country's resources.

However, when the heart-wrenching video of the torture of the two Bedouins surfaced, constituting evidence of the dozens of stories whispered during the months-long curfew in North Sinai, President al-Sisi's regime was too occupied preparing for the Economic Development Conference held in March 2015 that aimed to attract billions of dollars of investments and financial aid from across the globe. Ironically, the most important event Egypt had hosted since 2011 was held at Mubarak's favorite conference hall in Sharm al-Sheikh, and its attending royalties and high-ranking officials from over a hundred nations were accommodated at the very same hotels and resorts of Hussein Salem.

For al-Sisi, his regime, his loyalists, and the foreign governments and businesses that pledged billions of dollars in investments, the conference was successful, and anyone who dared speak a word that didn't enthusiastically celebrate this unprecedented achievement was immediately tagged a traitor, a Muslim Brotherhood sympathizer, or a bloodthirsty worshipper of Abu Bakr al-Baghdadi. Whether the economic conference succeeded or not, whether it raked in billions or a handful of empty promises, nothing will change the reality that some three hundred kilometers to the north, villages were being wiped off the face of the earth, Rafah's houses continued to be demolished, Sheikh Zuwayyed was left without water, electricity, phone networks, or fuel, and hundreds of businesses in al-Arish were on the edge of bankruptcy as the curfew continued.

Over 120,000 people of North Sinai's volatile corner stand hopeless between the lethal bullets and underground dungeons of the military-run state, and the beheadings and recruitment calls of al-Baghdadi's Sinai Province. Akin to Mubarak's post-2004 endeavor in Sinai, al-Sisi's regime may be able to defeat the insurgency with more brutality. But it wasn't the insurgency that called for, and accomplished, Mubarak's downfall in January 2011. Back then, the military was the savior at a time when the loudest chants, from Cairo's Tahrir Square to Rafah's al-Masoura, echoed "the people and the military are one hand."

Today, al-Sisi's regime is capable of ruling only as long as it maintains the iron-grip imposed by its tanks, Apache gunships, and the random fire of its AK-47s. Its only accomplishment is failing to plan for what will happen when the iron-grip loosens, and soon or later, in a country torn apart by polarization and an ailing economy, the grip will loosen.

NOTES

Chapter 1

1 Khalil Jabr died in June 2011, five months after documenting Mohamed Atef's death. His story was collected through various sources.

2 Masked with his traditional Bedouin scarf, the identity of Abdallah remains unknown even to those who witnessed him firing his machine gun on January 27, 2011.

3 Several interviews with Mostafa Singer in al-Arish, Sheikh Zuwayyed, and Cairo, 2011, 2012, and 2013.

4 Gen. Murad Mowafi is a military officer, a former head of the Egyptian Military Intelligence and Reconnaissance Directorate between 2004 and 2010, who was appointed governor of North Sinai in 2010 and replaced Gen. Omar Suleiman as head of the Egyptian General Intelligence Directorate on January 31, 2011.

5 In September 2011, during the Mubarak trial, former EGID head Gen. Omar Suleiman testified to the details of cabinet meetings, attended by Minister of the Interior Gen. Habib El-Adly, in which Hosni Mubarak was advised on the status of the January 25, 2011 protests. Suleiman stated that every member of the cabinet, including himself, underestimated the magnitude of the events. (See Hend Mokhtar, "al-Youm al-Sabi' tanshur shahadat Omar Suleiman allati addat ila al-hukm 'ala Mubarak wa-l-Adly bi-l-mu'abbad," *al-Youm al-Sabea*, 2 June 2012).

6 Several interviews with Ibrahim Abu Ashraf al-Menaei in al-Mehdiya and other parts of the Sinai Peninsula, 2011, 2012, and 2013.

7 Interview with Hassan al-Nakhlawi in al-Arish, 2012.

8 Several interviews with Col. Khaled Okasha in Cairo, 2012 and 2013.

9 Names of SSI officers mentioned in the book have been shortened to just initials.

10 Collected testimonies by the author during interviews with several people including activists, journalists, and tribesmen.

11 Interview with a Rafah native and member of al-Remeilat tribe, Rafah, 2013.

12 Observations from a tour by the author of the devastated SSI building in Rafah in 2012.

13 Over years of reporting in Sinai, the author has been aware of only three police or military personnel of Bedouin descent.

14 Testimony of Mohamed, Bilal al-Akhrasi's father, during an interview in al-Arish, 2012.

15 Interview with Hani Shukrallah in Cairo, 2013.

16 Ayman Noufal is a field commander of the Ezzidine al-Qassam Brigades. He was arrested in 2008 in the city of al-Arish and remained in prison until his escape in January 2011.

17 Abu Arrab al-Sawarka is one of a few aliases the trafficker went by. Through several tribal connections, he agreed to be interviewed in 2011, after threatening that revealing his real name would lead to "unpleasant consequences."

18 Cairo is surrounded by Bedouin clans, the majority of which are descendants of major tribes from the western and eastern deserts of Egypt and the Sinai Peninsula, others descend from North African tribes. Despite his vast knowledge, Abu Arrab refused to specify which clans were involved in attacking prisons in January 2011. But, given the far-flung locations of the prisons in different parts of Egypt, it is apparent that more than one clan and/or criminal syndicate were involved.

19 According to testimonies of several former government officials, including former Minister of the Interior Mansour el-Essawy. See, Yousef Hosni, "Khubara': muhakimat Mursi ila tastanid ila dalil," *al-Jazeera*, 23 December 2013.

20 Sami Shehab is the operational alias of Mohamed Youssef Mansour, a Hezbollah field commander arrested in Egypt in 2008 and sentenced to fifteen years in prison over charges of smuggling and plotting terrorist attacks. His trial along with twenty other defendants became known as the Hezbollah Cell Case.

21 In mid-2011, Mostafa al-Fiqqi made his statements during an appearance on "al-Qahira al-Youm," a widely viewed talk show hosted by prominent presenter Amr Adib on the pan-Arab Orbit Television Network. See, https://www.youtube.com/watch?v=cQ9xKpJmvNg

22 For Major al-Dardir's on-air testimony, see https://www.youtube.com/watch?v=2FUGeWRIydA

23 Human Rights Watch, *Egypt: Mass Arrests and Torture in Sinai*, 22 February 2005.

24 Figure provided by Hassan al-Nakhlawi, co-founder of Sinai Prisoners Defense Front, during an interview in al-Arish, 2012.

25 Throughout three and half years of reporting in Sinai, more than two dozen people described the exact same method of torture by hanging and electrocution. Several people interviewed also sustained permanent disabilities in their arms, allegedly due to the long hours of hanging.

26 In 2012, the author obtained a copy of the leaked document carrying the names of 'enhanced interrogation' officers across Egypt. More than half of the names on the list were referred to in interviews conducted across Sinai over a period of more than three years.

27 Figures provided by Hassan al-Nakhlawi, according to statistics of the Sinai Prisoners Defense Front.

28 Masaad Abu Fajr, "Kama'in mutaharrika: min al-Gharbaniyat ila Abu Za'bal," al-Dostor, 30 September 2011.

29 This was originally published on an online activist forum, which is no longer active.

30 Figures provided by Hassan al-Nakhlawi according to statistics of the Sinai Prisoners Defense Front, al-Arish, 2012. Other independent lawyers confirmed these figures.

31 Magda Salem, "Wazir al-Dakhiya: Jari al-ifraj 'an jami' mu'taqili Sini'," al-Youm al-Sabea, 23 February 2011.

32 Reuters and Barak Ravid. "Netanyahu warns outcome of Egypt revolution could be like Iran's," Haaretz, January 31 2011.

33 Meetings with several Israeli government officials, Jerusalem and Tel Aviv, 2013.

34 Interview with Ehud Yaari, Jerusalem, October 2013.

35 Mira Tzoreff, "Restless young Egyptians: Where did you come from and where will you go?" Sharqiyya 1.1, The Moshe Dayan Center for Middle East and African Studies (2010).

36 Interview with Mira Tzoreff, Tel Aviv, October 2013.

37 Observations of several Israeli government officials and independent politicians interviewed by the author in 2013.

Chapter 2

1 Collective testimonies of several people from the village next to the chamber.

2 Interview with Abu Sakl, al-Arish, 2012.

3 Interview with Mohamed Yahya, al-Arish, 2012.

4 Interview with Salman Abu Zeina, al-Arish, 2012.

5 The author accompanied Abu Draa to the bomb site a few hours after the explosion.

6   The "Alpha 6" fake bomb detector invented by British businessman, or rather hustler, Samuel Tree, and sold to Egypt and Iraq among several countries (despite confirmations that the device never passed the required tests, and certainly never detected bombs) is still used at checkpoints in Egypt. The so-called bomb detector was, not surprisingly, only sold to countries known for widespread corruption and, in October 2014, Tree was sentenced to jail along with his wife and business partner. This supposedly intelligent antenna isn't only rattled by explosive materials, but also by medications, shampoo, and deodorant—a disturbing fact that sometimes pushes security personnel to apply strip searches to transport buses only to find out that what triggered their suspicion was some diabetes pills as carried by millions of Egyptians who suffer from the wide-spread condition. ("Fake bomb detector husband jailed for three years," *BBC*, 3 October 2014).

7   Despite this appearance, their approach to security is often lax: they do not check vehicles thoroughly, or for any of those shoulder fired anti-aircraft missiles we constantly hear that the police seized on some random highway; they only glance at IDs and driver's licenses, if they do decide to be thorough.

8   Bedouins are known for their skill at following tracks and are normally sought after by the authorities and tribal customary courts (see chapter 5) to assist in gathering evidence in cases of theft and murder.

9   Interview with Ibrahim Abu Elayyan, at a tea shop on the highway between Bir al-Abd and al-Arish, 2011.

10 Interview with Abdallah Jahama, al-Arish, 2011.

11 al-Azhar Scholars Front, "Bayan jabhat 'ulama' al-azhar: ila jami' al-'amilin bi masani' tasdir al-ghaz al-masry ila al-yahud," 5 May 2008. Translations of Quranic quotes from www.quran.com

12 Case documents presented during an interview with Ambassador Ibrahim Yousri, Cairo, 2012.

13 "Egypt's Lost Power," *al-Jazeera*, 9 June, http://webapps. aljazeera.net/aje/custom/2014/egyptlostpower/index.html#top

14 Egyptian Center for Economic and Social Rights, "Hukm waqf tasdir al-ghaz li Isra'il," 17 July 2010.

15 "Mahkama misriya tu'ayyid istimrar tasdir al-ghaz li Isra'il," *Reuters Arabic*, 2 February 2009.

16 "Nanshur haythiyat hukm al-idariya al-'ulya fi qadiyat bi' al-ghaz al-misri ila Isra'il," *al-Youm al-Sabea*, 11 March 2010.

17 Interview with Ehud Yaari, Jerusalem, October 2013.

18 "Egypt's Lost Power," *al-Jazeera*.

19 Interview with Mira Tzoreff, Tel Aviv, October 2013.

20 This incident/information was confirmed by two police sergents based in Sinai, who spoke on condition of anonymity.
21 Bedouin guards and several tribal elders who cooperated with security authorities gave details on tactics known to be used by criminals in Sinai. They failed to explain why authorities failed to employ such knowledge in fighting crime.
22 Several interviews with Col. Khaled Okasha in Cairo, 2012 and 2013.
23 Phone interview with Abu Eid (al-Arish, 2012), who insisted on being identified only by his alias.
24 Harriet Sherwood, "Egypt cancels Israeli gas contract," *The Guardian*, 23 April 2012.
25 Rana Taha, "Salem and Fahmy imprisoned over Israel gas deal," *Daily News Egypt*, 28 June 2012.

Chapter 3

1 Mohamed Fawzy, *Harb al-thalatha sanawat 1967–1970* (Cairo: Dar al-Wehda Press, 1988), 151–72, 375–82.
2 Mohamed Abdel-Ghani al-Gamasi, *Mudhakirat al-Gamasi: Harb uktober 1973* (Cairo: General Egyptian Book Organization (GEBO), 1989), 123.
3 Chaim Herzog, *The Arab–Israeli Wars* (New York: Random House, 1982), 165.
4 Fawzy, *The Three Years War*, 151–72.
5 Interview with General Fouad Hussein, Cairo, 2011.
6 Gen. Fouad Hussein wrote several books including *The Holy Sinai*, and dozens of articles on the Sinai Peninsula. He continues to be a regular guest on various television shows.
7 Several interviews with Mohamed al-Filistini in Sheikh Zuwayyed and al-Arish, 2011, 2012, and 2013. Fearing intimidation by the authorities due to the sensitivity of his comments, he preferred to be referred to by his alias.
8 Fawzy, *The Three Years War*, 151–72.
9 Phone interview with Adnan Abu Amer, Cairo–Gaza, 2014.
10 Alan Cowell and Douglas Jehl, "Luxor survivors say killers fired methodically," *New York Times*, 23 November 1997.
11 John Daniszewski, "Islamic Group taunts Egyptian president after massacre," *Los Angeles Times*, 21 November 1997.
12 Interview with Ali Eddin Helal, Cairo, 2011.
13 Besides the film that featured him, Ezzat Hanafi's story was told extensively by the media at the time of his downfall. See, for example, Ibrahim al-Garhi, "Suqut Shamshun fi qariya al-nakhayla," *BBC*, 1 March 2004; Mamdouh Thabet, "Tanfith hukm al-i'daam fi Ezzat Hanafi wa shaqiqihi fi sijn burj al-'arab," *al-Masry al-Youm*, 16 June 2006.

14 Interviews and informal talks with various personalities (who did not want to be named) in Sinai and other parts of Egypt, many involved in smuggling, who have provided such "services" to police personnel on more than one occasion.

15 al-Garhi, "Suqut Shamshun fi qariya al-nakhayla."

16 Thabet, "Executing Ezzat Hanafi and his brother in Burj al-Arab Prison."

17 Several interviews with Gen. Mohamed Okasha, Cairo, 2011, 2012, and 2013.

18 Several interviews with Abu Suleiman al-Tarabin in North and South Sinai, 2012 and 2013. Like Abu Arrab al-Sawarka, he insisted, with a tacit threat, that he was only to be identified by one of his aliases.

19 Interview with Gen. Fouad Allam, Cairo, 2013.

20 Several interviews with Col. Khaled Okasha, Cairo, 2012 and 2013.

21 Figure provided by Hassan al-Nakhlawi, co-founder of Sinai Prisoners Defense Front.

22 Sarah El-Deeb, "Bedouins lead hunt for Sinai bombers," *Boston Globe*, 7 February 2005.

23 John Ward Anderson and Molly Moore, "Palestinian leader Arafat dies in France; Burial in West Bank on Saturday," *Washington Post*, 11 November 2004.

24 Nicolas Pelham, "Gaza's Tunnel Phenomenon: The Unintended Dynamics of Israel's Siege," *Journal of Palestine Studies* 41, Institute For Palestine Studies (2011/2012).

25 "Abbas declared victor in Palestinian election," *CNN*, 11 January 2011.

26 Scott Wilson, "Hamas sweeps Palestinian elections, complicating peace efforts in Mideast," *Washington Post*, 27 January 2006.

27 "WikiLeaks: Suleiman vowed to prevent Hamas rule in Gaza," *YNet News*, 11 February 2011.

28 "Hamas rockets," Global Security, n.d.

29 Matthew Levitt, "Hamas: Towards a Lebanese-style war of attrition," *Policywatch* 367, The Washington Institute for Near East Policy (26 February 2002).

30 Azriel Lorber, "The growing threat of unguided Qassam rockets," *Nativ* 1.17, Ariel Center for Policy Research (January 2004).

31 Israel Ministry of Foreign Affairs, "Gaza: Lists of controlled entry items," 4 July 2010.

32 Palestinian Ministry of National Economy in cooperation with the Applied Reseach Institute – Jerusalem (ARIJ), *The economic costs of the Israeli occupation for the occupied Palestinian territory*, September 2011.

33 Israel Intelligence Heritage and Commemoration Center, "Anti-Israeli terrorism in 2007 and its trends in 2008," Israel Ministry of Foreign Affairs, 5 June 2008.

34 The only other soldier kidnapped in Gaza was Cpl. Nahshon Waxman; he was killed after his abduction in 1994. See Clyde Haberman, "Kidnapped soldier is killed as Israeli troops attempt rescue at captors' hideout," *New York Times*, 15 October 1994.

35 David Rosenberg and Gwen Ackerman, "Israel ready to use extreme tactics to free soldier," Bloomberg, 28 June 2006.

36 Rosenberg and Ackerman, "Israel ready to use extreme tactics to free soldier."

37 Human Rights Watch, *Under Cover of War*, 20 April 2009.

38 Figure provided by Rafah Terminal Security officers during unofficial talks with the author in 2012. Egypt and the Palestinian Authority never officially stated the number of those who fled into Sinai in 2007.

39 Interview with Hamid al-Shaer, Gaza, 2012.

40 Figures quoted in "Gazans make new border wall hole," *BBC*, 25 January 2008.

41 Figures quoted in Sarah El-Deeb, "Border breach temporary boost for Gaza," Associated Press, 28 January 2008.

42 Steven Erlanger, "Palestinians topple Gaza wall and cross to Egypt," *New York Times*, 24 January 2008.

43 See, for example, Abdel-Halim Salem, "Ahali Ghaza yataqaddamuna nahw al-Arish ba'da tafjir al-hudud," *al-Youm al-Sabea*, 23 January 2008.

44 All three smugglers refused to be identified by their real names or even their usual aliases. Interviews and other unofficial talks took place in Rafah, Sheikh Zuwayyed, and the village of al-Mehdiya in 2012.

45 Information gathered through interviews and unofficial talks with smugglers, tunnel owners, and residents of the border area, 2011, 2012, and 2013.

46 Interviews and informal talks with smugglers and tunnel owners. Some traffickers of African migrants were said to have turned to arms smuggling due to their powerful connections in Sudan, Eritrea, and Ethiopia, from where most of the victims of African migrant trafficking come.

47 Amos Harel and Avi Issacharoff, "Hamas gets Iranian plans for improved Qassams," *Haaretz*, 28 March 2008.

48 Matthew Levitt, "Hezbollah's man in Egypt," *Perspectives on Terrorism* 8.2, Terrorism Research Initiative and the Center for Terrorism and Security Studies (2014).

49 Charlie Szrom, "Iran–Hamas relationship in 2008," Iran Tracker, 27 March 2009.

50 Yoram Cohen and Matthew Levitt, "Hamas arms smuggling: Egypt's challenge," *Policywatch* 1484, The Washington Institute for Near East Policy (2 March 2009).

51 Several interviews with Gen. Mohamed Okasha, Cairo, 2011, 2012, and 2013.
52 Cohen and Levitt, "Hamas arms smuggling: Egypt's challenge."
53 Several interviews with Col. Khaled Okasha, Cairo, 2012 and 2013.
54 These comments may seem far-fetched, but in mid-2012, the author wit-
    nessed two heavy trucks being customized at a mechanic shop in the village
    of al-Mehdiya, while another one was being taken apart piece by piece,
    allegedly to be smuggled into Gaza through the tunnels.
55 Seham Abdel-Aal, "al-Muwajiha!" *al-Ahram*, 11 March 2000.
56 Olivia Holt-Ivry, "Arms control in civil society: Controlling conventional
    arms smuggling in Sinai," in *Arms control and national security: New horizons*,
    edited by Emily B. Landau and Anat Kurz, Memorandum No. 135 (Tel
    Aviv: Institute for National Security Studies, 2014).
57 Nissan Ratzlav-Katz, "Shteinitz: FM Livni Withheld Egyptian Smuggling
    Video from US," *Arutz Sheva* 7, 24 December 2007.
58 Mohannad Sabry, "Arms smuggling explodes across Egypt–Libya border,"
    McClatchy Newspapers, 8 September 2011.
59 Sabry, "Arms smuggling explodes across Egypt–Libya border."
60 The author visited Rafah's Masoura market twice in 2012, while it was still
    known as Misrata market.
61 Tim Lister and Mohamed Fadel Fahmy, "Smuggling weapons to Gaza –
    the long way," *Security Clearance*, CNN, 12 November 2012.
62 Christopher Hope, "WikiLeaks: Suleiman told Israel he would 'cleanse
    Sinai of arms runners to Gaza,'" *The Telegraph*, 9 February 2011.
63 Interview with Yossi Kuperwasser, Jerusalem, October 2013.

Chapter 4

1 Ghazi al-Sorani, "Anfaq Rafah wa atharuha al-iqtisadiya wa-l-ijtima'iya wa-
   l-siyasiya," *al-Hewar al-Motamaden*, 14 December 2008.
2 Wafiq al-Agha and Samir Abu Mudallala, "Iqtisad al-anfaq bi qita' Ghaza:
   Darura wataniya, am karitha iqtisadiya wa ijtima'iya?" *al-Azhar University
   in Gaza Magazine* 13 (2011), 16.
3 Interview with Adnan Abu Amer, Cairo–Gaza, 2014.
4 Interview with Hamid, Gaza, 2012.
5 al-Agha and Abu Mudallala, "Iqtisad al-anfaq bi qita' Ghaza," 18.
6 Human Rights Watch, *Razing Rafah*, 18 October 2004.
7 Interview with Ehud Yaari, Jerusalem, October 2013.
8 On May 14, 1948, in reaction to David Ben Gurion's declaration of
   the independence of the state of Israel, Egypt, Jordan, and Syria waged
   war against the newly founded state. Despite Egypt's military success
   and taking of the Negev and major parts of the Palestinian territories,
   it was soon driven out by Israeli military forces and encircled in the

Mediterranean coastal enclave that became known as the Gaza Strip. Egypt remained in full military control of Gaza until Israel occupied it along with the Sinai Peninsula in June 1967.

9   Steven Erlanger, "Hamas leader faults Israeli sanction plan," *New York Times*, 18 February.

10   Interview with Benedetta Berti, Tel Aviv, October 2013.

11   al-Agha and Abu Mudallala, "Iqtisad al-anfaq bi qita' Ghaza," 10–15.

12   Several interviews with Gen. Mohamed Okasha, Cairo, 2011, 2012, and 2013.

13   Interviews with Hussein, al-Arish, 2012 and 2013. Traumatized by his former experience with State Security Investigations, he requested his identity remain hidden.

14   Several interviews with Mohamed al-Filistini in Sheikh Zuwayyed and al-Arish, 2011, 2012, and 2013.

15   al-Agha and Abu Mudallala, "Iqtisad al-anfaq bi qita' Ghaza," 17.

16   The description of tunnel building operations was provided during interviews with several smugglers and tunnel owners in both Sinai and the Gaza Strip.

17   Nicolas Pelham, "Gaza's Tunnel Phenomenon: The Unintended Dynamics of Israel's Siege," *Journal of Palestine Studies* 41, Institute For Palestine Studies (2011/12).

18   Pelham, "Gaza's Tunnel Phenomenon."

19   Pelham, "Gaza's Tunnel Phenomenon."

20   al-Agha and Abu Mudallala, "Iqtisad al-anfaq bi qita' Ghaza," 21.

21   Pelham, "Gaza's Tunnel Phenomenon."

22   al-Agha and Abu Mudallala, "Iqtisad al-anfaq bi qita' Ghaza," 20.

23   al-Agha and Abu Mudallala, "Iqtisad al-anfaq bi qita' Ghaza," 18.

24   Interview with Mubarak loyalist and businessman, conducted in Cairo, 2013.

25   Interview with Emad in Rafah, 2012. He requested his identity not be revealed.

26   Several interviews with Col. Khaled Okasha, Cairo, 2012 and 2013.

27   Amnesty International, *Israel/Gaza: Operation "Cast Lead": 22 days of death and destruction,*" 2 July 2009.

28   Pelham, "Gaza's Tunnel Phenomenon."

29   Interviews with tunnel owners and smugglers operating on both sides of the border, 2011, 2012, and 2013.

30   *Salafi* is the general term used to refer to the many variations of conservative Islamist ideologies, all of which see themselves as followers of the Holy Quran, Prophet Muhammad's teachings, or *sunna*, and the methods of *al-salaf al-saleh*, or the Righteous Ancestors. The Salafi current recognizes jihad, or holy war, but doesn't go beyond verbally and intellectually

endorsing it. The jihadist current, also known as *al-salafiya al-jihadiya*, is a more extreme current within the broader spectrum of Islamist movements; it permits and adopts the use of arms against what it defines as enemies of Islam and Muslims—a broad concept that even includes Muslims who are viewed as aggressors. The *takfiri* current is the most extreme of all Islamist ideologies: it views almost everyone as pagans and infidels. Some interpretations within the *takfiri* current excuse the non-believers for ignorance and believe they shouldn't be fought until informed; this minority is normally isolated, while the majority of *takfiris* permit the taking up of arms against non-believers and allow their murder and the seizure of their possessions.

31 Interview with Gen. Fouad Allam, Cairo, 2013.

Chapter 5

1   Several interviews with Asaad al-Beik, al-Arish, 2011, 2012, and 2013.
2   The Quran, Surat Yusuf, verse 40, translation from www.quran.com
3   Yahya al-Ghoul, *al-Qada' al-'urfi fi Sina'* (Cairo: al-Maktab al-Arabi Lil Maaref, 2010), 85–104.
4   Naum Shoucair, *The History of Sinai, New and Old, and Its Geography* (Sinai: Library of St. Catherine's Monastery, 1907), 398–422. The first edition was published in 1907 by Shoucair himself. The book continues to be published by the independent Library of St. Catherine's Monastery in South Sinai.
5   Interview with Yahya al-Ghoul, al-Arish, 2012.
6   Aya Nabil, "al-Sheikh 'Abd al-Hadi: Mubarak ikhtara qada min al-Badu wala'uhum al-awwal lahu," *al-Youm al-Sabea*, 29 February 2012.
7   Several interviews with Hamdin Abu Faisal at his courthouse, during which the author witnessed many hours of hearings, Sheikh Zuwayyed, 2011, 2012, and 2013.
8   The author visited sharia courts in Ismailiya and Marsa Matrouh. The occasional acceptance of sharia courts' verdicts by state courts was confirmed by several judicial workers in off-the-record conversations with the author.
9   Informal talk with David Ignatius, Cairo, 2012.
10 Translation of Quranic quote from www.quran.com, Surat al-Baqara, verse 109.
11 Tribal and sharia judges said almost a dozen cases of *tawthiq* occurred in the five years before Mubarak's downfall. Including other cases involving individuals rather than clans, they said the number would significantly increase.
12 Several interviews with Kuraiem Abu Rukba, Sheikh Zuwayyed, 2012 and 2013.
13 Salah al-Bolok and Osama Khaled, "al-Jama'a al-salafiya bi Sina' tunshi' lijanan li fadd al-munazi'at wa 6 alaf musallih li tanfidh al-ahkam," *al-Masry al-Youm*, 9 August 2011.

14 Interview with former deputy justice minister, Cairo, 2012.

15 Interview with Nageh Ibrahim, Alexandria, 2013.

Chapter 6

1   Naum Shoucair, *The History of Sinai, New and Old, and Its Geography* (Sinai: Library of St. Catherine's Monastery), 352. The first edition was published in 1907 by Shoucair himself. The book continues to be published by the independent Library of St. Catherine's Monastery in South Sinai.

2   The title was given to Sheikh Hassan Khalaf by his fellow fighters in the Sinai Mujahedeen Association; he remains widely known for it until today.

3   Testimonies of several followers of Sufi clerics in North and South Sinai.

4   Several interviews with Gen. Mohamed Okasha, Cairo, 2011, 2012, and 2013.

5   Sara Abou Bakr, "Farag Fouda: Assasination of the word," *Daily News Egypt*, 8 June 2013.

6   Chris Hedges, "Egyptian premier escapes car bomb," *New York Times*, 26 November 1993.

7   Youssef M. Ibrahim, "Egyptian militants blamed in attack on security chief," *New York Times*, 18 August 1993.

8   Craig Turner, "Egypt's leader survives assassination attempt: Africa: Muslim extremists suspected in attack on Mubarak's motorcade in Ethiopia. President is unharmed," *Los Angeles Times*, 27 June 1995.

9   Alan Cowell and Douglas Jehl, "Luxor survivors say killers fired methodically," *New York Times*, 23 November 1997.

10 SSI is the name of the department, the trials are carried out by the state security prosecution and the state security court.

11 Interview with Gen. Fouad Allam, Cairo, 2013.

12 Muhammad Abdel-Salam Faraj's *al-Faridha al-ghayba* and Sayyed Imam al-Sharif's *al-'Umda fi i'dad al-'udda* remain two of the most widely circulating manuscripts among radical Islamist circles.

13 "Death toll rises, Islamist group takes responsibility for Taba bombings," *al-Jazeera*, 9 October 2004.

14 Figure provided by Hassan al-Nakhlawi, founder of the Sinai Prisoners Defense Organization.

15 "Bombers kill 88 at Egyptian resort," *The Guardian*, 23 July 2005.

16 "Egypt police kill Sinai bomb suspect," *al-Jazeera*, 29 September 2005.

17 "Triple blasts rock Egypt resort," *BBC*, 25 April 2006.

18 Interview with a Sinai Bedouin, who did not want to be named, in al-Arish, 2012.

19 "Maqtal za'im jund ansar Allah bi Rafah," *al-Jazeera*, 15 August 2009.

20 Several interviews with Mohamed al-Filistini, al-Arish and Sheikh Zuwayyed, 2011, 2012, and 2013.

21 Interview with Nageh Ibrahim, Alexandria, 2013.

22 Remarks by Nageh Ibrahim in Alexandria 2013. Other convicted Islamists who preferred not to be identified spoke at interviews in Cairo, 2012 and 2013.

23 Ahmed al-Khatib, "Mu'taqilu al-jama'at al-islamiya al-mufraq 'anhuma salihihum al-amn wa rafdihim al-mujtama'…fa asbahu qunbula mawquta," *al-Masry al-Youm*, 20 May 2007.

24 al-Khatib, "Mu'taqilu al-jama'at al-islamiya al-mufraq 'anhuma."

25 al-Khatib, "Mu'taqilu al-jama'at al-islamiya al-mufraq 'anhuma."

26 Mohamed Abu Shama, "Dr. Fadl Manthar al-jihadiyin: Kitab al-Zawahiri kidhb wa buhtan wa mughalitat fiqhiya wa talbis 'ala al-qari'," *al-Sharq al-Awsat*, 18 November 2008.

27 A former minister and security officer commented, on condition of anonymity, on Hosni Mubarak's approach toward Islamist movements since the rise of his son, Gamal, and the subject of his potential run for presidency. Separate interviews, Cairo, 2012.

28 In 2012, the number of industrial zones in Upper Egypt reached thirty-eight, with investments reaching le60 billion. In 2013, the ceiling of investments was raised to le100 billion and eight more industrial zones were introduced. See, "Ziyadat al-manatiq al-sina'iya bi-l-Sa'id ila 46 mintaqa bi ijmali istithmarat 100 milyar jinayh wa 224 alf fursat 'amal," *Bawabat ma'lumat Misr*, March 2013.

29 Munir Adib, "3,000 jihadi ya'uduna ila Misr min Afghanistan wa-l-Shishan wa-l-Bosna wa-l-Sumal wa Iran," *al-Masry al-Youm*, 31 March 2011.

30 Quoted in Hossam Bahgat, "Who let the jihadis out?" *Mada Masr*, 16 February 2014.

31 "al-Maqrizi yanshur al-nass al-kamil li muqabalat al-Shaykh al-Muhandis Muhammad al-Dhawahiri," al-Maqreze Centre For Historical Studies, 21 August 2012.

32 Mohamed Khayal, "'Abbud al-Zumur: na'tadhir li-l-sha'b al-misri 'an qatl al-ra'is al-Sadat," *al-Shorouk*, 8 October 2011.

33 Hossam Tamam, "Entrenching revisions," *Al-Ahram Weekly*, 30 September–6 October 2010.

34 Interview with Ahmed Ban, Cairo, 2013.

35 Hossam Tamam, *The Salafization of the Brotherhood: The decay of the Brotherhood approach and the rise of Salafism* (Alexandria, Egypt: Bibliotheca Alexandrina, 2010), 26.

36 Loai Ali, "Nasr Farid Wasil yastaqil min ri'asat al-hay'a al-shar'iya li-l-huquq wa-l-islah," *al-Youm al-Sabea*, 11 July 2011.

37 Amir Lashin, "Dr Muhammad Yusri…:al-dustur al-islami jahiz wa bi-muwariqat al-ikhwan," *al-Akhbar*, 28 July 2011.

38 Phone interview with a Salafi activist, speaking on condition of anonymity, Cairo–Alexandria, 2013.
39 "al-Ikhwan al-muslimun: yu'ayyiduna al-ta'dilat al-dusturiya fi Misr wa baqi al-harakat al-siyasiya yata'rrid," *BBC Arabic*, 14 March 2011.
40 Amr al-Hadi, "Ya'qub: Intasarna fi ghazwat al-sanadiq wa-l-balad baladna wa-l-sha'b qala na'm li-l-din," *al-Masry al-Youm*, 21 March 2011.
41 Interviews with voters in Salloum at polling stations, March 2011.
42 Ahmed Selim and Hasnaa al-Sherif, "100 mulththam musallah bi-l-madafi' yuhajimuna qism thani al-Arish li muddat 9 sa'at" *al-Ahram*, 31 July 2011.
43 Salah al-Bolok, Ahmed Abu Draa, and Osama Khaled, "al-Masry al-Youm takhtariq al-tanthimat al-musalliha wa taltaqi 2 min manaffidhay ahdath al-Arish," *al-Masry al-Youm*, 2 August 2011.
44 Mohamed Arafa, "Dahlan umm al-Qa'ida wara' fauda Sina'?" *al-Wafd*, 1 August 2011.
45 AviIssacharoff, "Report: Three Egyptians took part in terrorist attacks on southern Israel," *Haaretz*, August 24 2011.
46 Interview with Lt. Col. Peter Lerner, Jerusalem, 2013.
47 Quoted in Isabel Kershner and David D. Kirkpatrick, "Attacks near Israeli resort heighten tensions with Egypt and Gaza," *New York Times*, 18 August 2011.
48 "Israeli airstrikes target Gaza after multiple attacks," *CNN*, 19 August 2011.
49 Different senior commanders of the Popular Resistance Committees applauded the attack during several interviews with local press in Gaza.
50 Several interviews with Gen. Mohamed Okasha, Cairo, 2011, 2012, and 2013.
51 Interview with Abdel-Aziz in Sheikh Zuwayyed, 2012.
52 The video was not broadcast by television channels or online news outlets until 2013 when it was featured in the al-Jazeera documentary "The Masked Man," about the repeated gas pipeline bombings. See http://www. aljazeera. net/reportslibrary/pages/c5066bd1-0836-467a-ada4-e48941c00a0c
53 Yosri Mohamed, "Istimrar al-infilat al-amni bi Sini' yadfa' al-misriyin li-l-mutalabat bi-ta'dil Camp David," *al-Sharq al-Awsat*, 2 February 2012.
54 Aymen Mohsen, "Akef: al-Ikhwan tarfud "Camp David" wa laysa min haqq-ihim ilgha'uha," *Sada al-Balad*, 9 March 2012.
55 Kadri boasted publicly about his time in prison with the Muslim Brotherhood's deputy leader Khairat al-Shater, until the ouster of Mohamed Morsi in July 2013 when he started denying his solid ties to the organization.
56 Interview with Kadri, al-Arish, 2012. After the ouster of Mohamed Morsi in 2013, the author received several warnings not to reveal the identity of Kadri who spoke on the record in 2012. Despite his strong and publicly known ties to the Muslim Brotherhood's Khairat al-Shater, the smuggling businesses, and North Sinai's militant groups, he remains in al-Arish until today.

57 See "Mana' murashshah al-ri'asa Sabbahi min dukhul madinatay al-Sheikh Zuwayyid wa Rafah," *Sinai Now* YouTube Channel, 25 April 2012, https://www.youtube.com/watch?v=vI7gdhoStcg

58 Interview with Azzam Sinjer, Sheikh Zuwayyed, 2012.

59 Hamdi Qassem and Yasser Shemis, "al-Alafat bi-l-Buhayra yushi"una shahid ahdath al-'Abbasiya Samir al-Kayyal," *al-Masry al-Youm*, 5 May 2012; "Hasr al-qatla fi 'ahd al-majlis al-'askari," *WikiThawra*, 2012.

60 "Mursi yasif al-yahud bi-l-qirda wa-l-khanazir . . . wa yatabarra' min tasrihihi," *al-Arabiya*, 17 January 2013.

61 Joel Greenberg, "Gunmen from Egypt's Sinai Peninsula attack Israeli workers, killing one," *Washington Post*, 18 June 2012.

62 Thomas Joscelyn, "Al-Qaeda linked group claims responsibility for attack in Israel," *The Long War Journal*, 19 June 2012.

63 Greenberg, "Gunmen from Egypt's Sinai Peninsula attack Israeli workers, killing one."

64 David Kirkpatrick, "Blow to transition as court dissolves Egypt's parliament, " *New York Times*, 14 June 2012.

65 "English text of SCAF amended Egypt Constitutional Declaration," *Ahram Online*, 18 June 2012.

66 Aaron Y. Zelin, "New video message from Jamā'at Anṣār Bayt al-Maqdis: If You Return (to Sins), We Shall Return (to Our Punishment)," Jihadology. net, 24 July 2012.

67 Transcript from Ayman al-Zawahiri's speeches titled "Messages of Hope and Glad Tidings to our People in Egypt," published periodically on jihadist forums since February 2011.

68 Interview with Gen. Saleh al-Masry, North Sinai Security Directorate, al-Arish, 2012.

69 Several interviews with Abu Arrab Al-Sawarka in Rafah, 2011, 2012, 2013.

70 The comments of both Mohamed al-Zawahiri and Hamdin Abu Faisal were featured in the 2013 al-Jazeera documentary "The Masked Man."

71 Bahgat, "Who let the jihadis out?"

Chapter 7

1 Ron Friedman and Michal Shmulovich, "US follows Israel's lead and issues Sinai travel warning, after Hamas frees terror chief," *Times of Israel*, 4 August 2012.

2 "Israel renews Sinai travel advisory amid threats," *Jerusalem Post*, 2 August 2012.

3 Yaakov Katz, "The Sinai attack: Blow by blow," *Jerusalem Post*, 6 August 2012.

4 Avi Issacharoff and Gili Cohen, "Israeli air strike kills Palestinian militant riding motorcycle in south Gaza Strip," *Haaretz*, 5 August 2012.

5 Interview with Mohamed, Rafah, 2012.

6 Interview with Abu Sallam, Rafah, 2012.

7 Interview with Ibrahim al-Menaei, Rafah, 2012.

8 Katz, "The Sinai attack: Blow by blow."

9 Mohamed Abdel-Raouf and Yousri Mohamed, "Misr tuwad'i shuhada' Rafah fi janaza mahiba bi-hudur Tantawi wa bi ghiyab Mursi," *al-Sharq al-Awsat*, August 8 2012.

10 See the official facebook page of President Mohamed Morsi, https://www.facebook.com/Egypt.President.Morsi/posts/397078020348121; presidential spokesman Yasser Ali made his statement in a televised appearance.

11 Interview in Cairo, 2012.

12 "Anba' al-Anadoul 'an ra'is al-mukhabarat: kanat ladayna ma'lumat tafsiliya hawla hadith Rafah wa-l-'anasir al-munaffidha lahu," *al-Ahram*, 7 August 2012.

13 Speech by President Mohamed Morsi aired in the aftermath of Rafah massacre, 5 June 2012. See https://www.youtube.com/watch?v=AjXBWbBTor4; Omar, Samir, "Mursi yazur Rafah marratayn fi usbu'," *Sky News Arabia*, 11 August 2012.

14 Mohamed al-Zahar, "Mursi sacks military and security chiefs," *Sky News Arabia*, 8 August 2012.

15 "Mursi yaghli al-i'lan al-dusturi al-mukammil wa yahil al-mushir Tantawi wa ra'is al-arkan ila al-taqa'id," *France 24*, 13 August 2012.

16 Sara Gamal, "Mursi wa ikhwanihi wa-l-Sisi: min wazir al-difa' bi nakhat al-thawra wa nushrif an yakun akhana li mas'ul 'an qatl al-thawwar," *al-Bedaiah*, 18 January 2015.

17 "We had detailed information on the Rafah attack," *al-Ahram*.

18 " We had detailed information on the Rafah attack," *al-Ahram*.

19 Several interviews with Gen. Mohamed Okasha, Cairo, 2011, 2012, and 2013.

20 Mostafa Bakri, "Lughz hadith Rafah al-halaqa al-ula," *al-Watan*, 28 February 2012.

21 Emad Ahmed, "Kawalis laylat 'azl Tantawi wa tawalli al-Sisi wizarat al-difa'," *al-Seyyasi*, 16 August 2012.

22 Interview in Sheikh Zuwayyed, 2012.

23 Interview with Ahmed Abu Draa, al-Arish, 2012.

24 " Maqtal jundi wa isabat 9 ashksas fi 'amaliya li-l-jaysh al-misry shimal Sina'," *BBC Arabic*, 16 September 2012; Yosri Mohamed, "Sina': Muwajaha 'anifa bayna al-shurta wa mutashaddidin," *al-Sharq al-Awsat*, 17 September 2012.

25 Interview with Kuraiem Abu Rukba, Sheikh Zuwayyed, 2012.

26 Several interviews with Ibrahim Abu Ashraf al-Menaei in Sheikh Zuwayyed, Rafah, 2011, 2012, 2013.

27 Fathi Sabbah, "Majlis shura al-mujahidiin yanfi mas'uliyatahu 'an hujum al-ahad fi Rafah," *al-Hayat*, 8 August 2012.

28 Statement 19. Mujahedeen Shura Council in the Environs of Jerusalem, October 10, 2012. Published on jihadist forums.

29 "Bayan al-salafiya al-jihadiya fi Sina'," al-Maqreze Centre for Historical Studies, 14 August 2012.

30 Several interviews with Abu Arrab al-Sawarka, al-Arish and Sheikh Zuwayyed, 2011, 2012, and 2013.

31 Several interviews with Mohamed al-Filistini, al-Arish and Sheikh Zuwayyed, 2011, 2012, and 2013.

Chapter 8

1 Maha Abu Oweim, "Hamas tuhadhdhir min infijar fi Ghaza idha istamarr hadm al-infaq," *al-Riyadh*, 1 October 2012.

2 "Haniya: satughliq al-anfaq ma'a Misr bi mujarrad tawaffur al-bad'il," *el-Fagr*, 7 September 2012.

3 Ahmed Ahmed, "Limadha yataharrib Mursi min al-qasas li-l-junud al-misriyin," *al-Arab*, 18 March 2013.

4 Interview with Lt. Col. Peter Lerner, Jerusalem, October 2013.

5 Interview with Yossi Kuperwasser, Ministry for Strategic Affairs, Jerusalem, October 2013.

6 Interview with Mousa Abu Marzouk, Cairo, 2013.

7 During an interview in Cairo in 2013, Muslim Brotherhood sources, demanding anonymity, said that Mohamed Morsi refused to include members of the Brotherhood-rivals al-Daawa al-Salafiya and al-Nour Party in the delegation to Sinai.

8 Ahmed Abu Draa, Abdel-Qader Mubarak, and Sherif al-Doukhaly, "al-'Amaliya nasr tawaqqafat ba'd ijtima' wafd al-ri'asa ma'a al-jihadiyin," *al-Masry al-Youm*, 27 August 2012.

9 "al-Qiyadat al-jihadiya wa sirr tawqif 'amaliyat nasr fi Sina'," *Sinai News*, 28 August 2012.

10 Salahuddin Hassan, "Jihadiyin yursiluna li Mursi adilla tawarrut al-mosad wa Dahlan fi Rafah," *al-Watan*, 2 September 2012.

11 Hassan, "Jihadists send Morsi evidence of Mossad and Dahlan's involvement in Rafah."

12 Interview with Magdi Salem, Cairo, 2013.

13 James Dorsey, "Contours of future Israeli-Palestinian battles emerge on the soccer pitch," *Huffington Post*, 30 March 2015.

14 Hillary Rodham Clinton, *Hard Choices* (New York: Simon & Schuster, 2014), 401.

15 Jeffrey Goldberg, "Hillary Clinton: 'Failure' to help Syrian rebels led to the rise of ISIS," *The Atlantic*, 10 August 2014.

16 Interview with Nageh Ibrahim, Alexandria, 2013.

17 Interview with Ahmed Ban, Cairo, 2013.

18 Hossam Tamam, "Fi tanaqudat al-harakat al-jihadiya," *al-Sharq al-Awsat*, 29 January 2010.

19 " Qandil yanfi tarhil aqbat min Rafah wa huquq al-insan tu'akkid," *al-Arabiya*, 29 September 2012.

20 Anas Zaki, "Morsi ya'ed Sina' bi-l-tanmiya wa raf' al-thulm," *al-Jazeera*, 5 October 2012.

21 For Mohamed Morsi's full speech on the 39th anniversary of the 6 October War, see https://www.youtube.com/watch?v=z_rkQwbWEc4

22 Yahya Zakaria, "Ahali Sina' yurahhibun bi qarar tamalluk al-aradi wa yutalibun bi-l-intiqal li marhalat al-ta'mir," *Sada el-Balad*, 3 November 2012.

23 The exception was investors, who operated in the southern tourist resort areas, as they deemed it destructive to their businesses because they were often either dual nationals or relied on partnerships with foreign nationals.

24 The Egyptian military institution has its own separate judicial system and prosecution, and has the constitutional right to issue and impose laws on any military-related matters.

25 Mohamed Tantawi, "Wazir al-Difa' yusdir qararan bi hathr tamalluk al-aradi al-mutakhima li-l-hudud al-sharqiya," *al-Youm al-Sabea*, 23 December 2012.

26 "Qandil yanfi tarhil aqbat min Rafah wa huquq al-insan tu'akkid," *al-Arabiya*, 29 September 2012.

27 Mohanned Sabry, "Morsi's popularity sinks after crash kills 51 children on bus," *al-Monitor*, 19 November 2012.

28 Mohameda l-Hakim, "al-Yazal: Iqamat mukhayyamat li-l-laji'in al-falastiniyin bi Sina' yuhaddid amnina al-qawmi," *Masrawy*, 18 November 2012.

29 Giora Eiland, "Rethinking the two-state solution," *Policy Focus* 88, The Washington Institute for Near East Policy (September 2008).

30 Saul Sadka, "Gazans belong in Sinai, says Chief Rabbi Metzger," *Haaretz*, 29 January 2008.

31 Taha Farghali, "Mashayikh al-qaba'il: sanamna' tawtin al-ghazawiya fi ardina wa law bi-l-damm," *al-Watan*, 21 November 2012.

32 Remarks made during meetings with Israeli politicians and independent figures in Jerusalem and Tel Aviv, 2013.

33 Mahmoud Bayomi, "Badi': la mani' min mukhayyamat li-l-filistiniyin fi Sina'," *al-Masry al-Youm*, 21 November 2012.

34 The Atlantic Council, "Unofficial English Translation of Egypt's Draft Constitution," *EgyptSource*, 30 October 2012.

35 Mohamed, Khaled "Ra'is al-arkan li Sudan: Halayeb wa Shalatin misriya . . . intaha," *al-Watan*, 1 May 2013.

36 The author attended the summit in the Valley of Firan on April 5, 2013.

37 Summit in the Valley of Firan, April 5, 2013.

38 Interview with Salem Eneizan, Nuweiba, 2013.

39 Abigail Hauslohner, "Egypt's government struggles to exert authority in the Sinai desert," *Washington Post*, 2 June 2013.

40 Interview with Ahmed al-Herish, St. Catherine's, 2013.

41 Interview with Ahmed Abu Zeina, Rafah, 2013.

42 Interview with former military officer, Cairo, 2013.

43 "Wadi al-Natrun, from the revolution to the Mufti," *Freedom and Justice Gate*, 16 May 2015.

44 Hend Mokhtar, "al-Youm al-Sabi' tanshur shahadat Omar Suleiman allati addat ila al-hukm 'ala Mubarak wa-l-Adly bi-l-mu'abbad," *al-Youm al-Sabea*, 2 June 2012.

45 Mokhtar, "Omar Suleiman's testimony that led to jailing Mubarak and El-Adly."

46 Ibrahim Qassem, "Nanshur adillat al-thubut fi qadiyat Wadi al-Natrun...," *al-Youm al-Sabea*, 9 July 2013.

47 Khaled Lotfi, "Bawabat al-Ahram tanshur haythiyat hukm mahkamat musta'nif al-Isma'iliya fi qadiyat tahrib sujana' Wadi al-Natrun," *al-Ahram*, 23 June 2013.

48 "'Essam 'Abdel-Magid li-tamarrud: sata'uduna li-l-juhur yawm 1 yulyo," *al-Arabiya*, 10 June 2013.

49 For President Morsi's last speech, see ONTV's YouTube channel, https://www.youtube.com/watch?v=O0Uqap-cX8Y

50 Interview with Bedouin driver in Rafah, 2013.

Chapter 9

1   Patrick Kingsley and Martin Chulov, "Mohamed Morsi ousted in Egypt's second revolution in two years," *The Guardian*, 4 July 2013.

2   Mohannad Sabry, "Egypt's North Sinai under curfew following deadly clashes," *al-Monitor*, 5 July 2013.

3   Sabry, "Egypt's North Sinai under curfew."

4   Figures gathered by the author from official government statements, the independent *al-Masry al-Youm* newspaper, and al-Arabiya's news website.

5   This specific statement of Col. Ahmed Ali was erased from his official Facebook page. After his removal from the post in April 2014, many more of his statements were systematically erased.

6   Egyptian Center for Economic and Social Rights, "al-Markaz al-misri tutalib bi-l-tahqiq fi hadith maqtal tifla badawiya bi rasas al-jaysh fi shimal Sina'," 11 July 2013.

7   "al-Beltagi ya'tarif dimniyan bi dulu' al-ikhwan fi ahdath Sina'," *al-Arabiya*, 8 July 2013.

8   Hamza Hindawi, "Source of Egypt's coup: Morsi gave free hand to Islamic militants, ordered military to stop crackdowns on jihadis," *TPM News*, 19 July 2013.

9   Lally Weymouth, "Excerpts from Washington Post interview with Egyptian Gen. Abdel Fatah al-Sissi," *Washington Post*, August 5 2013.

10 Dalia Othman, "al-Mutahaddith al-'askari yu'lin tafasil 'amaliyat al-quwwat al-musalliha al-akhira bi Sina'," *al-Masry al-Youm*, 7 August 2013.

11 Human Rights Watch, "Egypt: Retry or free 12,000 after unfair military trials," *HRW News*, 10 September 2011.

12 "Israeli drone strike kills suspected Islamic militants in Egypt," *The Guardian*, 9 August 2013.

13 Since Col. Ahmed Ali's departure from his position as military spokesman, many of his Facebook statements were erased. But despite his denial, several unnamed military sources confirmed to western media that the attack was carried out by an Israeli drone.

14 David Barnett, "Ansar Jerusalem and MSC in Jerusalem comment on death of jihadists in Sinai," *The Long War Journal*, 10 August 2013.

15 Interview with tribal leader, al-Arish, 2013.

16 Ahmed Eleiba, "Point of no return," *Al-Ahram Weekly*, 15 August 2013.

17 After *Al-Ahram Weekly*'s report was published, the author was contacted by four different western Middle East Security experts, all of whom inquired about the authenticity of the information the report contained and the sudden change in tone toward Bedouin figures. The inquiries prompted article explaining the stance of Bedouin tribes regarding the ongoing unrest. See, Mohannad Sabry, "Bedouins deny harboring militants as Sinai attacks escalate," *al-Monitor*, 21 August 2013.

18 Figures from Human Rights Watch, "Egypt: Rab'a Killings Likely Crimes against Humanity," *HRW News*, 12 August 2014; see also WikiThawra's statistics, https://wikithawra.wordpress.com/2013/09/03/rabiadisperal14aug/

19 Ahmed Saleh, "17 shahidan baynahum 15 min al-shurta wa 65 musaban hasilat al-hajamat al-irhabiya fi Sini' ba'da fadd i'tisam raba'a wa al-nahda," *Sada el-Balad*, 15 August 2013.

20 Hamdi Alkhshali and Ali Younes, "Egypt: 25 soldiers killed in Sinai Peninsula ambush," *CNN*, 19 August 2013.

21 Author observations and several testimonies collected in interviews during two trips to North Sinai's al-Arish and Sheikh Zuwayyed in the aftermath of Morsi's ouster and the bloody dispersal of the pro-Morsi sit-ins.

22 The driver, who doesn't want to named, told the author his story as they waited for more than six hours at al-Midan checkpoint, west of al-Arish in 2013. The commanding officer of this checkpoint insulted the stranded

people, including the author and driver, for complaining and fired his machine gun above our heads.

23 Interview with Mahmoud on the day of the suicide attack, his real name has been concealed for his safety.

24 Details provided by Ibrahim Abu Ashraf al-Menaei and two others who attended the convention.

25 Col. Ahmed Ali's statement posted on the army's Facebook page, September 3, 2013.

26 Post by Ahmed Abu Draa on his Facebook page on 5 September, 2013.

27 *al-Youm al-Sabea* newspaper erased the photos of Abu Draa published on their website after severe condemnation from the local media community.

28 Mohmed Mekled, "Jund al-Islam bi Sini' tatabanna tafjirat mabna al-mukhabarat bi Rafah," *al-Watan*, 12 September 2013.

29 Col. Ahmed Ali held the conference in the military's media department in eastern Cairo on 15 September, see https://www.youtube.com/watch?v=unsxZvprRSY

30 "Tawasil 'amaliyat Sina' wa itiham al-jaysh bi-l-'iqab al-jama'i," *al-Jazeera*, 16 September 2013.

31 Hussein al-Qayyem, "Ittihad sahafi Sina' yudin qabd 'ala morasili al-shorouq," *al-Masreyoon*, 23 September 2013.

32 "al-Hukm 'ala al-sahafi al-sinawi Ahmed Abu Draa bi-l-habs 6 ashhur ma'a iyqaf al-tanfiz," *al-Shorouk*, 5 October 2013.

33 Amr al-Wesimy, "Wasfi: al-Inqilab ya'ni tawalli al-'askariyin manasib fi-l-dawla," *al-Mesreyoon*, 28 January 2014.

34 Ahmed Marei, "Istishhad 4 wa isabat 5 min quwwat kamin al-Risa fi infijar sayyara mufakhakha," *al-Youm al-Sabea*, 10 October 3013.

35 "Infijar qurb mabna al-mukhabarat al-harbiya fi-l-Isma'iliya bi Misr," *al-Arabiya*, 19 October 2013.

36 Mohannad Sabry, "Al-Qaeda emerges amid Egypt's turmoil," *al-Monitor*, 4 December 2013.

37 The video statements documenting terrorist attacks were published by Ansar Bayt al-Maqdis on various jihadist websites.

38 "Foreign fighters in Iraq and Syria," *Radio Free Europe/Radio Liberty*, 29 January 2015. An Egyptian security officer, speaking on condition of anonymity, says Egypt has no record of the number of Egyptians who joined ISIS and believes it's impossible to have an accurate estimate due to the lack of security monitoring of travelers between 2011 and 2013.

39 Interviews in Rafah, 2012. The author met several Syrian refugees arriving at Nuweiba seaport in 2012 and 2013, all of whom arrived from Jordan's Aqaba seaport.

40 Mahmoud Nasr, "Tahqiqat al-niyaba fi qadiyat ightiyal Muhammad Mabruk," *al-Youm al-Sabea*, 11 May 2014.

41 Interview with former SSI officer speaking on condition of anonymity, Cairo, 2013.

42 Mohamed Sabry, "The details of assassinating Mohamed Mabrouk," *al-Ahram*, 18 November 2013.

43 Author's translation of the Ansar Bayt al-Maqdis statement published on jihadist forums on 9 November 2013.

44 Interview with a Sheikh Zuwayyed resident, who requested for his identity to be hidden, in al-Arish, 2013.

45 For more on this, see Mohannad Sabry, "The Muslim Brotherhood fights for legacy, not for Morsi," *al-Monitor*, 2 July 2013.

46 Ahmed Abdelnour, "Mousa demands al-Sisi strike Gaza," *Veto*, 10 September 2010.

47 Interview with Yossi Kuperwasser, Jerusalem, 2013.

48 Testimonies collected by the author from relatives of North Sinai detainees speaking on condition of anonymity, Cairo, 2013 and 2014.

49 Egyptian Center for Economic and Social Rights, "Ba'd 100 youm min al-'amal:yat al-'askariya al-muwassi'a intihakat manhajiya mustamirra wa ma'ana khaniqa fi Sina'," 22 December 2013.

50 Interview with Abdel-Rahman, al-Arish, 2014.

51 Observations and remarks from several activists and residents from Sheikh Zuwayyed, Rafah, and their surrounding villages.

52 "15 dead, 134 injured in Egypt's Mansoura explosion," *Ahram Online*, 24 December 2013.

53 Shadia Nasralla, "Egypt designates Muslim Brotherhood as terrorist group," *Reuters*, 25 December 2013.

54 Alistair Beach, "Cairo bomb attacks: Four killed and dozens wounded on eve of revolution rallies in Egypt," *The Independent*, 24 January 2014.

55 David Kirkpatrick, "Militants down Egyptian helicopter, killing 5 soldiers," *New York Times*, 26 January 2014.

56 Ahmed Abdel-Azim, "Nass bayan al-quwwat al-musalliha li-tafwid al-mushir al-Sisi li-ri'asa," *al-Watan*, 27 January 2014.

Chapter 10

1   Amr al-Wesimy, "Wasfi: al-Inqilab ya'ni tawalli al-'askariyin manasib fi-l-dawla," *al-Mesreyoon*, 28 January 2014.

2   See, Mayy El-Sheikh and David Kirkpatrick, "Amid Egypt's Sweeping Crackdown, North Sinai Residents in Crossfire," *New York Times*, 29 March 2014; Reuters, "Special Report: Egyptian militants outwit army in Sinai battlefield," 16 March 2014.

3   Interviews, phone interviews, and unofficial talks with several residents of North Sinai's al-Arish, Sheikh Zuwayyed, Rafah, and their surrounding villages, 2013 and 2014.

4   Quoted in Ali Shtewy, "Hasr 350 alf shajara muthmera tadararat fi shamal Sina'," *Mobtada*, 15 May 2014.

5   "Misr: Shadi al-Mani'i al-qiyadi fi ansar bayt al-maqdis fi Sina'," *BBC Arabic*, 23 May 2014.

6   Interview with North Sinai high-ranking government official, speaking on condition of anonymity, Cairo, 2014.

7   Interview with Osama Ali, Cairo, February 2011. The author met Ali while covering the humanitarian aid convoys to Libya, and saw him for the last time in April 2011. The last of his Facebook posts was in July 2011 after which he disappeared. The first mention of him after that was in the ABM video in July 2014.

8   A few days later, after reporting on the aid convoy, the author received a call from Ali who politely asked him about any job opportunity he happened to know of.

9   Kareem Fahim, "Attack kills at least 21 Egyptian soldiers at checkpoint in Western Desert," *New York Times*, 19 July 2014.

10 David Kirkpatrick, "31 Egyptian soldiers are killed as militants attack in Sinai," *New York Times*, 24 October 2014.

11 Ansar Bayt al-Maqdis published a video on jihadist forums, titled "Sawlat al-Ansar," showing its armed members as they attacked Karm al-Qawadis checkpoint in North Sinai and executed its military personnel.

12 Comments made during phone interviews by several people who were evacuated from Rafah's buffer zone, Cairo, 2014.

13 Soliman Gouda, "Ija'aluha nihaya li kull kha'in," *al-Masry al-Youm*, 25 October 2014.

14 Patrick Kingsley and Manu Abdo, "At least 32 killed in Egypt as militants attack army and police targets in Sinai," *The Guardian*, 30 January 2015.

15 Col. Mohamed Samir's statement on his official Facebook page on January 29, 2015, see https://www.facebook.com/Egy. army.Spox?fref=ts

16 Quoted in Hend Mokhtar, "al-Youm al-Sabi' tanshur shahadat Omar Suleiman allati addat ila al-hukm 'ala Mubarak wa-l-Adly bi-l-mu'abbad," *al-Youm al-Sabea*, 2 June 2012.

17 Links to photos of torture victims were published by military spokesman Col. Mohamed Samir on Facebook, claiming they were terrorists killed in action.

18 Mohamed Ibrahim is the minister of the interior who oversaw the mass killings of Morsi supporters in Rabaa al-Adawiya Square in August 2013. It was described by Human Rights Watch's executive director Kenneth Roth as "The worst mass unlawful killings in the country's modern history." (Egypt: Rab'a Killings Likely Crimes against Humanity," *HRW News*, 12 August 2014).

SOURCES

The following are profiles of the key individuals interviewed by the author for this book.

Adnan Abu Amer: dean of the Faculty of Arts and head of the Press and Information Section, as well as a lecturer on the history of the Palestinian issue, national security, political science, and Islamic civilization at al-Ummah University Open Education. He holds a doctorate in political history from Demashq University.

Ahmed Abu Draa: the most prominent news reporter in North Sinai to date. A descendant of the powerful Sawarka tribe and native of al-Muqataa village, south of Rafah, Abu Draa was detained along with his brothers in the aftermath of the Taba bombings in 2004. After the launch of the brutal military campaign in Sinai after Morsi's ouster in 2013, Abu Draa was detained for exposing the losses inflicted on civilians by the military's indiscriminate shelling of villages, including his own. He stood military trial in October 2013 and was sentenced to a suspended six-month jail term.

Ibrahim Abu Flayyan: the secretary general of the Independent Arab Tribes Union, a non-governmental organization established in 2004 to tackle and resolve issues of Bedouin tribes, not only in Sinai but across Egypt, in addition to preserving the Bedouin heritage. Abu Elayyan is known for his community work in Sinai and his fierce opposition to oppressive regime policies.

Mousa Abu Marzouk: deputy head of the political office of the Islamic Resistance Movement, Hamas. After departing Damascus at the outbreak of the Syrian revolution in 2011, he moved to Egypt and resided in a fortified villa in eastern Cairo.

Kuraiem Abu Rukba: a 26-year-old Salafi Bedouin from the village of al-Sadat, Rafah. During the 2011 uprising, he joined the popular committees formed to protect residential areas in the aftermath of the downfall of security authorities; he later became a member of the Rights Retrieving Committee, formed by the sharia courts to resolve community disputes.

Abu Sallam: an eyewitness to the first Rafah massacre. A bearded Salafi, Abu Sallam was met face-to-face by the militant who commandeered the armored vehicle and stormed the Karm Abu Salem Terminal in an attempt to carry out a terrorist attack inside Israeli territories.

Salman Abu Zeina: a resident of al-Arish, Abu Zeina witnessed the first attack on the natural gas pipeline that shipped Egyptian gas to Israel from 2008. During the first bombing, his poultry farm, which stood next to the targeted facility, was destroyed.

General Fouad Allam: former head of the State Security Investigations, a security analyst, and expert on radical Islamist movements and militancy.

Ahmed Ban: a former member of the Muslim Brotherhood and one of the founders of its Freedom and Justice Party, Ban defected from the organization in 2012 to protest the radical transformation that took place under the leadership of Supreme Guide Mohamed Badie and his deputy Khairat al-Shater. He is also a researcher of Islamist movements and radical ideologies.

Asaad al-Beik: the founder of North Sinai's Salafi bloc known as Ahl al-Sunna wa-l-Jamaa. Al-Beik is known for being one of the oldest sharia judges in the peninsula, his courthouse operated before and after the downfall of Hosni Mubarak in 2011. In 2013, he was detained by military forces and sentenced to jail by a military tribunal.

Benedetta Berti: a research fellow at the Institute for National Security Studies (INSS), a Young Atlanticist at the Atlantic Council, and a member of the faculty at Tel Aviv University. Benedetta is also a post-doctoral fellow at the Hebrew University.

Mohamed al-Filistini: an Egyptian resident of North Sinai of Palestinian origins and an expert on arms movement in the Sinai and Palestine. In the aftermath of the January 2011 uprising and the ensuing relative freedom in Egypt, al-Filistini agreed to speak at several interviews using his alias, which could be one of many he uses.

Yahya al-Ghoul: a native of North Sinai, al-Ghoul inherited his position as a customary judge from his father, Sheikh Mohamed al-Ghoul. He wrote a book on the history and mechanism of the tribal customary justice system, titled *al-Qada' al-'urfi fi Sina'* [Customary justice in the Sinai Peninsula].

Hamid: a native of the Gaza Strip, Hamid is known for being one of the first people to dig and operate a tunnel between the Strip and the Sinai Peninsula. His tunnel, along with hundreds of others, was demolished in 2013 after the launch of Egypt's military campaign in Sinai.

Ahmed al-Herish: in his fifties, al-Herish is a powerful and revered leader of al-Gararsha tribe, whose territories extend through the Valley of Firan in south Sinai. The tribe has been providing security for churches and monasteries in the valleys for hundreds of years. In the aftermath of Egypt's January 25 revolution, al-Herish cooperated with the military in matters of security, helped release kidnapped tourists and mobilized his tribe's youth to hunt criminals. Despite his reputation and community efforts, a police officer attempted to murder al-Herish in the town of St. Catherine's in June 2013; the state did not respond to the incident.

Hussein: a native of North Sinai's al-Arish. After failing to find a decent job to support his family and build his future, Hussein worked as a purchases manager for a tunnel owner. In 2009, he was detained by the SSI, tortured, and jailed without trial for almost one year.

General Fouad Hussein: former Egyptian military intelligence officer. In 1968, Hussein was charged with overseeing the operations of close to seven hundred Bedouins who operated as covert combat and reconnaissance units in the Sinai Peninsula during the Israeli occupation.

Nageh Ibrahim: a former member of al-Jamaa al-Islamiya who was convicted and jailed for his participation in the 1981 attack on the Asyut Security Directorate. In 1997, Ibrahim embarked on a campaign of ideological recantations and was released in 2005.

Abdallah Jahama: former parliamentarian under the regime of Hosni Mubarak and former head of the Sinai Mujahedeen Association, an independent outfit that was established after the 1973 war to include the covert Bedouin fighters who operated under the command of the EMIRD throughout Israeli occupation of Sinai.

Kadri: a native of the border town of Rafah, he was jailed on charges of arms trafficking before the outbreak of the January 2011 uprising. During his time in prison, he shared a jail cell with Khairat al-Shater, the Muslim Brotherhood's deputy leader. Kadri became one of the most powerful smugglers in North Sinai after 2011.

Yossi Kuperwasser: the former director general of the Israeli Ministry of Strategic Affairs. He is a former senior officer in the Israeli Military Intelligence Directorate, (Aman).

Lt. Colonel Peter Lerner: the official spokesman of the IDF for foreign media.

General Saleh al-Masry: former security chief of North Sinai. During his time in office, the natural gas pipeline was bombed fourteen times and the first Rafah massacre took place, leaving sixteen military conscripts dead and several others injured.

Ibrahim Abu Ashraf al-Menaei: head of the independent Sinai Tribes Union. A native of al-Mehdiya, south of Rafah, al-Menaei was jailed under Hosni Mubarak with an administrative emergency law detention warrant. He has been a fierce opposition figure both before and after the Egyptian uprising in January 2011; his loud condemnation of the military campaign launched in Sinai after Morsi's ouster in July 2013 led to the demolition of his house, his son's, and his Bedouin guesthouse at the hands of Egyptian military forces.

Ibrahim al-Menaei: a native of Rafah and a witness to the first Rafah massacre. He helped carry the bleeding corpses and the injured soldiers to Rafah hospital, and testified to seeing one of the alleged militants in the vicinity of the military post before the attack took place.

Hassan al-Nakhlawi: leftist political activist and native of Sinai. After the administrative detention of his two brothers in the aftermath of the Taba terrorist attacks in 2004, he co-founded the Sinai Prisoners Defense Front. He was detained and tortured in 2006 for his political activities and fierce opposition to Hosni Mubarak's regime and the brutality of his security authorities.

Colonel Khaled Okasha: the former head of North Sinai's Civil Defense Department and commander of the governorate's fire brigade and explosives specialists. He retired from police work in 2012 to become a security analyst and commentator on Egypt's security turmoil. In 2013, he testified at the infamous Wadi al-Natrun Prison Break Case, in which former President Morsi was accused of plotting the attacks on prison facilities across Egypt and then sentenced to death in 2015.

General Mohamed Okasha: a former airforce pilot and military intelligence officer. During the Israeli–Egyptian war between 1967 and 1973, Okasha led a squadron of jet fighters and remained an active combatant until the ceasefire was brokered in 1974.

Magdi Salem: prominent lawyer of Islamist movements, including the Egyptian Islamic Jihad. He was the speaker of the presidential delegation convened by former President Morsi to lead the dialogue with Sinai's militant jihadists in the aftermath of the first Rafah massacre in August 2012.

Abu Arrab al-Sawarka: an arms smuggler from the outskirts of Rafah, North Sinai. Abu Arrab is one of several aliases he bears. In the aftermath of the January 2011 uprising, he agreed to speak of his experience and illegal activity, with the aim of exposing the corruption of security authorities and the state's policies of ignoring, if not at times sponsoring, the movement of arms across Egypt and Sinai.

Hani Shukrallah: one of Egypt's most prominent journalists and political analysts. He is the former editor-in-chief of *Ahram Online* and *Al-Ahram Weekly*, the English versions of the state-owned *al-Ahram* newspaper. His courageous writing and insistence on overhauling the policies of the news outlets led to his continuous intimidation by the Egyptian authorities.

Mostafa Singer: Egyptian activist and writer, resident of Sheikh Zuwayyed and descendent of the Sanajreh clan that moved from the Gaza Strip to North Sinai in 1948. For years, Singer's writings have been published by various Egyptian media outlets; he is considered one of Sinai's most active leftist figures.

Azzam Sinjer: a jihadist native of Sheikh Zuwayyed, Sinjer was a member of the militant group that led an attack on the presidential campaign of Hamdin Sabbahi in North Sinai in 2012. Threatening to fire their weapons at a scheduled rally, Sinjer and his fellow militiamen banned the rally from holding any events in Sheikh Zuwayyed.

Abu Suleiman al-Tarabin: an arms smuggler and native of the Sinai Peninsula. In the aftermath of the January 2011 uprising, Abu Suleiman agreed to speak on his illegal activities during a string of interviews held in different parts of the peninsula. Akin to Abu Arrab al-Sawarka, his main goal of speaking was to expose the corruption of security authorities and shed light on the causes behind Sinai's rampant arms-smuggling operations.

Mira Tzoreff: professor of humanities, the Moshe Dayan Center for Middle Eastern and African Studies at Tel Aviv University. Tzoreff has written extensively about Egypt, the Middle East, and Israel.

Ehud Yaari: prominent Israeli political analyst and television presenter. For years, Yaari has written about the region's security, especially that of Egypt, the Sinai Peninsula, and its impact on Israel. Like many Israeli political and media figures, he maintained close relations with figures in Hosni Mubarak's regime.

Ibrahim Yousri: former Egyptian ambassador to Algeria and former head of the International Law and Treaties Department of the Egyptian Ministry of Foreign Affairs. As soon as Egypt began exporting natural gas to Israel in 2008, Yousri launched a campaign opposing the agreement. He won several legal rounds against the regime of Hosni Mubarak, with the aim of terminating the murky deal.

BIBLIOGRAPHY

Abdel-Aal, Seham. "al-Muwajiha!" [The Confrontation!] *al-Ahram*, 11 March 2000.

Abdel-Azim, Ahmed. "Nass bayan al-quwwat al-musalliha li-tafwid al-mushir al-Sisi li-ri'asa" [Text of Military Council statement on al-Sisi's candidacy for presidency]. *al-Watan*, 27 January 2014.

Abdel-Ghani al-Gamasi, Mohamed. *Mudhakirat al-Gamasi: Harb uktober 1973* [Memoirs of al-Gamasi, The October 1973 War]. Cairo: General Egyptian Book Organization (GEBO), 1989.

Abdelnour, Ahmed. "Mousa demands al-Sisi strike Gaza." *Veto*, 10 September 2013.

Abdel-Raouf, Mohamed and Yousri Mohamed. "Misr tuwad'i shuhada' Rafah fi janaza mahiba bi-hudur Tantawi wa bi ghiyab Mursi" [Egypt bids farewell to martyrs of Rafah massacre in massive funeral attended by Tantawi, while Morsi is absent]. *al-Sharq al-Awsat*, August 8 2012.

Abou Bakr, Sara. "Farag Fouda: Assasination of the word." *Daily News Egypt*, 8 June 2013.

Abu Draa, Ahmed, Abdel-Qader Mubarak, and Sherif al-Doukhaly. "al-'Amaliya nasr tawaqqafat ba'd ijtima' wafd al-ri'asa ma'a al-jihadiyin" [Operation Eagle stopped after presidential delegation met with jihadists]. *al-Masry al-Youm*, 27 August 2012.

Abu Fajr, Masaad. "Kama'in mutaharrika: min al-Gharbaniyat ila Abu Za'bal" [Mobile Checkpoints: From al-Gharbaniyat to Abu Za'bal]. *al-Dostor*, 30 September 2010.

Abu Oweim, Maha. "Hamas tuhadhdhir min infijar fi Ghaza idha istamarr hadm al-infaq" [Hamas warns of Gaza explosion if tunnels demolition continues]. *al-Riyadh*, 1 October 2012.

Abu Shama, Mohamed. "Dr. Fadl Manthar al-jihadiyin: Kitab al-Zawahiri kidhb wa buhtan wa mughalitat fiqhiya wa talbis 'ala al-qari'" [Dr. Fadl: Zawahiri's book is lies, false claims, flawed jurisprudence, and misleads the reader]. *al-Sharq al-Awsat*, 18 November 2008.

Adib, Munir. "3,000 jihadi ya'uduna ila Misr min Afghanistan wa-l-Shishan wa-l-Bosna wa-l-Sumal wa Iran" [3,000 jihadists return to Egypt from Afghanistan, Chechnya, Bosnia, Somalia, and Iran]. *al-Masry al-Youm*, 31 March 2011.

al-Agha, Wafiq, and Samir Abu Mudallala. "Iqtisad al-anfaq bi qita' Ghaza: Darura wataniya, am karitha iqtisadiya wa ijtima'iya?" [The tunnels economy in Gaza: A national necessity or an economic catastrophe?]. *al-Azhar University in Gaza Magazine* 13 (2011).

Ahmed, Ahmed. "Limadha yataharrib Mursi min al-qasas li-l-junud al-misriyin" [Why doesn't Morsi avenge the Egyptian soldiers]. *al-Arab*, 18 March 2013.

Ahmed, Emad. "Kawalis laylat 'azl Tantawi wa tawalli al-Sisi wizarat al-difa'" [Behind the scenes of sacking Tantawi and appointment of Sisi to the Ministry of Defense]. *al-Seyyasi*, 16 August 2012.

al-Ahram. "15 dead, 134 injured in Egypt's Mansoura explosion." *Ahram Online*, 24 December 2013.

———. "Anba' al-Anadoul 'an ra'is al-mukhabarat: kanat ladayna ma'lumat tafsiliya hawla hadith Rafah wa-l-'anasir al-munaffidha lahu" [Anadolou News quoting intelligence chief: We had detailed information on the Rafah attack and the elements executing it]. *al-Ahram Gate*, 7 August 2012.

———. "English text of SCAF-amended Egypt Constitutional Declaration." *Ahram Online*, 18 June 2012.

Ali, Loai. "Nasr Farid Wasil yastaqil min ri'asat al-hay'a al-shar'iya li-l-huquq wa-l-islah" [Nasr Farid Wasil resigns his position as head of the Legitimate Council for Rights and Reform]. *al-Youm al-Sabea*, 11 July 2011.

Alkhshali, Hamdi, and Ali Younes. "Egypt: 25 soldiers killed in Sinai Peninsula ambush." CNN, 19 August 2013, http://edition.cnn.com/2013/08/19/world/meast/egypt-sinai-ambush/

Amnesty International. *Israel/Gaza: Operation "Cast Lead": 22 days of death and destruction* .2 July 2009.

al-Arabiya. "'Essam 'Abdel-Magid li-tamarrud: sata'uduna li-l-juhur yawm 1 yulyo" [Essam Abdel-Magid to Tamarrod: You will return to your hideouts on July 1]. 10 June 2013.

———. "al-Beltagi ya'tarif dimniyan bi dulu' al-ikhwan fi ahdath Sina'" [al-Beltagi implies Muslim Brotherhood's involvement in Sinai's events]. 8 July 2013.

————. "Infijar qurb mabna al-mukhabarat al-harbiya fi-l-Isma'iliya bi Misr" [Explosion near Military Intelligence building in Ismailiya]. 19 October 2013.

————. "Mursi yasif al-yahud bi-l-qirda wa-l-khanazir . . . wa yatabarra' min tasrihihi" [Morsi describes Jews as monkeys and pigs, denies his statements]. 17 January 2013.

————. "Qandil yanfi tarhil aqbat min Rafah wa huquq al-insan tu'akkid" [Qandil denies evacuating Copts from Rafah, human rights organizations confirm]. 29 September 2012.

Arafa, Mohamed. "Dahlan umm al-Qa'ida wara' fauda Sina'?" [Dahlan or al-Qaeda, behind Sinai's anarchy?]. *al-Wafd*, 1 August 2011.

The Atlantic Council. "Unofficial English translation of Egypt's draft constitution." *EgyptSource*, 30 October 2012.

al-Azhar Scholars Front. "Bayan jabhat 'ulama' al-azhar: ila jami' al-'amilin bi masani' tasdir al-ghaz al-masry ila al-yahud" [Statement from the al-Azhar Scholars Front: To all working in exporting Egyptian gas to Israel]. 5 May 2008.

Bahgat, Hossam. "Who let the jihadis out?" *Mada Masr*, 16 February 2014.

Bakri, Mostafa. "Lughz hadith Rafah al-halaqa al-ula" [The riddle of Rafah's attack, episode one]. *al-Watan*, 28 February 2013.

Barnett, David. "Ansar Jerusalem and MSC in Jerusalem comment on death of jihadists in Sinai." *The Long War Journal*, 10 August 2013.

Bawabat Ma'lumat Misr [Egypt's information portal]. "Ziyadat al-manatiq al-sina'iya bi-l-Sa'id ila 46 mintaqa bi ijmali istithmarat 100 milyar jinayh wa 224 alf fursat 'amal" [Increasing industrial zones in Upper Egypt to 46 zones with total investments LE100 billion and 224 thousand jobs]. March 2013.

Bayomi, Mahmoud. "Badi': la mani' min mukhayyamat li-l-filistiniyin fi Sina'" [Badie: No problem with Palestinian camps in Sinai]. *al-Masry al-Youm*, 21 November 2012.

BBC. "Misr: Shadi al-Mani'i al-qiyadi fi ansar bayt al-maqdis fi Sina'" [Egypt: Shadi al-Menaei, leading ABM figure killed in Sinai]. *BBC Arabic*, 23 May 2014.

————. "Fake bomb detector husband jailed for three years." *BBC News*, 3 October 2014.

————. "Gazans make new border wall hole." *BBC News*, 25 January 2008.

————. "al-Ikhwan al-muslimun: yu'ayyiduna al-ta'dilat al-dusturiya fi Misr wa baqi al-harakat al-siyasiya yata'rrid" [Muslim Brotherhood endorse constitutional amendments and remaining political movements oppose it]. *BBC Arabic*, 14 March 2011.

———. "Maqtal jundi wa isabat 9 ashksas fi 'amaliya li-l-jaysh al-misry shimal Sina'" [One soldier killed, 9 injured in military operation in North Sinai]. *BBC Arabic*, 16 September 2012.

———. "Triple blasts rock Egypt resort." *BBC News*, 25 April 2006.

Beach, Alistair. "Cairo bomb attacks: Four killed and dozens wounded on eve of revolution rallies in Egypt." *The Independent*, 24 January 2014.

al-Bolok, Salah, Ahmed Abu Draa, and Osama Khaled. "al-Masry al-Youm takhtariq al-tanthimat al-musalliha wa taltaqi 2 min manaffidhay ahdath al-Arish" [al-Masry al-Youm infiltrates militant organizations, meets two of al-Arish attackers]. *al-Masry al-Youm*, 2 August 2011.

al-Bolok, Salah, and Osama Khaled. "al-Jama'a al-salafiya bi Sina' tunshi' lijanan li fadd al-munazi'at wa 6 alaf musallih li tanfidh al-ahkam" [The Salafist group in Sinai establishes committees to resolve disputes and six thousand men to execute verdicts]. *al-Masry al-Youm*, 9 August 2011.

Clinton, Hillary Rodham. *Hard Choices*. New York: Simon & Schuster, 2014.

Cohen, Yoram, and Matthew Levitt. "Hamas smuggling: Egypt's challenge." *Policywatch* 1484. The Washington Institute for Near East Policy, 2 March 2009.

Cowell, Alan, and Douglas Jehl. "Luxor survivors say killers fired methodically." *New York Times*, 23 November 1997.

CNN. "Abbas declared victor in Palestinian election." 11 January 2005.

———. "Israeli airstrikes target Gaza after multiple attacks." 19 August 2011.

Daniszewski, John. "Islamic Group taunts Egyptian president after massacre." *Los Angeles Times*, 21 November 1997.

El-Deeb, Sarah. "Bedouins lead hunt for Sinai bombers." *Boston Globe*, 7 February 2005.

———. "Border breach temporary boost for Gaza." *Associated Press*, 28 January 2008.

El-Sheikh, Mayy and David Kirkpatrick "Amid Egypt's Sweeping Crackdown, North Sinai Residents in Crossfire." *New York Times*, 29 March 2014.

Dorsey, James. "Contours of future Israeli-Palestinian battles emerge on the soccer pitch." *Huffington Post*, 30 March 2015,

Egyptian Center for Economic and Social Rights. "Ba'd 100 youm min al-'amaliyat al-'askariya al-muwassi'a intihakat manhajiya mustamirra wa ma'ana khaniqa fi Sina'" [100 days into military campaign, systematic violations and a struggle in Sinai]. 22 December 2013.

———. "al-Markaz al-misri tutalib bi-l-tahqiq fi hadith maqtal tifla badawiya bi rasas al-jaysh fi shimal Sina'" [ECESR demand investigation into death of Bedouin child from military fire in North Sinai]. 11 July 2013.

———. "Hukm waqf tasdir al-ghaz li Isra'il [Ruling to stop natural gas exports to Israel." 17 July 2010.

Eiland, Giora. "Rethinking the two-state solution." *Policy Focus* 88. The Washington Institute for Near East Policy, September 2008.

Eleiba, Ahmed. "Point of no return." *Al-Ahram Weekly*, 15 August 2013.

Erlanger, Steven. "Hamas leader faults Israeli sanction plan." *New York Times*, 18 February 2006.

———. "Palestinians topple Gaza wall and cross to Egypt." *New York Times*, 24 January 2008.

el-Fagr. "Haniya: satughliq al-anfaq ma'a Misr bi mujarrad tawaffur al-bad'il" [Haniyeh: Tunnels will be closed as soon as alternatives are provided]. 7 September 2012.

Fahim, Kareem. "Attack kills at least 21 Egyptian soldiers at checkpoint in Western Desert." *New York Times*, 19 July 2014.

Farghali, Taha. "Mashayikh al-qaba'il: sanamna' tawtin al-ghazawiya fi ardina wa law bi-l-damm" [Tribal sheikhs: We will stop the resettlement of Gazans in our land with blood]. *al-Watan*, 21 November 2012.

Fawzy, Mohamed. *Harb al-thalatha sanawat 1967–1970* [The Three Years War 1967-1970, Memoirs of General Mohamed Fawzy]. Cairo: Dar al-Wehda Press, 1988.

France 24. "Morsi yaghli al-i'lan al-dusturi al-mukammil wa yahil al-mushir Tantawi wa ra'is al-arkan ila al-taqa'id" [Morsi annuls constitutional declaration and retires Tantawi and the chief of staff]. 13 August 2012.

Freedom and Justice Gate. "Muhattat hazliyat Wadi al-Natrun min al-thawra ila al-mufti" [Wadi al-Natrun, from the revolution to the Mufti]. 16 May 2015.

Friedman, Ron, and Michal Shmulovich. "US follows Israel's lead and issues Sinai travel warning, after Hamas frees terror chief." *Times of Israel*, 4 August 2012.

Gamal, Sara. "Mursi wa ikhwanihi wa-l-Sisi: min wazir al-difa' bi nakhat al-thawra wa nushrif an yakun akhana li mas'ul 'an qatl al-thawwar" [Morsi, his brothers, and al-Sisi: from Defense Minister with a revolutionary flavor to responsible for killing the revolutionaries]. *al-Bedaiah*, 18 January 2015.

al-Garhy, Ibrahim. "Suqut Shamshun fi qariya al-nakhayla" [The downfall of Samson in Nekheila village]. *BBC Arabic*, 1 March 2004.

al-Ghoul, Yahya. *al-Qada' al-'urfi fi Sina'* [Customary justice in the Sinai Peninsula]. Cairo: al-Maktab al-Arabi Lil Maaref, 2010.

Global Security. "Hamas rockets." n.d.

Goldberg, Geffrey. "Hillary Clinton: 'Failure' to help Syrian rebels led to the rise of ISIS." *The Atlantic*, 10 August 2014.

Gouda, Soliman. "Ija'aluha nihaya li kull kha'in" [Make it an end to every traitor]. *al-Masry al-Youm*, 25 October 2014.

Greenberg, Joel. "Gunmen from Egypt's Sinai Peninsula attack Israeli workers, killing one." *Washington Post*, 18 June 2012.

The Guardian. "Bombers kill 88 at Egyptian resort." 23 July 2005.

———. "Israeli drone strike kills suspected Islamic militants in Egypt." 9 August 2013.

Haberman, Clyde. "Kidnapped soldier is killed as Israeli troops attempt rescue at captor's hideout." *New York Times*, 15 October 1994.

al-Hadi, Amr. "Ya'qub: Intasarna fi ghazwat al-sanadiq wa-l-balad baladna wa-l-sha'b qala na'm li-l-din" [Yaacoub: We triumphed in the Battle of the Ballot Boxes...]. *al-Masry al-Youm*, 21 March 2011.

a l-Hakim, Mohamed. "al-Yazal: Iqamat mukhayyamat li-l-laji'in al-falastiniyin bi Sina' yuhaddid amnina al-qawmi" [al-Yazal: Building refugee camps for Palestinians in Sinai threatens our national security]. *Masrawy*, 18 November 2012.

Harel, Amos, and Avi Issacharoff. "Hamas gets Iranian plans for improved Qassams," *Haaretz*, 28 March 2008.

Hassan, Salahuddin. "Jihadiyin yursiluna li Mursi adilla tawarrut al-mosad wa Dahlan fi Rafah" [Jihadists send Morsi evidence of Mossad and Dahlan's involvement in Rafah]. *al-Watan*, 2 September 2012.

Hauslohner, Abigail. "Egypt's government struggles to exert authority in the Sinai desert." *Washington Post*, 2 June 2013.

Hedges, Chris. "Egyptian premier escapes car bomb." *New York Times*, 26 November 1993.

Herzog, Chaim. *The Arab–Israeli Wars*. New York: Random House, 1982.

Hindawi, Hamza. "Source of Egypt's coup: Morsi gave free hand to Islamic militants, ordered military to stop crackdowns on jihadis." *TPM News*, 19 July 2013.

Holt-Ivry, Olivia. "Arms control in civil society: Controlling conventional arms smuggling in Sinai." In *Arms control and national security: New horizons*, edited by Emily B. Landau and Anat Kurz, Memorandum No. 135. Tel Aviv: Institute for National Security Studies, 2014.

Hope, Christopher. "WikiLeaks: Suleiman told Israel he would 'cleanse' Sinai of arms runners to Gaza." *The Telegraph*, 9 February 2011.

Human Rights Watch. *Egypt: Mass Arrests and Torture in Sinai*. 22 February 2005.

———. "Egypt: Rab'a Killings Likely Crimes against Humanity." *HRW News*, 12 August 2014.

———. "Egypt: Retry or Free 12,000 After Unfair Military Trials." *HRW News*, 10 September 2011.

———. *Razing Rafah*. 18 October 2004.

———. *Under Cover of War*. 20 April 2009.

Hosni, Yousef. "Khubara': muhakimat Mursi la tastanid ila dalil" [Experts: Morsi's trial has no evidence]. *al-Jazeera.net*, 23 December 2013.

Ibrahim, Youssef M. "Egyptian militants blamed in attack on security chief." *New York Times*, 18 August 1993.

Israel Intelligence Heritage and Commemoration Center. "Anti-Israeli terrorism in 2007 and its trends in 2008." Israeli Ministry of Foreign Affairs, 5 June 2008.

Israel Ministry of Foreign Affairs. "Gaza: Lists of controlled entry items." 4 July 2010.

Issacharoff, Avi. "Report: Three Egyptians took part in terrorist attacks on southern Israel." *Haaretz*, August 24 2011.

Issacharoff, Avi, and Gili Cohen. "Israeli air strike kills Palestinian militant riding motorcycle in south Gaza Strip." *Haaretz*, 5 August 2012.

al-Jazeera. "Death toll rises, Islamist group takes responsibility for Taba bombings." *al-Jazeera.net*, 9 October 2004.

———. "Egypt police kill Sinai bomb suspect." *al-Jazeera.com*, 29 September 2005.

———. "Maqtal za'im jund ansar Allah bi Rafah" [Leader of Ansar Jund Allah killed]. *al-Jazeera.net*, 25 August 2009.

———. "Tawasil 'amaliyat Sina' wa itiham al-jaysh bi-l-'iqab al-jama'i" [Sinai operations continues, army accused of collective punishment]. a*l-Jazeera. net*, 16 September 2013.

Jerusalem Post. "Israel renews Sinai travel advisory amid threats." *Jerusalem Post*, 2 August 2012.

Joscelyn, Thomas. "Al-Qaeda linked group claims responsibility for attack in Israel." *The Long War Journal*, 19 June 2012.

Katz, Yaakov. "The Sinai attack: Blow by blow." *Jerusalem Post*, 6 August 2012.

Kershner, Isabel, and David D. Kirkpatrick. "Attacks near Israeli resort heighten tensions with Egypt and Gaza." *New York Times*, 18 August 2011.

al-Khatib, Ahmed. "Mu'taqilu al-jama'at al-islamiya al-mufraq 'anhuma salihihum al-amn wa rafdihim al-mujtama'…fa asbahu qunbula mawquta" [The released Islamist prisoners, reconciled with security and refused by security: A ticking bomb]. *al-Masry al-Youm*, 20 May 2007.

Khayal, Mohamed. "'Abbud al-Zumur: na'tadhir li-l-sha'b al-misri 'an qatl al-ra'is al-Sadat" [Abbod al-Zomor: We apologize to the Egyptian people for killing President Sadat]. *al-Shorouk*, 8 October 2011.

Kingsley, Patrick, and Manu Abdo. "At least 32 killed in Egypt as militants attack army and police targets in Sinai." *The Guardian*, 30 January 2015.

Kingsley, Patrick, and Martin Chulov. "Mohamed Morsi ousted in Egypt's second revolution in two years." *The Guardian*, 4 July 2013.

Kirkpatrick, David. "31 Egyptian soldiers are killed as militants attack in Sinai." *New York Times*, 24 October 2014.

———. "Blow to transition as court dissolves Egypt's parliament." *New York Times*, 14 June 2012.

———. "Militants down Egyptian helicopter, killing 5 soldiers." *New York Times*, 26 January 2014.

Lashin, Amir. "Dr Muhammad Yusri. . .: al-Dustur al-islami jahiz wa bi-muwariqat al-ikhwan [Dr. Mohamed Yosri Salama: The Islamic Constitution is ready, with the consent of the Brotherhood]. *al-Akhbar*, 28 July 2011,

Levitt, Matthew. "Hamas: Towards a Lebanese-style war of attrition." *Policywatch* 367. The Washington Institute for Near East Policy, 26 February 2002.

———. "Hezbollah's man in Egypt." *Perspectives on Terrorism* vol 8 (2). Terrorism Research Initiative and the Center for Terrorism and Security Studies (2014).

Lister, Tim, and Mohamed Fadel Fahmy. "Smuggling weapons to Gaza – the long way." *Security Clearance*, CNN, 12 November 2012.

Lorber, Azriel. "The growing threat of unguided Qassam rockets." *Nativ* 1.17. Ariel Center for Policy Research (January 2004).

Lotfi, Khaled. "Bawabat al-Ahram tanshur haythiyat hukm mahkamat musta'nif al-Isma'iliya fi qadiyat tahrib sujana' Wadi al-Natrun" [Al-Ahram publishes the verdict report by Ismailiya court in Wadi al-Natrun prison break case]. *al-Ahram*, 23 June 2013.

al-Maqreze Centre For Historical Studies. "al-Maqrizi yanshur al-nass al-kamil li muqabalat al-Shaykh al-Muhandis Muhammad al-Dhawahiri" [Text of interview with Sheikh Mohamed al-Zawahiri]. 21 August 2012.

———. "Bayan al-salafiya al-jihadiya fi Sina'" [Statement by Salafi jihadist group in Sinai]. 14 August 2012.

Marei, Ahmed. "Istishhad 4 wa isabat 5 min quwwat kamin al-Risa fi infijar sayyara mufakhakha" [4 killed, 5 injured in al-Rissa Checkpoint bomb attack." *al-Youm al-Sabea*, 10 October 2013.

Mekled, Mohamed. "Jund al-Islam bi Sini' tatabanna tafjirat mabna al-mukhabarat bi Rafah" [Jund al-Islam takes responsibility for Rafah bombing]. *al-Watan*, 12 September 2013.

Mohamed, Khaled. "Ra'is al-arkan li Sudan: Halayeb wa Shalatin misriya . . . intaha" [Chief of Staff to Sudan: Halayeb and Shalatin is Egyptian, end of story]. *al-Watan*, 1 May 2013.

Mohamed, Yosri. "Istimrar al-infilat al-amni bi Sini' yadfa' al-misriyin li-l-mutalabat bi-ta'dil Camp David" [The continuation of instability in Sinai pushes Egyptians to demand amendment of Camp David]. *al-Sharq al-Awsat*, 2 February 2012.

———. "Muwajaha 'anifa bayna al-shurta wa mutashaddidin" [Sinai: Violent confrontations between police and radicals]. a*l-Sharq al-Awsat*, 17 September 2012.

Mohsen, Ayman. "Akef: al-Ikhwan tarfud "Camp David" wa laysa min haqqi-him ilgha'uha [Akef: The Brotherhood rejects Camp David but don't have the right to trash it]. *Sada al-Balad*, 9 March 2012, http://www.el-balad. com/102485. aspx

Mokhtar, Hend. 2012. "al-Youm al-Sabi' tanshur shahadat Omar Suleiman allati addat ila al-hukm 'ala Mubarak wa-l-Adly bi-l-mu'abbad" [Omar Suleiman's testimony that led to jailing Mubarak and El-Adly]. *al-Youm al-Sabea*, 2 June 2012.

Nabil, Aya. "al-Sheikh 'Abd al-Hadi: Mubarak ikhtara qada min al-Badu wala'uhum al-awwal lahu" [Abdel-Hadi Eteik: Mubarak chose Bedouin judges loyal to him]. *al-Youm al-Sabea*, 29 February 2012.

Nasr, Mahmoud. "Tahqiqat al-niyaba fi qadiyat ightiyal Muhammad Mabruk" [Prosecutor's investigation into Mohamed Mabrouk's assassination]. *al-Youm al-Sabea*, 11 May 2014.

Nasralla, Shadia. "Egypt designates Muslim Brotherhood as terrorist group." *Reuters*, 25 December 2013.

Omar, Samir. "Mursi yazur Rafah marratayn fi usbu'" [Morsi visits Rafah twice in one week]. *Sky News Arabia*, 11 August 2012,

Othman, Dalia. "al-Mutahaddith al-'askari yu'lin tafasil 'amaliyat al-quwwat al-musalliha al-akhira bi Sina' [Military spokesman announced details of military operations in Sinai]. *al-Masry al-Youm*, 7 August 2013.

Palestinian Ministry of National Economy in cooperation with the Applied Research Institute – Jerusalem (ARIJ). *The economic costs of the Israeli occupation for the occupied Palestinian territory*. September 2011.

Pelham, Nicolas. "Gaza's Tunnel Phenomenon: The unintended dynamics of Israel's siege." *Journal of Palestine Studies* 41. Institute for Palestine Studies (2011/12).

Qassem, Hamdi, and Yasser Shemis. "al-Alafat bi-l-Buhayra yushi"una shahid ahdath al-'Abbasiya Samir al-Kayyal" [Thousands mourn Abbasiya martyr Samir al-Kayyal]. *al-Masry al-Youm*, 5 May 2012, http://www. almasryaly-oum.com/news/details/176801

Qassem, Ibrahim. "Nanshur adillat al-thubut fi qadiyat Wadi al-Natrun…" [The Wadi al-Natrun evidence...]. *al-Youm al-Sabea*, 9 July 2013.

al-Qayyem, Hussein. "Ittihad sahafi Sina' yudin qabd 'ala morasili al-shorouq" [Sinai Journalists Union condemns detention of Shorouk reporters]. *al-Masreyoon*, 3 September 2013.

Radio Free Europe/Radio Liberty. "Foreign fighters in Iraq and Syria." 29 January 2015.

Ratzlav-Katz, Nissan. "Shteinitz: FM Livni Withheld Egyptian Smuggling Video From US." *Arutz Sheva* 7, 24 December 2007.

Reuters. "Special Report: Egyptian militants outwit army in Sinai battlefield." 16 March 2014.

Reuters and Barak Ravid. "Netanyahu warns outcome of Egypt revolution could be like Iran's." *Haaretz*, January 31 2011.

Reuters Arabic. "Mahkama misriya tu'ayyid istimrar tasdir al-ghaz li Isra'il" [Egyptian court approves continuation of gas exports to Israel]. 2 February 2009.

Rosenberg, David, and Gwen Ackerman. "Israel ready to use extreme tactics to free soldier." Bloomberg, 28 June 2006.

Sabbah, Fathi. "Majlis shura al-mujahidiin yanfi mas'uliyatahu 'an hujum al-ahad fi Rafah [MSC denied responsibility for Rafah attack]. *al-Hayat*, 8 August 2012.

Sabry, Mohamed. "Tafasil ightiyal al-shahid Muhammad Mabruk" [The details of assassinating Mohamed Mabrouk]. *al-Ahram*, 18 November 2013.

Sabry, Mohannad. "Arms smuggling explodes across Egypt–Libya border." McClatchy Newspapers, 8 September 2011.

———. "Bedouins deny harboring militants as Sinai attacks escalate." *al-Monitor*, 21 August 2013.

———. "Egypt's North Sinai under curfew following deadly clashes." *al-Monitor*. 5 July 2013.

———. "Morsi's popularity sinks after crash kills 51 children on bus." *al-Monitor*, 19 November 2012.

———. "The Muslim Brotherhood fights for legacy, not for Morsi."
　　al-Monitor, 2 July 2013.

———. "Al-Qaeda emerges amid Egypt's turmoil." *al-Monitor*, 4 December 2013.

Sadka, Saul. "Gazans belong in Sinai, says Chief Rabbi Metzger." *Haaretz*, 29
　　January 2008.

Saleh, Ahmed. "17 shahidan baynahum 15 min al-shurta wa 65 musaban hasilat
　　al-hajamat al-irhabiya fi Sini' ba'da fadd i'tisam raba'a wa al-nahda" [17
　　killed, including 15 police personnel, and 65 injured in Sinai after Rabaa
　　and Nahda dispersal]. *Sada el-Balad*, 15 August 2013.

Salem, Abdel-Halim. "Ahali Ghaza yataqaddamuna nahw al-Arish ba'da tafjir
　　al-hudud" [Gazans advance toward al-Arish after border bombing]. *al-Youm
　　al-Sabea*, 23 January 2008.

Salem, Magda. "Wazir al-Dakhiya: Jari al-ifraj 'an jami' mu'taqili Sini'" [Min-
　　ister of Interior: The Release of Sinai Prisoners is Underway]. *al-Youm
　　al-Sabea*, 23 February 2011.

Selim, Ahmed, and Hasnaa al-Sherif. "100 mulththam musallah bi-l-madafi'
　　yuhajimuna qism thani al-Arish li muddat 9 sa'at" [100 masked men attack
　　al-Arish police station for nine hours]. *al-Ahram*, 31 July 2011.

Sherwood, Harriet. "Egypt cancels Israeli gas contract." *The Guardian*, 23 April
　　2012.

al-Shorouk. "al-Hukm 'ala al-sahafi al-sinawi Ahmed Abu Draa bi-l-habs 6
　　ashhur ma'a iyqaf al-tanfiz" [Ahmed Abu Draa sentenced to six months
　　suspended term]. 5 October 2013.

Shoucair, Naum. *The History of Sinai, New and Old and Its Geography*. St. Cath-
　　erine's, Egypt: Library of St. Catherine's Monastery in South Sinai, 1907.

Shtewy, Ali. "Hasr 350 alf shajara muthmera tadararat fi shamal Sina'" [350
　　thousand trees destroyed in North Sinai]. *Mobtada*, 15 May 2014,

Sinai News. "al-Qiyadat al-jihadiya wa sirr tawqif 'amaliyat nasr fi Sina'" [Jihad-
　　ist figures and the secret behind ending Operation Eagle]. 28 August 2012.

al-Sorani, Ghazi. "Anfaq Rafah wa atharuha al-iqtisadiya wa-l-ijtima'iya wa-l-
　　siyasiya" [Rafah tunnels and their economic, social, and political impacts].
　　al-Hewar al-Motamaden, 14 December 2008.

Szrom, Charlie. "Iran-Hamas relationship in 2008." Iran Tracker, March 27,
　　2009.

Taha, Rana. "Salem and Fahmy imprisoned over Israel gas deal." *Daily News
　　Egypt*, 28 June 2012.

Tamam, Hossam. "Fi tanaqudat al-harakat al-jihadiya" [The contradictions of
　　jihadist movements]. *al-Sharq al-Awsat*, 29 January 2010.

————. "Entrenching revisions." *Al-Ahram Weekly*, 30 September–6 October 2010, http://weekly.ahram.org.eg/2010/1017/eg10.htm

————. *The Salafization of the Brotherhood: The decay of the Brotherhood approach and the rise of Salafism*. Alexandria, Egypt: Bibliotheca Alexandrina, 2010.

Tantawi, Mohamed. "Wazir al-Difa' yusdir qararan bi hathr tamalluk al-aradi al-mutakhima li-l-hudud al-sharqiya" [Defense minister issues law banning land ownership in border areas]. *al-Youm al-Sabea*, 23 December 2012.

Thabet, Mamdouh. "Tanfith hukm al-i'daam fi Ezzat Hanafi wa shaqiqihi fi sijn burj al-'arab" [Execution of Ezzat Hanafi and his brother in Burj al-Arab Prison carried out]. *al-Masry al-Youm*, 16 June 2006.

Turner, Craig. "Egypt's leader survives assassination attempt: Africa: Muslim extremists suspected in attack on Mubarak's motorcade in Ethiopia. President is unharmed." *Los Angeles Times*, 27 June 1995.

Tzoreff, Mira. "Restless Young Egyptians: Where did you come from and where will you go?" *Sharqiyya* 1.1. The Moshe Dayan Center for Middle East and African Studies, 2010.

Ward Anderson, John, and Molly Moore. "Palestinian leader Arafat dies in France." *Washington Post*, 11 November 2004.

al-Wesimy, Amr. "Wasfi: al-Inqilab ya'ni tawalli al-'askariyin manasib fi-l-dawla" [Wasfi: A coup means militarymen occupying leadership positions]. *al-Mesreyoon*, 28 January 2014.

Weymouth, Lally. "Excerpts from Washington Post interview with Egyptian Gen. Abdel Fatah al-Sissi." *Washington Post*, 5 August 2013.

Wilson, Scott. "Hamas sweeps Palestinian elections, complicating peace efforts in Mideast." *Washington Post*, 27 January 2006.

YNet. "WikiLeaks: Suleiman vowed to prevent Hamas rule in Gaza." YNet News, 11 February 2011.

WikiThawra. "Hasr al-qatla fi 'ahd al-majlis al-'askari" [Count of casualties during the rule of SCAF]. 2012.

————. "Statistics for the clearance of Alatsamin and related events 14–30 August 2013," n.d.

al-Youm al-Sabea. "Nanshur haythiyat hukm al-idariya al-'ulya fi qadiyat bi' al-ghaz al-misri ila Isra'il [Transcript of ruling by Supreme Administrative Court regarding sale of Egyptian gas to Israel]. *al-Youm al-Sabea*, 11 March 2010.

al-Zahar, Mohamed. "Mursi yuqil qiyadat 'askariya wa amniya" [Morsi sacks military and security chiefs]. Sky News Arabia, 8 August 2012.

Zakaria, Yahya. "Ahali Sina' yurahhibun bi qarar tamalluk al-aradi wa yutalibun bi-l-intiqal li marhalat al-ta'mir" [Sinai welcomes Land Ownership Law]. *Sada el-Balad*, 3 November 2012.

Zaki, Anas. "Mursi ya'ed Sina' bi-l-tanmiya wa raf' al-thulm" [Morsi promises Sinai with development and ending injustice]. *al-Jazeera*, 5 October 2012.

Zelin, Aaron Y. "New video message from Jamā'at Anṣār Bayt al-Maqdis: If You Return (to Sins), We Shall Return (to Our Punishment)." Jihadology.net, 24 July 2012.

INDEX